THE PREZ

THE PREZ

DAVID SPITERI

HarperCollins*Publishers*

HarperCollins*Publishers*

First published in Australia in 2012
by HarperCollins*Publishers* Australia Pty Limited
ABN 36 009 913 517
harpercollins.com.au

HarperCollins*Publishers*
Level 13, 201 Elizabeth Street, Sydney NSW 2000, Australia
31 View Road, Glenfield, Auckland 0627, New Zealand
A 53, Sector 57, Noida, UP, India
77–85 Fulham Palace Road, London, W6 8JB, United Kingdom
2 Bloor Street East, 20th floor, Toronto, Ontario M4W 1A8, Canada
10 East 53rd Street, New York NY 10022, USA

National Library of Australia Cataloguing-in-Publication data:

Spiteri, David.
  The Prez/ David Spiteri.
  ISBN: 978 0 7322 9487 8 (pbk.)
  Motorcycle gangs.
  Organized crime.
  Subculture.
364.1066

Cover design by Darren Holt, HarperCollins Design Studio
Cover image supplied by the author; all other images by shutterstock.com
Typeset in 10.5/14.5pt Minion by Kirby Jones
Printed and bound in Australia by Griffin Press
70gsm Classic used by HarperCollins*Publishers* is a natural, recyclable product made from wood
grown in sustainable forests. The manufacturing processes conform to the environmental
regulations in the country of origin, Finland.

5 4 3 2 1   12 13 14 15

This is not an orthodox work of non-fiction. For reasons which should require no explanation the author cannot name names or identify real people in this story. Although this book is a recollection of events which actually happened, the names along with any identifying characteristics of the central characters have been changed as well as the names of clubs and the places where these events took place.

Foreword

I was born to be a bikie. But it wasn't until I was in the sixth grade and saw Marlon Brando in *The Wild One* that I realised what being a bikie was all about.

This story is a true account of the birth of Outlaw Motorcycle Clubs in Australia. There was no template for us. Clubs just evolved, with a simple creed: loyalty to the club and respect for your brothers.

In the early 1960s US soldiers on R and R from the Vietnam War came to Sydney with full pockets, wanting marijuana. We saw there was money to be made and that money soon changed a lot of blokes. Treachery and greed became commonplace, as did strife and chaos, but most clubs survived.

Without knowing it, we were being used by a variety of people, for example police, politicians and lawyers, but now we are using them, and our money opens a lot of doors. For obvious reasons I have changed the club names and events. If you were there at the time you will nod your head and agree. This story has not been told before.

David Spiteri

Chapter 1

Shovelling shit is no way to spend a Saturday morning, but that's what Peter Winifred and his mate Brian Corrigan did when they were twelve. They mucked out the stalls at Fairfield trotting track, collecting and shovelling horseshit into sugarbags and selling it to punters. They took turns pulling and pushing the billycart, hard work when the shit was wet, but at six shillings a bag, it wouldn't take long before they each had enough to buy a 125 cc BSA Bantam motorcycle and race up on Snow's Mountain with the other kids.

Their customers wanted to get a healthy garden going in their backyards, and prized the cheap fertiliser delivered to their door. The boys got to know them all and formed an opinion on everyone's character. Old Joe, the Ukrainian loner, they reckoned was a Second World War concentration camp guard hiding in Sydney's west. He just grunted when he got his two bags and counted out their twelve bob. Mrs Tweedy and her husband always offered them a glass of lemonade. Hauling shit was hard work and the lemonade was a hit. The other customers were mainly new Australians, immigrants from the Mediterranean, trying to grow fruit and vegies in their tiny, identical backyards.

After a couple of months Winnie and Brian had enough cash to know they wouldn't have to do it forever, and that knowledge kept them going. The person they credited for the turning point in their lives was Mrs Wright, who lived on Chapel Hill in a neat bungalow with nice roses. She'd owed the boys thirty bob for five bags for two weeks. She refused to answer the door, but whenever they went to collect and heard music playing inside they knew she was home. It pissed the boys off that the mingy bitch wouldn't cough up and she taught them a valuable lesson: cash only, no credit.

On Saturday nights at Winnie's, his dad, who'd had a few down the pub with his mates, fell asleep in his chair next to his mum, who was watching a black and white television movie while enjoying her weekly ration of six chocolates. One Saturday night Winnie had a bath after dinner and went to the room he shared with his older brother. Warren toiled in a nail factory for a pittance and every Saturday night he went to a church dance. Winnie reached under his bed to add his daily takings to his horseshit money. Eleven pounds and seven shillings — only a few more weeks before he had the fourteen quid to buy Kevin Hinchey's Bantam. Kev wanted to upgrade to a 500 cc Matchless. Winnie stashed the box then went to kiss his mother goodnight, making a big fuss about how tired he was. Engrossed in her movie, she kissed him lovingly and told him to sleep well. From a traditional Italian family, she was ever-patient and forgiving. Even though his father was a dinky-di Aussie, the kids in the area picked on Winnie and his brother because they weren't one thing or another. The wogs didn't accept them, and nor did the Aussies, so they were fair game for the neighbourhood bullies.

That Saturday night Winnie and Brian had a job to do. Winnie turned off his light, changed out of his pyjamas into his jeans and climbed out the window. He walked down the road to meet Brian, who pulled out a small tomahawk. Winnie laughed and called it 'good thinking'. They made their way to Mrs Wright's house, where the lights blazed and laughter roared inside. Brian crept up the path to the rose bushes and chopped them all off at the ground. The bastards inside wouldn't be laughing next morning.

On Sunday mornings Winnie's mum made him get up and go to church with her. They had to leave early because she arranged the altar flowers. She and Father Pius were thrilled to see the bunch of fresh, beautiful roses left at the presbytery door. While she arranged them, Winnie hung around outside the front door of the church where his schoolmate Ocker earned a quid manning a newsstand. When they saw Mrs Wright pull up in her flash car Winnie told Ocker about the night before and they pissed themselves laughing. Winnie hoped she liked the flower arrangements.

After mass Winnie had a quick bite then changed clothes to meet his mates. The last thing he heard was his mother calling out, 'Don't be late for tea.' In those quiet days of the late 1950s just about everyone had a baked dinner on Sundays and the whole family got together because the pubs were closed. Winnie's old man turned on his charm and proved quite funny when sober.

He raced down his street, past the identical Housing Commission three-bedroom fibro houses. From some he heard angry shouting and snatches of arguments. It unsettled him; he'd never shouted in his whole life. He reckoned he was pretty lucky that his home was a happy one: no raised voices, no argy-bargy. He met the boys on the corner and they headed up Snow's Mountain. On Sundays in Sydney's western suburbs, too far from any beach, it was all about motorbikes; Snow's Mountain had a twisting bush track, ideal for dick-swinging, derring-do riding and bravado.

Big Kev tried to ride his Bantam up Snow's Mountain but he was so big and heavy the gutless little motor couldn't make it without a huge run-up and he had to push it up the last hundred yards. He was as anxious to sell it as Winnie was to buy it. There were no roads or houses on the hill, just tracks made by kids on motorbikes driving around and about. A big gang had gathered up there that Sunday and the top dog was a bloke everyone called Twister. His mates hung around him like flies and he thought he owned the mountain. He rode a 500 cc Triumph, the most powerful bike of the lot.

Winnie and Twister shared a bit of history, going back to a time after school when Twister got stuck into Winnie's brother Warren with his fists. Winnie didn't hesitate. He picked up a length of timber and gave Twister a good thumping, with some full-blooded belts. Twister never forgot it, but still thought he was a tough cunt. When Twister saw the boys walking towards him he gunned his bike and sprayed Winnie, Brian and Kev with gravel, then headed off, laughing.

'That Twister is a real queer cunt,' Big Kev snarled. 'Wait until I get my Matchless …'

Kev never liked Twister at the best of times; all Kev had a mind to do was to beat him around the track, if not about the ears.

Winnie saw the fire in Kev's eyes. 'Hey, Kevvie, don't wreck my bike before I can buy it.'

Twister took off and easily outsprinted Kev on his tiny Bantam.

When the boys headed down the hill they found Kev revving the motor and saying 'Fuck, fuck, fuck' under his breath.

'The cunt nearly put me over the edge.'

Brian had an idea. 'Come on, leave the bike here. Help me with this.' Brian found a log. When they heard Twister starting on another lap they dragged it across the track on a blind corner and hid in the bushes. Twister came roaring around the corner. To avoid running into the log, he dropped the big bike and slid off into the bushes arse over tit.

The boys ran home laughing while Brian shouted, 'Don't get mad, get even!' Twister was two years older and tougher, and probably smart enough to work out who'd brought him undone, but at that moment they couldn't have cared less.

That night at tea, Warren glared at Winnie then dropped a bombshell. 'You didn't go to mass today. Mary from youth group told me you were out at Ocker's paperstand yakking it up the whole time.'

Winnie was caught dead to rights. His first thought was that Warren was a prick for dobbing him in and then he tried to come up with some excuse. His mum just looked at him and said, 'That's alright, Peter.' As soon as Warren realised their mum wasn't going to get up Winnie, he was full of self-righteous anger.

On their way to school the next morning he asked Winnie, 'Didja do your homework?'

'Nah, too busy riding motorbikes.'

They shared a good laugh. Warren didn't ride bikes — he just wasn't interested — but he liked girls and there were plenty of them at the youth dances. It rained on the way to school; low scudding black clouds made the sky look eerie. In class Winnie noticed Brother Michael staring at him with his little blackcurrant eyes. Winnie thought it most unusual. Every time he looked up he saw those black eyes boring into him. After prayers, and without even saying 'Good morning', Brother Michael told the class to get out their homework, then he marched straight to Winnie's desk. Winnie shit himself. Here comes trouble, he thought.

'Where's your homework, Winifred?' Brother Michael never asked for homework first; something was up.

Winnie fiddled with his bag, pretending to look for what he knew wasn't there.

'You never did your homework, did you?'

Before Winnie said a word, Brother Michael grabbed him by the throat and dragged him out the front of the class, banged his head against the blackboard and shouted, 'Why didn't you do your homework, Winifred?'

Winnie tried to speak but nothing came out.

'You didn't do it,' Brother Michael paused for dramatic effect, 'you didn't do it because you were too busy riding motorcycles.'

Brother Michael was squeezing so tightly Winnie couldn't breathe. When his face went red, Brother Michael loosened his grip and dragged him to the back of the classroom, lifted him up and hung him on the hat pegs. Winnie's feet dangled a foot off the ground and he squirmed like a bug on a pin while Brother Michael headed back to the front of the class. Winnie's Brylcreem had made a greasy stain on the blackboard.

The class giggled at Winnie's predicament and turned to look at him hanging there, each secretly glad it wasn't him.

'Get him down!' Brother Michael shouted to no one in particular, struggling to regain his composure.

Brian and 'the Rat' Rassock, two of Winnie's mates, hurried to the rear of the classroom and lifted Winnie down, desperately trying not to laugh. Winnie knew Warren had given him up to Brother Michael, and while he couldn't work out why his own brother would do that, in time he would forgive him; he loved his brother, but he would never forget. Lesson learned: never rat on anyone, ever.

Right there and then Winnie made a vow: no bastard would ever make a fool of him again. He didn't mention the episode to anyone, especially his parents, because they always believed whatever the Brothers said. But he decided then that school and he weren't meant for each other. That little episode delivered another simple lesson: he and his mate Brian were not going straight. They didn't have long to wait to find out what not going straight meant.

One Saturday the Fairfield racetrack had a gymkhana and all Winnie could think about was more horses, so tons more horseshit. If they could sell it all that day they'd have enough for the bikes. Brian arrived at Winnie's carrying extra sugarbags.

'This might be the last week.'

To find extra customers they went to a new area and knocked on doors. Kids they knew from school laughed at them. It wouldn't have mattered if there hadn't been any girls around, but there were, so they pulled out their air rifles and took a few pot shots at the boys and told them to get fucked. Stung from the slugs, the kids yelled back insults but scurried off like rats. The extra sales resulted in a pocketful of cold cash, almost double their normal return, but there was trouble that night. The police hauled them off to the police station over the slug guns. Winnie told the cops that he'd been robbed; he was only trying to defend himself and make an honest quid. The cops wrote up a report and gave it to Sergeant Burrows. Like most cops, Burrows seemed a big, blue brute and the boys had no idea that their caper was of little concern to him, so they packed shit. Burrows told them they couldn't just go around shooting kids because they thought they were 'about to rob them'.

'Do you understand that?' he roared and they both shit themselves.

'Now because you're making an honest quid I'm going to be lenient. We'll keep your slug guns and I'll give them back only if you come back with your parents. Now fuck off home!'

The boys thought they'd got off lightly and had a good laugh about it, but they never told their parents and never went back for the guns. At home they counted up the takings; it had been a big day and they finally had enough money to buy their bikes and give the horseshit caper the flick for good.

The next Sunday Brian, Kev and Winnie went up to Snow's Mountain. Big Kev rode his Matchless and the boys rode their BSA Bantams, 'beezers' they were called. Twister was up there with a few of his mates but that didn't worry the boys. This was the day Twister would meet his match in Big Kev. Twister thought he was king shit and got up them straight away.

'You bastards put that log on the track! I nearly killed meself.'

The boys said nothing and tried to look innocent.

'What log, Twister?' Big Kev asked. He was big enough to take shit from no one, and that included Twister. 'Get fucked.'

Twister gunned his bike. 'You wanna race, Kev?'

Kev was ready. They agreed on three laps around the hill and lined up with motors running. Someone yelled three, two, one, go, and off they went. Twister got in front and cut Big Kev off whenever he tried to overtake. Kev backed off and waited until Twister turned around to see what was happening behind him and then he shot through on Twister's blind side and led until the finish. The boys cheered loudly — it was the first time anyone had beaten Twister; when he and his mates left, no one said a fucking word.

One night Winnie watched *The Wild One* on television. He suddenly knew what he wanted to do with his life; something to do with motorbikes and a band of mates, to feel the wind in his face just like Marlon Brando and his gang. He was impressed with the way they carried themselves, and knew then and there that he was going to be a bikie, whatever that was and whatever it took. After his run-in with Brother Michael he determined to spend the least amount of time at school and Brian agreed.

'We've got to get out of this place, mate.'

School was bad enough, but the Catholic shit was way too much.

'First they try to shove it down your throat and when that fails, they try sticking it up yer arse,' said Brian, and they laughed long and hard.

The decision to quit wasn't entirely theirs, though, because the truant officers eventually took them to juvenile court and they were sent to different reform schools until they reached fifteen. Brian went to Mount Penang on the Central Coast and Winnie to Mittagong Boys' Home.

Since they had no trade, they were probably destined to work in the local factories but when they came out they had learned separate, valuable skills: Brian knew how to steal motorcycles, grind the engine and frame numbers off, stamp on new numbers, paint and register them and resell them for a fat profit, while Winnie had grown a foot, filled out and learned how to lead men by quietly applying his steely will. He reckoned someone had to be in charge and it might as well be him. As soon as they could, they opened their own little factory in the garden shed in Winnie's backyard and resold a few stolen bikes. Soon Ocker and Big Kev quit their factory jobs and joined in, because Winnie and Brian offered better hours, conditions and pay to do shit they liked — simple choice, really.

On Friday and Saturday nights in the early 1960s three or four hundred bikies from all over Sydney met at the Centennial Hotel at Woollahra to hit the piss and show off their British bikes. In those days Harley-Davidson bikes were rare; blokes reckoned they were too noisy and that they sounded like tractors. Winnie and about twenty of his mates would ride into Sydney and drag each other from the traffic lights. Big Kev once chucked a wheelie and nearly ran over a couple who were slow to clear a crossing. He soon developed a reputation as a hard cunt. When Winnie pulled up at the next traffic lights he leaned over to Kev and told him, 'You're going to kill someone one day.'

'Yeah, I know,' Kev yelled and raced off to the next light wearing a grin a yard wide.

Outside the pub, boys bragged about their motorbikes. Under a full moon the chrome glistened on a long, menacing line of motorbikes parked at the kerb. When a roar announced the arrival of a pack of fifty bikes the pub emptied to watch the new arrivals park wherever they liked. Kev recognised Twister.

'Hey, Winnie, fucking Twister's gotten big.'

'Yeah, but he's still ugly.'

Twister and a few mates walked over. 'Ah, the little boys are here.'

Big Kev stepped out of the shadows and Twister's face turned white. He hadn't seen Kev for a while. Kev was over six foot four and built like a Mallee bull. Twister stuck his hand out to Winnie. 'How're you going, boys? Nice bikes you've got here. Why don't you come inside and have a beer?'

Winnie spoke up. 'Maybe later, Twister.'

Twister headed into the pub followed by his mates.

'I don't trust that cunt, Winnie,' said Ocker.

'Me neither, Ocker. He's a snake. Anyway, we have a little work to do before pleasure.'

They wandered down the line of bikes and made their selection of the ones they liked, recording the numberplates for Ocker. His brother worked in a motor registry office and would slip them the addresses. The boys would turn up, nick the bike and do a 'rebirth' in the shed. It was just that easy.

Their work done, the boys made their way into the Centennial, ordered beers and watched the band. They found a table near the dance floor filled with girls in tight jeans and t-shirts that showed off their tits. A young one with long blonde hair, dressed in imitation leopard-skin tights, danced alone. Winnie thought she didn't fit in. Maybe it was her age — she was a kid.

'Hey, Winnie,' Big Kev called out, 'it's your shout', but Winnie didn't hear a word.

'You can't keep your eyes off her, can you, mate?'

Winnie made his way into the bar where Twister held court and told jokes. 'Hey, Winnie, aren't you going to have a beer?'

'I'll have one with you out at Little Bay, if you're going.'

'We'll be going. I heard you've got a business going and I reckon we might do something together.'

'I don't think so, Twister.'

Back at the table Winnie set the beers down in front of his mates. 'Hey Brian, Ocker, I want to tell you something.' The boys leaned in. 'Twister must know what we're up to with the hot bikes. He just put it to me that he'd like to do business with us. I'm just wondering how he knows. Has anybody said anything?'

The boys looked blank.

Brian spoke at last. 'We sold a hot Triumph to that bloke with Twister.'

'Twister's going to have a beer with me out at Little Bay; I'll see what else he has to say.'

The band played and Winnie checked out the crowded dance floor for the girl in the imitation leopard-skin tights but she was gone. Big Kev, who kept an eye on everything, yelled over the band, 'I think she went to the little girl's room, mate.'

The beer soon had an effect on everyone and eventually a fight on the dance floor turned into a full-on brawl; blokes from all sides ran in and started swinging fists. The band unplugged and walked off while the bouncers stood back and watched. It went on for a few minutes until the sound of sirens signalled arriving cops and the pub emptied like magic. It was almost ten o'clock — closing time — so the boys pooled their cash and Ocker raced off to get a few dozen at the bottle-o. Ocker stowed their beer in saddlebags while the pigs made a few arrests, then three hundred bikies started their engines and took off into the night; the noise could have awakened the dead. Big Kev sidled up to Winnie and nodded towards a girl standing in the shadows outside the pub.

'There she is, Winnie.' She stood alone and looked scared. Kev nudged Winnie. 'You better be quick, mate, before someone else grabs her.'

Winnie pulled his idling bike onto its stand and made his way over. There was no time for niceties. 'Do you want a ride to the party?'

She nodded.

He pulled down the rear foot pegs, showed her where to put her feet and yelled, 'Have you been on a bike before?'

'No,' she mouthed.

He mounted up. 'Hop on and hang tight.'

He found first gear and shot off in a hurry, heading for Little Bay. It turned out to be a fast ride on twisting and curving roads. Winnie felt her tits rubbing on his back and it gave him high hopes for a night of quiet fucking in the dunes by the sea. He followed the other bikes to the party but made his way to a place away from the fire. The boys followed him. They probably thought they were onto an onion, a gangbang, but Winnie had other ideas as he turned off the engine and helped the girl off his bike. He noticed her eyes were glazed.

'What's your name?'

'Mimi.'

He was a bit worried: she didn't look right. 'Are you pissed or what?'

'No, stoned.' She smiled.

'What do you mean, stoned?'

Winnie was in the dark. He hated feeling ignorant but he'd never heard the word before.

'Marijuana,' she said. 'You bikies haven't heard of it?'

Winnie said nothing: what he knew and what he didn't know was his business. He called the boys over to introduce them to Mimi. The boys salivated.

'Do any of you blokes know what stoned is?'

Ocker always knew everything. 'Yeah, it's when you smoke dope, Winnie. The surfers are into it.'

She leaned over and whispered in Winnie's ear, 'Would you like some?'

He nodded and grabbed her hand and they walked off into the dark towards the sand dunes. The boys wanted to come but Winnie turned and shook his head. They wouldn't follow unless he signalled them. Winnie had a feeling about her. She differed from the scrags and wannabes he met.

She pulled out a tobacco pouch and rolled a cigarette. 'This is a joint. What's your real name?'

'Peter Winifred, Winnie to me mates.'

'I enjoyed that ride tonight. It was the first time I've ever been on a bike.'

'Do you always go to that pub?'

'No, tonight's my first time, my father told me to keep away. Not from the pub, but from bikies.'

'How come you went, then?'

'Just curious.'

'Where do you live?'

'Rose Bay. And you?'

'Fairfield.'

'That's out west, isn't it?'

'At least I know where Rose Bay is,' Winnie muttered and lit the joint.

He felt insecure for a second — she was putting him down because of where he lived — but after his first puff he couldn't have cared less. It changed him almost immediately. He just smiled at her and handed back the joint. He felt terrific, the effect was calming and very private and he just stared at her thinking she was the most beautiful girl he'd ever met. They lay on the sand and she reached over and tousled his hair. He closed his eyes and listened to the waves and smelled the salt air. After a while he came out of it and asked, 'Where can I get some marijuana?'

'Down at Bondi from the surfers. They buy it up the North Coast and bring it down.'

Winnie had no idea what she was talking about so he just nodded. He knew this was better than beer and he wondered if there might be a good earn in it for him and his mates; he just had to find out how. Lying there next to her he couldn't believe he was with this girl. Normally he'd be groping her tits and going for it but she was no onion, that he knew.

Suddenly Mimi leaned over and kissed him. Winnie's heart almost stopped. He lay there and stared into the night sky and said nothing. In the distance Winnie heard the roar of approaching motorbikes followed by a police siren.

'What's that?' Mimi looked scared.

Winnie stood up and grabbed her hand and led her back to his mates. Two blokes on motorcycles came roaring into the party site. They laughed as they got off their bikes and yelled out how they'd outrun the coppers. The siren sounded closer and Twister and his drunken mates gathered around Winnie and Mimi, probably looking for a good time. The police car pulled up, lights flashing, and two cops got out and said they wanted to talk to the last two riders. The gathered crowd laughed as one.

'You find them,' Twister called out. The coppers realised they were heavily outnumbered and were just about ready to get back in their car when someone chucked a bunger that exploded near them. That changed things quick smart; the cops got on the blower and called for reinforcements.

'There's going to be trouble now,' Winnie whispered in Mimi's ear, 'let's blow.'

'Peter, you have to get me out of here. I'll be in big trouble if I'm caught.'

Big Kev and Brian came over. 'Don't forget we're next, Winnie.'

Winnie shook his head. 'Get fucked, this one is different. Is there a way out of here?' He didn't want to get caught up in Twister's shit either.

Ocker piped up. 'Hey, Slippery knows how we can get away.'

Approaching sirens got louder.

'Follow me, we don't have much time.' Slippery took off.

Winnie mounted up, kick-started the bike and waited for Mimi to climb on, then he gave it a handful and took off after Slippery. Mimi wasn't happy, Winnie could hear the panic in her voice. He followed Slippery behind a hill and turned off his lights. The three other boys followed. Five police cars passed them heading in the opposite direction. Winnie didn't know if five cars would be enough to quell the crowd; they were all drunk and probably more than a match for ten coppers. The boys followed

Slippery down a track and back onto the road and they were off, free as birds.

Winnie gave Slippery the thumbs up and roared past him for Elizabeth Bay. The boys were still hoping for a gangbang but there was no chance; Winnie wanted to 'sheriff' her, to keep her for himself; he just didn't know how he was going to lose the boys. Ocker rode up next to him and smiled and looked at Mimi. Winnie pulled over and parked and the boys pulled up alongside and gave him the 'What the fuck's going on?' look. Before Winnie could answer they heard more police sirens nearby. He seized the opportunity and yelled out, 'I'll see you blokes tomorrow', taking off in a cloud of blue smoke.

'Good luck,' Big Kev shouted as Winnie headed east.

Winnie thought he'd died and gone to heaven. Fuck, I'm in like Flynn, he thought, but he didn't have a clue where to take her in the Eastern suburbs. The police reinforcements drove by but paid no attention to them. He stopped at a light and Mimi got off, ran across the street and hailed a taxi. Before she closed the door she mouthed 'Thank you', and that was that. Winnie just shook his head. The boys wouldn't believe it. She and the taxi were long gone before he came to. He kicked his bike into life and then it struck him, it was going to be a long ride home and he didn't even get her number.

The next morning was Sunday. His mum had long since stopped trying to get him to mass. He heard the sound of motorbikes pulling into his drive. He was lying in bed trying to recall what had happened the night before; all he could think of was Mimi — he could still smell her perfume — but he couldn't work out exactly what had happened. He opened the back door and saw his mates lounging around the backyard.

'You sheriffing cunt,' Brian yelled. It was a good thing he smiled.

'I know. Do you want to know what happened?'

'Yeah,' they all answered, anticipating a lewd story.

'When we went for our stroll in the sand dunes we sat down and she rolled me a smoke of marijuana.'

'The bikies in the States are into that,' said Kev. 'What was it like?'

'Better than piss, mate. We both just lay there smoking while I played with her titties. Fuck, they were nice.'

'Yeah, I noticed,' Brian said and grabbed his crotch.

'Go on, Winnie, what happened?' Ocker always wanted to know every dirty detail.

'It turns out she's some rich cunt's daughter from Rose Bay. You wouldn't believe it, after you blokes left I was trying to think where I could take her when she jumped off, got in a taxi, said thank you and fucked off. I still can't believe it.'

'Bullshit,' said Kev and the boys laughed until they almost cried.

'Fucking oath, boys, I suppose she's telling her rich girlfriends all about it by now. The only good thing about last night was the marijuana. There could be a decent earn in that for us. We'd better look into it.'

Brian piped up. 'You see the headlines, Winnie?' He read from the Sunday paper: 'Riot at Little Bay. Bikies steal a police motorcycle. Forty-five police battle bikies after police chase. Sixty-five arrests made. Police continuing their investigations.'

'I guess we don't go to the Centennial for a while then, eh? I'm sick of hanging around with those meatheads anyway. If we're going to get into shit it had better be for what we do instead of those cunts. Did they get Twister?'

'I hope so,' Kev said smiling. 'Come on, let's go up to the shed.'

They walked up the backyard and Kev asked Winnie if he was sweet on Mimi.

Winnie thought he was but said 'She was just another slut' and left it at that. Kev shook his head as they walked into the shed and sat down to discuss business.

Ocker asked if anyone got the numberplates of the bikes they wanted.

Winnie had. 'Yeah, I got three new bikes, so they should be insured. When we sell one more I reckon we're going to have to get somewhere else to do this. My old man is getting suspicious of us bringing bikes here at night.'

The news took a minute to digest.

Brian said, 'Why don't we open a shop?'

Winnie looked at him while he gave the idea some thought, then he said, 'That'd be pretty easy, there are plenty of places to rent. We could do modifications, sell spare parts. Ocker could spray and Kevvie could do repairs. We could sell the hot bikes from the shop. How much do you reckon it'd cost?'

'Well, when we sell this bike there should be enough in it to cover our start-up costs. I can bring my old man's tools in, that will save us, and Slippery can do the sign-writing.'

Winnie was suddenly interested in the idea. 'What would we call the shop?'

A few ideas were aired. Brian started to write some names down then he looked up and said, 'What about Snow's, after Snow's Mountain?'

The boys cracked up. 'Yeah, Brian, it's not a bad name. Where would we set up?'

'What about Parramatta? It's central.'

Winnie laughed. 'Sounds alright to me, and if we have any complaints we can refer them to Snow, 'cos he'll never be in,' and the boys laughed some more.

'Right then, I'll go and see a real estate agent tomorrow,' said Brian.

The boys talked about getting a few bikes to go in the new shop and Winnie put a stop to it right away. 'Can you blokes wait until we rent a shop? I don't want to upset the old man.'

'Sure, Winnie, it's only a night's work.'

After they sold the last hot bike they had enough to rent a workshop in a back alley behind the Parramatta business district. It had a small display area and a dirt floor soaked with years of oil and grease.

'At least it's cheap,' Brian said.

'It'd want to be,' Winnie said, looking around at the mess.

Brian was already planning where he was going to set up his spare-parts section. 'This could be the start of something big, Winnie.'

Winnie wasn't too sure. 'If we don't run out of money first.'

'I saved some money, mate. We can use that to get started.'

'Good to know.' Winnie raised an eyebrow. He had no idea Brian had saved a penny.

'Hey, you blokes remember Rat Rassock from school?' Winnie was thinking out loud.

The boys all nodded. 'Well, he's into surfing and he might know how to get onto the blokes with marijuana. He still lives around here, I see him now and then driving a yellow Zephyr with a surfboard on top. I'll see what he knows.'

Ocker and Big Kev brought in a bike they quickly renumbered and repainted. They changed the handlebars, added a few accessories and finished it so well that the original owner could have bought it back and not known it was his in the first place. The boys knew that their work was superior and they wanted to put the word around that they were in business. Slippery sign-painted 'Snow's British Motorcycles Sales and Service' on a board they hung in the front window and the boys stood outside and admired his work.

'It looks like a pro shop now,' Brian said proudly. 'How about we have a grand opening? Slippery said he can make t-shirts with our name on to sell. It's free advertising.'

Brian was quick with a good idea, a natural marketing whiz.

Instead of closing at twelve on Saturdays like the other shops, they decided to stay open until three o'clock. It gave the blokes who worked on Saturdays a chance to come in and nose around, and they made some of their best sales then. For the grand opening most of their mates came; even Twister put in an appearance to have a sniff around. Sometimes he was a real good bloke and other times a cunt; that's why they called him Twister. He filled Winnie in on what had happened at Little Bay. Turned out it was a full-on riot; the police didn't give a fuck who they bashed. Twister and a few of his mates escaped, including his cousin Kero Ken from the country. Kero Ken was the bloke who stole the police bike in the first place. He was a real mad prick and dumb as a post; he got his name by putting kerosene in his bike instead of petrol, and the name stuck.

Winnie asked Twister, 'Are you blokes going to Bathurst this year?'

'Of course. Why don't you ride up with us?'

'I don't think so; you're not exactly Kev's best mate.'

'Fuck Big Kev, who's running this show?'

Just then Kev walked into the shop. Twister turned and without batting an eyelid tried to turn on the charm. 'Kev, I was just telling Winnie what a great shop you have.'

Kev looked unimpressed.

Twister took the hint. 'Anyway, guys, I have to go now. We have a run down to Wollongong tomorrow.'

After they closed shop they sat around drinking beer while Brian counted the takings.

'That wasn't a bad idea with the t-shirts; let's get some more. We made enough to cover our set-up costs and once we start selling bikes this shop is going to be a nice little earner.'

'It won't be like this every week. We'd better stay on the dole for a while.'

'We make good money from the hot bikes, Winnie.'

'Yeah, but how long do you reckon we'll get away with it, if we just sell hot ones? The pigs will be onto us for sure. But if we just slip one in every now and then we'll do alright. I promised myself when I got out of reform school that I'm not going back. We have to be smarter than the pigs and the only way to do that is to not get greedy.'

Brian nodded.

'What was Twister after today?' Kev asked.

Winnie laughed. 'He wanted us to ride up to Bathurst with him and his boys.'

'Yeah, like fuck!' Kev roared.

'Settle down, mate. I told him he wasn't on your Christmas card list.'

'What did he say to that?'

'Fuck-all. You came out of the workshop and that's when he pissed off.'

'Good,' Kev said with a smile.

'He also said what a good-looking shop we had.'

'If he says anything good about us, we should be careful. He's still a cunt, remember that.'

Chapter 2

The next Saturday night the boys met at the bike shop, excited about their first ride into Sydney since the Little Bay incident. The Centennial Hotel had been sold and painted purple and turned into a poofters' pub so they headed to Kings Cross. Thick Saturday night traffic slowed them down and they snaked under garish neon lights and past the girlie shows, parking their bikes wherever they could. Drunks slept in doorways, hookers plied their trade and spruikers yelled at the punters about the exotic tricks their dancers got up to. In the crush they saw Twister's cousin, Kero Ken, who made his way over and held out his leg-of-lamb-sized hand. Kero shook Winnie's hand and Winnie introduced him to his mates.

'This is Kev and Brian.'

'Yeah, we met you with Twister out at Little Bay.'

'That's right, Twister tells me you blokes have a bike shop out Parramatta way. Maybe we can do some business one day.'

The boys laughed. 'Like fuck! We don't deal with Twister.'

Kero went back to spruiking. 'Check the girls out, boys, no charge for you.'

'Fucken oath,' said Brian. 'You coming, Winnie?'

'No, mate, I might go for a wander.'

'I'll come with you, mate,' Kev said.

Brian and a few of the boys disappeared inside the strip club. Kev stopped to talk with the strip-joint bouncers he knew from boxing school.

One of their mates, Porky, stayed to keep an eye on the bikes and chatted to a couple of girls wearing leather jackets and tight slacks. The girls laughed at Porky's jokes. Kev squeezed each girl on the arse. 'I'll take both,' he growled as they squealed and jumped out of his grasp. Their tits bounced and Winnie and Kev had a good laugh.

Kev shook his head. 'Just playing, girls.' They were telling more jokes and flattering the girls when Kero Ken waved to Winnie and Kev. 'Come here, boys, there's trouble inside.'

'You stay with the girls, Porky,' Kev shouted over his shoulder as they ran towards Kero.

'What's up?'

'There are some footy players in there and they're not getting on very well with your blokes.'

Kev barrelled down the stairs and saw Brian pinned up against the wall with two footy players giving it to him. Winnie pulled a large shifting spanner out of his jeans and whacked one bloke on the shoulder until he heard bone snap. Then he turned his attention to the other bloke, whose face he recognised from the sports pages. Winnie whacked him on the nut and the bloke collapsed like a sack of spuds, joining his moaning mate on the floor. Winnie reckoned he wouldn't look so familiar now. Brian was bleeding from the mouth and his forehead sported a huge welt.

'I'll be right,' he said, but he was glassy-eyed and wobbling.

Big Kev and the other boys swung chains, intending to bash anyone else who wanted it. Punters poured out the exit doors. Kero Ken showed them the fire door leading out to the back alley and told them to bugger off in a hurry because the cops were on their way. They sauntered back to the street and Brian wiped the blood from his mouth.

'Are you alright?' Winnie asked.

'Yeah,' Brian laughed a little nervously, putting on the bravado. 'They can't hurt me.'

They headed for their bikes. The girls were still talking to Porky, oblivious to the shenanigans in the club.

'What happened down there, Winnie?'

Winnie nodded at Brian and smacked his right fist into his left and then raised his finger to his lips and winked at Porky. Porky had the sense to shut up. They looked down the road and saw the police trying to make sense of what the two footy boys were trying to say. They looked in rough shape and their clothes were spattered with blood. Winnie thought that right about then was as good a time as any to get the buggery out of the Cross. Porky grabbed one of the girls and the other one looked to see who she would go with. She'd started to walk over to Winnie when Brian grabbed her by the arm. His self-esteem needed a bit of boosting. 'Come with me.'

She looked at his fat right eye. 'You poor thing,' she said, and climbed up behind Brian. He said later he could tell it wasn't her first time on a bike. The boys took off, adrenalin pumping. They roared past the El Alamein Fountain and down to Woolloomooloo, past Harry's Café de Wheels, Sydney's famous pie and peas caravan, then across the Cahill Expressway, over the Harbour Bridge and down to the smiling face of Luna Park at Milson's Point. They mounted the footpath and parked on the grass under the bridge.

Brian thanked Winnie. 'I was in a bit of trouble in there.'

'How did it start?'

'A couple of them footy hero loudmouths put shit on the girls and I told them to shut up. They didn't like it and got stuck into me.'

The girl Brian brought along for the ride brushed his hair off his forehead and kissed his eye. He grabbed her hand and led her into the shadows. The boys had the other slut undressed in the moonlight while Big Kev unbuckled his belt.

'After a fight, Winnie, there's nothing like a good fuck.'

He dropped his jeans and slid them down around his ankles. The boys whispered to each other about who'd be next. Ocker decided he was going last so he could take her home for the night. While Brian had his turn, Winnie and Kev sat in the park and sipped rum and watched the ferries and fishing boats crisscrossing the harbour.

'I think Brian's in love,' Big Kev sneered. 'He's had that sheila to himself all night, the bastard.'

Kev was getting restless and Winnie yelled out, 'Come on, Brian, it's time to get out of here.'

Brian brought the girl over. 'Gina, meet Winnie and Kev.'

'G'day, boys.'

'G'day,' they replied. They were pretty unimpressed that Brian had attached himself so quickly to a slut from the Cross.

'Okay, I'm going to give Gina a lift home.'

'See you on Monday.' Ocker was fucking the other girl on the grass in the shadows and all they could see was his waving hand and the moonlight bouncing off his bare arse.

Brian turned up about ten o'clock on Monday, a black eye but all smiles.

Winnie asked if he still had the slut from the other night and Brian's face darkened. He grabbed Winnie by the throat.

'Don't ever call her that again.'

The boys had never seen him flip out before. His eyes turned steely. He'd obviously done his balls over the slut overnight.

Winnie grabbed Brian's wrist, twisted it off his throat and said very quietly and calmly, 'Don't ever touch me like that again.' Big Kev and Ocker watched silently. 'What's her name?'

'Gina.'

'Well, I'm sure you and Gina are going to be happy together.' Winnie's voice turned dry and his eyes black.

Suddenly Brian realised what he'd done. He knew it should never have happened and was eager to make amends. No one spoke for about five minutes as they got on with their jobs. Brian called out, 'Have a gander at this.' On the front page of the morning paper were photos of the two footy players who'd belted Brian. The article said they'd been selected to play a rugby league Test for Australia against England, but they wouldn't be playing for a while. It went on to say they were having a quiet few beers when they were attacked by about fifteen bikies..

'Yeah, like footy heads always have quiet beers,' said Kev sarcastically.

'Hey, boys,' Brian whispered as he pointed outside the shop at two cops in suits.

Winnie asked Brian if he had the paperwork for the bike. 'Don't be smart, just go and see what they want.'

Brian walked over. 'You interested in that bike? I can give you a good deal.'

'We're from the motor squad and we believe this Triumph is stolen.'

Brian passed them the paperwork. They carefully checked the numbers.

'I think you might be making a mistake. I have the address of the person I bought it from.'

The senior cop handed the papers back. 'A lot of motorcycles are getting nicked.'

The younger cop was on his knees with his torch out. 'It's legal, boss.'

Brian could hardly hold in his laughter until they left.

Winnie shook his head. 'You wouldn't believe it if you didn't see it with your own eyes. That was lucky, but there's gotta be another way for us to make an earn. I've been reading about what's going on in the States with marijuana. Ocker, do you know where we can find Rat Rassock?'

'The Granville pub.'

'Let's see if he knows where we can get some. The way I see it, it's easy enough to grow and if we can get hold of a supply and sell it to our mates, we could do alright with it. We could go a quarter each, just like the shop. Whaddya reckon?'

Brian was naturally cautious until he had a firm idea of what was going to happen next. 'Wait a minute, Winnie, not so fast. How are we going to sell it?'

'We know enough blokes, start from there and see how we go. It could be big. Why don't we wait until we talk to the Rat then make a decision? Have any of you tried it?'

The boys shook their heads.

'Okay, wait until you try it.'

Outside the pub they saw other bikes and inside they found the Rat lining up a shot on the pool table.

'There's your man, Winnie. Fuck, he sure looks like a rat.'

With beady eyes and a stringy goatee beard, the Rat indeed resembled his namesake. He looked up and made his way over.

'Long time no see, boys.' He shook hands with them. 'What's going on?'

'That's what we were going to ask you, Rat.'

The Rat's face drained of colour; his eyes darted from Kev to Winnie then back to Kev.

'Don't worry, mate, there's no problem. I haven't seen you since school. I was just wondering what you've been up to.'

'Surfing, mate, that's the go. Fuck staying out here in the suburbs. I go to the northern beaches, lots of mates there. We're off to Hawaii soon, they reckon the sheilas fall over you there.'

'What we want to know about is marijuana,' Brian said.

'Do you want some?' The Rat pulled a joint out of his pocket.

'Here?'

'Yeah, nobody knows what it is out here yet.' He lit the joint and passed it around. Everyone coughed trying to inhale and by the time they'd finished the boys were laughing at pretty much anything.

'Fuck, Rat, I had a joint the other night but it was nothing like this.'

'What do you think?'

'Yeah, it's pretty good.' Kev smiled, off his face.

'You do know it's illegal?' The Rat looked serious.

'Of course, mate, no tax then,' Winnie replied with a cheeky smile. 'So what's the go, can you get us some?'

Rat smiled with shining eyes. 'Fucken oath I can, Winnie. Me and me surfie mates have a syndicate. You blokes could have one too, it's just too easy. Don't bring anyone else in and wholesale it, there's a piss-pot of money in it.'

Winnie wanted to get down to business. He knew it was time to shit or get off the pot; he wanted to do it but he wanted to underplay his hand. 'Okay, Rat, just start us off.'

'You should get a pound, it'll set you back three hundred bucks.'

Three hundred was a lot of money. With Easter and Bathurst looming, Winnie wondered if they could afford it.

Rat read their faces. 'Take it on credit; there are sixteen ounces to a pound, you sell ten at $30 a bag, that's your three hundred and the rest is profit. You'll make about $180 a pound, depends how much you smoke yourselves. I'll drop it off at the shop tomorrow morning. Tell you what, I'll pass you my customers on this side of town; you'll be doing me a favour.'

'Okay, Rat, good one. Drop it off in the morning.'

'So how did you and your mates get into it?' Brian asked.

'I know surfers up the far north coast. They got friendly with some farmers who grow it for them, hundreds and hundreds of pounds of the stuff.' The Rat was stoned and a little loose. 'You should see how it is on the northern beaches, the whole peninsula is stoned. It's better than piss and you make money into the bargain. Anyway, I'll see you tomorrow.'

Winnie turned to the boys. 'Fuck, they must be making some money out of it if only half of what he said is true.'

They ordered beers and enjoyed their high. Kev nudged Winnie. 'Have a look at that, Winnie.'

Two of Twister's boys leaned against the bar. They wore sleeveless denim jackets and embroidered on the back was a tiger's head with the words 'Tigers' on top and 'MC' on one side with 'Sydney' underneath.

'Let's have a chat with them. Brian, you and Ocker go out to the beer garden; we'll be out in a minute.'

'Isn't that bloke with the long hair in the Tigers jacket Ian Wells?' said Kev.

'Yeah, that's Wellsie. Let's have a word.' They sauntered over.

'G'day, Winnie, Kev. I heard you opened a bike shop.'

'That's right, Wellsie. If you or your mates need work done on your bikes, come and see us.'

'How do you like our club colours? Alright, eh? We meet here Thursday nights; you and your boys should come and join us.'

'Maybe, mate. Don't forget we'll do you a good deal on any work.' Kev and Winnie grabbed a few beers each and walked out into the beer garden.

Kev asked, 'What do you mean, maybe?'

'Never let them know what you're thinking, Kev. No point in telling them to get fucked, is there? They were only trying to be friendly. They probably have no idea what Twister's like … What did you blokes think when you saw the Tigers patch?'

'I thought it was an ad for Esso,' said Ocker and they laughed as one.

'That aside,' says Winnie, 'it wasn't bad, but I reckon we could do better.' Everyone nodded.

Brian got up, drained his beer and announced, 'I'm going over to Gina's for tea, see you in the morning.'

When Brian turned to go, Winnie raised his eyebrows to Kev and Ocker. He had a funny feeling in his water bag about that Gina.

Over the next few weeks everything ran smoothly in the shop. Bikes wheeled in and out and they made an honest dollar doing first-class work. The word soon spread. Brian sold two hot bikes one week and they started doing business with the Rat. He dropped off the pound and brought scales and showed them what to do. He even brought bags to put the weed in.

'There you go, boys, it's that easy. Now, Winnie, here's my phone number. Keep the scales, ring me when you want more. You'll have to pay for the first pound before you get more, so don't piss all the money away at Bathurst.'

'Hey, Rat, you'll get paid, don't worry.' Winnie laughed. 'Do you have to drive that bloody yellow thing around?'

The Rat looked mildly puzzled. 'It doesn't stick out, does it?'

'Not on the northern beaches, mate, but it does out here.'

The Rat just shrugged. 'Seeyas.'

On the Thursday night before the Bathurst weekend Brian added up the week's takings: over $2960 in the kitty and rent paid.

Winnie wanted to know about the pot money and Brian was on top of it.

'I keep that separate. It's going alright too. With the Rat's friends buying, we only have seven ounces left. We should take an ounce to Bathurst with us and introduce it to the boys.'

'Another good idea, Brian.' Winnie respected Brian's eye for an earn.

'How much do we want to pay ourselves?'

Brian suggested $300 each and to keep the pot money separate and build it up. He was pretty sensible like that. They all agreed. Life looked sweet.

On Good Friday, the boys' first holiday since Christmas, the sun shone and Winnie's mum cooked up a big breakfast for him, probably his last decent feed for a few days. Winnie wheeled his Triumph out of the shed and marvelled at how beautiful it looked, all black and chrome and gleaming, with matching four-inch mirrors. He strapped the sleeping bag on the back, primed the carburettors with two kicks and the motor roared into life.

When he reached the shop he smelled marijuana in the air. Kev was pulling on a joint.

'I hope you haven't given all our stuff away?' Winnie asked, half seriously.

'No way, Winnie. Fuck that, we're selling it at full price.' Then Kev turned serious and said, 'Have a look inside, mate, at what Brian has with him.'

'You remember Gina, don't you?'

Winnie cringed; it was the last thing he wanted, a girl on their boys' weekend. After the last episode he'd learned how protective Brian was, so all he felt he could do was give her a tight smile and say hello. She smiled back.

'I've heard so much about you, Winnie. It's like I already know you.'

Yeah, like fuck you do, he thought.

'Hey, Brian, we're going at ten o'clock.' He wanted Brian to tell her to fuck off but Brian was his mate, so he bit his tongue.

Winnie made his way outside to Kev and Ocker, standing in a cloud of marijuana smoke. Winnie boiled over. 'It was going to be a good ride. Doesn't he know that taking her will just fuck everything up?'

'Don't worry about him, mate, I already told him to keep her out of the way,' assured Kev.

'The silly cunt, I bet he puts her up the duff and has to marry her.' Winnie was frustrated at the situation his mate was getting into, especially since the business looked ready to take off.

'I wouldn't bet against it,' said Kev. 'She looks like the trapping and using type to me. Poor bastard. Hey, Winnie, remember Squizzy Taylor? He's coming too.'

'Isn't he at university?'

'Law,' said Squizzy from behind him. 'Good to see you, Winnie.' They shook hands.

'What are you going to be? A solicitor?' Winnie laughed. 'Maybe we can use you one day.'

'It's five minutes to go, Winnie. You better let Romeo know,' said Kev.

They left Parramatta and rode up the Great Western Highway, weaving through traffic up the Blue Mountains over twisting roads, where the bikes came into their own. Their first stop was the Railway Hotel in Katoomba, the only pub that served the riders of about two hundred bikes parked outside. Kev smiled and rubbed his hands together. There was nothing he liked more than a beer and a chat about bikes.

They recognised plenty of familiar faces from the Centennial Hotel days. One bloke stood out: Swannie from Hurstville. He made his way over and shook Big Kev and Winnie by the hand. 'Who are you with, mate?'

'A few of the boys,' Winnie replied.

'You want to ride up with us?'

'Well, we're not staying here long and we want to get a good camp site, we're leaving pretty soon.'

'Sounds alright to me, Winnie, we'll join you.'

A couple of blokes did burnouts on the road when the bells from the railway crossing started ringing. One bloke revved his bike, did a wheel stand and headed towards the crossing. The crowd stepped off the footpath to watch and cheered madly as he went flat out up the road and over the lines just seconds before the boom gates shut behind him. On the other side a car pulled out of a side street and centre-punched him, sending him flying through the air just before the train sped through and blocked their view. When the train had passed, people rushed up to him. He'd landed head first on the road. His mates realised he was dead immediately. They knelt around him on the road and cried. The pub crowd hushed, shocked by the suddenness of the death. People slowly moved back to the pub and gave them space. An ambulance pulled up a few minutes later.

'He's dead, mate,' Winnie said quietly to Brian.

'Silly cunt,' Gina said as if the poor bastard had deserved it.

Winnie felt as though she had hit him. Right then his fears were confirmed and he knew what sort of cunt Brian had. Winnie looked at Brian and then at Gina, shook his head and walked away.

Gina looked at Brian. 'What did I say?'

After Katoomba a few more blokes joined their pack. When they reached the Golden Mile coming into Bathurst they saw the highway patrol on bikes and in cars on both sides of the main strip. The boys were amazed to see thousands of British bikes all polished and gleaming — there was not a Jap bike in sight — their riders lolling about on the grass.

Ocker asked, 'When are we going to roll up the joint?'

'We'll do it tonight. I told a few of the boys and they're all excited. That's what we want. Ocker, remember this is business. We don't want to be stoned and fuck up.' Winnie knew it could be a great business and he wanted to make money.

A pack of bikes roared past, led by Twister and his Tigers in their club colours. They looked good with denim cut-offs over their leather jackets, each with the embroidered Tigers patch. It stirred the crowd; it was all new, very American. The Australian way had been to paint an emblem on the leather jacket, but most of those early clubs had long disbanded; they were a different generation.

'We should think about starting up a club,' said Kev, staring at Twister's boys. 'You know I'd love to be in a club but I don't want to ride with some of those queer cunts.'

Brian said, 'Fuck 'em. I'm taking the girl, we're going to set up camp. I'll see you up there.'

Winnie shouted after him, 'Hey, if we start a club up, this will be the first and last time she comes on our run, mate.' Ocker and Kev laughed as Brian got on his bike.

Swannie from Hurstville came over with a few of his mates. Winnie introduced him around and noticed Twister moving in his direction with a mob of Tigers. Twister looked like he was the Prime Minister on a walk; he remembered names and shook hands everywhere.

'How're you going, Winnie?'

'Good, Twister, good.' Winnie noticed the gleaming gold 'President' badge on his cut-off.

'How do you like it?' Twister spread his palms out and did a slow turn. 'You should come for a ride with us, join our club.'

'We'll see.'

'Kero Ken went to see your shop. He says it's a good little business and it's getting a good name.'

'We try. Oh, Kero, thanks for helping us out at the Cross.'

'No worries, mate. Those footballers were giving me the shits too; anyway, I'm out of there now. I'm working with Twister. Where are you camping tonight?'

'Up the hill.'

'We'll most probably go there too. Let's have a beer later.' He strolled back over to Twister.

'I can't stand that poncy cunt,' Swannie sneered at Twister's back.

Winnie smiled. He didn't want to get involved, so changed the subject. 'Alright, let's go and make camp.'

At last the boys headed for Mount Panorama and watched the cops isolating the Tigers, who stood out like dogs' balls in their patched cut-offs. When the boys reached the main gate they saw the last of the qualifiers practising for the next day's races. Winnie was awestruck; he'd always wanted to race and watching the bikes on the track made the urge stronger. The service road swirled with dust from hundreds of bikes going in both directions. Bandanas came in handy. They found a shady spot under a tree and collected wood and watched the sun set over the western plains that stretched to the horizon.

Brian strolled over with Gina. 'Hey, Winnie, when are we going to have a joint?'

'Real soon, but first we need to have a talk about the weed. Get your girl to go for a walk and I'll get Kevvie and Ocker.'

The four of them sat for a chat and Winnie pulled out the pot.

'Now,' said Winnie, getting serious, 'don't forget this is business. We have to find a market for it. Tell only people who you know that it's for sale at the shop. Thirty bucks a bag. Any questions?'

'All right, Winnie, let's roll that joint.' Ocker laughed. 'Party time tonight, fellas.'

Brian took some to smoke with Gina. Kev and Winnie headed off for a beer and Swannie joined them. They talked about the poor cunt at the railway crossing. Swannie knew a little more than they did. 'They say he did it everywhere. Fuck, it looked good. Poor cunt, who was he?' No one knew, so they raised a drink for the guy who went out in style.

Squizzy Taylor made his way over with beers.

'Hey, Squizz, what are you up to? How's the solicitor caper?'

'Expensive, Winnie, I dunno if I can afford to keep paying all my fees. I might have to sell my bike.'

Winnie gave it a moment's thought. 'Well, we could sell it for you … or you could sell some of our pot to your uni mates. Whaddya reckon?'

'Fucken oath, mate, they're all on it there. I'll come and see you next week.' Squizzy walked off to join a crowd around a fire.

The cops normally didn't come up the hill at night but that year they built a compound and brought in back-ups. They wanted everyone to know who was in charge and cruised around in Land Rovers daring anyone to cause trouble. Whenever crackers went off they sped off to investigate and they were in so much of a hurry they ran over some bloke's bike. It never took long for an alcohol-fuelled crowd to gather and soon the cops were on the radio calling for back-up. The police had no idea what to do — the bike was stuck under the Land Rover. A few blokes in the crowd chucked some bottles and cans and then a Molotov cocktail exploded near the cops and about then they roared off to their compound, leaving the Land Rover behind. Another Molotov cocktail landed on the Land Rover's roof and it went up in flames. The crowd went wild and the fire lit up the faces of about three hundred cheering people. Out of the darkness the police, protected by shields and waving truncheons, charged the mob but retreated under a hail of rocks.

'Fuck this,' said Winnie, 'I'm going back to our camp.'

The police charged again and belted anyone within reach with their sticks and made a few arrests. The boys heard some blokes squealing from the blows.

'Fuck, do you hear that? Well, if any of them copper cunts wants to do that here there'll be trouble,' snarled Kev.

Two coppers walked up to their campsite. They just stared at the thirty blokes lying around drinking but didn't say a word and soon disappeared into the darkness. Laughter erupted around the fire. They sipped rum and stared into the fire, alone with their private thoughts. After a while Kev spoke up.

'I never saw anything of Twister and the Tigers. What happened to them? They really stand out with those Tigers patches, don't they? Have you given any thought to us starting up a club of our own, Winnie? A lot of blokes we know would join.'

'As a matter of fact, I have, mate. Let everyone interested know and we'll have a meeting on Thursday night at the shop.'

The next morning the result of the previous night's rioting was evident: the squashed bike and the cops' Land Rover were a tangle of burnt-out black metal sitting in a halo of scorched grass. During the night more police arrived and regrouped around the compound. No doubt they had arrested a lot of people, whether they were involved or not. The boys decided to head home as soon as the races finished, reckoning it wasn't going to be much fun up there the next night. As they rode out they passed roadblocks and cops pulled over riders, taking down names and issuing notices for minor defects. The cops had a bad case of the shits with everyone. On the slow ride home they bypassed the fatal boom gates.

Back in Parramatta they pulled up at the shop in a group of about fifteen and entered the workshop. By unanimous decision, the shop shouted everyone a beer. They were lounging around drinking and rehashing the weekend when Brian drove up minus his girl. He came in all smiles and the blokes took the piss out of him.

Brian cracked a beer, smiled and said, 'Well, at least I got some pussy. Here, smell this.' He grabbed his crotch and invited blokes to smell his hand.

Winnie cleared his throat. 'Well, blokes, what do you think about starting up a motorcycle club like the Tigers?'

Suddenly everyone perked up, all talking at once, shouting different names for it.

'Hold on!' shouted Big Kev.

Winnie took a breath. 'Listen, everyone who wants to can write down ideas for the club's name and some rules. Bring them along on Thursday night at seven o'clock.' With that most of the blokes headed off home and left the four of them alone.

'Brian, where's the money and the pot?' asked Winnie.

'I'll get it.' Brian counted out the proceeds.

'I don't think it's a good idea keeping the money and the pot together,' said Kev. 'Or leaving it in the shop. There's some low cunts around who'd like to break in, especially if they know it's here.'

Ocker offered to take the pot to his place and bring in a couple of ounces the next day.

'But no taxing it, okay, Ocker?' Winnie knew Ocker well enough to know it might happen.

'Come on, Winnie, I'd never do that.' They laughed; they both knew.

'Brian, will you sort out the books?'

'Sure, mate, I'll get Gina to help me.'

'Oh, Jesus, Brian, come on, you've only just met her. We don't want just anyone knowing our business.' Winnie was annoyed; Gina seemed to be coming up all the time.

'But she's a fair dinkum bookkeeper. Besides, I'm going to marry her.' Brian blurted it out, maybe before he was ready.

The boys stood and stared in amazement. Kev said, 'I told you, he's done his balls.'

'Fuck, Brian! You've only just met her.' Winnie was incredulous.

'I know, but I bloody love her, mate, and she feels the same way. Anyway, she's had a pretty tough life and now it's her turn for a bit of the good stuff.'

'What about her oldies?'

'Just her mother. Her stepfather's in jail. She reckons her mother wants her out of the way before the stepfather gets out. Gina says she can remember the lewd looks he used to give her. The mother doesn't want any sexual rivals around when he gets out. What a cunt.'

Yes, Winnie thought, like mother like daughter. He shook Brian's hand and wished him all the best, knowing Brian wouldn't change his mind. 'Best of luck, mate. I'm off. Don't forget to take the cash home with you.'

Winnie gave it all some thought — not too much, just enough to work out it wasn't the best news he'd had all day. The shop was busy the next week thanks to the under-the-counter pot selling. By Wednesday only four ounces remained; they'd recouped the $300 outlay for the first pound and stood to make $180.

'Not too bad!' Ocker said. 'We have to get onto the Rat and get some more before Thursday night.'

Brian whistled. 'You were right, Winnie, we're going to make a good earn out of this pot.'

Winnie arranged to see the Rat the next day. He arrived in his Zephyr with a plastic bag full of pot.

'You're up early!' said Winnie.

'Yeah, surf's up, Winnie, got to get it while it's there.' Ocker weighed up a pound. 'See, mate, just like I said. I tell you, it's like the northern beaches. You're in the box seat here; pretty soon you could do five pounds a week.'

'Sure, Rat. Hey, next time you come to the shop, take those surfboards off the car, they stand out like dogs' balls.'

The Rat looked puzzled; he didn't think he stood out at all.

On the Thursday night twenty of the boys turned up to decide on a few club rules and a name. Big Kev got everyone's attention and asked for suggestions.

'What do you think, Winnie? The club's your idea.' Everyone shut up.

'Well, I reckon the Miners Motorcycle Club, to celebrate the gold-diggers who rebelled down in Victoria. They swore by the Southern Cross to stand by each other and fight to defend their rights. We could use their Eureka Stockade flag and put the name MINERS MC in the middle. Instead of getting gold underground, we'll get ours above ground.'

'Hey, that's not a bad idea, Winnie. I'll drink to that,' said Kev swigging his rum.

The boys gave it some thought and warmed to the idea, though some didn't have a clue what the Eureka flag looked like. Winnie brought out a couple of drawings and passed them around. The boys start nodding, signalling their approval.

'I like it, it's really Australian,' said Big Kev.

'Okay, so that's it, we're now the Miners Motorcycle Club, otherwise known as the Club.'

The boys shook hands with the men who became their brothers from that moment onwards.

'Everyone here tonight is a founding member of the Miners. Now we have to elect a President, Treasurer and Sergeant-at-Arms.'

Slippery proposed Winnie for President.

'Yeah!' the boys shouted and Big Kev grabbed Winnie's hand and raised it as if he'd won a prize fight.

'How yer going, Prez?' Kev embraced Winnie and whispered in his ear, 'I've always wanted a brother.'

Brian shook Winnie's hand and told him, 'You're the one, mate. You organised the horseshit, you can organise the club.'

They both laughed at the memory, and Winnie said, 'All right, we need a Treasurer and I nominate Brian.'

'Yeah, thanks, mate,' said Brian and the boys voiced their approval.

'I trust you,' said Winnie, patting him on the back.

'Now what about our Sergeant-at-Arms?'

As if there were any doubt who it would be. They all looked at Big Kev, all six foot four of him, standing with his arms folded and legs apart. No one said a word, then Ocker stood up and aped Big Kev. He stood just five foot seven inches, and the boys had a good laugh.

'Well, that's it, then!' said Winnie. 'What about the rules of the Club? Everyone think about it and we can draw them up next week. Just remember we don't want too many rules — that's why we chose this lifestyle. Anyway, why don't we go for a ride and a beer?'

Winnie's suggestion didn't need any seconding and they saddled up and took off with a noisy roar for the Locomotion Hotel, their pub. A big crowd hung around outside, waiting to get in to see Billy Thorpe and the Aztecs, one of Sydney's best bands. Some had never ventured so far west of Sydney in their lives. As long as they didn't cause any shit, there wouldn't be any. The crowd built up and the doormen kept letting people in until some idiots started tossing beer cans. The band's security manager made his way over to their table just as Brian lit up a joint.

'G'day, boys, my name's Lee Dillow.' He extended his hand to Winnie. 'Listen, fellas, there's a big crowd here tonight and I don't think we can control it. When Billy comes on to play we don't want any cans flying around. If you can help us out I'll get a few cases of beer for you and your boys.'

'What do you reckon, Kev?' Winnie was up for it but he left it to Kev.

'Piece of piss, mate.'

'Okay, Lee, we'll pick the grog up after the show.'

When Lee left they laughed their guts out. Piece of piss indeed.

'All right, Kev, tell those boys to stop throwing the fucking cans.'

When the band finished the set, Dillow went to the microphone and thanked the crowd and the Miners Motorcycle Club for providing 'security'. The boys were dumbfounded. How did he know?

Brian confessed. 'I told him.'

'That's one way of going public,' Winnie laughed. In the crowd the drunken dickheads moved out slowly. One sang out, 'Watch out for the minor bikies.' That brought about more laughter. In a flash Winnie grabbed the smart-arse by the throat. He smacked him in the snout and dropped him in a second. Kev grabbed two of them in a headlock and knocked their heads together and let them fall to the floor. In a flash the place became a free-for-all and the boys used whatever came to hand — chairs, boots and, best of all, a big shifting spanner.

'That'll teach you cunts to fuck with the Miners,' shouted Winnie. They walked out of the pub leaving behind a bunch of fucked-up, unhappy punters, bleeding and horizontal.

'Now, let's go and get our beer — we earned it.' They rode down to the river to celebrate their first victory as a club. Winnie proposed a toast to the Club, then Big Kev looked at George, one of the blokes who came to the meeting. 'How come you never got involved?'

'Well, you had it under control.'

'Get fucked! We agreed, one in, all in,' Big Kevvie roared.

George took a step back, but not quickly enough. Kev kicked him in the crotch and George tumbled backwards and landed on his arse.

'There's few rules here, mate, but it's one in, all in. Now fuck off and don't come back, you cunt.' George tried to avoid another dose of Kev's size twelve boots but it was too late and the boys heard ribs snap.

'Kevvie, that'll do, mate. Come and have a beer,' Winnie shouted. George crawled away into the darkness.

'Now that's going to be one of our rules. Anyone who doesn't agree can leave now,' growled Kev.

'One in, all in!' they shouted together.

Brian wanted to know what they'd do with George's bike.

'We'll sell it and the proceeds go to the Miners and that goes for anyone who gets thrown out. Big Kev can find out where George lives and get him to sign his bike over to the Miners MC. Brian, you can sell it through our shop and since you're the Treasurer you better start up a bank account in the Club's name.'

Winnie was on top of it. There wasn't room to fuck around.

'Is that it for tonight?' Brian said he wanted to get home to his girl.

'Who, your mother?' Kev laughed.

'Smart cunt,' Brian was angry. 'Her name's Gina! Orright?' No one said a word. 'I'll see you tomorrow.'

The next morning at the shop Brian leaned on the counter and quietly announced, 'I'm getting married this Friday.'

'Fuck me dead, mate, congratulations!' Ocker yelled, shaking hands with a beaming Brian.

He looked pretty happy, Winnie thought, as he shook Brian's hand.

'Doing it at the Registry, then off to the Loco. They're putting on a spread and it's our treat. Bring a girl.'

Big Kev shook Brian's hand. 'I'm happy for you, mate.'

'We might be able to help with the costs,' said Winnie. The pot was starting to make a good quid, just like the Rat said it would. 'I have blokes who want three pounds.'

'Yeah and I want two,' said Ocker. Brian wanted three.

'That's eight pounds, fuck me,' said Winnie, and they all started laughing. 'What about you, Kev?'

'No, none for me.'

'Don't worry, mate,' said Winnie, 'you've got better jobs to do in this business. Now listen, Brian, remember Mrs Wright with the roses, who never paid for her horseshit? Well, we give no bastard credit. If anyone gives credit, they pay any loss, fair enough?'

'Sure, Winnie, no credit!' they all agreed.

Winnie did a quick calculation. 'Looks like you're going to have a good wedding, mate. I reckon if we put fifty dollars on every pound and the Rat gives it to us cheaper if we buy ten pounds at once, we're on a winner. If we can sell ten pounds a week we could clear an extra couple of grand a week. If the shop keeps going good, we'll kill it. After I meet Rat I'm seeing an embroiderer in Fairfield to make up our Club patches. I'm off now.'

Winnie left, not too happy about Brian's news, but determined to put his bad feelings to bed and support his mate.

Chapter 3

Winnie had arranged to meet Rat at the Hornsby Hotel.

'Good place to sit, mate, near the stinking toilet.'

Rat smiled, 'Yeah I know, mate. We can talk in peace.'

The penny dropped. 'Well, you were right about the pot. We want ten pounds.'

'Good one, Winnie, you can have it for $280.'

'Fair enough. What about credit?'

'Okay, you pay for five, five on credit.'

'Sounds good, mate. When can we get it?'

'Two days, mate.'

'Tell me, Rat, how many pounds can you supply if we need it?'

'Don't worry, you'll be right. The blokes I know are big time.' Draining his beer the Rat wiped his thin moustache with the back of his hand. 'I'm off, mate, business.'

When Winnie told the boys back at the shop about Rat's offer they were amazed.

'Fuck, credit. That's all right, Winnie.'

'Yeah, I know, but that doesn't mean we have to give it, so let your buyers know it will be here on Thursday. We need fifteen hundred bucks to pay Rat. Can you organise that, Brian?'

Brian nodded; money was becoming less of an issue.

On Thursday night, Miners' meeting night, the boys closed the shop after the last member came in. Kev boomed out, 'Shut up, you lot, a bit of quiet.'

'Alright, here are the rules for our Club.' Winnie held up a piece of paper and read aloud:

1. If ever a Miner is attacked, everyone there helps.
2. No thieving from one another.
3. No one tries to hit onto another member's girl, even if they're no longer together.
4. A Miner wearing his patch rides only a British or American bike.
5. Members must pay dues at each meeting.
6. Anyone thrown out of the Club gets bashed and their bike goes to the Club.
7. What goes on in the Club does not get repeated to anyone not in the Club.
8. Your family comes first, then the Club. That way the Club becomes your family.

'Has anybody got anything else they would like to ask? Or anything they don't like?'

'Yeah, Prez.' Slippery stood up and looked around, a little uncertainly. 'About the girls, what if a bloke wants to go out with a member's ex? Is that alright?'

'No, mate, it'll only cause trouble. Oh, there's one more rule. Rule number nine: no old ladies allowed on Club runs. Okay?' The boys nodded. 'The Club patches'll be ready next week but we start paying fees tonight. Ten dollars a week and give it to Brian. Now for those of you who don't know, Brian is getting married tomorrow.'

The boys all congratulated Brian. Ocker brought out a couple of cases of beer and an ounce of pot and the boys got stuck in.

Big Kev talked to Winnie. 'Hey, Prez, we're going to have to find a clubhouse for our meeting. The workshop is too small and I don't want everyone leaving their mess in here.'

'I know, mate, I'm going to look around for one next week.'

The wedding was a pretty low-key affair, first the hitching at the Registry office and then a bit of grog and a feed at the pub. Just before Brian and Gina left for the honeymoon Gina asked Winnie, 'Have you got a kiss for the bride?'

'Sure, Gina!' He gave her a kiss on the cheek and she looked up at him.

'You don't like me much, do you, Winnie?'

'Fuck me, what brought that on?'

'Just a feeling I have.'

'Well, you're wrong, I'm happy for both of you.'

'Thanks, Winnie, that means a lot to me.'

'Just take good care of him.'

After a few months they found a clubhouse in an industrial estate and started attracting new members. They changed their meeting night to Friday and when the members arrived the nominees had the bar stocked and the barbecue ready to go. A separate room was set aside for the meeting.

Big Kev roared out, 'Meeting in five minutes!' The members grabbed extra drinks and moved into the meeting room. Brian collected fees, and Big Kev called the meeting to order.

Ocker started to read out the minutes from the last meeting. There were a few members behind with Club fees. Winnie stood up. 'Listen, you cunts, we have rent and other expenses running this clubhouse. If you can't pay your fees, fuck off. We don't want losers in this Club.'

Nestor, one of the founding members, spoke up. 'Winnie, a few of us are out of work.'

'Get fucked, Nestor, you lazy cunt. You sit around watching TV and drinking piss. You're an outlaw, aren't you? Maybe you don't like working in a factory but there are other ways to make a decent earn and that goes for everyone. You can sell pot — find a big factory and get someone inside to sell it for you. If you don't want to sell, steal motorcycles and we will help you to do the numbers for a small fee. That pays for the original stamp. You only have to do one every two months.'

'But there's good movies on during the day.' That brought the house down.

'Next, Ocker?' asked Winnie.

'Right, those Commando cunts have been seen hanging around and they should be told to keep away from our bikes. Wherever they go a couple of bikes disappear and they don't give a fuck who they hit.'

'I heard they got one of the Tigers' bikes.'

'And what did Twister do about that?'

'I don't know. I heard he went to see them and it turns out Twister is doing some sort of business with them. If Twister told his Tigers the Commandos would never steal from them he probably believed it and so did the Tigers.'

'Well, still, we'd better go and have a talk with them.'

'Fucken oath!' Kev yelled, 'Does anybody know where they'll be tonight?'

'Sure,' Ocker said. 'I know a slut one of them is fucking and she told me that they drink at the General Grant.'

'Good, let's go now,' said Winnie. 'We can finish the meeting next week. There's nothing urgent, is there? Grab whatever you need. There's plenty of baseball bats around, chains, whatever you feel comfortable with. When we arrive at the pub keep everything out of sight. Kevvie and me will go and talk with them. If you see trouble brewing, just get into them. We don't know how many there will be, but just get into them.'

The General Grant pub is in Balmain, an inner Sydney suburb. There were about twenty-five Miners but only about twelve Commandos and a few odd blokes hanging around in groups of three or four. Winnie told everyone to go into the pub while he and Big Kev found out who to talk to. When the boys headed for the bar, the new Miners patches stood out like the Southern Cross in the night sky. Big Kev nodded as two of the dirtiest cunts he'd ever seen headed towards him. They could barely make out the Commandos Patches under all the dirt. Their patch had a soldier astride a motorcycle holding a rifle. They didn't look too impressive.

As they approached, one bloke reached out his hand. 'Rastus is the name, and this is Spike.'

They were both about the same size and arse-ugly, wearing beanies with Commandos MC embroidered on the front. Both sported short black beards. Winnie didn't know what to make of them.

'Yeah, Winnie's the name,' he shook their grubby hands, 'and this is Big Kev.'

'Yeah, I've heard about you from Twister.'

'All bad I hope,' smiled Kev.

'Yeah, you tried to kill him up on Snow's Mountain when you were kids.' They all laughed and that broke the ice.

Rastus pointed to a table. 'Let's have a beer.' Rastus snapped his fingers and a nominee came over and took their orders.

'Where are you from, Rastus?' Winnie asked.

'Victoria. We thought we'd have a look around in Sydney.'

'And how do you like it?'

'It's not too bad.'

'What's wrong with Melbourne?'

'Too much competition, there's a club down there in every suburb. It's only new up here.'

'Well,' said Winnie, 'We just want to tell you that if any of our bikes go off there'll be trouble.'

Rastus unwrapped a small cigar and stuck it in his mouth, which was missing three front teeth. 'We know what the go is, mate. We don't take Club bikes.'

'That's not what Twister says,' Winnie lied and they both laughed.

'That cunt would say that.'

'I'll talk to him about it,' said Winnie.

The boys spread out in the pub and Kev let them know everything was all right and to mingle with the Commandos. They drank and laughed together and passed around joints and tried to outdo each other.

'You haven't got into the Harleys up here yet, have you?'

'No, fuck 'em; they're never on the road.'

'Yeah, you have to work on them a bit but they're getting better and once you ride one you'll never ride another Triumph.'

'They're too slow,' said Winnie.

'You reckon?' Spike said.

'What do you mean?' Big Kev asked Spike. Their mutual love of mechanics was evident.

'Come on, I'll show you,' said Spike and they grabbed their beers and headed out to the parking lot.

'How do you know Twister, Rastus?' Winnie asked.

'One of my cousins is in his Tigers.'

'And did you get one of their bikes?'

'Come on, Winnie,' Rastus said with a grin. 'You've known him a while.'

'Yeah, and he is a Twister.'

'I am glad you came down tonight, Winnie. I've heard about you.'

'And what's that?'

'No bullshit, and that's what I like.'

'You should bring your boys back to our clubhouse,' Winnie said. 'We'll organise a few strippers.'

'Sounds all right, I'll let my boys know.' Rastus reached out his hand. 'It's good to meet you, Winnie.'

'Same, Rastus, I reckon we have a lot in common.' Winnie walked over to the boys. 'Hey, Ocker, do you reckon you can organise a few strippers for the clubhouse tonight? I've invited the Commandos back.'

'Are you sure they're all right, Winnie?'

'Yeah, mate, they're just like us, only dirty cunts.'

Big Kev came back into the pub grinning. He said the Commandos might look dirty but their bikes were immaculate.

'And what are you so happy about, Kev?' Winnie wanted to know.

'Nothing, mate!'

'I invited them back to the clubhouse.'

'Oh good, now we can see how fast their Harleys go.' Kev set off to get all the Miners out of the pub and let them know about the party with the Commandos.

Brian came over to Winnie. 'So, mate, they seem alright, eh?'

'Yeah, mate, I think so. Come on, let's go.'

Winnie headed towards his black Triumph, jumped on and kicked it into life. The high-pitched motor roared. The other Miners did the same. Next Rastus and his Commandos kicked their Harleys into life. It was the first time that most of the Miners had heard that many Harleys at once and the sound of them booming in sequence drowned out the noise of the Triumphs. Winnie led the pack out of Balmain and through the back roads, where the Harleys had trouble keeping up with the lighter and nimbler Triumphs.

At a set of traffic lights, Spike from the Commandos idled up to the front where Big Kev and Winnie sat revving their engines, waiting for the green light. Spike revved his bike and looked across at them with a big smile on his face that said, 'I'll show you how this Harley goes.'

When the lights turned green, Kev did a wheelie and took off down Parramatta Road. The Harley chugged off slowly at first until it picked up revs, then in a heartbeat Spike made up ground on Winnie and Big Kev, accelerated past them and damn near disappeared into the distance, leaving Winnie and Kev way behind until he pulled up at the next light.

'Fuck me,' Winnie mouthed to no one and shook his head.

At the clubhouse, one of the nominees unlocked the front gate and let in the pack. Winnie asked Rastus and Spike what they'd like to drink.

'Rum,' they said in unison and Rastus lit another of his cigars.

'Fuck, they stink,' Big Kev said.

'Yeah, they're rolled by these virgins in Cuba, they use their thighs,' and he gave an impersonation by rubbing a stogie back and forth on his leg.

'They don't smell like any virgins I know,' laughed Kev. 'Fuck me, Spike, you sure have your Harley tricked up.'

'You don't have to do too much to them. Everyone thinks of the Harleys they used in the war. They were like tractors, but these are 1200 cc shovelheads. Rastus has the panhead. Once you get into them you'll never go back to your Triumphs.'

'What about the Sportster?'

'Nah, they're a sheila's bike. We call them half a Harley.'

'Come on, Spike, tell me all about them.' Kev and Spike went outside to look over the Harleys.

Ocker organised the strippers and haggled over the cost and what they would do for the money. He settled on the fruit and vegie act.

Winnie brought Brian over to meet Rastus and they shook hands.

'Brian is not only a Miner, but my business partner. We run a bike shop with Kevvie and Ocker. Hey, Ocker, come over here, and meet Rastus.'

Rastus was in fine fettle. 'Owyergoin', mate? You've got the girlies, eh? When do they come on?' He giggled wildly.

'As soon as I see what they've got on offer. I've got to personally inspect them.' Ocker winked and took the girls out the back with a huge smile on his face.

'Can't wait, I love the sluts,' Rastus said. 'I'll have another rum.' He pulled out a wad from his pocket. put fifty dollars on the bar, announced to Winnie, 'That's from the Commandos.' The smell of marijuana filled the air. 'I love the pot,' Rastus smiled.

Brian pulled a three-paper joint out of his pocket and sparked it up then passed it to Winnie, who didn't normally smoke. He took a few tokes and passed it to Rastus, who puffed on it until he looked like a steam train ready to take off.

'Fuck, I love the pot. Not much of it down our way; you Sydney blokes are a mile in front.'

'Well, Rastus, we can talk about that later. Here come the girls.'

When their music came on, the boys roared encouragement and Rastus made his way to the front row with his rum in one hand and a cigar in the other. Winnie and Brian stayed back at the bar and talked about the prospect of more business. The girls really got into the party mode and Rastus disappeared outside with a girl in tow. When the sun rose, most of the boys started to leave. Each one came over and shook everyone's hand as they left. Rastus got his boys together.

'Hey, Winnie, I'll drop into your shop next week so we can have a yarn. Thanks for the night; your girls are real friendly.'

'No worries, Rastus, I'll talk to you then.' Winnie wondered how Rastus could drink rum all night and still be fine to ride as he watched them roar off on their Harleys.

Kev came over to Winnie. 'That Spike sure knows his Harleys. He let me know a few of his tricks. Turns out there are special V stamps you need when you do a number job.'

'Well, mate, I reckon we might need a set of stamps like that. The only problem is there aren't enough Harleys around.'

'Not yet, mate, but I bet there will be pretty soon. Spike let me take his for a ride while the party was on. Fuck, it felt good.'

Winnie spoke quietly. 'This pot business looks good, but there'll be trouble if too many clubs start up in Sydney unless the clubs here look after their own areas.'

'How are you going to get everyone to agree to that?'

'Dunno yet, but I'm going to see the Twister next week and work something out. Where are the Tigers drinking?'

'I went for a ride with Gina last week and there must have been about thirty of them down at the Scarborough Hotel on the old coast road,' said Brian.

'Hey, Kev, can you come with me when I see Twister?'

'Sure, Winnie.'

'How's the pot money going, Brian? The bank should be building up now.'

'Eight and a half grand so far, Winnie.'

'Well, I reckon we take a thousand each and if our pot business keeps going, we should be able to get a grand each fortnight.'

'Fuck me, Winnie, we could close the bike shop and just do pot,' said Ocker.

'Yeah, like fuck we will. The shop keeps us busy and it's a good front for us. We have to be seen to be working and idle hands breed idle minds. I don't want to end up like our parents, living in Commission homes. Not me.'

'Anyway,' Brian said, 'I'm starting to save for a home for Gina. I want to be the first person in my family to own a home.'

'Yeah, good move, Brian.'

'Not me,' Big Kev said, 'I'm going to save up for a new Harley.'

Winnie agreed. 'Yeah, me too, Kev. I fell in love with them last night after Spike blew me off at the traffic lights.'

Ocker said, 'Fuck that, I'm off to the ponies to double my money.'

'Okay, next thing, the shop. Brian, now we're doing alright with the pot we should stop doing the hot bikes through the shop. We can still do makeovers for any of our members, but they can sell them to other shops or privately. Blokes are getting more security conscious and there's no way I want any of us four getting shot just for stealing a bike when selling five pounds of pot gives us the same profit.'

'Yeah, good move, Winnie,' Ocker said. 'My brother is getting a bit nervous about passing out the addresses.'

'Have you been paying him, Ocker?'

'Yeah, he just reckons it's getting a bit risky.'

'Fair enough, we'll just use him for special occasions. How's the rest of the shop going?'

'Well, there are a couple of our members who have to pay for work done.'

'Well, fuck 'em, it doesn't matter if they're Miners or not, everyone pays for any work. It's still our shop and not the Club's. Who owes?

'Nestor owes a fair bit.'

'That cunt, he'd better tidy his act up. You speak to him, Brian. The Club's not for bludgers. He owes Club dues too. We'd better keep an eye on him; if he doesn't lift his game, out he goes. Okay, Kev, that's your job.'

'Sure thing, Prez.'

'Who else owes, Brian?'

'Bikie Billy owes for a battery.'

'He's cool, but just keep an eye out. It's up to us not to let them get slack. We want the Miners to last. We have to be staunch: the Club comes first.'

Brian looked in his ledger. 'Well, not counting what's owed, and after we take wages, we still have about eighteen hundred. I'm going to the bank next week to find out how much deposit I need to buy a house. They're putting in a new housing estate up on Snow's Mountain.' Besides, there's something I haven't told you. Gina's pregnant.'

The boys looked stunned. Winnie stood and grabbed him by the shoulders. 'Congratulations, mate!'. Ocker and Kev did likewise. Brian seemed genuinely surprised and his eyes started to moisten.

'I love you blokes.'

They raised their glasses of bourbon and clinked them together.

Brian asked, 'Is business finished?'

'Yeah, mate.'

'Well, I'm off home. What are you up to?'

'Nothing,' said Winnie. 'Just having a rest here for a bit.'

He lay back in his chair with his hands behind his head, stretched his legs out and stared at his denim jacket with the one per cent badge and President's embroidered patch. It had been a good night — they'd made a good contact with the Commandos and might do some business with them, no blood had been spilled and they'd all had a bloody good time. He was pleased with himself and his mates.

'Hey, Ocker, where'd those girls go?

'I've got one coming back later.' Ocker played all the angles when it came to women.

'Dirty cunt,' said Winnie and laughed out loud. 'What are you up to today, Kevvie? Feel like playing?'

'Yeah, you beauty,' said Kev and rubbed his hands. He wore an identical cut-off jacket except for the Sergeant-at-Arms patch on his left side.

'Ocker, give her a bell and see if she's got any girlfriends she can bring.'

Ocker went to the bar to use the phone.

Brian stood up. 'I'm off, boys, looks like you're in for a good day. You know, this may sound a bit funny, but it doesn't interest me. I'm quite happy to go home to Gina.'

'Good, mate, more for us.'

Brian headed to the door and shook hands as he left. 'I'll see you at the shop Monday morning. Oh yeah, Winnie, you have to come over for a meal one night. Gina cooks a good roast dinner. She told me to ask you.'

'Okay, mate, I'll talk to you next week.' When Brian headed out, Winnie noticed how good the Miners MC patch looked.

'I reckon she must have been his first fuck,' Kev said.

'Nah, she was his second; he gave up waiting for his first one.' They both laughed.

Ocker entered the clubhouse smiling. 'You owe me a drink; the girls are on their way. Bourbon, please.'

'Why are you smiling, Ocker?' Kev said as he turned up the Rolling Stones to ear-splitting volume.

'Well, the go is there are only two of them but they're both party girls and they should be here pretty soon. I told them to grab a taxi. Sandy was waiting for my call, dunno about the other one. Anyway, we'll know soon enough.' A car horn blared outside. Ocker darted outside.

'Do you want a game of pool?' Winnie asked.

'Yeah, you set them up, I'll be the buster.'

Kev selected his favourite cue, flicked the white ball with the cue to where he wanted to break from and chalked up.

'Fuck me, Kev, you're arsing around like an old moll.'

Kev scattered the balls just as Ocker entered the clubhouse with two gorgeous dolls. The boys turned their heads and watched him lead the girls over.

'Winnie and Big Kev, this is Sandy and this is Robyn.' Sandy had shoulder-length red hair, red lipstick, halter top, tight slacks and high heels. Robyn wore the same, except she had short blond hair and pale lipstick, a real surfie type.

Robyn said, 'I've never been in a bikie's clubhouse before. I'm not going to get raped, am I?'

Winnie turned from the pool table after missing his shot. 'You'll get whatever you want here and nothing you don't.'

'Oh, goody,' Robyn giggled as she sat cross-legged on a bar stool and sipped her drink.

Kev lined up his shot and sank it.

'Oh, good shot,' Robyn gasped.

'Thank you, ma'am,' Kev said, bowing, and moved around to sink the black ball and end the game. 'Good game, Winnie.' They shook hands.

Kev caught Robyn's eye and nodded towards Winnie. 'He hasn't been able to sink a ball since you came in. I think he's in love with you.' Winnie almost blushed.

'I'll give you a game, Kev.' Robyn jumped off her stool and reached into her pocket for change.

'What a beautiful arse,' said Winnie.

Robyn turned and patted it. 'That's what I get paid for. Just a stripper's arse.'

The boys laughed at her honesty.

Ocker began rolling up a joint. 'Here, put some of this with it.' Sandy gave Ocker what looked like a piece of chocolate. Ocker pulled the mull bowl away to protect it.

'No, Ocker, it's hash, hashish — haven't you seen it before? It's stronger than pot. It'll make the joint the best you've ever smoked.'

'Okay, I've got to see that,' said Winnie.

Kev lined up the pool balls. 'Have you ever played before, Robyn?'

'No, but I've seen lots of games,' she said, while Kev scattered the balls around the table. Kevvie passed the cue to the girl and she lined it up. Her hand wobbled and when she took her shot the balls rolled all over the table.

'You're right, you haven't played before, have you?' Winnie said.

'Maybe you can help me.'

'Maybe I can,' he smiled, as Kev sank ball after ball. 'Hey, Ocker, how's that joint coming along?'

'It's coming. Calm down, will you?'

Sandy held a lighter under the hash, and then sprinkled some over the pot.

Cue in hand, Robyn grabbed Winnie by the hand. 'Come on, you're going to help me beat your Sergeant-at-Arms, aren't you, Prez?'

'We'll see, you just line your shot up.'

Robyn lay along the pool table and Winnie lay on top of her, one foot on the table's edge. He grabbed her elbow with his right arm, his head directly behind hers, and whispered in her ear what to do; his left hand steadied hers.

'Now just line up the white ball, look at the ball, look at the spot you want to hit it, then draw the cue back and hit it firmly.'

She drew the cue back and let her shot go and sank the ball in the corner pocket. She danced around as if she'd won the lottery.

'I could have shown you how to do that,' Kev said.

'You could have, too, but the Prez was closer.'

Kev sank the rest of the balls and ended the game.

'Hey, fellas, have a look at this — Sandy's rolled a real three-paper joint, neat as a pin.'

Kev put on another Rolling Stones cassette.

'Here, Prez, your light.'

'No, roller first,' and he flicked his Zippo for Sandy, who took a huge puff on the joint to get it cracking before passing it to Winnie.

'Slowly,' she said, exhaling a long stream of smoke.

'Hey, Sandy, where'd you get this hash?' Winnie asked.

'One of the bouncers up in the Cross.'

Robyn was wandering around looking at different posters and photos on the wall.

'That's pretty good,' Winnie said slowly as he exhaled the smoke. He felt the effects immediately. He went over to Robyn, who was standing in front of a poster advertising an upcoming rock festival at Freemans Reach, west of Sydney. It had a good line-up of Aussie rock bands.

'Are you going to this, Prez?'

'Thinking of it.'

Ocker strolled out to the back room with Sandy, smiling over his shoulder at Winnie.

'Where are you from, Robyn?'

'Down the coast, past Nowra.'

'Come up to the big lights, eh? Want to be a stripper?'

'No, I'm a dancer but there's not a real lot of work for dancers. Stripping pays well and they look after you, but I'm not a pro.'

'Never said you were.' Winnie rubbed her arse and squeezed it enough to make her wiggle and giggle. 'Jesus, Robyn, that's good.'

'Oh, Catholic, are you?' she quipped, then she pulled his face towards her with both hands, kissed him passionately and ground her hips against him. 'I'm in love with you, Prez. The first time I saw you this feeling went right through me. That's the man for me, I thought.'

'Fuck off, it's the joint speaking.' Winnie tried to change the topic.

She smiled coyly and did pirouettes.

Winnie watched her carefully. She spun around and came back and stopped in front of him and he pulled her towards him and kissed her, crotch rubbing crotch. Kev had seen enough and went outside after grabbing another drink, leaving Winnie inside with Robyn. As soon as the door shut they ripped at each other's clothes, raw passion, no bed, just a barstool and a wall.

'God, that was good, Prez, just what I needed.'

Winnie stroked her hair. 'Yeah, me too.'

'I think I'm in love with you.'

God, he thought, don't start that again. 'No, it's just a fuck. A bloody good one, but just a fuck.'

'We'll see,' she said and pulled her clothes on.

Ocker and Sandy walked into the bar and Ocker replaced the Stones tape, midway through 'Jumping Jack Flash', with a Pink Floyd tape.

Kev immediately got the shits. 'What do you think you're doing?'

'Settle down, Kevvie, you'll like this.'

'I better, or off it goes.'

Kev probably couldn't have cared less about the music; he wanted to spend time alone with Sandy.

49

'Don't worry, Kev, you're not going to miss out.'

'It's not that, Ocker.'

'Don't give me the shits, Kev. You think we're going to sheriff the girls on you? Sandy told me she wants to fuck you. Just leave it for a while then grab her by the hand and take her out the back.'

'Are you sure?' Kev smiled at last.

'Fucken oath, mate.' Ocker and Kev headed to the bar where Winnie was entertaining the girls.

'So neither of you is from Sydney?'

'I'm from Queensland,' said Sandy. 'And where are you boys from?'

'We all grew up together, out here.'

'Yeah,' said Kev, 'I've been looking after them all their lives.' They all laughed.

'So you boys are pretty close?'

'We're brothers,' Ocker said proudly.

'I'll drink to that,' Sandy said. She drained her glass and put it on the bar for Winnie to refill. 'Have you boys ever had a trip?'

'Yeah, all the time,' Kev said. 'We go to Bathurst and down the coast to —'

Sandy cut him off, laughing. 'No, not those sort of trips.' She pulled out a plastic bag that held a dozen small pills. 'It's acid. You know, LSD.'

'What do they do?'

'They let you look at everything in a different way.'

'Yeah, I've heard about 'em. I'll have one.' Ocker was into anything for fun.

'Why not?' Winnie shrugged and reached out for one and soon they'd all dropped one each.

'What else have you got in that bag?' Kev asked Sandy.

'Wouldn't you like to know, big fella?' she flirted.

With that, Kev grabbed her by the hand and dragged her off like a cave man. She trotted along behind and smacked his arse, saying 'Bad boy, Kev'. They disappeared out the back.

After half an hour the effects of the acid overcame them. They turned up the music and danced and laughed and didn't even notice Kev come back in until he started laughing while reaching out in front of him, stopping and reaching out again as if he was trying to catch a fly.

'What are you up to, Kev?' Winnie asked.

'There's a swirly thing that comes at me and when I reach out to grab it, it pulls back again.'

They all started imitating Kev and laughed until their guts ached. Sandy whispered in Ocker's ear, 'Pick some sexy dance music for Robyn and me, we'll put on a show.' Ocker couldn't get the music on quickly enough. 'We'll show you something special.'

Ocker winked at the boys and leaned against the bar and rubbed his crotch. 'Show time, boys.'

'You're a dirty little cunt, Ocker,' said Kev, still trying and failing to catch whatever swirled before him. 'How are you feeling, Prez?'

'Don't really know. How long do they last?'

Sandy reckoned about three hours.

'Well, I might as well enjoy it.'

He gently rubbed Robyn's back and stroked her with the tips of his strong fingers. She shuddered when he touched her spine.

'You should do your stage act for us,' he whispered.

'Sandy and I spoke about it. Just wait for a bit, and then you'll see what we can do.'

'Can't wait,' Winnie said and grabbed a handful of hair and massaged the back of her head. He felt waves of the acid sweep over him.

Kevvie yelled and clapped, thinking the show was about to start. He sang out, 'Fuck, I love these trips! It's show time, girls.'

Sandy told Robyn, 'Come on, we're on.'

Winnie sat beside Kev and draped his arm over Kev's shoulders. 'How're you going mate, orright?'

'I'm fucken crazy. All these things were coming at me but they're gone now. I can't wait for the girls to come on. Ocker bloody loves it, look at the little bugger.' Ocker danced on the spot as if in a trance.

Sandy called out, 'Ocker, we're ready.'

'Yeah, so am I,' said Kev, standing up and unzipping his pants.

Ocker got on his case straight away. 'Put 'em back, Kev, it's show time,' and he cued the dance music. The girls made their entrance with their hair and make-up redone. They looked the part and they danced around the pool table and teased the boys. Kev started yelling 'Take it off!' and wolf whistling as they wiggled out of their tight slacks.

The girls didn't have much left to take off when Sandy came over to Kev. 'Undo my buttons for me, please.' She stuck out her chest.

'Fucken oath,' he said, reaching out and pulling her closer so he could rub her titties.

'No, Kevvie, just the buttons,' she whispered as he pulled open her top.

'That's what I want,' said Kev, when Sandy undid Robyn's buttons and rubbed her breasts. Robyn arched back with pleasure. They danced around shedding clothes until they were down to their undies. They rubbed each other's breasts and slid their fingers up and down each other's pussies.

'If this is the special, I love it,' said Winnie. The girls lay on the pool table and licked each other all over. Sandy slipped off Robyn's undies then ran her tongue along her cunt. Robyn moaned and played with her nipples and gyrated her hips while the boys yelled encouragement.

'Fuck, I've never seen this before,' said Ocker. He dropped his pants and pulled out his prick and gently rubbed it. The girls started to really get into it and Sandy pulled her head out of Robyn's cunt, turned and cocked a finger to Kev to get him to fuck her from behind. She didn't have to ask twice and he stood up and entered her. Winnie moved around the table toward Robyn with his prick hanging out. She stroked him then began to suck him off. Ocker stood behind the bar pulling himself off until he groaned and reached for a bar towel.

'Fuck, you're a dirty cunt, Ocker,' Kev yelled as Ocker dropped his load into the bar towel. Kev kept pounding away while Sandy yelled, 'Fuck me, Kev!' Robyn kept sucking Winnie until he moaned and fell back against the bar. Kev collapsed on top of Sandy and hooted like an owl.

'Fuck that was good,' Kev said to no one. Winnie zipped up his jeans while Robyn licked her lips as if she'd just eaten an ice-cream. Whatever was in that acid worked wonders for everyone.

'Let's have a drink,' said Winnie, heading for the bar.

Ocker chucked his used bar towel into the trash basket. 'Sure thing, Prez. Not a bad day, eh mate?'

'Couldn't be better,' he said while the girls gathered their gear and headed out the back to 'straighten up'.

The acid began to wear off. 'Thank fuck,' said Kev, 'I don't think I like those trips after all. They're good girls, Ocker. Is that Sandy married or anything?'

'What do you want to know for?'

'You never know, mate.'

'I don't know her that well. You ask her.'

'Do you reckon they're dykes?'

'Nah, that's just their show. Not bad, eh?'

'Fucken oath.' Kev winked at Winnie.

The girls came out from the back room and approached the bar. They looked as good as ever. Sandy grabbed the drinks and passed Robyn hers.

'Very good,' Winnie applauded and the girls bowed.

Ocker rolled another joint.

'We have to leave soon,' said Sandy as she handed Ocker the leftover hash. 'We have to work Saturday night, it's the busiest night of the week. Can you call us a taxi?'

Winnie moved over to the phone and Robyn followed.

'I loved that, Prez. Can I see you again?'

'We might be going to the rock festival at Freemans Reach; maybe I'll see you there.'

In the bar Sandy sat in Kev's lap. He smacked her lightly on the bum. She jumped and said, 'You'll get yours, mate.'

'Yeah, when's that, then?'

When the girls left, Ocker opened the main gate for them and waved goodbye.

Winnie and Kev watched the cab drive off. 'Not a bad way to spend a Saturday, eh, Kevvie?'

A smiling Ocker walked back into the clubhouse. 'How was that, boys?'

'You're my man.' Kev grabbed Ocker in a bear hug and planted a big wet kiss on his lips then pushed him away laughing.

Ocker stepped back and licked his lips. 'Mmm, I taste fish.' The boys cracked up.

Kev said he felt a bit fucked and wanted to head home. He said he'd see the boys on Monday morning and walked out the door. Then he stopped and turned and looked really serious for a minute. 'You know that Rastus from the Commandos? I still can't get over how ugly he is.'

'But the girls like him,' Ocker said.

'What's he got?'

'He makes 'em laugh.'

'Yeah, but we make 'em happy,' Kev said and rubbed his crotch, and then he was gone.

'Well, I'm going home, Ocker,' said Winnie. 'I've got a bloke coming over to pick a couple of pounds up. Business first.'

Chapter 4

Monday morning at the shop everyone was chirpy except Brian. He was moody and erratic in his behaviour.

Big Kev taunted him. 'Hey Brian, what's up with you? Sick of marriage already?'

'No, mate, I love her. I feel bad when I see her crook in the morning.'

'Oh, isn't that just so loving?'

'Get fucked, you wouldn't know.'

'Hey, Winnie, are we going to the concert at Freemans Reach?'

'Yeah, I reckon. I'll bring it up at the next meeting.'

'The girlies are going down,' Kev announced.

'How do you know that?'

'Because the dirty cunt went to the strip club on Saturday night and went back to their place with them,' Ocker said with a smile.

All Kev could do was stand there and smile, holding his groin with one hand and licking his lips. 'Yeah, I love it.'

'Good on you, Kev,' Winnie said. 'Now let's get down to work; remember, the shop comes first. How are you going with the backlog, Kev?'

'Well, Spike is coming over this week with his Harley and he's going to show me how to service it. I think we can change our sign at the front to say Snow's British and American Motorcycles. I'll buy a couple of workshop manuals for them.'

Brian brightened. 'I can help you with that, Kev; I have a salesman who drops by. I'll let you know when he comes in.'

'Yeah, thanks, Brian, and mate, I was only mucking around before about your missus.'

'Yeah, I know,' Brian said. 'You know, I reckon you're right about the Harleys — they could be the next big go. I saw this new bike magazine from the States called *Easy Riders*. Every issue shows how to fix different problems on Harleys. I'll see if I can line up a few copies.'

'Good one, Brian,' and Kev grabbed him in a bear hug. 'I love you, mate.'

'Okay, what else is going on?' said Winnie, getting everyone back on track. 'What about you, Ocker, how's the spray booth going?'

'Well, to tell you the truth, I could do double my work if I had a bigger compressor.'

'Well, you'll have to find one but don't go over the moon with it.'

'Rightio, mate, I know what I want. I'll have a look and get back with a price.'

'Hey, Brian, do you think we need a shop ute? Blokes always want bikes picked up and it'd be good for getting spare parts.'

'Yeah, you're right, Winnie, it'd be good for other business too. I'll look around for one, mate.'

'Well, I'm off to organise some pounds with the Rat, and Kevvie, later on today we'll go and have our talk with Twister and let him know we're onto his little game with the Commandos about the stolen bike.'

'Fucken oath, Prez.'

'Okay, I'm off. The Rat has me running all over Sydney for our meetings. He's a cagey bastard. This time it's a pub in Hurstville.'

Winnie pulled into the parking lot of the pub where the Rat had parked his yellow Zephyr. The good thing about the Rat was he was always on time. Winnie bought some beers and sat at his table. They shook hands and talked about the surf and then Winnie got down to business.

'Well, mate, the pot's been a real good earner. Could you get us twenty pounds this week?'

'No worries, mate.'

'Same deal, cash for half and half on credit?'

'Sure, mate, you're right. You're better at paying than some.'

'What do you mean?'

'Well, this cunt called Bruce who lives over on the northern beaches ripped me off for six grand and he's too big for me to look after.'

'Well, what about the blokes you get it off, what do they say?'

'They don't give a fuck; I cop the loss.'

'I might be able to help you. Me and Kevvie might collect the money and you can pay us.'

'I'd make it worth your while.'

'What do you reckon it's worth, Rat?'

'Don't worry, mate, I'll pay.'

'Okay, give me his address and name and we'll talk to you when you drop the pot off. There's something else I'd like to know — if you grow the pot, that's where the money is, eh?'

'It's the growers who make most of the money.'

'Yeah, I thought so. What's involved with growing it?'

'Bugger all, I can show you how.'

'I might hold you to that, Rat. So when can you drop the pounds off?'

'Thursday, mate.' Rat got up, drained his beer, shook Winnie's hand and headed out to his Zephyr. Winnie walked into the main bar. It was his first time in Hurstville. He looked around and thought the surfies looked the same as bikies, only they had blond hair.

His Miners patch was copping a fair bit of attention; blokes were looking his way and whispering. Winnie was pretty sure they didn't like bikies. He looked around and spotted Swannie, who he hadn't seen since the Bathurst Easter weekend.

'How ya going, Swannie?'

'Real good, Winnie. Meet Chris and Wayne, a couple of mates of mine.' They shook hands.

'Are you still riding, Swannie?'

'No, lost me licence. I get it back in a couple of months. I'm building a Harley chopper at home.'

'Well, if you need anything for it, give us a ring at the shop. We've got a good spray man, he does pretty nice work.'

'Yeah, I've heard about him. Ocker, isn't it? He's a funny cunt.'

'That's him.'

'Yeah, I reckon I'll drop my tanks and guards over. I'm rebuilding a Harley panhead I bought all pulled down. My old man's helping.' Swannie nodded to the bar girl and she pulled another four beers. 'So what are you up to, Winnie?'

Winnie never said more than he had to. He asked Swannie why the punters didn't seem too friendly.

'Because Twister and his Tigers were here a couple of weeks ago and bashed a few of the locals selling pot. Seems they wanted to get their mates in.'

'So what's going to happen, mate?'

'Don't worry about that. I hate Twister and his bloody Tigers. They'll find out who runs the show over here.'

'Be careful of him, Swannie.'

'Yeah, I will, mate, don't you worry.' He took a long look at Winnie's patch. 'It looks good. Real good. When I get my chopper on the road I'll have to come for a ride with you. Do you want to have a joint with us, Winnie?'

'Where?'

'Out the back, in the beer garden. We'll be right.'

They found a table and Swannie fired up the joint and passed it to Winnie. He wanted to know how Winnie was doing with his pot out west.

'Bloody oath, mate, it's all over the place. There's a good earn in it for everyone.'

'Do you reckon it'll last?'

'Well, alcohol has. I think it'll only get better. Are you doing much, Swannie?'

'A couple of pounds a week. I could do more but the supply isn't always there.'

'What would you say if I could help you out?'

'How much a pound?'

Winnie calculated what it cost and how much he wanted in an instant. 'For you mate, $320.'

'Well, that's cheaper than what I pay. When?'

'Bring your guards and tanks over later on this week and I'll have it at the shop.'

'Can you supply every week?'

'Sure can, mate. Now I have to get going; business to do.' Winnie got up to leave.

'I see you're still riding the Triumph, mate,' said Swannie. 'Wait until you ride a Harley, you'll never go back.'

'See you later, Swannie. Ta for the beers.' Winnie kicked the Triumph into life and roared out of the car park, giving Swannie a wave.

When Winnie arrived back at the shop he saw a cop car parked in front and almost shit himself. Kev came out looking worried. 'What's up, Kev?'

'Dunno, mate, they're in there talking to Brian.'

'Well, we better find out.'

Brian was behind the counter talking to two cops. When he saw Winnie the relief was plain on his face.

'Hi boys, what's the problem?'

The senior constable asked Winnie who he was.

'I'm a part owner of the shop.' Winnie smiled confidently.

'If you're the President of the Miners then I want to talk to you. What's your name?

'Peter Winifred, just call me Winnie.'

'My name is Senior Constable Carter and this is Constable Cole. Now, we give you a fair go around here and then you go and shit in your own backyard and rip off people who can't afford to lose their televisions and stereos. We have information you lot are responsible for it.'

'Well, your information is wrong,' Brian piped up.

'Settle down, mate.' Winnie, calm as he could be, the calm that comes from knowing he was telling the truth, looked the cop in the eye and spoke quietly, just above a whisper. 'Officer, your information is wrong. All of us were brought up on the Housing Commission estate. We know those people, we *are* those people; we wouldn't have anything to do with it.'

Winnie smiled at the cop, who looked into their faces for the clues to a concealed lie. He saw nothing and finally spoke. 'I bloody hope so, for your sake, because if I find out it was you blokes you'll get another visit from us and a short ride in a black van. You follow me?'

'Yes, constable,' said Winnie. He walked out the front with the cops and watched them leave.

'Fuck, I wonder why he's so worried about bloody television sets.'

Brian said he thought the cop's parents lived there; he'd seen a cop car parked there over the years and always wondered why.

Kev and Ocker came into the shop. 'Fuck, he had the shits, eh?'

'You heard him, then. It'd be no one we know, I hope. He's right though, you can't shit in your own backyard.'

'I'm pretty sure I know who it is,' Kev said. 'It's that lazy cunt Nestor. I heard the other day he had TV sets for sale. But if he's doing it, how come he hasn't got the money for Club fees and getting his bike back on the road? His bike's been sitting here for a month waiting for him.'

'Well, what happened to all his money? Maybe he's a gambler,' Winnie said. No one said a word. They looked at each other and shrugged shoulders. 'Okay, we'll sort it out Friday night.' Winnie was furious. 'We don't need coppers coming around visiting us. Hey, Ocker, do you remember Swannie from Hurstville? I ran into him today. He's building a Harley chopper and he's going to drop his tanks and guards over for you to spray-paint.'

'What's he building?'

'An old panhead.'

'I wouldn't mind having a look at that,' said Kev.

'What are they like, Kevvie?'

'I'll get the manual and show you.' He was gone for all of thirty seconds. 'Here it is. Can you see why they call them panheads? Look at the rocker covers, they look like saucepan lids.' The boys crowded around and looked. 'These Harleys interest me more every day.'

Ocker had work to do and disappeared into his spray booth, and Brian had a customer to serve.

Winnie said to Kev, 'Hey, the Rat told me he was ripped off by one of his customers for six grand and he wondered if we'd like to get it back for him for a share.'

'Six grand? Jesus, the Rat must really be into the pot business in a big way.'

'Yeah, I suppose so, but it's not all his dough; he's just responsible for it. That's the pot business for you, and that's how we have to do it. No one gets credit; it's either cash or no sale, eh?'

'So when do you want to do it?'

'Tonight. I'll borrow my dad's car. The bloke's in Dee Why.'

'Okay, Winnie.' Kev smiled at the prospect. He had no idea what was going to happen, but he didn't care, and he was big enough and ugly enough not to have to.

Brian came in rubbing his hands with glee. 'I just sold one of the bikes — a bloody great way to start the week.'

Winnie hugged Brian. 'That's it, mate, we all contribute in our own way. Now, I'm off, I won't be back today.'

'Where're you going, mate?'

'To see a bloke about a farm. Tell you all about it tomorrow.'

Brian and Kev looked at one another; they didn't know what he was talking about. 'What's he up to?' Brian asked. He knew something big was on.

'Dunno, mate, but whatever it is, it'll be good for us.' Kev continued to work on the motor and whistled while he worked.

Winnie rode northwest, towards Windsor on the Hawkesbury River. In those days there wasn't much on either side of the road but market gardens, owned mainly by Chinese and Maltese. They had huge glasshouses growing tomatoes or cut flowers, and the occasional chicken farm. Winnie had arranged to meet a Maltese bloke called Joe he knew from school. When Winnie wheeled into the service station at Vineyard he saw Joe sitting at the takeaway food bar, next to his Ford Falcon with tassels hanging from the windows. It really looked like a wog's car. Winnie rode up next to it and pulled his bike up onto its stand.

'Owyergoin, Winnie?' They shook hands.

'Good, Joe, nice-looking car, mate. Don't know about the tassels, but it's the only way to have one, eh?'

'Got to dress 'em up,' Joe said. 'So you're President of the Miners, eh? I always knew you were a leader. So what can I do for you?'

'Joe, I heard you inherited a farm and I was wondering what you're doing with it.'

'Nothing much, mate, they're all empty right now. What do you want to grow, tomatoes or something? I didn't think that'd be your go, Winnie.'

Winnie looked Joe straight in the eye and leaned forward and said really quietly, 'I want to grow marijuana, Joe. Pot.'

'Geez, Winnie, I'd never thought of that.' Joe turned serious.

'No, not you, mate, me. I want to grow it. I'll lease the property off you under a bodgie name. You won't have to go near it.'

'Thinking about it, I wouldn't want to go near it.'

'There'll be no connection between us.'

'How much will you pay?'

'I'll give you five hundred now and when the crop comes in we'll see how much profit there is and I'll cut you in for a share.'

'Fuck, Winnie, that sounds alright to me, but can you make much out of pot?'

'We'll just have to wait and see, mate.'

'Okay, I'll be in it, as long as there's no connection. Come on, I'll take you to see the farm. We can go in my car. Leave your bike here and I'll get my auntie to keep an eye on it for you.'

Winnie sat in Joe's car and took off his Miners patch. Joe watched as he folded his colours and put them on his lap. Winnie noticed Joe looking so he explained that he only wore his colours on the bike. After a ten-minute drive, Joe pulled up outside a locked gate at the end of a long driveway. He unlocked the gate and they drove past row upon row of glasshouses, all of them invisible from the road. Each glasshouse was a bit bigger than a tennis court, with a large packing shed at the back.

'Whaddya reckon, Winnie?'

Winnie looked around and worked out how much room he'd have to plant. He reckoned he could grow about two thousand plants in each glasshouse.

'Perfect, mate!' Winnie pulled out a wad and counted out five hundred dollars and handed it over. 'Listen, mate, let me tell you what's going to happen now. I'll get a lease written up with some cunt's name on it and that's all you need to know. It's our little secret. You can't talk to anyone about this, so the less you know the better. If anything happens and there's a bust, you just stick to your story. They'll never suspect you.'

'Deal's a deal, Winnie. Here's the key to the gate and good luck, mate.'

While Winnie rode into the city he calculated what sort of money they were likely to make if everything went to plan. They would be the grower and the distributor, with a chain of sellers in place. It wasn't just the money, it was also the fact that there would be fewer people in the know, and the fewer knowing their business the better, as far as he was concerned.

Winnie took off in his dad's car and pulled up outside Kev's place. Kev jumped in and they said very little. He looked as if he didn't want to be there.

'What's up, mate? You're not going soft on me, are you?'

'No, mate, it's just that, well, I got a letter from the Army today. Seems like I won the lottery. My number came up. Looks like I'm in the Army now.'

'Fuck me, Kev, I'm sorry to hear that. When do you have to go?'

'I've got to report in ten days, just when my life is starting to pay off.'

'Don't worry, Kev, I'll keep your colours and you'll still be a partner in the shop and the pot business. By the time you get out of the Army you should have enough for a new Harley.'

'Yeah, that's if I come back alive.'

'Well, I'll tell you what, mate, let's take it out on this Bruce cunt who owes the Rat. He won't suspect a thing. The Rat says he sells his pot from his house and people come and go all the time.'

'What if he won't cough up the money? How far will we go with him?'

'This is the plan, mate. As soon as we get in you just hit the cunt with the baseball bat. As soon as he goes down I'm going to stick this in his mouth.' Winnie pulled a handgun from his jacket.

'Where did you get that from, Prez?'

'It's the old man's — he kept it from the war — but I can't find ammo for it anywhere. He'll pay up all right, plus whatever else he has on him.'

'Good, mate, I'm just in the mood for it, too.' Kev had a dark look on.

They drove for about twenty minutes until Winnie pulled up outside a dingy house with an overgrown garden out front. They walked up the path and knocked on the front door.

A big surfie appeared behind the screen door. 'Hello, what can I do for you?'

'Are you Bruce?'

'Yeah.'

'The Rat told me we could score some pot from you.'

'The Rat. Okay.' He opened the screen door. 'Sure, fellas, come in, how much do you want?' The boys followed him down the hallway and he never knew what hit him.

Kev whacked him a few times until he hit the floor and his legs rattled the lino.

'Fuck, what's going on, man?' he groaned just before Winnie stuck the gun into his bleeding mouth. His eyes opened wide and his face turned deathly pale.

'Now, cunt, just listen,' said Winnie in a menacingly quiet voice. 'You owe our mate Rat and we're here to collect. If you understand just nod.'

Bruce's eyes flitted back and forth between Winnie and Kev, and he nodded very slowly.

'If you make a single noise, someone will find you with your brains all over the floor. Do you understand?'

He nodded again; this was fair dinkum and he wasn't about to play the hero. Winnie pulled the gun out of Bruce's mouth and wiped the bloodied barrel over his face.

'Now where's the money?'

'In my bedroom.'

'Right, let's go get it.' They followed Bruce into the bedroom and he headed towards his wardrobe.

'Hold on, just tell us where it is.'

'In the top drawer.'

'Check it out, Kev.'

Kev pushed Bruce out of the way and searched the drawer until he found the wad of notes.

'You can't take it all,' Bruce moaned. 'There's eight grand there, I only owe him six.'

'Shut your mouth, cunt, the rest is interest. Just cop it sweet and don't be such a cunt in your business dealings in the future. If you go squealing to the pigs you can expect more, you understand?'

'Don't worry, I won't.'

Kev pocketed the money and he and Winnie walked out into the street, got into the car and drove off.

Neither of them spoke until they got onto Pittwater Road and were headed home. When they pulled up at the first set of lights they looked at each other and started laughing. It was the first time they had ever done a job like that. It was almost too easy. They could hardly believe it.

'Would you have shot him, Prez?' asked Kev.

Winnie didn't answer, he just smiled at Kev. 'Well, mate, it looks like we got ourselves a bonus tonight. We'll pay Rat his six grand and keep the extra two for us. We'll see how much Rat reckons it's worth to get his six back.'

They were well pleased with themselves.

Kev thought for a while and then asked, 'You want to come up the Cross and see Robyn and Sandy with me?'

'No, I'll drop you off, though. You're really sweet on Sandy, aren't you?'

Kev grinned. 'What do you think of her?'

'You're not getting married too, are you?'

'Get fucked, mate, she's just a fuck,' Kev said, a little too defensively.

Winnie thought he'd seen this all before with Brian, but he loved his mate and he wasn't going to get into it.

At the top of William Street at Kings Cross the traffic slowed; the cross-streets were filled with punters looking for a good time.

'Here, mate, I'll let you out here. I don't feel real good hanging around up here with all this money and a gun on me. I'll see you tomorrow, same time, mate.'

'That was a good night, Winnie.' Kev got out and disappeared into the thronging crowds and Winnie headed home, at or under the speed limit the whole way and with an eye on his rear-view mirror.

The shop formed the central part of the boys' lives and Brian and Ocker were hard at work when Winnie arrived the next morning.

'What did you do with Kevvie last night, Prez? He's usually here by now.' Brian believed in regular hours.

'Well, fellas, he got some bad news yesterday. He's been called up for the Army. I don't think he's too happy about it, so he went up the Cross to see Sandy last night.'

'Fuck me,' said Ocker. 'What will we do for a mechanic now?'

'I don't know, mate, we'll have to talk with Kev about it.' They got on with their work until they heard the sound of a motorcycle coming down the lane. Kev roared into the back of the shop, parked his bike and turned off the engine. He just sat on the bike on its stand and stared into space.

'We were just talking about you, mate,' said Winnie. 'I told the boys about what's happened with the Army.' Brian and Ocker looked sadly at Kev.

'Fuck, Kev,' said Ocker, 'we're sorry to hear about your call-up. What can you do?'

'Fuck-all.'

'Well, we were just saying, what are we going to do about a mechanic?'

Kev snapped, 'Is that all I am to you blokes?'

'Just joking, Kev,' Ocker said quietly, but he'd said the wrong thing and he knew it.

Kev's mood was pretty dark, and there was no point in pissing him off any more, but Winnie knew they needed a mechanic and that there wasn't time to stuff around. 'Is there anybody you know who could do the job?'

'Yeah, I've been thinking about it too. I reckon we should ask Spike from the Commandos. There's nobody else in our Club who could do it.'

'Well, it won't hurt to ask him. Rastus and Spike are coming over to pick up their pot today; do we all agree we should ask him?'

Brian and Ocker nodded in agreement: Spike was an ideal replacement and they liked and trusted him.

'Hey, Prez, weren't you going to tell us about your trip out to Windsor yesterday to look for a farm?' Brian wanted to know.

'That's right, I was too,' Winnie said with a grin. 'Now we're in the pot business as suppliers and middlemen, we make a nice earn. Imagine if we grew it ourselves, how much more could we make.'

'We're not farmers, Prez,' Ocker moaned.

'No, but I read up on it and it's not that hard; all we need are seeds, water, fertiliser and sunshine. The Rat knows a fair bit about it and he's due here today. You can see how much money we're going to hand over to him. Think about the profit we could make. Let's wait until he gets here and let him tell us all at the same time, orright?' There was no point in arguing with the Prez; he gave every idea a thorough airing and they would have a chance to voice concerns later, but not then.

The Rat pulled up a half hour later in his yellow Zephyr with the surfboard on top. He bounced into the workshop. 'Fucking hell, Winnie, you done it, you beauty. I'll dance at yer wedding.' He grabbed Winnie in a bear hug and laughed. 'Thanks, mate.'

'Did what?' Brian looked puzzled.

'You done it,' Rat said again. 'Bruce.'

'Did Bruce call you? What did he have to say?' Winnie could hardly wait to hear the story from the other side.

'You must have put the wind up him. The big cunt was all apologetic, telling me he intended to pay me and that there was no need to get those mad bikie cunts onto him.'

'Do you reckon he'll go to the cops?' Kev asked.

'No, the queer cunt really had shit dribbling out of his mouth about how sorry he was.'

'Good,' was all Winnie said, 'and here's your six grand, Rat.'

'Thanks, Winnie, I'll keep four and here are two for you and Kev — does that seems fair enough? Bruce reckons you got ten grand off him.'

'He's a lying cunt. There was eight, that's a bonus four for you and four for us, done deal. Happy?'

'Fucken oath, mate.' The Rat beamed.

'So, Rat, have you got our pounds?'

'Too right, Winnie.'

'Okay, Brian, you pay the Rat, and Ocker, could you take the pot to our stash hole? Now, Rat, there's something you can do for us. Remember we talked about growing pot? Well, I've organised a hothouse on a market garden farm; can you come out with me to Windsor and show us how we can grow our own?'

'Sure thing, Winnie, when do you want to go?'

'No time like the present, is there?'

'Okay, we'll go in the Zephyr.'

Winnie turned to Brian, who looked a little confused. 'I'll be back around two this arvo, when Rastus and Spike come. Get them to wait. We need to talk.'

'Sure thing, Prez.'

With that Winnie and the Rat walked out and jumped in the Zephyr.

Ocker and Brian turned to Kev. 'What did you and Winnie get up to last night?'

'Mate …' a grin came over Kev's face while he related the story. The boys' eyes stood out like chapel hat-pegs as they listened.

'Fuck, this drug business is getting real fair dinkum.' Brian was a bit shocked.

'It's the only way to deal with anyone who wants to rip us off. We just can't allow it to happen. The Rat may not be in our Club but he's on our side as far as the business goes, and we have to look after our business.'

'Too true,' Ocker said with a smile. 'I always knew Winnie was hard.'

'You ain't seen nothing yet,' said Brian. 'I've known him a long time. I've yet to see anyone get the better of him.'

'That's why he's the Prez,' Kev replied.

Later that afternoon Rastus and Spike turned up in a battered ute. They looked exactly the same as the first time the boys met them, except they weren't wearing their Commandos colours.

The smell of cigar smoke preceded them into the shop.

'Don't you ever wash?' Brian asked when they shook hands.

'Once a month, whether we need it or not,' said Rastus, his laugh like breaking glass. 'Where's your Prez?'

Kev told them Winnie would be back around two, and then he spoke quietly to Spike and Rastus.

'While you're waiting, Spike, I have a proposition for you. You wouldn't read about it, but I've been called up for the Army. It's only until I get out, about a year, I think. It's just an idea, but how would you like to work with us as the chief mechanic? Whaddya reckon?'

Spike looked at Rastus before answering. 'Okay by me, mate, if I can help out. I'd earn a quid, eh?'

'Too right, mate, we're doin' alright. In fact, we're doing great.'

'All right, Kev, there's nothing I like better than working on bikes. Let's talk it out when Winnie gets here, okay?'

Chapter 5

'Here's the Prez,' said Brian when he looked out the window and saw Rat dropping Winnie off. Rastus asked Winnie if he'd been surfing.

'Yeah, sure I have,' Winnie answered, smiling as they shook hands. 'How're you going, Rastus?'

'Good, Winnie, how about you?'

'No complaints, mate. You after ten pounds?'

'Yeah, can we get them today?'

'Hey, Ocker, will you bring back ten pounds for our mate here?'

'Sure thing, Prez.'

'Come with me, Rastus.' They joined Kev and Spike poring over a bike. 'Has Kev spoken to you about working for us?'

'Yeah, Winnie, I'll be glad to help you out.'

'Good on you, mate. There's only one rule: what goes on in this shop stays in the shop.'

'Fair enough, Winnie.'

'Oh and another thing, there's a decent earn in it for you, Spike. We're busier by the day. Does that sit well with you both?'

'Yeah, Winnie, Rastus can keep our little earn going and I can work with you blokes. Beauty!'

Ocker handed over the pounds and Rastus stashed it in his ute. 'Hey, Rastus, there's a rock festival on this weekend at Freemans Reach.'

'We'll find it. Come on, Spike, we have to go, people are waiting.'

'Okay,' said Spike. 'Let me know when you want me to start, Winnie.'

When the Commandos had left, the four boys gathered around the table.

'Now I suppose you're wondering about the farm,' said Winnie. 'I just took Rat out to have a look and he reckons we could get two crops a year off it. We're going to grow it in some hothouses. We need a couple of blokes to work it for us. The Rat reckons we should be able to get four hundred pounds a crop.'

'Fuck, Prez, we're going big time now.' Brian was amazed.

'Yeah, and it'll be all profit instead of having to buy from the Rat.'

Kev wanted to know who Winnie had in mind to grow it.

'I've thought about that. What do you reckon we get Nestor and another member to live in a caravan on-site? We don't want too many people to know or be involved.'

'I don't know about Nestor, Prez,' Ocker said.

'No, it'll be good for him; we can keep an eye on him plus get him out of the way for a while. It'll give him an earn. That's what being in the Club is all about. He might be lazy but he's staunch as far as the Club goes. Do we all agree?'

No one hesitated. They liked Nestor even if he nicked poor people's television sets, and besides, he owed the Club money. 'Yes, Prez.'

'Okay, Brian, we're going to need money from our bank to set it up. It already owes me five hundred. We'll need to find a decent old caravan for them to live in and get hold of a shotgun in case of snoopers.'

'You can have mine, it's an old single-shot,' Kev said. 'I won't need it where I'm going.'

'Okay, Kev, they'll probably give you a machine gun. Also I want you both to know I told Kev he's still in our business while he's away. Orright? Brian, we can put it to Nestor before the Club meeting tomorrow night.'

'Is that all, Prez?' Brian said. 'I have to take Gina to the doctor.'

'Okay, Brian. Hey, here's Swannie. He said he was coming. He wants some pounds, plus he wants you to do some painting for him, Ocker.'

Winnie jumped up and went out to greet Swannie.

'Hey, good to see you, Swannie. Come in and say hello.'

'Where can I put these, Winnie?' Swannie held a mudguard in each hand and had a petrol tank stuck under each arm.

'Here, let me take some of that off you. Follow me, mate.' Winnie led him out the back towards Ocker's spray booth and put the guards and the tank on Ocker's bench.

'Hey, got some work for me, eh?'

'Well, I've heard you do a good job.'

'Are you trying to piss in my pocket, mate?' Ocker made Swannie laugh.

'Yeah, sure he is,' Kev said. 'How're you going, Swannie?'

'Not bad, mate.'

'Winnie told me you were building an old panhead. What colour do you want?'

'Black, mate, black as black. I can't wait to take it for a ride.'

'You should come with us to Freemans Reach next weekend, it's Kevvie's last weekend of freedom.'

'What, are you going to jail?'

'No, mate, into the Army. Fucking conscription.'

'Yeah, a few of my mates are going too. It's fucked, isn't it?'

'You're telling me nothing, Swannie.'

'Hey, Swannie, you still interested in some pounds?'

'Sure am, Winnie. I want to check it out first. They won't buy shit over my way.'

'Pot's pot, mate.'

'No, mate, it's not. They don't like any seed in it.'

'We haven't had any complaints about it yet, but that's cool, mate. Hey, Ocker, have you got any pot on you? Swannie wants to check it out.'

'Here you are, Prez.' Ocker handed Winnie a bag.

'There you go, Swannie.'

Swannie opened it, had a sniff and felt for seed in the buds.

'Yeah, that'll do nicely, Winnie. I'll take three. How much do I owe you?'

'Nine hundred and sixty dollars cash, Swannie.'

Swannie handed it over. 'See you next week, Winnie.'

'Nice doing business with you, Swannie.'

When Swannie had left, Winnie turned to Kev. 'How'd you go up the Cross last night? Did you see the girls?'

'Yeah, mate, I waited until they finished work and went home with them. Robyn is really keen on you. They're both going to the festival. Just thought I'd let you know.'

'She's just a fuck to me, mate. I don't want anyone in my life,' said Winnie dismissively.

'Well, Sandy's the best girl I've ever met, Winnie. She does everything for me.'

'You're not going to get married too, are you, mate?'

'No, not yet. I'll see what happens when I get back from the Army.'

'Kev, I want you to come with me and talk with Twister before the meeting tomorrow night up at the Granville pub.'

'Sure, mate.'

They rode up and saw a line of bikes outside — nearly all of Twister's Tigers must have been inside. One of their nominees outside scurried inside to inform Twister of their arrival.

Big Kev pushed open the door of the pub and it banged loudly. Heads turned in his direction. Kev strode over to the bar and ordered beers. Kero Ken came over and shook their hands.

'Where's the Twister, Kero?'

'Out the back, follow me.'

The boys followed Kero and as they did they heard voices saying, 'That's the President of the Miners.' When they walked past the pool table Kev bumped the table and balls flew everywhere. One of the Tigers was about to say something when Kero Ken turned and told him to shut up. Twister sat at a table with a couple of sheilas who looked distinctly underage. As Kev and Winnie approached him he told the girls to leave them and go into the bar. When they passed Winnie they gave him the 'come fuck me' look. Winnie smiled back. Twister stood up to shake hands.

'How're you going, Winnie? Kev?'

'Not bad, Twister. How're you going, orright?'

'So to what do I owe this pleasure, Winnie?' Twister took a long look at the Miners patches. They were fresh and clean and really stood out. 'The Miners … you two would have looked good in Tigers colours. Each to their own though, eh?' One of the Tiger nominees put their beers down on the table. 'You lot are getting real friendly with those Commandos up from Melbourne. Do you have an alliance with them?'

'No, Twister, we have no alliances with anyone and it'll stay that way. Our problems are our own and their problems are theirs. It doesn't help when you spread stories, though.'

'Just a joke, Winnie. I knew you'd find out that they never stole bikes off us.'

'No, it was you who stole a bike from your own member,' said Kev.

'He was a queer cunt, Kev. As soon as we got his bike we threw him out of the Tigers.'

'Anyway, let's forget that,' said Winnie. 'There's more serious business to discuss.' He took a long pull on his beer, then leaned in closer to Twister. 'It's in everyone's interests to keep the number of bike clubs down to a few who can run their own areas. Otherwise we'll be warring all the time and that will only bring the heat down on us, and that's not good for business.'

'Is that what you came over for? To tell us what to do?'

'No, not at all, Twister, but that's what happened in Melbourne and I know that you're a businessman. If you want that kind of situation the only cunts to win will be the pigs.'

'He makes sense, Twister,' Kero Ken said.

'How do we know where each club's area is?'

'Well, first in, best dressed. Wherever we have people selling for us, you just don't go and try and muscle in like you done down the Hurstville pub.'

'What, is that Swannie cunt working for you? Well, he and his mates gave it to a couple of my boys last week.'

'That's exactly what I mean, Twister. We have supplied him for a while and if there's any more bother with Swannie you'll have to deal with us.' Winnie put his half-finished beer down, as if there was going to be trouble. His unwavering eyes glowed black.

Twister puffed up like a cockatoo. Before he spoke again he paused just long enough to show Winnie he understood the implied threat. 'I've got twice as many members as you, Winnie.'

'You of all people should know I don't give a fuck about that, Twister.'

'Just joking, Winnie.' Twister laughed and the moment passed. 'Alright, that's that, I hear you. We'll develop our own areas and we'll keep off each other's turf, orright?' Twister winked at Kero to organise more beers. Winnie put up his hand and winked at Kero as if to say, 'Don't bother, we're leaving.' Kero nodded.

Twister wanted to know how the shop was going.

'Pretty good, Twister. We're getting into Harleys now.'

'I heard that, good luck with them.'

Business was over as far as Winnie was concerned. He'd come to deliver a message and Twister seemed to get it; there was no point in sitting there any longer.

'Come on, Kev, let's go.'

'Hey, Winnie, are the Miners going out to Freemans Reach next weekend?'

'Yeah.' As Winnie walked back through the Tigers the bar grew unusually quiet and the Tigers members showed them respect by making way.

Riding into the clubhouse Kev chucked a wheel stand on his bike and the Miners cheered and shouted. They all knew about Kev's looming service in the Army.

Nestor walked over to shake Kev's hand. 'You'll win the war all by yourself.'

'Would you like to swap places with me?'

'No, Kev, I have a bad heart, I wouldn't pass the medical.'

'That's because you haven't got a heart, Nestor.' Nestor tried to look cool but Kev's words cut to the quick. 'Don't worry, the Prez has a job for you. Just don't fuck it up.'

'What's that?'

'He'll tell you.' Kev headed to the bar.

Brian sidled up to Nestor, grabbed him by the elbow and walked him outside. 'Come on, cunt, me and the Prez want to have a word with you.'

'What's up, Brian?' Nestor wasn't a guy you could put the frighteners on easily, but he was suddenly scared.

Brian led him out to Winnie at the back of the clubhouse. 'Come over here, Nestor, and sit down.'

'What's up, Prez? Have I done something wrong?' Nestor sounded nervous.

'You're a silly cunt, Nestor. Not only are you lazy, but you're dumb.' Nestor started to twiddle his fingers. 'We had a visit from the coppers at our shop the other day. Apparently somebody's been breaking into houses and thieving television sets from Housing Commission homes and we reckon it's you. Tell us the score without any bullshit, orright?'

'Well, Winnie, you told me to earn a quid and that's how I did it. At least I can pay my club fees now and get my bike fixed.'

'Yeah, but we never expected you to rob our people,' Brian snarled.

Nestor's head dropped further. He feared he was going to get bashed and thrown out of the Club. 'All I want is to be a good member of the Miners.' He didn't blubber, but he could feel it coming.

'Well, Nestor, we're going to give you one big chance to prove it. One.'

'I'll do anything, Prez.'

'Okay, this is what we have for you. We want you to become a farmer for us.'

'But I never farmed anything in my life.'

'Just shut up and listen, you silly cunt!'

'Okay, okay.' Nestor looked very uncomfortable, but he listened closer than he'd ever listened to anyone before or since.

'This will be easy — we'll show you everything. All you have to do is what the Rat shows you, nothing more. You got it?' Nestor gulped and wondered what he was supposed to know about farming. Farming what?

'We want you to grow our pot for us. You'll be housed and we'll look after you, and if you're smart, you won't say a word to anybody about this.' The picture became clearer by the second. 'If people ask what you're up to, tell them some bullshit. You're also going to have to find a partner. Is there anyone you know?'

'Yeah, Winnie, the new nominee, Nick,' said Nestor, looking more relaxed by the second.

'How long have you known him?'

'All his life: he's my nephew.'

'Good, I'll take you out next week. The Rat is going to teach you how to grow it, then it will be up to you to look after it. You'll live in a caravan at the farm. Security is important, but if you keep your mouth shut about what you're growing, there should be no problems. To make it easier on you, I won't even tell you where it is until you get there.'

Nestor stood up and his head swam. He wanted to cry from relief.

'Meeting time,' Big Kev's voice boomed out. The members grabbed drinks and filed into the meeting room. Big Kev called the meeting to order. Brian gave his treasurer's report, informing the members how much they had in funds, and called for a few delinquents to pay outstanding fees. For the first time in months Nestor wasn't among them. The members cheered when Brian told them that Nestor was up to date.

'Next!' Kev shouted over the hubbub.

Brian read the minutes from the previous meeting. Then he said, 'The Prez had a meeting with the Tigers and he wants to give you his report.'

'We met Twister and Kero Ken,' said Winnie. 'They reckon they were only mucking around about the Commandos nicking their bikes. I think he felt threatened by the Commandos and thought he could cause trouble between us — that's Twister for you. We also told them that we want no blues over territory. If we sell our drugs in one area they won't move into that area, and we won't move into their areas. Does anyone have any questions?' No one said a word. 'There'll be no warnings; the first time anyone does it, we hit them hard. Orright?'

'Orright!' the Miners shouted in unison. A few blokes yelled, 'Goodonya, Winnie! Beauty!'

'Next order of business. You all know Big Kev is going into the Army, and we're going to need a Sergeant-at-Arms. It'll be up to him to pick who he wants, okay, Kev?'

'Sure, Prez.'

'Okay, next weekend we're riding up to the festival at Freemans Reach; I want everyone to go. We leave the clubhouse at ten on Saturday morning. Brian, I want a couple of the nominees to organise a tent and we'll take our own piss in the Club ute. We should take a few baseball bats in case there's trouble. A lot of you don't know Swannie from Hurstville. Well, he and his boys are coming, so make them welcome. If things go right with them, we might think about starting up a new Chapter of the Miners on the Southside, but we have to see how they fit in. Is there anything else we have to discuss?'

'No, that's everything,' Brian said.

'Okay, meeting's over. Let's have a beer.' A cheer arose from the Miners as they got up and walked into the bar.

Chapter 6

Monday morning, the shop was abuzz. Spike came early to watch Kev work his last week as head mechanic and find out where everything was. The Rat arrived early as well, to take Winnie and Nestor up to the farm. They drove for forty minutes, and when they arrived Winnie handed Nestor the key to unlock the gate, let the car through and then relock it behind them. The Rat parked and Nestor helped him unload all the gear Rat had brought with him.

They all pitched in with the digging and so on. Once the trays were all filled with soil and laid out on the ground, the Rat produced a bag of seeds from his pocket. He pushed the seeds into the soil in rows and patted them down gently. Nestor walked next to him and watched carefully — he'd been told to learn quickly and he was doing his best.

'It's important you don't let them dry out. They'll take about three to four days to germinate and then they'll start to pop up all over the place. Once that starts you have to water them in and that's about all there is to it. Now let's go over to the hothouses. This is the hard part. You have to dig two rows.' The Rat grabbed a mattock and started to rake long parallel rows in the soil. He made sure Nestor watched closely.

'Spread the fertiliser down each row and water it in. When the seedlings are about six inches high, that's the time to transplant them into the ground. It isn't hard, but you have to be gentle with them. I'll come back out in a few weeks to see how you're going.'

'Okay, Nestor, you know what to do?' Winnie was pretty sure Nestor was up to the task.

'Sure, Prez.'

'Well, you get into it. I'm going to get you a caravan to live in. Have you told Nick yet?'

'Yeah, Prez, but I didn't know I had to stay here. What about supplies … and a TV?'

'Geez, you have to have TV, don't you? Don't worry, we'll set you up, you'll be comfortable. So get on with it and I'll come back later today with supplies. I'll bring you smokes. Anything else you want?'

'A couple of sheilas might be the go.' They all laughed. Nestor shook hands with the Prez and the Rat. 'See you later, Prez.'

'Yeah, mate, see you. Don't worry, it'll be worth it, Nestor. Give me the key to the gate. Come on, Rat, let's go.'

Winnie came back later in the afternoon with a caravan loaded with groceries and a television set and some cartons of smokes and grog. He reversed the caravan inside the packing shed. 'This'll keep you out of the weather. How're you going, Nestor?'

'I've got three of the hothouses ready. We'll be able to finish the rest tomorrow.'

'You realise why you have to stay here, don't you?'

'Yeah, to keep the seedlings moist.'

'Not only that, mate — we have to keep out snoopers and make sure there are no rip-offs. If this goes alright there's going to be a good earn in it for everyone. Come on, let's bugger off and you can come back with Nick tomorrow. Just explain to him the need to keep his mouth shut. Oh, and tell him to bring plenty of clothes. That goes for you too.'

'Sure, Prez.'

'Good, Nestor. I'll drop off food and beer every week.'

'You're the boss, Prez.'

Early on Saturday morning the Miners arrived on their bikes at the clubhouse and Swannie and his boys turned up in one big pack. Swannie had finished his rebuilt Harley, and it stood out among the British bikes. Kev came over to admire Swannie's panhead. 'Looks really good, Swannie.'

Ocker said, 'I like the paintwork.'

'Yeah, great job, Ocker.'

Ocker liked hearing that, and it was a very nice paint job.

Brian called out, 'Everyone in the clubhouse!'

Winnie gave a short speech. 'Now listen, if any of you don't know Swannie and his boys, introduce yourselves. If there's any trouble with the Tigers at the show, Swannie's boys are with us. There's bound to be undercover coppers there, so no selling any drugs. Okay, that's all. We leave in fifteen minutes so make sure you all have full fuel tanks, we're not stopping.'

Big Kev and Winnie had a quiet word. 'I picked Smouch to replace me as the new Sergeant-at-Arms.'

'Is he hard enough, Kev?'

'For sure, Prez. He's smart, too.'

'Does he realise it's only till you get back?'

'Yeah, mate.'

'Okay, we'll make the announcement at the show. Bring him over for a chat.'

Smouch saw Kev nod and he walked over, as proud as punch.

'Congratulations, Smouch, Kevvie's spoken highly of you. Just remember you have big shoes to fill.'

'Thanks, Prez.' Smouch was half-excited and half-nervous. Did he have it in him? Winnie wondered. Kev thought so and that was good enough for the Prez.

'We'll tell the boys out at the show. Alright, Smouch, your first job is to let the boys know we're leaving in five minutes.'

Smouch turned on his heel, walked outside and in a booming voice announced, 'Mount up!'

Winnie winked at Kev. 'At least he's loud enough.'

The sound of fifty bikes starting never failed to set the adrenalin pumping; the roaring engines made Winnie glad to be alive. Fuck, it's good to be on a run again — it's been too long, he thought as they headed northwest towards Freemans Reach on the Hawkesbury River. The traffic slowed and gave way to the pack led by Winnie and Brian. They rode at the speed limit to keep the pack together and joined what seemed like half of Sydney heading to the show. At one point Winnie pulled the pack over and a nominee collected everyone's entrance fee to save them all stopping at the gate.

At the festival entrance the nominee handed the security guard a wad of cash. 'You'll find it's all here, mate.' The guard quickly counted the bundle of fives and tens. 'Where's a good spot to set up camp?' He directed them to a shaded area under the gums by the creek, where they had a good view of the stage.

The nominee stayed until the pack rode through. Like the nominee said, all the money was there.

The boys rode single file through the site, past lines of waving girls whose blokes stood back and avoided eye contact and whispered to one another as they watched the Miners and Swannie's mob pull up on the banks of the creek under an old river gum.

Winnie made a simple announcement. 'Okay, you know Kevvie is going into the Army, so we need a new Sergeant and it's his choice.'

Big Kev stood and took off his Sergeant's badge. 'Thanks for all your support, boys. I've chosen a new Sergeant-at-Arms and I want you to give him the same loyalty and support as you've given me. I want you to welcome Smouch.' The boys cheered and lined up to thank Kev first and wish him well, and then they congratulated Smouch with slaps on the back and hand shaking. Kev was a mass of mixed emotions but he had one more announcement: 'Now it's time to party!' The boys cheered again.

Winnie congratulated Smouch and gave him the drum. 'You're in charge of security now. If there are any problems with the cops or security, don't wait, come and get me, orright?'

'Rightio, Prez.'

'Come on, Kevvie, let's go for a walk around.'

They strolled around the festival under the blazing summer sun. Most of the punters kept to the shade and the beer tents did a roaring trade. The security guard and his mate on the gate came over.

'Looks like you're going to be busy tonight,' Kev reckoned.

'We can handle them,' the taller of the two said. 'It's your lot we worry about.'

'You won't have any trouble with us,' Winnie assured them. He extended his hand and shook theirs firmly, looking them straight in the eye. 'I'm Winnie, what are your names?'

'Slim.'

'Mick.'

'Well, Slim, what are you worried about?'

'There's another club over the other side, the Tigers, and they've been getting on the piss since this morning.'

'I see, well *they're* your problem. Don't confuse us with them, they're undisciplined cunts.'

Slim smiled. 'Fair enough, Winnie. Have a good party, boys.'

'Ta, mate, you too.' They continued their walk through the crowd and after a minute or two had got the lay of the land. In the heat the best idea seemed to be to go back and have a few beers and watch the topless sheilas cooling off in the creek. Winnie and Kev cracked a beer each and relaxed on their sleeping bags.

Swannie came over for a sit-down with Winnie. 'My boys are keen to join the Miners.'

'I'll tell you what, Swannie, I'll put it to the members next week and there shouldn't be a problem. It'll be good to have you with us, but since it's a fair distance for you to come every week, maybe we should have a Miners Chapter over your way, and you should be their President. Whaddya reckon?'

Swannie gave the idea some thought and then broke out in a big grin. He was thrilled, it was plain on his face.

'That's a great idea, Winnie.' Swannie shook hands and then he hugged Winnie. 'I won't let you down, Prez.'

Winnie gave him a hug back and said quietly, so quietly even Kev, standing a few feet away, couldn't hear, 'I wouldn't if I were you.'

'I'll drink to that.' Kev raised his beer and took a long swig. 'Fuck, I'm going to miss you blokes.'

'Don't worry, Kev, it'll go quick enough. Just don't get yourself shot in Vietnam.'

Kev and Winnie were getting stuck into the grog under the trees when Sandy and Robyn in high heels, tight jeans and skimpy tops walked towards them, smiling. Heads turned, following every delicate footstep.

Kev stood and grabbed Sandy. 'I've been waiting for you,' he growled and pulled her towards him with a big hand on each cheek of her arse. He whispered in her ear and she giggled and pulled away.

Robyn sat down next to Winnie. 'How're you going, Prez? Good day for a party, eh?'

Winnie might have been happy to see Robyn, but he showed little emotion. He wasn't sure he wanted the girls around.

'Yeah, looks like it.' The sound from the stage cranked up just as Robyn sat down.

'Have you missed me, Prez?'

'No, should I have?' He was as non-committal as he could be. She rubbed his thigh. Swannie got the hint and wandered away.

Kev led Sandy by the hand towards the stage, where Steppenwolf belted out 'Born to Be Wild'.

'They're playing your song, Prez,' Robyn whispered and nibbled his ear before giving him a lingering kiss. Despite his misgivings Winnie couldn't help himself; he got a bit worked up and his crotch bulged, and Robyn reached down and stroked him.

'Oh, nice, Rob. Could you grab me another beer?'

'Jesus, you're a hard man, Winnie.'

'I know, gotta be alert at all times.'

Robyn bounced back with the beer and he pulled her on top of him. 'I want you, Prez,' she said, rubbing herself against him as Winnie pulled a sleeping bag over the both of them. 'I've been waiting for this since we were last together.'

Winnie unbuckled his belt and opened his jeans and she stroked him while he pulled her jeans off. She slid on top of him and kissed him deeply. Winnie entered her slowly and Robyn rocked back and forth and began to moan. 'Fuck me, Prez, don't stop.'

He was in no hurry, he just enjoyed her and lost himself in her, and the world could have ended right there and then and each of them would have heard and felt nothing but the other. Robyn started to quicken her rocking pace and suddenly she growled and bucked and twisted and arched her back and just as suddenly she lay still for a moment before collapsing, utterly exhausted, on top of him. When Winnie finally opened his eyes he saw a couple of nominees standing in the darkness looking in his direction. Winnie waved them away then swigged from his beer.

'Mmm, that was nice.'

'It was for me too.'

'No, I meant the beer.'

'Fuck, you're a cold cunt, Winnie.'

'It's just a fuck, Robyn.'

'Not for me, Winnie. I love you.' Christ, he'd heard that little song once too often, he thought, and wondered what it was with chicks and bikies.

'Come on, let's go for a walk.' Winnie stood and zipped up while Robyn adjusted her clothes and brushed her hair. 'Do you want to grab something to eat and we can check out the bands?'

She nodded. He didn't see she was crying in the dark.

Walking up towards the crowd Winnie spotted Miners chatting up chicks. As he drew closer he recognised Smouch and Brian. 'How's it going, boys? This crowd is really rocking.' The air was full of the unmistakable smell of pot.

'There should be more of these, Prez. They must be making a fortune but they're not very security conscious. They just take the money from the beer tents and the gate over to that caravan and they're probably sitting in there and counting it.'

'Any trouble?'

'Not yet, but most of the Tigers are tripping and anything is liable to happen.'

'Just keep an eye on it. We don't want any strife.'

Winnie saw a pack of bikes he didn't recognise and noticed the blokes wore patches he'd never seen before. A couple of them clutching beers headed in his direction. They got quite close before Winnie could make out the spider on their patch and the word 'Redbacks' with 'Newcastle' underneath. He'd never heard of them before. The taller of the two blokes stuck out his hand.

'How are ya, mate? Not a bad party, eh? My name's Sorrow, this is Fred.'

'Winnie's the name.'

'Yeah, we heard you got a bike shop at Parramatta that sells used bikes. One of our members bought his bike from you, reckons it was a good buy.'

'Well, that's what I like to hear.' Winnie hoped it was a 'good' bike and not a hot one.

'We're opening a new shop in Newcastle, maybe we can do some business together?'

'There's a good chance, Sorrow. Give us a call or come down for a ride, you're only an hour or two away on the new expressway.'

'Geez, you're dead-set right. What a good ride that is, new road and all.'

'Yeah, well when you come down you'll be welcome at our clubhouse. I'll catch you later. Have fun, boys.' Winnie winked at them and led Robyn off into the crowd.

'Geez, you bikies have funny names,' Robyn said.

'Whaddya mean?'

'Well, his name is Sorrow — what sort of name is that?'

Winnie had an answer for everything. 'You have to be called something.'

They were retracing their path, searching for Smouch and the Miners, when he saw security guards running towards the stage area. He saw Smouch and headed over.

'What's the score, mate?'

'The fucking Tigers are running amok. Some stoned cunt ripped off a sheila's top and when her boyfriend stood up to him they bashed him.'

'Fuck, they're queer cunts; all they'll do is bring the heat down on all of us.' The sound of wailing sirens and the flash of blue lights meant the cops had been waiting for an excuse to enter the site.

'Smouch, put the word out for our blokes to go back to our site.'

Kevvie was already there with Sandy and they couldn't keep their hands off each other. Winnie and Robyn sat down on the grass and watched them. 'You two look as if you had a good time,' Winnie said.

'Good enough,' said Kev, who was a bit pissed and a lot happy.

'You've heard about what's going on up there?'

'A little, Prez. Whaddya reckon?'

'Seems the Tigers are all off their heads on acid trips, then the pigs came in. I wouldn't be surprised if they lump us all in together.'

There was a sudden silence. Someone must have pulled the plug on the music. The quiet was eerie. 'The shit's hit the fan.' Winnie stood up to get a better view and saw three patrol cars racing down the track and screeching to a halt. The cops jumped out.

'It looks like they mean business. Robyn, you and Sandy had better clear off for a bit, I don't want you copping it.'

'But Winnie ...'

'Just shut up and go!' The girls grabbed hands and sprinted into the dark.

The head uniformed copper walked over to Winnie. 'Alright, get your boys lined up.'

'We haven't done anything, we've been here all night.'

'Do as you're fucking told!'

'We can take them,' one of Swannie's boys said, but Winnie had other ideas.

'No, we play it their way.' The cops searched the boys one by one.

Winnie whispered to Smouch to tell any Miners with drugs to toss them into the darkness. A couple of the boys were too pissed and a bit slow and the cops found some pot and handcuffed them and threw them into the bull wagon.

The senior cop stuck his face into Winnie's face. The smell of alcohol on his breath was rank. 'We're fucking sick of scum like youse destroying everyone's fun.'

'That's what I was just saying about you, Pig.'

'Smart cunt, eh?' He was raising his hand to smack Winnie when a voice rang out.

'That'll do, Constable, that'll do!'

Winnie never forgot a voice or a face. He knew who that disembodied voice belonged to, and thanked his lucky stars.

'I know that face,' Smouch whispered. 'It's Sergeant Burrows.'

Burrows was dressed in a cheap suit; he looked like he was on his way to church. When he drew closer to Winnie he turned to the uniform and told him to back off.

'I'll remember you,' the beer-breathed uniform said in Winnie's face.

'Me too,' said Winnie in as low and menacing a voice as he could muster. He wanted to laugh at the cop but he bit his tongue.

'Right, what have you been up to?'

Winnie pretended not to know who the plain-clothes cop was but he knew alright. 'Nothing. We were just enjoying ourselves when suddenly you turned up.'

Burrows looked around at Winnie.

'I remember you. You're Peter Winifred. Don't you own Snow's Bike Shop in Parramatta?'

'Me and my mates do, yeah.'

'Alright.' Burrows leaned in. 'If you and your mates had nothing to do with the shit over there just nod your head.' Winnie nodded.

'Okay, keep your members down here and out of the way.' Burrows shouted to the uniforms to get back to the main stage, where the trouble was.

'Hey, what about my blokes you grabbed?'

'They'll be charged and bailed and back by morning.' With that the coppers got back in their cars and racked off.

The boys cheered and called the cops cunts once they were out of earshot. Other members scrambled on their hands and knees in the dark, trying to find the drugs they threw away. Every now and then someone would cheer when a bag was found.

'Fuck, this has turned into a real shit fight,' Brian said to no one in particular.

'Fucken oath,' said Winnie. 'Who have they got locked up?'

'Ocker, Smithy and one of Swannie's boys.'

'Fuck, I thought Ocker was smarter than that.'

'Yeah, he is, but apparently they never saw the cops till it was too late. They were having a session behind the club truck.'

'Hey, Smouch, let the boys know that as soon as we get our members back from the pigs we're leaving.'

'Sure thing, Prez.'

'Hey, Brian, let's go see what's happening. Smouch, we're going for a wander. Make sure everyone stays here.'

When they got close enough to see what was going on, everything looked normal and the band was heading back on stage. Slim the security guard came over. One of his eyes had started to darken and close but he had a big smile on his mug. 'Fuck, I hate those Tigers.'

'Where have I heard that before?' Winnie laughed. 'What was the problem?'

'Well, they were just funny at first, then things started to get nasty as the trips kicked in. They started ripping off sheilas' clothes and bashing their boyfriends and intimidating everyone. Then they knifed some poor cunt — it wasn't pretty.'

'How did you get that black eye?'

'Who knows? It was pretty wild, then the coppers turned up with big batons and they really gave it to the Tigers and locked 'em all up. I tell you something for free: this'll be the last outdoor gig I do.'

'Okay, catch you later, Slim. Let's go, Brian.'

On the way back to the camp site Winnie asked Brian, 'How's Gina going with the baby, mate?'

'Well, she's over the sickness, only a couple of months to go before it's due. She'd like you to come over for dinner, Winnie.'

'Okay, Brian, you make the plans.'

As they approached the campsite Big Kev walked over. 'Prez, do me a favour while I'm away? Drop around to my mum's place and give her some money every couple of weeks, please. Don't let Sandy in the clubhouse, either. I don't want blokes I know hitting on her.'

'Are you falling in love, Kev?'

'No, but I really like her.'

'Okay, mate. When do you have to report, Kev?'

'Tuesday. This is the last you'll see of me for a while.'

'Here comes Ocker, Prez.'

Sure as shit he's strolling down the hill with the other blokes who got busted. 'Come here, you silly cunt.' Ocker had a smile on his face. 'What happened?'

'They took us to Windsor Police Station and charged us with possession. We have to go to court in two weeks.'

'Good, I was worried they were going to mix you up with the Tigers.'

'No, they're fucked, they took them to Parramatta. Sergeant Burrows looked after us.'

'I wonder what he's up to.'

'Who knows,' Ocker said. 'I don't much care. One thing I do know is they do nothing for nothing.'

'It's puzzling, Winnie,' Brian said. 'Maybe he's just a good copper.' They all laughed at that.

'Okay, Brian, get Smouch to get the boys together. We're going.'

Chapter 7

The next day at the shop Spike walked into Winnie's office.

'G'day, Spike. Kevvie's told you what's going on in the workshop?'

'Sure has, boss. This is my thing.'

'Well, I'll leave you to it. Oh, by the way, I thought you were going out to the rock festival?'

'No, fuck 'em, Winnie, you have no control over them, and by what I read in the newspapers, I'm glad we didn't. Why give your money to some other cunts when you're better off running your own show?'

'You reckon, Spike?'

'Yeah, like incorporating a custom bike show with it.'

'Not a bad idea, Spike.'

Ocker walked into the shop and laid a newspaper on the table.

The front page headline said it all: 'Bikies Ruin Rock Festival'.

Members of rival bikie gangs war with each other, rape women and knife innocent bystander.

The story went on:

Following a vicious weekend brawl at Freemans Reach members of the Miners and Tigers motorcycle gangs were arrested at the scene and charged with various offences ranging from 'public affray' to 'possession of prohibited drugs'. A police spokesman today stated that the organisers have now stipulated that motorcycle gangs be banned from attendance at any future concerts.

'Fuck, they can bullshit,' said Ocker.

'Who cares?' Winnie said. 'We'll run our own.'

'What do you mean, Prez?'

'I'll let you know, Ocker.'

As it turned out, for the next couple of months the boys could hardly go for a ride without getting pulled over by the pigs and getting hassled and booked for very little or nothing.

Brian and Gina had a baby girl and they asked Winnie to be the godfather. As they pulled up at the church for the christening, most of the Club was already there and Winnie noticed Sandy at the top of the stairs.

'How're you going, Sandy? I never thought you'd be here.'

'Gina invited me. I met her with Kevvie a few times.'

'Have you heard from him?'

'I've had a couple of letters. He can't write too well, so he's enlisted a mate to write them for him.'

'Yeah, I know. Has he got much to say?'

'Very little, Prez, and Robyn's gone back down the coast to where she comes from.'

'I didn't think the city suited her.' Winnie was distracted.

The priest ushered everyone inside without a second glance, as if he had bikies in his church all the time.

At the end of the christening Winnie shook Brian's hand and gave Gina a kiss. He took a silver bracelet from his pocket, engraved with the name Kitty, and gave it to Gina. He told them, 'I'll take this godfather thing seriously.'

Brian was really happy. 'I know you will, mate, that's why we asked you. I've got a keg on at my place, are you coming? We have to wet the baby's head!'

Winnie smiled. 'Is the Pope Italian?'

The aroma of cooking meat wafted through the air. Ocker and Winnie drank beer standing beside the barbie, watching the snags sizzle.

'They make a nice couple.'

'Sure they do, mate.' Winnie's sarcasm was barely disguised.

'What do you mean, Prez?'

'Nothing, mate, nothing.'

'Look at Sandy over there, a real miss prim and proper today.'

'What do you mean by that, Ocker?'

'Well, she's supposed to be in love with Kevvie but the slut's going out every night of the week with the Yanks on R and R up the Cross.'

'Fair dinkum?'

'Fucken oath! I've seen her sometimes with one on each arm!'

'Does she know you saw her?'

'No, too busy having a good time!'

'Well, let's keep it our little secret; you're not to let on to Kevvie.'

'But he should know.'

'Not from us, he doesn't; she can tell him if she wants, but not us. Okay?'

'Sure, Prez.'

Rat turned up early next morning. Winnie was raring to go. 'Come on, Ocker, let's go. Brian, Ocker and I are going to the farm, we'll see you tomorrow.'

The Rat headed towards Windsor in the traffic for a bit, then he turned to the boys and said, 'Hey, I've got some good news and some bad news. What do you want first?'

'Don't play games with us, Rat. Give us the bad news first.'

'Well, the price of pot has gone up.'

'How come?'

'Well, with all the Yanks on R and R in town, they're willing to pay more. Also there are more locals smoking, so the good news is your crop is doubling in price every month.'

'How much a pound now?'

'To you, Winnie, nine hundred a pound.'

'I suppose that's the good news.'

'Fucken oath it is, Winnie!' Ocker said. 'Work it out — if we get a four hundred pound crop, that's three hundred and fifty grand, minimum.'

'Fuck me!' said Winnie. 'Let's get to the farm, pronto!' Winnie's head swam; his little gardening venture was turning out trumps.

Nick was waiting for them at the locked gate, key in hand.

'Where's Nestor, Nick?'

'He's watering.'

'Jump in, I want to see the crop.'

Rat pulled up near the packing shed and Nestor emerged from one of the hothouses. He was wearing a torn singlet, a dirty pair of jeans and boots covered in mud, and had an old slouch hat perched on his head.

'How're you going, Prez?'

'Good, Nestor. You even look like a farmer!' He laughed. 'Come on and show us what you've been up to.' They walked into the hothouse and the size of the plants totally knocked them out.

'Fuck, Nestor, you must have a green thumb!' The Rat whistled and bent down and pulled out a huge plant and chucked it on the ground.

'What are you doing, Rat? Hey, Prez, what he's doing?'

'Fucking hold on, Nestor, listen to the Rat.'

'See these little balls,' Rat started to explain as he pointed to the obtrusions. 'This is a male plant, so when these little sacs open, the pollen blows over the females and that fertilises them and they become full of seed. It renders the crop almost useless.'

'You have to check every plant every day. Are you listening, Nestor?'

'Sure, Prez. I'm keen to produce a bumper crop, it's like these are my babies.'

'Well, let's go and check the rest of your kids!'

By the time they'd finished they'd had to pull out ten per cent of the crop.

'You're still going to have a good crop, Winnie.'

'Thanks, Rat. Now you and Nick go for a wander; we've some Club business to talk about.'

Nestor opened the caravan door and motioned the boys inside. 'What's happening with the Club, Prez? I heard about the shit fight at the music festival on the radio.'

'A couple of Twister's Tigers went to jail over it, that's all; the coppers could hardly get anyone to testify. Smouch is the new Sergeant-at-Arms till Big Kev gets back and Swannie from Hurstville started a Miners Chapter over in the Southside. Brian and his missus had a baby girl, Kitty.'

'Has anyone asked where I am?'

'Yeah,' Ocker says. 'We told them we had to shoot you.'

'Did you?' And with that, everybody had a good laugh.

'No, mate,' said Ocker, 'I told them you were away on Club business; there's no need for anyone to know.'

'Nestor, I'm really proud of what you've achieved,' said Winnie. How's Nick handling it?'

'He's a bit worried about not being able to go to Club meetings.'

'Tell him not to worry; he'll get his colours when we think he's ready.'

'Do you need anything out here, Nestor?' asked Ocker.

'No, but I'd like to know how long before the harvest.'

'Hey, Rat,' Winnie called out the door, 'how long do you think before we can harvest?'

'In these hothouses, about two months. We'll need a team to trim the heads and then weigh it up, that's the best part!'

'Wouldn't selling it be the best part?'

'Well, yeah, it is. Winnie, you're going to have a good crop!'

Winnie turned back to Nestor. 'Have you had any visitors?'

'No, Prez, quiet as a mouse out here.'

'Good. Come on, Ocker, let's go.'

The next Friday night Swannie and his Southside boys came over to share a drink and a joke before sitting down to discuss their various business ventures. Many members from the Chapters had interests in common. Some were into rebirthing bikes and cars and others were big on selling pot and acid. One common thread among most of the members was running their own 'legitimate' businesses. A few just got by doing whatever they had to, but what they shared first and foremost was not bludging on the Club. They took that seriously, and were one hundred per cent behind each other.

Brian read the minutes from the previous meeting and then called for any new business.

Winnie spoke. 'What I have to say will only work if we have the full support of the Club. Now, you blokes were out at the rock festival and saw how many people were there and the money they took.' Winnie's dark, serious eyes scanned the room. 'What if we put on a rock and custom motorcycle show for American and British bikes?'

Murmurs filled the room and then quickly hushed as he continued. 'We provide trophies, sell the piss, pay the bands and keep the gate. There'll be lots to organise but it'll be our little do. So what do you think, boys?'

Most members were enthusiastic. Some blokes couldn't imagine what Winnie had in mind but they swam in a school and if the Prez thought it would work, it would work.

Swannie wanted to know, 'Are we going to let just anyone come?'

'I thought about that. Do you mean Twister and his Tigers, Swannie?'

Swannie nodded.

'I know what you mean, mate,' Winnie said. 'They did nothing to us, so if we invite them and get them to act like boy scouts, imagine the amount of respect we'll get from everyone.'

The boys all nodded. They'd seen Twister and his mob go off the deep end; maybe this was a way to settle things down a bit. But Winnie hadn't finished. 'I'm going to make certain that I visit Twister and invite the Tigers. I'll wait until he's sitting there smiling and thanking me, then I'm going to pull a gun on him, point it straight at his head' — the boys looked stunned — 'and say, "If just one of your blokes gets pissed, I'm going to shoot the fucker, and I don't care who it is. It's that or don't come at all." Then I'll put the gun away. You reckon that'll work?'

The boys were silent for a moment. They saw the look in Winnie's eyes and knew he wasn't fucking around. The Tigers had caused enough shit for everyone, including the Miners; they were sick of it. It was unanimous. 'Fucken oath, Prez!'

'Who's going to see him with you, Prez?'

'You, Swannie. And Smouch and Brian.'

'What about the show, who do we invite?'

'I met a few of the Redbacks from Newcastle and I wouldn't mind inviting them,' Winnie said.

'We'll invite anyone and everyone.'

'Hey, we could have wet T-shirt competitions.'

'First we have to decide where to have it.'

'Well, what about here?' Brian said.

'Do you reckon it'll be big enough?'

'We've got a couple of acres here. If we keep all the cars out, just allow show bikes and our bikes, there should be plenty of room.'

'That sounds good,' Winnie said. 'Ocker, you can organise the bands. Do you want strippers?'

'Yeah!'

'Good, we'll have them in the clubhouse for after the show, Ocker. Most people will leave when we shut the outdoor bands down, and we'll host the bike show during the day. With the piss, I reckon we just sell cans of beer, bourbon and soft drinks. So we don't have to worry about cash we'll have a booth selling tickets they can exchange for drinks.'

'What about any drunks?'

'We'll be responsible for the security. Now, if anyone does cause trouble, we don't want to bash them; just lead them out to the main gate and piss them off, understand?' Winnie ensured they'd all got the message. 'We don't want any trouble inside.'

'When are we going to have the show, Prez?'

'Well, it'll take a bit to put together … Say just before Christmas, in two months.'

'End of meeting! Let's have a drink!'

On the way out of the meeting, Winnie pulled Swannie aside.

'Listen, mate, you're President of the Southside Chapter, there's no need to call me Prez.'

'You'll always be the Prez to me, Winnie. I'm just glad to be a Miner.'

'Come on, Swannie, I'll buy you a drink.'

Ocker was at the bar in full swing, telling bad jokes.

Swannie whispered to Winnie, 'You know you can't trust that Twister cunt, mate.'

'Yeah, I know, mate, but he knows I'm as good as my word. I'll shoot the bastard if I have to. We can't have the heat on all us bikies because he can't control himself or his boys. When we're there, I don't want you to say anything, Swannie. Just sit there, give him your best stare. You know what he's like, he doesn't give a fuck about anybody. Even his own Tigers say he's only interested in money and making himself look good.'

After Winnie had met with Twister, he spoke briefly about their exchange. 'Twister nearly shit himself when I pulled the gun on him and it went exactly as I said, only he reckoned that if any of his boys played up at the show, he'd shoot them himself.' He couldn't be pressed into saying much more and the boys knew if the Prez said little, then that was all there was to say.

'I don't think we'll have any more problems with the Tigers.'

'How's your pot business going, Swannie?'

'Like crazy, mate!'

'Sorry to tell you, mate,' Winnie said, 'but the price is going up.'

'I heard that. It won't stop them from buying it.'

'How high do you reckon it'll go?'

'Who knows?'

'How's your Harley, Swannie?'

'Pretty good. I'm going to put it in the bike show. I don't think there's too many panheads entered.'

'I reckon I'll be getting a Harley soon. Should I buy a new one or build one — what's your take?'

'I'd just buy a new one and customise it to suit yourself, Prez, otherwise you'll end up taking ages to finish it, like I did.'

'Yair, that sound the go.'

'I'm off now, I'll see you soon.'

'See ya, Swannie.'

'Brian, get our stash tin out, it's time we paid ourselves. I'm buying a new Harley.'

'Sure thing, Winnie!' Brian brought out the cash box stuffed with bundles of notes.

'How much have we got?'

'Thirty-two grand.'

'Fuck!' Ocker couldn't believe it. It was enough to buy a house and a car.

'How much will we take out, Prez?'

'We'll take seven each; keep Kevvie's separate and Ocker can take five hundred to drop into Kev's mother. I'm off to buy a new shovelhead. I already picked it out and I'm paying cash!'

'Good!' Brian said. 'Gina and I've been looking at a new house up on Snow's Mountain. I'm going over to see the estate agent and give him five as a deposit.'

'What are you going to do with yours, Ocker?'

'Well, I've been thinking of opening a tattoo shop. One of Swannie's boys is a tattoo artist and I'm setting it up.'

'Good on ya, Ocker, good thinking. How's Spike going in the workshop, Brian?'

'Yeah, good, he told me he has something for you.'

Winnie walked out to see Spike busy working.

'I've got something for you.' He handed a bundle to Winnie.

'What're these, Spike?'

'They're original Harley stamps, straight from the Harley factory in the States. I know a Yank mechanic in Melbourne, and he worked there. They're originals. He brought a couple of sets with him. Once you renumber the motors, they're like factory jobs.'

'Are you entering your Harley in our bike show, Spike?'

'Too right, I'm already working on it now.'

The day Winnie went to pick up his new Harley he was nearly drunk with anticipation. He'd been into the store and looked around a few times in the week before; he wanted to think about what he wanted, and he took his time. He finally decided on the cream shovelhead. He'd seen it the first time he went in and he never forgot how sweet it looked. He walked over to it and breathed in the intoxicating smell of his new motorcycle.

The salesman was dressed in jeans and looked like a rider too. He left Winnie alone for a few minutes then he sauntered over. 'Good looking, aren't they?'

Winnie said he thought so and stuck his hand out. 'Winnie, mate. I think I'll take this one. Don't suppose you'd mind if I paid in cash?'

The salesman stuck out his hand. 'In cash we trust.'

They both stood and admired the bike a bit longer and then sat down to do the paperwork. Once that was done, Winnie took the opportunity to hang a few posters for the bike show at Burling & Simmons, and everywhere else. 'All we need is for the punters to turn up.'

When Winnie stopped at the traffic lights on Parramatta Road he noticed admiring glances from motorists and pedestrians. There were few Harleys around, let alone new ones. He could hardly wait to show it off to the boys. At the clubhouse he revved the motor and the members flooded out and admired his new bike.

'Onya, Prez, it's a honey,' said Ocker and offered to buy Winnie a beer. When they approached the bar Winnie saw Nestor's cousin Nick.

'Hey, Nick, shouldn't you be out at the farm with Nestor?'

'No, Prez, he told me it was okay to have a couple of days off but to come and let you know my old man died; we buried him today. I'll go back to the farm tomorrow.'

'Geez, Nick, I'm sorry to hear that. Let's have a drink to him. What was his name?'

'Bert.'

'Okay, here's to Bert, may he rest in peace.'

'Thanks, Prez.'

Chapter 8

Show day was sunny, promising good business at the beer tents set up near an outdoor stage on the back of a semitrailer. Another tent served as the registration area, where entrants could register their bikes for the show. Brian had organised trophies for all the different categories: best Harley, best British, best paint job, best custom and best 'rat bike', though Winnie wondered why anybody would want to win that. They opened the gates at nine and at ten people were streaming in. No one could believe it; even Winnie was amazed.

From down the road he heard a dull roar: Rastus and his Commandos.

Rastus looked around at the gathering crowd. 'Geez, Winnie, this is a great turn-out, you'll do alright today.' The boys, like excited schoolkids, walked around and checked out the bikes and winked at the girls.

'Rastus, if you're going to be one of the judges, no favouritism, okay, mate?'

'Not at all, Winnie.' Rastus grinned and pulled his beanie down over his forehead.

'Geez, he can look like a real drongo, eh?' Ocker laughed.

'Whaddya think of your new shovelhead, Winnie?'

'I love it, Rastus! The power, the ride — couldn't be happier with it. There it is, pretty as a picture.' The cream shovelhead cranked up on its stand at a jaunty angle glowed in the bright sunlight and the chrome sparkled.

'Oh yeah, mate, it's nice alright.' They walked around it and Rastus pulled out one of his small cigars, lit up and said thoughtfully, to no one in particular, 'Beautiful.'

A member pointed to two girls standing by the gate. 'A couple of sheilas want to come in. Should I let 'em?'

'How old are they?'

'They look eighteen, but I bet they're only sixteen.'

'Let them in, they're welcome, but not in the clubhouse.'

The beer tents sold lots of grog and then the band started playing. It turned out a nice afternoon, and the kids had fun with the free games and sausages. Ocker asked Winnie if he should get the bands to stop playing and announce the results of the bike competition and present the trophies. They were still talking about the presentation when the roar of approaching bikes announced the arriving Tigers. Winnie and Swannie walked over to welcome them.

Winnie pointed Twister to a parking area and the Tigers rode in. No doubt their actions at the rock festival were still fresh in everyone's mind. Once they'd parked and mingled with the crowd the punters relaxed and the good vibe returned.

'Not a bad show you put on, Winnie. Bit of work, eh?' Twister looked around at the crowd.

'We're happy with it, Twister.'

The two young girls who'd come in earlier wandered straight over to Twister. They giggled and flirted with him. He put one under each arm. 'Hey, Winnie, you want some pussy?'

Winnie looked at them and smiled. 'No, you keep 'em, Twister. I don't play and work at the same time.'

Ocker, the master of ceremonies, got up on stage to do the presentations.

'Attention and welcome, friends. Good to see you all and we hope you're having a good time.' A loud cheer arose. 'Welcome to the first Miners' Bike show! We're now going to present the trophies for the different bike categories. First trophy is for best custom and it goes to Swannie for his panhead!' The crowd cheered. 'He put a lot of effort into getting it ready and it shows. Congratulations, Swannie.'

After Ocker presented the trophies for the different categories he picked up the last one and held it high above his head, saying, 'This is for the best paint job and it goes to ...' he paused for dramatic effect, 'me!' Everyone booed in response but Ocker smiled and leaned into the microphone, saying with a laugh, 'I was the only entry, so next year, if there are any painters out there, get your work in!'

'Now here's something for the ladies. I have one hundred dollars here for you — the crowd will judge the winner. Whoever gets the loudest cheer wins the money.' Ocker glanced around at the women and continued, 'Come on, girls, who wants to win one hundred dollars?'

About ten girls of varying sizes and ages mounted the stage and Ocker poured water over the front of each one, exposing their titties. He stood behind them and announced each one's name then pointed the microphone towards the audience to hear their cheers. He'd already decided on the winner, a tall blonde with huge tits, and as it turned out, she was the popular choice according to the cheers. Ocker gave her a hug, slipped her the hundred and whispered in her ear. Then he ushered the girls off the stage. The band started playing, the dancing started up and the party began again.

When the sun set, the show wound down a bit and Twister made a point of thanking Winnie for the day. 'Good clean fun, mate, really had a good time. You put on a good one!'

Winnie asked him about the two young girls. 'Are you going to leave them for us?'

Twister looked over his shoulder; the girls were waiting for him with Kero Ken.

'It wasn't that good, Winnie.' With that he grinned and headed to his bike.

The Tigers mounted up and waited for him. He climbed on, kicked his bike into life and they roared off.

Winnie and Swannie stood at the gate and watched them go. 'Thank fuck,' said Swannie. 'Now we can relax.'

Brian came out of the back counting the take. 'Well, I'd say we cleared around seven grand.'

'Fuck, that's not bad for a day's work.'

'Are you staying for the party tonight, Brian?'

'I'll stay a while; I want to get home to Gina and Kitty.'

'You love being the family man, eh?'

'Nothing wrong with that is there, Prez?'

'No, not at all, mate. Say hello from me.'

When the crowd left, it was time for the Miners' party. Ocker had a blonde in tow. He introduced her to Winnie.

'Hey, Prez, Sharon here wants to meet you. Come and share a joint with us.'

'Yeah, I reckon that's just what I need, Ocker; it's been a long day, but a good one. Let's go.'

Ocker whispered in Winnie's ear, 'She's a good party girl, mate.'

'Let's go right now, then.'

Ocker laughed. He took out the joint and gave it to Winnie then pulled Sharon's top down to expose her tits and rubbed them as she lay back and moaned with pleasure.

'You love that, don't you?'

'Yeah, I love it,' she purred.

'I thought you came out for the joint, Ocker?'

'What, you don't want some of this, Prez?'

'What part can I have?'

'Any part you like,' Sharon replied.

Winnie pulled out his cock. 'How about sucking this?'

'With pleasure.' Sharon began stroking and licking his cock urgently.

Ocker passed the joint back to Winnie, then resumed rubbing Sharon's tits.

'You sure get good girls, Ocker!' Winnie said after he came. 'Not a bad effort, Sharon.'

He zipped up his jeans, patted them both on the head, said, 'I'll leave you two love birds to it', and went back to the party.

Winnie made a beeline for Swannie.

'It was a good day, Prez. What was it like financially?'

'Not too sure yet. Any profit we get we share sixty-forty with your Chapter.'

'You don't have to do that, Prez.'

'Yeah, mate, we're all in this together; your blokes helped.'

Sorrow from the Redbacks rocked up. 'I'm not interrupting, am I?'

'No, not at all. Swannie, do you know Sorrow from Newcastle?'

'No. How are you going, mate?'

'Good show you put on today, and fuck, those Tigers were bloody well-behaved!'

'That was good to see.' Winnie was pleased; his little visit to Twister had paid off.

Swannie spoke to Sorrow. 'You've got a few Harleys in the Redbacks — are there many more in Newcastle?'

'Quite a few, mate. One of our boys has a shop. You'll have to drop in and see us.'

'I might just do that,' Swannie said.

'Did you build your panhead, Swannie?'

'Yeah, and Ocker did the paintwork.'

'Well, you both did a good job with it.'

Winnie asked if Sorrow and his boys were staying the night.

'Yeah.'

'Well, we've bunged on some strippers for later.'

'The boys'll like that.'

'Good. I'm going to find Rastus, Swannie, I'll catch you later.'

It was never hard to find Rastus. Winnie headed for a gaggle of girls and Rastus was in the middle of them.

'Winnie, how are you, mate?'

'Good now, Rastus.'

Rastus moved a girl away, patted the seat next to him and invited Winnie to sit down next to him.

'Good show today, Winnie. Twister was very quiet.'

'You know what he's like, Rastus, if he isn't the centre of attention.'

'Well, I'm glad they didn't stay tonight.'

Walking into the back room they saw a naked Ocker gently spanking Sharon's arse with a rolled newspaper.

'You're a naughty girl. Who's a naughty girl?'

'I am, I'm a very naughty girl.'

Rastus said straight off, 'If you get tired, Ocker, I'll take over.'

'Give me time, mate,' Ocker replied and stroked his cock.

'God, you're dirty cunts!' Winnie said and shook his head.

'How are your boys settling in Sydney, Rastus?'

'They love it, mate. We found a place in Balmain; it's just like Melbourne but with a big harbour.'

'You have the Yarra.'

'No comparison, Winnie.'

'I'm going to take my Harley for a dawn ride before the traffic starts.'

On Monday morning Winnie rode in on his new Harley.

'Hey, Spike, could you service my bike?'

'No worries, Winnie.' Spike wheeled the bike up to his spot near the bench and looked at the speedo. 'Fuck, you put some miles on.'

'Yeah, I went for a ride on the weekend just to get to know it. Couldn't stop, too much fun.'

Brian and Ocker were discussing the show in the shop; every so often Ocker howled like a wolf and every time he did it Brian laughed.

Winnie walked in. 'There's no need to ask what you're telling him, Ocker, you dirty cunt.' Ocker howled again and went back to his spray booth.

'Brian, have you worked out the finances from the show yet?'

'Yeah, mate, after all expenses we made ten and a half grand, not bad for our first effort.'

'I'll tell you what, Brian, give four grand to Swannie's Chapter.'

'That's fair enough, Prez. Who's their treasurer?'

'Thommo.'

'Get a hold of him and give it to him. I'm going back out to the farm with the Rat to check on the crop.'

'We'll be in the money big time when that comes in.'

'Don't count your chickens yet, mate.'

While driving to the farm Winnie asked the Rat if he thought the plants would be ready. 'If they are, Rat, this could be your last trip out here.'

They pulled up at the gate and Nick let them in.

Nestor came out looking pretty pleased. 'How are you, Prez, orright?'

Winnie smiled and nodded. They walked over to the first hothouse.

'What was the bike show like, Prez?'

'Went off like a bomb, mate.'

'I won't miss the next one. Come on, let's check out the crop.' Nestor pulled open the door.

The place was crammed with hundreds of tall, healthy pot plants, so dense Winnie couldn't see through them.

'Fuck, look at this!' Rat was stunned. 'I've never seen plants like this before!' He pulled branches down, smelling them and inspecting the heads closely.

'Fuck, Winnie, you've hit the jackpot here.'

'Are they ready, Rat?'

'Fucken oath, mate!'

'We've got two more hothouses just like this,' said Nestor. 'What do we do now, Prez?'

'Ask Rat, Nestor.'

The Rat pulled a plant out, shook the soil loose and then headed towards the packing shed with the boys in tow. He hung it on a clothes line upside down.

'This is what you do, Nestor. Let it dry for four to five days,' Rat explained. 'See the big leaves? Take them all off and keep them separate,

I have a market for them. What you're left with are buds; that's where the money is. You just cut them off and weigh them up into five-pound lots, and there you go.'

'How many pounds do you think we have, Rat?'

'I'd be surprised if you don't get four hundred. Burn all the stalks when you've finished — you don't want to leave any evidence around.'

Winnie smiled at Nestor and Nick. 'Bloody good job, boys, bloody good.' He shook their hands. 'Good work, Nestor. You were born to do this. Thanks, Nick, great work. Sooner we get on with it, sooner we can sell it. Nestor, you and Nick better get into it. I'll come out on the weekend with Brian and Ocker to help you blokes. We'll bring bags and secateurs to cut the heads off. See ya Sunday. Come on, Rat, let's go.'

They fairly floated back to the bloody yellow Zephyr. Winnie's head spun. They were looking at a fair chunk of change when they unloaded it all at the going rate of $900 a pound.

'I tell you what I'll do, Rat: if you have a market for the leaf you can have it for helping us.'

'It's a deal, Winnie.'

Winnie, Ocker and Brian drove up the next weekend and walked into the packing shed. Brian and Ocker had no idea what to expect. When Winnie pulled the door back he stood speechless. Nestor and Nick stood in front of their crop and smiled proudly. Winnie had never seen Brian and Ocker so excited, they were bouncing around on the balls of their feet.

Brian was incredulous. 'This is unfuckingbelievable, Winnie. It's almost too much pot.'

Ocker wanted to howl like a wolf, but all he could say was 'Fuck me, fuck me rigid.'

'Come on, save that for later, we've got work to do.' Winnie wanted to get the packing over and get out of there quick smart.

Nestor was the boss of the production line and Nick his offsider. For once Winnie, Ocker and Brian took instructions. They carefully snipped off the heads, which resembled cat's paw, and packed them in five-pound bags. Then they stripped the plants and stashed the leaf in two huge bags for the Rat. It took the five boys almost two full-on, twelve-hour days before they had finished snipping, packing and tidying up the evidence. With due care, they set to work weighing it all up.

'How many bags did you get, Brian?'

'Eighty-five five-pound bags.'

'Fuck, I think it's time to celebrate!'

'Have you smoked it, Nestor?'

'Fucken oath, Prez. It's good!'

'Nick, here's some money. Go to the pub and get some piss.'

Once Nick was gone, Winnie called the boys together.

'Ocker, is your stash hole big enough for this? I don't want to leave it out here.'

'No problems, Prez.'

'Well, it's your job to get it transported.' Winnie stared at Nestor. 'When we get some money in, you and Nick will be first paid. Your share will be thirty grand — give Nick ten and keep twenty for yourself.'

'No problem, Prez.'

'Do you want to do it again?'

'Give me a couple of weeks off, Prez, and I'll be back into it. I don't think Nick is real keen. He really wants to get his colours and he's more worried about that than making money. He has great potential. I've had a lot of talks with him since we've been here.'

'Well, Nestor, you pick your new offsider, but he has to come from the Club. Just let me know.'

'Sure, Prez.'

Nick turned up with the grog and Nestor built a little fire out the back in an old 44-gallon drum and burnt the stalks and all the evidence. Then they had a barbie around the glowing coals and a bit of a session, with a lot of laughs.

Everything went along really well for the next few weeks until Winnie got wind of a new club calling themselves the Southern Stars. There would have been no conflict with them except they used the Miners' patch!

'They've been told about us, but the smart cunts say they don't give a fuck.'

'Don't they?' Winnie's eyes narrowed while he weighed his options.

'What are we going to do, Prez?' Swannie asked.

'Do you know where they drink?'

'At the Seabreeze Hotel.'

'Well, that's where we'll hit them. Hit them hard; take their colours and burn them.'

'What? Burn their colours, Prez?'

'Fucken oath, we want everybody to know there'll be no hiding. I want it to be public; I want the whole Club involved in this, no exceptions. We'll leave here next Saturday and hit them in the afternoon. Then no hanging around — straight in, do the job and out. Smouch, I want you to organise the burning of their bikes, the rest of us'll hit the maggots. Only baseball bats, boys, no guns or knives. We'll isolate the pub's phones so they can't ring the pigs. We'll call the pub and when they answer, leave the phone off the hook and that'll put their phone out of order. It should give us about ten minutes to do the job.'

On the Saturday morning, both Chapters gathered at the clubhouse. The members were pretty animated and spoke with bravado, but it was mostly to hide their nervousness, since no one really knew exactly what would happen. They strapped bats and clubs to their bikes and waited for the Prez to give the signal. This was war. The boys followed the Prez out of the clubhouse and headed down the coast. A couple of miles from the Seabreeze the pack pulled into a servo to fuel up.

'Smouch?'

'Yes, Prez?'

'Ring the pub when we're all ready.'

As the Miners pulled into the Seabreeze, the Southern Stars, the queer cunts, all smiled and waved. They hadn't a clue what was about to happen till the boys entered, brandished their weapons, and got stuck into them. Their women started screaming and crying out for the blokes to fight back but it didn't do much good. They were on the back foot from the word go and not prepared. Some tried to use pool cues as weapons but they were of little use against bats and chains.

The Miners only went after the blokes wearing patches and the whole affair was over in less than five minutes. They tore off the cut-offs bearing the Southern Star name patches and left the pub in mayhem. The women screamed obscenities at them and they were so loud and so rude it might've been funny except for their moaning, beaten and bloodied boyfriends. Smouch and a couple of members torched the Southern Stars' bikes and as they rode off, one exploded in a massive fireball.

The ride back to the clubhouse was pretty quick; they wanted to put as much distance between them and the Seabreeze as they could before the pigs were alerted. It worked a treat. The next day an article in the paper alleged that the Southern Stars had 'paid the penalty for stepping out of line in their outlaw society'. The civilians had escaped unhurt and the police didn't give a fuck about what the clubs did to each other. It enhanced the Miners' reputation. Everyone 'in the know' knew never to fuck with the Miners.

The proceeds from the pot crop gave everyone involved a good earn. Nestor and Ocker bought themselves new Harleys and Brian and Gina paid a big cash deposit on their new house on Snow's Mountain. Winnie paid Joe the Maltese musician ten grand as well. Joe was very thankful for it but wanted to know nothing about where the money came from. Life took on a rosy glow for a few weeks as the boys luxuriated in the sure knowledge that their 'farming' caper had paid off. Everything was going as sweet as a nut until Winnie drove over to the Southside in his car to see Swannie. A highway patrol car pulled him over.

'What can I do for you, officer?'

'Your rear number plate is hanging down.'

'I never noticed,' Winnie replied. 'I'll fix it.'

'No, I want to look in your boot, so open it up.'

'What for?' Winnie got that sinking feeling that comes when you know there's something in the boot that you don't want anyone to see.

'Just open it up!'

A sudden dryness came into his throat and the next thing, another patrol car pulled up. He must've called for back-up. The Pig opened the boot and pulled out a bag.

'What's this?'

'Don't know, officer, I've never seen it before.'

The coppers laughed. 'Sure, you haven't!'

The cop looked inside the bag and pulled out a handful of pot.

'Lock your car up, you're coming with us the station!'

While Winnie waited to be charged, he noticed a familiar face passing the charge room; it was Sergeant Burrows. 'Fuck, he gets around,' thought Winnie, but there was no way he could get his attention.

The copper who pulled him over came in to take a statement. In reply to every question Winnie gave the same answer: 'Not talking without a legal representative.'

'Righto, come on.'

'Where are we going?'

'We're taking you down for fingerprints. Is this the first time you've been in trouble with the law?'

'First time, but am I going to get bail?'

'We'll have to see what the Sergeant says.'

Back in the charge room the copper came back with Sergeant Burrows. Burrows winked at Winnie when he walked in, but acted coolly.

'How're you going, Peter? Got yourself in the shit, eh?'

'I know nothing about it.'

'Do you know him, Sarge?'

'We've met before. Are you still living at home?'

'Yes, Sarge.'

'Okay, we'll give you self-bail. You'd better get yourself a lawyer, too. We've set your court appearance for next week.'

Back at the shop, Winnie told the boys what had happened.

'Fuck, Prez, what happens now?'

'First, I have to get a solicitor. Do we know one?'

'What about Squizzy Taylor? He's doing law at uni and he'll know someone for sure, Prez,' Ocker replied. 'He's still living at home so I'll get him to come and see you. I sell him pot and he sells it at uni — that got him through.'

'Thanks, Ocker.'

'How much did they get you with, Winnie?' Spike asked.

'Five pounds, mate.'

'Bad luck, Winnie. If you'd been in Melbourne, good chance they would have just taken it and sent you on your way.'

Brian asked if Winnie wanted him to come to court with him. 'I'll bring Gina and the baby. You might get some sympathy.'

'Don't bring her, Brian, but I wouldn't mind you coming along for some moral support.'

'Sure thing, Prez.'

Next day Squizzy Taylor arrived in a suit and with his hair cropped short. 'A bit different from your hippie days, eh, Squiz?'

'How're you going, Winnie? You're in a bit of strife, mate. I won't be able to appear for you, 'cos I'm not qualified, but I spoke to a mate who'll do it. I just want to find out the story for him.'

After Winnie told him, Squizzy wasn't sure how he'd go. 'How long have you owned the car?'

'A couple of weeks.'

'Have you changed the registration over yet?'

'No, not yet, I was on my way to do it after I dropped off the pot.'

'I'll talk with John Baker. He's a good lawyer and there just might be an out for you. Do you have your charge sheet?'

Squiz read it and then sat and thought for a minute. 'It's a good thing you didn't admit anything. Turn up next week and we'll see you in court. This is a first offence, so don't worry too much. There could be a way out of this, orright?'

Winnie was pretty unhappy; he reckoned he might be done for all money.

When Winnie walked into the courthouse Ocker and Brian flanked him.

Squizzy was with a tall bloke in a dark suit looking very spiffy, and they led Winnie to a private interview room.

Ocker and Brian smoked cigarettes outside. It was the first serious offence for any of the Miners and they had no idea how the law worked, or if there was any chance Winnie would cop it sweet.

About ten minutes later Winnie, Squizzy and the lawyer emerged from the room. Winnie had on a big grin.

'What's going on, mate?' Brian asked.

'Well, the lawyer reckons I might be able to beat it; it'll be hard for them to prove it was mine.'

'Hey, Prez, there's your mate Sergeant Burrows!'

Burrows walked over to Winnie and asked for a quiet word.

Squizzy whispered to Winnie, 'Be careful, you don't have to talk with him, you know.'

'It won't hurt to hear what he has to say.'

Winnie and Burrows moved away from the group. 'What can I do for you, Sergeant?'

'I know it's your pot and you might have a good story to tell the judge, but if you want to make sure you get off I can arrange it for you; the Crown Prosecutor is a mate.'

'How am I going to do that?'

'It'll cost you a thousand dollars.'

'How do I know this isn't a set-up?'

'You don't.'

'Well, I don't have that sort of money on me.'

'That's okay; I'll come over to your shop tomorrow.'

'Okay, I'll be in it.'

'Don't try to go back on it, Winnie.'

'You have my word.'

'That'll do.'

Winnie saw Squizzy talking with a glamour puss. He never forgot a face, especially not that pretty one. 'It's that Mimi slut I picked up at the Centennial Hotel and took to Little Bay.'

John Baker came over to announce Winnie's hearing was up next.

Winnie told Ocker to get her phone number.

'Good luck, Prez!' Brian called out.

When it was all over, John Baker smiled coolly and Winnie looked relieved.

'That was a good result, Winnie,' Baker said. 'No conviction. That prosecutor went easy on you.'

'John, thanks a lot for your help.'

Squizzy stood up as Winnie came out of court. 'How did you go, mate?'

'No conviction; they believed my story. Hey, Squizzy, do you know Sergeant Burrows?'

'No, but you didn't do a deal with him, did you?'

Winnie smiled at Squizzy and said nothing.

'You can't trust the coppers, Winnie.'

'Don't worry about it, Squiz. Hey, who was the girl you were talking to?'

'Mimi Gregson, she's a friend of a friend.'

'Okay, Squiz, I owe you for today. Come around to the shop and have a beer.'

'One day, Winnie.'

The boys asked Winnie how'd he got off the charge. 'You won't believe it,' he said, then stopped. 'Hang on a minute, I have to talk to someone.'

Walking towards Mimi, he had a feeling he'd never experienced before, a moment of self-doubt. He wondered if she'd remember.

'G'day, Mimi, what're you up to over this side of town?'

'Hello, Winnie, I never expected to see you again.'

'What are you doing with yourself?'

'A bit more than you by the look of things.'

'It's not the way it looks. It was just a mistake.'

'That's what they all say.'

'Just get fucked, slut, you have no idea. Go back to your up-themselves friends!' With that Winnie turned and walked over to Brian and Ocker. 'Come on, let's go!'

Winnie had been hurt by that little exchange. He didn't say a word but neither Brian nor Ocker asked what had happened — they were aware something was up.

Brian wanted to know how Winnie got off.

'Don't you remember Burrows? The bloke who took our slug guns. When I went for a walk with him, he put it to me that for a thousand dollars he'd be able to influence the Crown Prosecutor not to go too hard with the charges and put enough doubt in the judge's mind that I was just an innocent party to it all. Just because the pot was in the boot didn't necessarily mean it belonged to me — I only just bought the car.'

'So Sergeant Burrows's a bent copper,' said Brian. 'When do you have to pay him?'

'He's coming to the shop to pick it up tomorrow.'

'You know, it won't hurt to have a bent copper onside.'

Chapter 9

At the shop the next day, the Sergeant parked his unmarked car at the front door and motioned Winnie outside. 'Come on, Winnie, we'll talk in the car. Have you got something for me?'

'Yeah, here it is.' Winnie handed over the money.

The Sarge counted it and pocketed it. 'Correct weight, Winnie, and yeah, you done alright yesterday.'

'So did you, Sarge.'

'Well, have you ever tried to live on police wages?'

'No, never have and never expect to.'

'I love a bloke with a sense of humour, Winnie.'

'I don't intend getting caught again.'

'Good chance you will, Winnie. In your line of business it's an occupational hazard.'

'What, running a motorcycle shop?'

'Come on, Winnie, you're talking to me now. I know you're a major marijuana wholesaler.'

'What makes you say that?'

'I know it, Winnie; it's my business to know things like that.'

'Well, if you know everything, how come you haven't busted me?'

'Oh, don't worry, Winnie, I was getting around to it. You unfortunately got busted before I could give your operation my full attention. So far you're still relatively unknown.'

'Well, how can we do business?'

'Not do business — do *more* business. What happened at court yesterday was the start of it and it's all about money. I'm in charge of the drug squad, a good position to help you. Remember, there are people I can introduce you to who will help us both. I can tip you off about raids and some of our tactics so you can be out of the way when you need to.'

'And how much is this going to cost?'

'We'll start with, say, a thousand a week.'

'Fuck off! Who do you think I am, Al Capone? I don't make that sort of money.'

'Okay, Winnie, let's start with five hundred, and as your business grows, which it will, we can renegotiate down the track a bit. Just think of me as the taxman, and you know how they can be cunts.' His eyes narrowed. 'I wouldn't like you to see that side of me; it's not pretty, Winnie.'

'Well, how will I pay you?'

'We'll work it out.'

'I don't want you to come here.'

'I'll give you a phone call to let you know where we can meet. Don't come in your colours, it'll draw attention. Neither of us needs that.'

Burrows reached over to shake hands but Winnie ignored him. 'Let's just keep it on a business level.' When he turned his back to walk into the shop he heard Burrows laughing.

'I don't know what to make of that bent cunt.'

'What do you mean, Prez?'

'He seems to know fucking everything about me, about selling pot mainly. He offered me a deal. In exchange for letting us operate he wants five hundred a week, and that covers giving us the drum about when we might get raided.'

'Can we trust him, Prez?'

'I don't think we have a choice, but I'd like to get some insurance against him. He wants to meet me at different places of his choice, but there's going to be a time when I can get him to come to the shop. We can set it up with a camera. By then he won't be suspicious.'

Brian wasn't sure if cooperating with Burrows was a good idea.

'Well, mate, I don't think we have a choice; we either close down the pot business or go along with him.'

'Go along with him, Prez,' Ocker said. 'He has more to lose than we do.'

'He also mentioned that he has people we can do business with.'

'What does he mean by that?' asked Brian.

'I don't know yet. He's pretty cunning, I suppose he doesn't trust us yet, either. We'll see how it pans out.'

'Hey, Prez,' said Ocker. 'Squizzy's coming around to see you this arvo.'

'He's most probably got a bill for me — that's what solicitors are like. Alright, boys, do you agree to pay the Pig?'

Ocker was all for it. 'It looks like good insurance to me, Prez.'

'What about you, Brian?'

'I can't see any way out of it, unless we just go and give him up.'

'I really don't think that's an option.'

'Well, that's it then.'

All day Winnie fretted about the deal and wondered if he'd made the right decision. He didn't like it when he had no way out, and Burrows had played him perfectly. But in a way, Burrows had told him something worth more than the five hundred a week: the cops knew about the pot, so everyone had better tidy up the way they did business or the price they might all pay could be a lot higher. Once he came to that conclusion he relaxed a bit and got down to work.

Squiz walked in with a big grin. 'Hey, Winnie, where's that beer you offered me? Hope you're happy with yesterday's result?'

'Yeah, the best, Squizzy.' Winnie didn't have the heart to tell him that he gave the Pig a sling!

'Did you bring me a bill?'

'No, mate, John said to tell you it was free, but if anyone you know needs a criminal lawyer to keep him in mind.'

'Does he know something I don't know?'

'Just forward thinking, I suppose.' Winnie cracked a few beers and handed one to Squizzy.

'Here's cheers to yesterday.'

'Yeah, cheers, Squiz.'

'I had a phone call about you this morning, Winnie.'

'Oh yeah, and who would that be from?'

'Mimi Gregson. She said you two had a misunderstanding yesterday.'

'Did she just?'

'She asked me to give you her phone number.'

'What's she like, Squiz?'

'Well, we never socialised at all. She was with the "in" crowd — you know, parties, balls, the tennis club and so on. She's not a bad sheila. It's just that she's never known anything else; it's the lifestyle of the well-to-do. She works for her old man, who's a futures trader. We're on totally different sides of the law. I want to get into local politics. I already joined the Labor Party.'

'What do you want to be next, the Premier?'

'No, I want to study local government and become a ministerial advisor. They need blokes like me to help interpret the laws for development and so on. No courtroom work.' He pulled on his beer and looked around the shop. 'It looks like your shop is doing alright, but you want to be careful in the next few years. If we go the way of the Yanks they'll try to introduce laws enabling the government to confiscate any ill-gotten gains. Assets you may have that weren't obtained legally.'

'They can't do that, can they?'

'Bloody oath, they can. You just watch, I reckon you have about five or six years before they're introduced.'

'Where do you get this information?'

'A professor at uni came back from the States and he was involved in it. It might be good for you to talk to Mimi. I don't know how much money you have but she could advise you on a way to make it sink from view, you follow me?'

A light went on in Winnie's head. Sink from view. He thought it over; it seemed like a good idea. Squizzy walked around the shop and looked at the work in progress. 'Hey, Winnie, how's Big Kev doing in Vietnam?'

'Don't you read the newspapers? The shit is really hitting the fan there — it's a full-on war now, there are tons of casualties.

'I hope Kevvie is alright.'

'And so do I, Squiz.'

'I'd better get going now, Winnie. I'll keep in touch.'

'Hey, Squiz, once again, thank John Baker and tell him we'll use him as our club solicitor.'

Over Chinese that night, Winnie told Swannie about his court appearance.

'You won't believe what happened, but I've got a bent copper in my pocket. He calls himself the taxman without the paperwork. And we now have a Club lawyer called John Baker, on call twenty-four hours a day. Make sure if any of your members get busted they call him first, and say nothing until they get his advice.'

Swannie chewed the last of the Peking Duck and asked Winnie how much money his Chapter got from the bike show.

'Four grand, why? Don't you think that was enough?'

'No, that was fine, but I think we have a thief in our Chapter because our treasurer Thommo, the silly cunt, only passed on three grand.'

'You can't let that go, Swannie. What are you going to do with him?'

'First take his bike and colours, then break a leg.'

'Or two,' Winnie replied with a wry smile.

Next day Winnie rang Mimi.

'Hello, Winnie, how are you?'

'I heard you wanted to talk to me.'

'Yes, that's right. I think we got off on the wrong foot the other day. What do you say we go and have a drink and try again?'

'Sounds fine to me. Tell me where and when.'

'What about five o'clock Saturday night at the Brooklyn Hotel on George Street — do you know it?'

'I'll find it. See you then.'

Winnie pulled up on his Harley outside the pub. He wore a new leather vest emblazoned with his Miners colours. He saw the punters admiring his bike as he made his way into the bar. He ordered a beer and casually looked around. Mimi was sitting alone; he made his way over and bowed his head.

'Good afternoon, Miss, may I join you?'

Mimi ignored the sarcasm in his tone. 'Please do, Winnie.'

'You're a hot bitch, Mimi.'

'Do I take that as a compliment?' she replied, smiling.

'I'm still trying to work out why you pissed off on me all those years ago.'

'I was young and scared, Winnie, but I never forgot you. I just didn't know how to contact you to explain. I'm sorry for that. Tell me, Winnie, what's happened since? Are you married?'

Winnie looked surprised. 'No, Mimi, just to the Club.'

'You're the President, aren't you?'

'I'm also a partner in a motorcycle shop. It's going well. What about you?'

'Oh, the usual thing. I just finished uni.'

'It's not usual where I come from. The only person I know who went to uni was Squizzy.'

'Gary Taylor?'

113

'Yeah, Squizzy.'

'Winnie, you can be anything you want.'

'I want to be a bikie; you're right, though, Mimi, I do want to be the best at it.'

'And you will be, I can see that. Why were you in court?'

'I bought this car and two weeks later I got pulled over by the pigs. They found five pounds of pot in the boot. It wasn't mine, I told them, but they charged me. Justice was done, the judge believed me.'

'You see, Winnie, you can trust the system.' She looked into his eyes and smiled warmly.

Winnie smiled back at her. 'You're so naive, Mimi.'

'You think so?' She raised her eyebrows. Winnie wasn't so sure she'd missed the irony. He liked that. She was at least twice as sharp as he'd first thought.

'Squizzy told me what sort of business you're in. So what does a futures banker do?'

'We give financial advice to people and lend money to businesses and help them get up and running.'

'Maybe we can do business. I have fifty or sixty thousand to invest.'

'There must be a lot of money in motorcycle shops.'

'We get by. Have you got a man in your life, Mimi?'

'Yes, I'm engaged to Phil. We went to uni together. He's a real fun guy. Everyone likes him.'

'Including your parents, I suppose?'

'Yes, especially my parents.'

'How come you wanted to see me again?'

'I don't know, Winnie, just curious.'

'It's more than that, I can feel it.' Leaning back in his chair Winnie looked her straight in the eyes.

'Don't look at me like that, Winnie, you make me uncomfortable.'

'Is that what it is?'

'It can't be anything else. I have to go, Winnie. Would you like an appointment to meet my father about investing money?'

Winnie ignored her. He continued staring, and felt his blood rising. He remembered the little blonde cutie in the imitation leopard-skin tights dancing at the Centennial years before, and savoured the moment again. 'Where are you going tonight?'

'Phil and I have a dinner party.'

'Would you like to go for another ride, Mimi?'

'One day, not now. Give me a ring when you want to invest.'

'Does he ask many questions about where it came from?'

'No, money is money in his business. You'd be surprised at the people we do business with. Very few questions are asked, and fewer are answered.'

'That sounds good to me.'

'What sort of business are you in, Winnie, besides the bike shop?'

'I do a little farming.'

'Farming?' She appeared puzzled for an instant then glanced at her watch. 'I have to go.'

Winnie stood up, pulled her towards him and kissed her full on the lips. When he finished, her cheeks had flushed a bright red that matched her lipstick.

'See you, Mimi.'

'Give me a call, Winnie.'

Winnie stared at her as she walked out of the pub and thought he'd get her one day. He liked her face, her name. He said it aloud — 'Mimi Gregson' — as if he might forget it, but he knew he wouldn't, he couldn't.

Chapter 10

At the shop, Winnie asked Brian to show him the stash book; he wondered how much money he had. He wanted to invest some cash and he liked the idea of a pub or a bar — it had to make more than being bundled up in a safe. He had eighty-three grand and asked for sixty.

'I'll have it for you tomorrow.' Brian put almost all his money into the house and Gina spent whatever he gave her on furniture and whatever else she wanted. If it kept her happy, he didn't mind; he'd agree to almost anything to keep the peace.

'Ocker was up at Kev's mother's the other day,' Brian said. 'She said Kev'll be home in a month.'

'Great. We'll have to start organising a homecoming party. Is Kev's money here?'

'Yeah, all of it except for a few grand that Ocker gave his mother.'

Winnie stared at the gold lettering on the big double doors: Gregson & Gregson Futures traders. When he walked up to the receptionist sitting behind the meant-to-impress desk in the dimly lit foyer he thought it didn't look much like a bank. With his saddlebag slung over his shoulder he probably didn't look like a typical client, either.

'Good morning, I'm Peter Winifred, here to see Mimi Gregson.'

'One moment, sir. Please sit down, she'll be with you shortly.'

He turned his back and surveyed the mirrored ceiling, exotic flowers and modern art. He heard the receptionist giggle over the phone.

Mimi appeared suddenly. Winnie turned and said, 'Not a bad layout you have here. You'll have to come and see my shop some day.'

Mimi offered her hand under a tight little smile. Christ, she's gorgeous, he thought.

'This way, Mr Winifred.' He followed her into an office.

'I've never been in a place like this before. Where are the tellers?'

'We're not that type of bank, I told you that.'

'Well, Mimi, it's all new to me. I want to meet your old man.'

'I'll look after your account.'

'Sure you will, but I still want to meet the boss. If I don't feel right with him I'm not parking my money here. Or haven't you told him about me?'

Mimi gave Winnie a 'forcrissakes' look, rolled her eyes then stood up.

'Wait here a minute.' She might have had the shits with him, but it was his money and she knew it. Five minutes later she returned with a tall, well-fed man dressed in a grey pinstriped suit. Her father. Same good looks, long slender hands, bright blue eyes.

'This is Peter Winifred, Dad. He'd like to become a client.'

'Pleased to meet you, Mr Gregson,' Winnie said, holding out his hand.

'Likewise, Peter.' They shook hands warmly. Gregson indicated that Winnie should sit.

'Mimi tells me you're wondering if we need to know where or how you acquired your assets. We don't. We're traders, and currently we are not obliged to divulge any details concerning our clients. Your business is your business. Our business is to try and find investment opportunities that keep your money safe and give you a good return. That's it — it's that simple. Anything else you want to talk about?'

'Yes, I'd like to tell you you have a beautiful daughter.'

'Thank you, I already know that. I'll leave you two to get on with it. Nice to meet you, Peter.'

'Thank you, Mr Gregson.' Gregson left and closed the door behind him and Winnie turned his attention back to the daughter.

'Well, is that all the checking you want to do?' a slightly sarcastic Mimi asked.

'Yes, Miss Gregson.' Winnie was inwardly happy he'd irritated her a little.

'Okay, let's get down to business. I've worked out a balanced plan for your money. We'll keep some cash, find some quality bonds and shares and look for some emerging opportunities. I recommend we spread it around so if anything doesn't perform we can limit the loss.'

'How can I lose money?'

'Winnie, we're traders; not everything comes off. Sometimes we back the wrong horse — not very often, I might add, and that's why we're so successful. I think the best for you is not anything too risky, so we'll go for a mix of blue-chip stock and a few little new business plays.'

'Well, Mimi, I know nothing about it, but I like that you're looking after me. Let's go with that.'

'I need some particulars, your full name and address.'

'Why, do you want to visit me?'

'Very funny. It's for the records, or don't you want your money back?'

Winnie looked straight at her. 'We're made for each other, Mimi.'

She ignored him and continued. 'Where's your money, Winnie?'

He bent at the waist, opened his saddlebag, pulled out bricks of money and stacked them on her desk.

'Clients normally bring a cheque.'

'Is there a problem with cash?'

'No, I have to count it, that's all.'

Winnie liked that she'd have to count out his money.

'Do you remember Big Kev?'

'Vaguely, why?'

'Well, he's been serving in Vietnam and we're having a homecoming party at our clubhouse for him. Saturday night in three weeks. Would you come?'

'Can I ring you at the shop?'

'Please do; if I'm not there, leave a message.'

'Okay, once I get all the paperwork in order I'll send it. You'll have to forgive me but I have other clients to see. Goodbye for now.'

'I'll wait for your call.'

The women decorated the clubhouse and hung a banner emblazoned with 'Welcome Home Kev'. All the members turned up. Kev chucked his usual wheel stand on his new Harley and screeched to a stop. The members mobbed him in the doorway. They slapped him on the back and shook his hand and he hugged the girls and the men. At one point he let out a huge roar that sounded like it was good to be home.

'How're you going, you big cunt?' Winnie said, and they embraced. 'It's good to see you, mate.'

'Me too.' Ocker and Brian joined them in a group hug.

'Where are your war medals?' Ocker asked.

'Fuck the medals!'

'I take it you had a good war, mate?' Winnie asked.

Kev grinned. 'Where's the rum?'

'Hey, Kev, Sandy should be here soon.'

Kev's eyes sparkled. 'Thanks, Ocker, goodonya.'

Kev made his way to the bar and Winnie pulled Ocker aside.

'Don't bloody mention to him about Sandy going out with the Yanks.'

'No way, Prez, he's my mate.'

The party took off and when Sandy arrived she didn't leave Kevvie's side all night.

At 10.33, Mimi walked in. Even though the clubhouse was packed she turned heads. Winnie made his way over.

'You look beautiful, Mimi. Thanks for coming. Would you like a drink?'

'Vodka tonic, thanks.'

Gina made a beeline for Mimi. 'Where have you been hiding her, Winnie? You have to come and meet the girls, Mimi.'

'Later, Gina, she's mine for now.'

'Just trying to be friendly, Prez.' Gina smiled and left.

'You don't like her, Winnie, do you.' It wasn't a question; it was a statement of fact. 'You can be really sweet at times, Winnie.'

'You bring out the best in me. Come and meet Kev … Kevvie, say hello to Mimi.'

'Pleased to see you again, Mimi. I remember you from the night at Little Bay.'

'That's right, the night of our first joint.'

'The things you remember, eh?'

'Mimi, this is Sandy, Kev's girl.'

'Pleased to meet you, Sandy.'

Winnie seized her hand. 'Come on, Mimi, let me show you around.'

'Where's your motorbike?'

'It's outside.'

All eyes followed Mimi and Winnie out into the cool evening.

'What's the Club all about, Winnie?'

'What do you mean, Mimi?'

'Well, when people are in a surf club they patrol beaches, and save anyone who's in trouble.'

'We make sure no one puts shit on our friends; we keep peace in our own way. See all these factories around here? Since we moved our clubhouse here, not one has been robbed.'

'Where do your members come from?'

'All over. Most don't fit into straight society. We ask for commitment to one another and to the Club.'

'What happens to members who break the rules?'

'Put it this way, Mimi, we don't just pat their heads and tell them to leave. If we have trouble with anybody we sort it out ourselves.'

'You're a hard man to know, Winnie.'

'Come here.' He kissed her and grabbed her arse.

She pulled back and smiled. 'I'm no moll, Winnie.'

Brian called out 'Prez, you're needed!', and Winnie and Mimi went back inside. 'Mimi, this is Brian, my lifelong friend and Gina's husband. He was there the night we met.'

'Hello. I remember you, Brian.'

'Gina has a homecoming cake for Kevvie,' Brian said to Winnie. 'We'd like you to present it now.'

Winnie cleared his throat. 'Everyone listen up. We're here tonight to celebrate Kevvie's homecoming and we don't know what shit Kev has had to put up with while he was in Vietnam, but now he's home with his family, so raise your glasses. Here's to Kev and the Miners!'

Everyone shouted in unison, 'Kev and the Miners!'

Kev, a man of few words, simply said 'Thanks everyone' and grabbed Sandy in his arms.

Mimi watched silently and after a moment whispered, 'He's like a brother to you, isn't he, Winnie?'

'He's more than that; I don't expect you to understand.'

'You should have been born a hundred years ago,' Mimi laughed.

'What about your fiancé, Phil — are you going to marry him?'

'That's the plan.'

'I intend to make sure you don't.'

'And how are you going to do that?'

'I've been in love with you, Mimi, since the night we met. I didn't know if I'd ever see you again, but it's true: I always get what I want.'

'Well, not tonight. I have a big day tomorrow.'

'Let me take you home.'

'No, please stay for Kev. I have to go. I'll call next week. Come in to sign the paperwork. Maybe we can smuggle in a lunch.'

Winnie embraced her. They kissed, and his head swam. It might have been the single best moment he'd ever had — maybe better than when he bought his little BSA Bantam. He'd said enough; there wasn't anything left to say. She walked away. That might have been enough for him but then she turned and walked back and stood on tippy-toe and kissed him.

'Phil's gone forever.' That simple act iced his cake.

Winnie went back inside and Gina sidled up to him.

'That's a very pretty girl you have, Winnie. Classy, too!'

'What were you two talking about, Gina?'

'Just girl talk, Winnie. You wouldn't be interested.'

'Wouldn't I? Try me.'

'You have to promise not to say a word to Mimi; she has to tell you herself.'

'What? Don't fuck me around, Gina.'

'Okay, Winnie, she told me she was in love with you ever since the night at Little Bay.'

'Don't you say a word to anyone, Gina!'

'My lips are sealed, Prez.' She put a finger to her lips.

Chapter 11

Kevvie amazed everyone by turning up at work on Monday. Spike came out of the workshop. 'I kept your tools warm for you, Kev.'

'Good to see you, and Spike, thanks, mate. I heard you did a great job.'

When Winnie and Ocker came in they saw Kev hard at work. Winnie took one look and shook his head.

'Can't keep away from the place, can you, Kev?' Kev was all smiles. 'Hey, Spike, mate, take today off. We have some catching up to do with Kev. Come in tomorrow.'

'Okay, Winnie, I understand.'

'Come on, Kev, sit down, mate, and give us the scoop.'

'I hardly know where to start.'

'First thing — Brian, surprise him.'

'Okay, Kev, money first. How much do you reckon you might have from the pot business?'

'No idea, how much?'

'Over a hundred grand.'

'Fuck me, you have been busy!'

'Thank Winnie, Kev. We're growing our own on a farm — we grow it, distribute it and make all the profit; no more middlemen.'

Winnie chipped in, 'Swannie started up a new Southside Miners Chapter.'

'Yeah, I heard about his crew. How are they going?'

'On fire, mate. They have as many members as we do.'

'Enough surprises for you, Kev?' Ocker asked.

'Fuck' is all Kev said.

Winnie related the story about getting busted and how they paid off the bent copper.

'Do I know him?'

'You might — Sergeant Burrows. The cunt runs the drug squad now.'

'Can we trust him?'

'It works both ways, Kev — he has to trust us.'

'Are there any more surprises?'

Brian said, 'Gina and I bought a home up on Snow's Mountain.'

Kev rolled his eyes. Things *had* happened while he was gone, all good so far. 'What about you, Winnie?'

'Still the same, Kev, except for my new Harley.'

'And his new girl!' Brian couldn't wait to toss that in.

Winnie said nothing. He gave Brian a blank stare and then turned to Kev. 'What was your job, Kev?'

'Forward scout.' After a lengthy pause Kev looked up. 'One thing I learned is that if I have to kill anyone again, it has to be for a good reason. I'm out of the Army now and that's where I want to leave it. Fair enough?'

'Sure, Kev. You'll be pleased to know Nestor came good. He was our pot grower. I'll take you out and show you our set-up. How would you like Spike to work in the shop? We're getting pretty busy and if we have other jobs, Spike can keep the shop ticking over.'

Brian would talk it out with Spike.

'How are the Commandos going?'

'Real good, we see Rastus regularly. They buy a fair bit of pot, too.'

'So it's all working without me, Prez?' Kev pulled a face then burst out laughing.

The phone rang. After a short conversation Winnie hung up. 'Speak of the devil, that was Burrows. He wants to meet in an hour. I have to go now. It's good to have you back, Kev. Welcome home.'

Burrows was to meet Winnie in an old wharfie's pub for the end-of-shift drinkers. It was empty but for two other patrons. Winnie ordered a beer and spotted Burrows approaching.

'Hello, Winnie.'

'What do you want?'

'Not very friendly, are you, even after I did you a good turn.'

'You got paid.'

'Loosen up, Winnie; I have an offer for you.' The Pig lowered his voice and leant forward. 'I have acquaintances who have a product they want to distribute and they're looking for a long-term business arrangement.'

'Why me, Sarge?'

'You're young, you have a network in place and I trust you.'

'Who are the people and when do I meet them?'

'Not so fast, Winnie. They're legitimate businessmen and they don't know you like I do. They finance the operations and don't like to get their hands dirty.'

'Well, how come they need us?'

'Because they have five thousand kilos of Afghani hash wrapped in red cellophane with a gold seal. It's the real McCoy.'

Winnie tried to picture five thousand kilos of hash — it was a lot of smoke. 'Fuck, I can't hide that.'

'They won't give you all of it at once. You'll get a hundred kilos at a time at five thousand a kilo and wholesale it for eight. When you pay for that, you get more. There's only one problem, Winnie. Do you know Jerzy Bosinjak?' Winnie knew about Bosinjak, he was all over Sydney. 'He's distributing the hash now but he's too smart by half, thinks that he's important in the chain, that he's indispensable. The smart cunt is trying to get it cheaper and causing trouble, making threats. The people I know are fed up to the back teeth with his bullshit.'

'And you're going to tell him that, Sarge?'

'No, he'll work it out for himself. He's waiting for a shipment now that'll never come. You can have it if you're interested. He'll find out and come looking for you but I think you can handle it. Interested?'

Winnie thought about it and knew immediately there was more to it than simply agreeing with Burrows. 'What can you tell me about Bosinjak?'

'He's as mad as a cut snake and has a big Yugoslav offsider called Branko who's always around. How they work it is they'll set up a meeting, walk in, shoot and leave. End of meeting.'

'Men of few words, eh, Sarge?'

'You do have a sense of humour, Winnie. Listen, if he was no longer running the west it might make a few people I know a bit happier, you follow me?' Winnie said nothing but he listened hard. 'Don't take them too lightly.'

'Well, we could give it a bit of a think; I'll have to talk it over with the boys first. This Bosinjak, a bit of a tough nut, is he?'

Burrows just sat back and stayed mum. Then he leaned in and said under his breath, 'For a start he'll underestimate you; he doesn't know you. But don't you make the same mistake. Don't give him a chance.'

'What sort of heat do you think'll come down from your mob?'

'Don't worry, there won't be too many tears shed. This has been coming for a while.'

'If my boys say it's on, then what do I do next?'

'I'll let the people who run the show know you're in. Get your boys organised. Once this hash hits the street it won't take Bosinjak long to find out who's running it and he'll get the shits. Then it'll be up to you to do what has to be done. I'll call you tomorrow and let you know where to pick up the hash.'

'What do we have to pay you for this, Sarge?'

'Nothing, I'm being looked after. You're in the deep end now, Winnie, hope you can swim.'

While Winnie drove back to the bike shop his head spun. Delegate, he told himself; delegate and don't let anyone fuck up. He walked in to see Brian.

'Get the boys together, you won't believe it. Better close the shop, too; we don't want anyone walking in on us.' The boys gathered around. 'Well, fellas, the deal we've been offered is the entire hash market if we want it.'

The boys looked stunned.

'We get it for five thou a kilo and all on credit. If we want it, there are a few jobs to do first. Brian, get on to the Redbacks to see if they want in. I'll see the Rat, he has a good market. Kev, you talk with Spike. I'm sure the Commandos will be in on it and with our blokes that should just about cover Sydney. There's just one other thing I haven't told you yet — nothing this good comes easy.'

Kev asked quietly, 'And what would that be, Prez?'

'We're taking over someone else's business. They fucked up with the big end of town. They're trying to get it cheaper and they started getting heavy with the suppliers, who don't like it at all, so the big guys are cutting them out and giving it to us. Everyone got that?'

The boys nodded.

'They won't like it, Prez.'

'I know, Ocker, that's why I'm putting it to you. What do you think?'

Kev piped up. 'Nothing ventured, nothing gained, Prez.'

'Good,' Winnie said. 'I've already told them we'd be in it but I wanted your okay. Everybody hop to it. Kev, come with me, we have to plan this to a T.'

Kev followed Winnie out the back. 'Well, Kev, how do you think we should go about this? I've been thinking, it's going to have to be first in, best dressed. If they want to have a meeting with us, sure as shit they're going to try and hit us first. We'll meet them where there won't be too many witnesses. The good thing about it is they think we're just young, dumb bikie cunts. We might be, but we learn fast. We'll just have to wait until they contact us.'

Next day the phone rang and Ocker took the call. 'It's for you, Winnie.'

When Winnie hung up he turned to Ocker.

'Right, mate, this is your job. Go to the roadhouse at Taverner's Hill at eleven sharp tomorrow. Opposite the toilets there'll be a white Holden panel van with the hash in the back. The keys will be under the seat. Jump in and drive it to the shed. Brian can take you out there.'

'What do we do with the ute?'

'Keep it. Use it for our business. When we start to run out of pot, we'll sell the punters hash. No more quiet times.'

The pick-up went without a hitch and by the end of the week practically every suburb in Sydney and Newcastle had the hash on sale, with Rastus supplying his Melbourne mates. Bosinjak sent his mate Branko over to the shop inside a week. The boys were all heads down, arse up working when a huge cunt walked in and asked to speak to Winnie. Brian called out, 'Hey, Winnie, there's someone here to see you.' Winnie knew who it was before the bloke opened his mouth. When he did speak it was with a voice and an accent out of the Balkans. 'My friend wants to have chat with you.'

Winnie acted dumb. 'And who's your friend?'

'Jerzy Bosinjak.'

'What's this all about?'

'Mutual business interests.'

'Where?'

'You choose place,' Branko said. His eyes never left Winnie's and Winnie stared right back.

'Oasis Hotel beer garden in Bankstown, tomorrow night at seven-thirty.'

'He meet you there.'

Winnie sat with Kev and explained how they would handle it. 'I know the pub. There's a brick wall around the beer garden and a car park outside. I'll go in the front and check out where they're sitting. When I know, I'll come back to the car and tell you. You're the shooter, Kev. I have a pump action shotgun that should take care of them. Bring a box so you can see over the wall.'

Next afternoon Ocker stole a car over near Liverpool. They couldn't afford any slip-ups. Winnie went through all the details with Kev. Winnie would pick up any spent shells. 'Are you nervous, Kev?'

'Don't worry, Prez, I know my job. I just hope they're close. I left my nerves in Vietnam.' Kev's face was set hard.

Winnie parked out the back of the pub, strolled through the ladies' lounge and peered into the beer garden. He spotted Bosinjak and Branko sitting alone in the beer garden, backs against the wall, watching everyone coming and going. They didn't look behind them.

Winnie located them for Kev exactly.

'Good, let's do it.' Kev stood on the box and peeked over the wall, saw his target, bent down and then raised the shotgun. He aimed carefully, fired twice, then jumped to the ground. The explosions echoed, followed by a moment of silence, then women screamed. Winnie stuffed cartridges in his pocket and Kev heaved the box into the car. Ocker drove off, not too quickly, and Winnie watched Kev in the rear-view, breaking down the gun and wiping it clean, glad Kev was on his side.

'Good result, Kev? Both?'

'Order the lilies.' Kev wrapped the shotgun pieces in a sleeping bag. No one spoke, they didn't have to — the adrenalin had long ago kicked in and all they wanted was to get the hell out of there.

Back at the shop Brian waited. 'How'd it go?'

Winnie looked at Kev busying himself with the gun and nodded faintly. One year in Vietnam had changed Kev in unknowable ways.

The phone rang, Burrows's voice sounding as if he was at the bottom of a well. 'Well done, talk soon.'

'The Pig's already heard the job's done.' Winnie's head swam. 'I need a drink. You, Kevvie?'

'After a hard day's work, why not?'

Ocker passed beers around, but no one was too happy.

Brian broke the sombre silence. 'We're really in it now. I'm taking Gina on holidays to the new casino in Tasmania for five days.'

'Do you want us to come?'

'Very funny. I'm just letting you know.'

The boys sipped their beers and thought about Brian flying to Tasmania and getting away for a few days. It sounded pretty good.

It made the ten o'clock news, lead story. Police called to a Bankstown hotel where two men were shot dead in a gangland-style shooting. Bystanders saw nothing.

'Well, that didn't take too long, boys.' Kev said it matter-of-factly. Whatever effect it had had on him, he hid it well. Brian and Ocker headed off.

A silence hung over the shop. Winnie and Kev sat and cracked another beer. 'You don't talk much about what you got up to in Vietnam. How come, mate?'

''Cos it was a shithole — rain, heat, mud and fuckwit officers. They might have been clever in the head, but no common sense out in the field. Plus the fact it's an unjust war. If we got it wrong, sometimes innocents died. I saw the results. Fuck the Army, fuck the war.'

Kev and Sandy were looking to buy a flat and set up a brothel at the Cross for Sandy.

'Sounds like a good idea, Kev.'

'What about you, Prez? How's it going with Mimi?'

'Slowly, Kev. Big change in her life and mine, but this might be it.'

'Have you told her?'

'She thinks I just see her as another slut.'

'They're not all sluts, though, are they?'

'Yes, they are. She just has more class about it.'

The next day Brian spread the newspaper on the bench. The headline summed it up in two words: 'Gangland Murder'. The photo showed two unrecognisable, bloody-faced men sprawled across an upset table.

'It says it could be the result of an ongoing feud with the Gibbs brothers from Rozelle. "They reportedly had a falling out with Bosinjak's crew, say police."' Brian kept reading. 'It says Bosinjak's death was a welcome relief to both Sydney police and criminals, everyone lived in fear of them.'

The Pig called. 'Feeling good today, Winnie?'

'Couldn't be better.'

'Good. There's a booking at Fritz's for one o'clock in your name. It's on the Pacific Highway in North Sydney.'

Winnie went home, changed into civvies, drove to the restaurant. The maitre d' stopped him at the front desk. 'Good afternoon, sir. A booking in whose name?'

'Yes, the name's Winifred.'

'Right this way, sir.' The maitre d' led Winnie to a table and pulled out the chair. Burrows appeared within a minute and ordered beers.

'You impressed a lot of people, Winnie. No one knows a thing; no clues, not one patron saw a thing. The patrons heard two shots and that was it. A nice clean professional job, that's all. One thing, Winnie: what happens between us stays here.'

The maitre d' brought a menu that Winnie refused. 'I'll have steak and chips.'

'Tony, the Osso Bucco Milanese and more beers.'

Winnie asked about the Gibbs brothers. They ran the old SP, owned a few brothels — old guard. They reputedly imported heroin and were currently rebuilding their empire. The Pig said Winnie didn't want to get involved in their shit; they were rough as guts and didn't give a fuck about anyone. 'Are you moving the hash?'

'I tell you, everybody wants it.'

'Just be careful, Winnie. Do business with people you know. I heard a rumour.'

'Yeah?'

'Some undercover boy's infiltrated Southside Chapter. I don't know the name, but it doesn't matter, 'cos he wouldn't be using his own name anyway. But you can't shoot him.'

'What do I do?'

'Walk up to him, say you know he's a copper and tell him to fuck off. He has no useful information yet. Keep it that way.'

'Well, what's he look like?'

'A long, blond ponytail.'

'I'll get onto that straight away.'

'That information is going to cost you five grand, Winnie, or would you prefer I never told you?'

'No, five's fine.'

Tony brought their meals. Winnie's stomach churned. All he wanted was to find Swannie and sort it out. He had two small bites of his very well-cooked steak and didn't touch a chip. Burrows got stuck in and made a big deal about how good it was. Burrows saw Winnie's mind working.

'You in a hurry, mate? I take it you don't want dessert? Look, get going, Winnie. Lunch is on me, and don't forget, no harm comes to the narc. Orright?'

Winnie was gone in a flash. He called Swannie to meet him at the shop and told him about the narc and his long, blond ponytail.

Swannie knew who it was right off the bat. 'Jimbo, a fairly new nominee. Fuck. What do you think I should do, Prez?'

'Does he know much about your business?'

'No, fuck-all; he's only been around for a few months.'

'Try the simple way: go and see him with your Sergeant-at-Arms, tell him you know he's a Pig, get his vest and tell the cunt you don't ever want to see him again. Don't bash him, otherwise the jacks will come down on us like a ton of bricks.'

'Where did you get this information, Prez?'

'The Pig told me. It's going to cost your Chapter five grand. In future, we want their parents' and grandparents' addresses so we can check them out. All members are responsible for their noms. No more cunts coming in and nominating just anybody. We're lucky he hasn't found out much. Tell your members to clean up their homes, just in case.'

Winnie's old man died quite suddenly and peacefully at home. Winnie told the boys and took off. The family gathered, tears were shed and arrangements made. The day of the funeral they met Father Pius on the St Brendan's church steps. The church was packed with his mates, his family and the Miners in a show of respect. Winnie's mum's church friends came too and after the simple ceremony they all stood around talking and offering condolences. Mimi approached Winnie and offered hers. They hugged.

'Thanks for coming, Mimi. How did you know?'

'I rang the shop, and Brian told me. I was sorry to hear the news, Peter.'

She'd never called him Peter before. One of them at least was in love. 'Come and meet my mum.' He introduced Mimi to his dazed mother, who was encircled by church ladies. 'I'll call tomorrow. I have to look after Mum.'

He joined his mother in a car for the ride to the cemetery. Afterwards, he led his mother to the car and they went to a neighbourhood-catered wake at their place. The mourners stood around in little groups quietly nibbling sandwiches off the best plates and drinking all the grog.

* * *

Winnie spent some time on the phone renting a seaside cottage for his mum near her sister at Woy Woy, which she loved, before he returned to work. He was pleased when he heard how Swannie had fronted the narc and got rid of him quietly, as suggested. He called Mimi to arrange to sign the forms and have lunch.

Brian announced that he'd organised a welcome home run for the next weekend, after his little Tassie trip. He reckoned Newcastle was a good spot — not too far and a guaranteed party with the Redbacks.

At Gregson & Gregson, Winnie waited in the mirror-ceilinged foyer for Mimi. She shook his hand. 'This way, sir.'

As soon as her door closed, she kissed him.

'Is this the way you greet all your clients?'

'Only the special ones. Okay, Peter,' she passed him a stack of documents, 'sign where marked.' He signed and passed the papers back. Mimi checked them all and, when satisfied, placed them in a folder. 'All present and accounted for,' she said cheekily.

That night Winnie took Mimi to dinner at Fritz's, no expense spared. He was surprised but no less delighted when Mimi invited him to her home afterwards. Mimi opened the security door of a very classy block. Inside it was all marble and mirrors. They took the lift to her flat and Winnie watched her gracefully swaying body as she walked down the hallway. 'God, it's getting cold.' She shivered and tossed her bag onto the leather couch. 'Would you like a cup of tea?'

'No, I just want you,' he whispered, taking her in his arms. 'Come on, where's your bed, I want to lie down with you.'

She led him to bed, kicked off her shoes and lay down. 'The first night we met we lay down in the sand dunes of Little Bay. I'll never forget that night.'

'And you corrupted me with my first joint. It changed my life.'

'You didn't need my help.' She pulled him to her.

He kissed her neck, her eyes, her lips. Mimi moaned softly and kissed him back. She grabbed his hair and pulled him to her and whispered 'Yes, Winnie, yes.' Winnie unbuttoned her blouse. He wondered at her green bra and matching undies; he'd thought they only came in black or white. When he'd unzipped her skirt she wiggled out of it and slid into bed.

Winnie stood and undressed then rolled into bed beside Mimi. He kissed her nipples through her bra and rubbed her tits. She unhooked the bra and he pulled it off with his teeth. He wanted nothing but to lose himself inside her but he took his time and they kissed urgently. He slipped his hand onto her cunt and she moaned as he rubbed her. She pulled his head down and pushed her tongue down his throat. He licked her neck and shoulders and made his way down to her belly button. Mimi stroked his dick and sucked his fingers and Winnie slowly licked the sides of her cunt, searching for her clitoris, the little man in the boat, with his tongue. She dug her nails into his back and sputtered, 'Oh Peter, that feels so good.'

He sucked her clit and she moaned and her hips undulated then she pulled him on top of her, reached for his prick and guided him into her.

'Lie still,' she said, 'let me do it.'

She pressed against him, rose off the bed and began to rock slowly back and forth until she suddenly cried out, 'Oh Peter!' She arched her back and frantically bucked against him until she suddenly collapsed and lay still.

'Fuck me, Peter, slowly.'

Winnie began to fuck her urgently but she stopped him.

'No, just stay still, let me do it again.'

He looked into her eyes and suddenly she started to buck and moan and wrap her legs around him, and quickened the pace until they both exploded in an orgasm. Winnie had never experienced anything like it. She held him tightly. Winnie stared into her eyes and kissed her. He had no idea how long they lay like that but he knew sex had never been like that before. This wasn't just a fuck. It was the moment Winnie realised that sex could be like that, and the intimacy almost scared him.

Mimi tried to focus on Winnie's face, just inches from hers.

She whispered, 'And you even kiss after.' She pulled his face to her and told him, 'I love you.' Winnie said nothing. Whatever he felt, he kept inside, but he pulled her closer and they just stared at each other, till they closed their eyes and fell into a deep sleep in each other's arms.

In the morning Winnie awoke to the sound of traffic outside. It took him a few seconds to orient himself. He smelled coffee brewing and heard the running shower. Outside the bedroom doors was a garden; neighbours were having breakfast on their balconies. Winnie didn't think he should take a leak out there and made his way back into the flat. Mimi came out of the bathroom wrapped in a towel and smelling of expensive perfume.

Winnie kissed her; she smelled so nice, so fresh, he didn't know whether to take a leak or throw her on the bed.

Mimi had laid out a towel and a fresh toothbrush for him. Winnie was amazed at how organised she was, and he luxuriated in the memory of the night before. He walked into the kitchen where Mimi had poured coffee and put out a packet of Weet-Bix. Winnie was hungry but when Mimi bent over to sort out the Weet-Bix he grabbed her from behind and wrapped his arms around her. Mimi spun around, pulled him towards the bedroom and kissed him. Her towel unwrapped and slipped to the floor as they embraced. Winnie picked her up and carried her to the bedroom, and they fell onto her bed and had the other half of what they had started the night before. Mimi ran her nails over his shoulders and down his back and purred like a cat.

'That was very nice, Peter; you could win a gold medal at this.'

Winnie grinned. She was fantastic. This intimacy scared him a little, but he liked the feeling too. He said nothing, just lay there inside her.

Mimi broke the spell. 'How's your mother keeping?'

'She's doing fine. Her new place is what she always wanted, but never expected. It's good to give something back to her. She's always supported me.'

'You're a beautiful person, Peter. That was a wonderful thing to do; you're lucky you could afford it.' She stirred and Winnie rolled over as she sat up. 'I wish I could stay here all day but I have to go.' She went to her wardrobe and dressed. Watching her pull on her business suit, Winnie thought she looked pretty sexy. He felt like pinching himself.

'What are you doing tonight?'

She looked over her shoulder. 'Having dinner with my parents. Why?'

'Just wondering.' His eyes followed her as she walked to the door. She stopped and asked about his plans for the weekend.

'We have a Club run to Newcastle. We don't take girls on Club runs.'

'That's unusual.'

'That's us. I'll tell you what, we can go for a ride the weekend after if you'd like.'

'I'd like that, I still remember my first ride. I loved it.' She came back to kiss him goodbye. 'Have what you want, and just shut the door when you leave.'

Winnie had had the night of his life. He knew he should get up and go back to the shop but he just lay there thinking about the dinner and his night with Mimi. He was the boss, he didn't have to get up, so he just lay there enjoying it all.

Chapter 12

Brian came back from his holiday looking as if he'd been to a funeral. He told Winnie that Gina went to the casino and blew twenty grand on roulette.

'Fuck, twenty grand! You'll have to watch that.'

'She's addicted, mate, but at least it's drug money, so easy come, easy go.'

'How are we going with the hash money? The Pig wants the proceeds to pass on to his boys.'

'We have enough money to pay for the first ton and there's a big profit.'

Brian packed the cash in a big suitcase and Winnie waited for the Pig to call and arrange the handover later that day; he didn't want the money lying around. Winnie wanted to discuss a few matters with the Pig, including why Twister started a Tigers Chapter in Melbourne.

Ocker rode into the workshop, killed his motor and climbed off looking pretty unhappy. A couple of Tigers had visited his tattoo parlour and threatened his tattooist, told him to close down because it was too close to their shop. They walked in and tossed everything around and the tattooist had backed down.

'Leave it to me,' Kev said, in a voice full of intent.

The next morning on the radio the lead story in the news was about a firebombing in a tattoo parlour. Police were investigating. Ocker looked at Kev, who was wearing a half-smile.

'What'll Twister say about that?' Winnie wondered aloud.

Kev mumbled, 'Who fuckin' cares?'

Twister called an hour later and his screaming was audible from across the room. After a minute Winnie said, 'Are you finished?'

'What are you going to do about it, Winnie?'

'We'd better talk, Twister. Come around.' Winnie hung up, smiling. 'I don't think he's too happy.'

Twenty minutes later Twister and Kero Ken pulled up in a car. Kev followed Winnie out to talk with them.

Kev spoke up first. 'How're you going, boys? Long time no see.'

It caught Twister by surprise. He mumbled something that sounded like hello.

'Now what're you on about, Twister?' said Winnie.

'Someone firebombed our tattoo shop last night.'

'And what makes you think we were responsible?'

'Well, a couple of our boys went around to Ocker's shop yesterday. They were only mucking around, they never meant anything.'

'Not fucking much they didn't!' Kev roared. 'If you want trouble just bring it on. Don't fuck with us, our mates or anyone else in our Club. Whatever thinking was behind roughing up that tattoo parlour was stupid. You've got the whole city, why fuck with ours?'

Twister looked at Winnie. He tried to start a few times but Kev looming over him unsettled him. 'I'll make sure they keep away from Ocker's shop. We don't need a war, Winnie.'

'Good thinking, Twister.' For another moment Twister stared at Winnie while Kev stared at Twister and no one said a word. Everything that needed to be said had been said, and they got back in their car and left. Winnie winked at Kev.

'I liked the way you handled that, Kev.'

'My pleasure, Prez.'

Ocker and Brian wanted to know what Twister had had to say.

'Fuck-all, mate. You won't have any more trouble with them,' Kev said, his face set in a grimace.

Kev went back to working on a bike and Winnie followed Brian into the shop. 'I'll tell you what, Brian, you should have seen Kev in action out the back. I nearly shit myself when he roared at them.'

'He certainly has changed after his year in Vietnam. He's more confident and there's nothing wrong with that. Good on him.'

Winnie was impressed: Kev had learned that when the time came to fire, you had to fire first or die. He'd fired first. 'Brian, is the hash money together?'

'In the car.'

* * *

When the Pig called to arrange a pick-up he told Winnie that the Miners were going to get a little visit in an hour. Winnie announced to one and all to clear the shop of anything incriminating, pronto. Brian put the hash and the guns in the boot of his car with the hash money and parked in a side street a five-minute walk away. Whenever a car passed everyone looked up, then at each other and then shared a smile — there was nothing like waiting to be visited. Ocker made coffee and passed around a packet of biscuits. Anyone walking in would have found the shop on 'smoko', situation normal.

'This is the go,' Winnie said. 'Tell the truth about where you were last night, especially you, Kev.'

When the shop buzzer went off and two detectives walked in the door, Ocker offered them coffee.

One held up his hand like a kid in first class. 'Yes, please.' Everyone laughed.

'I'm Detective Simes and this is Detective Smyth. We have a warrant to search the premises.'

Simes handed Winnie the warrant. All Winnie could think about was, good cop, bad cop. 'What are you looking for?'

Smyth said, 'Whatever we can find.' He walked around aimlessly with his notebook in hand, pen at the ready. He picked up tools and inspected the bikes and their motors. What he was looking for wasn't clear but he wasted everyone's time by peering into Kev's toolbox and looking over the shelves stacked with bits and pieces. Satisfied that he was getting nowhere, he announced, 'I want all your names and addresses.'

He passed the notebook to Simes. Smyth went behind Brian's counter, and Brian jumped up straight away. Simes told him to sit down and stay where he was.

'Go,' Winnie said to Brian. Winnie spoke to Smyth softly. 'We don't trust anyone behind our counter. Who knows what you could put there?'

'We're not like that,' Simes said. 'Where were you last night?'

'At home with my mother.'

'A real mummy's boy, hey?' said Smyth.

Winnie looked at him then back at Simes and said in his coldest voice, 'My old man died a couple of weeks ago and I want to keep her company before she moves up the coast.'

Detective Smyth mumbled something to Simes about Brian's counter being clean. Simes turned to Brian and asked where he'd been the night before.

'At home with my wife and daughter.'

Simes wrote it all down, and then he asked Spike.

'Home by myself. I can tell you what was on TV if you like.'

The copper ignored Spike and turned to Kev. Kev gave the standard reply: 'At home with my girlfriend.'

Simes looked at Ocker. 'You have a tattoo shop, don't you?'

'Yeah, that's right.'

'Your opposition was firebombed last night. Anything to do with the fact that they came and turned your shop over the other day?'

'It might look like that but I had fuck-all to do with it,' Ocker said. 'I was up the Cross with a stripper from the Purple Onion club all night.'

'What was her name?'

'Mandy. You can check if you like.'

'Oh, we will,' said Smyth. 'You're all in the Miners Motorcycle Club?'

'Not me,' Spike replied, 'I just work here.' Smyth realised he was getting nowhere and drew himself up, tucked in his shirt and walked to the door and pointed a finger at Winnie.

'Look, we don't give a fuck what you do to each other, but when it affects the public we're going to come down on you.'

'Is that it, then? We want to get back to work. Having you here is no good for business.'

Simes told Ocker that they'd come back to see him later and then they left.

Winnie hoped Ocker's alibi would stand up. Everyone in the room knew that if they wanted to, the cops could make whatever they said stand up in any court.

Brian unloaded the car at a rental lock-up and left the money in a bag in the car in the shop. The Pig called Winnie and arranged to meet at a pub for the handover.

Before the Newcastle ride, Kevvie made sure of protection by packing a couple of shotguns in the back-up truck.

'We don't know if the Tigers'll retaliate, but it's best if we're prepared.'

Kev was in no mood to take shit from the Tigers; he was ready to just give it to them, boots and all.

The Miners waited at the clubhouse for Swannie and his boys. Ocker was on the phone to the Redbacks in Newcastle to make sure there was no change of plans, and when Swannie and his boys rode in the Miners went out to welcome them. Winnie talked about the bloody Tigers and that Twister might take a shot at a payback.

Swannie patted the side of his nose. 'I tooled up our truck.'

'Good, Swannie, we can have your truck up front and ours at the back.'

Ocker brought two-way radios, reckoning they might come in handy in the back-up trucks.

Kev yelled out for everyone to mount up and the Club grounds reverberated with the sound of fifty bikes filing out onto the road. Winnie and Swannie headed the pack towards the Newcastle Freeway through the Saturday morning traffic. Parents held their kids' hands and stared at the procession, fascinated by the commotion and frightened by the unknown, in equal amounts. The pack stuck to the speed limit until they hit the Freeway then opened it up and hogged the fast lane, creating even more interest as they roared past the traffic heading out of town. Near the Newcastle turn-off, Ocker rode up beside Winnie, pointed to his radio and shouted, 'Police roadblock up ahead.'

They slowed to the speed limit and the police motioned them to pull over. Winnie spread the word for everyone to take it easy and just sit there.

In a loud voice the head copper yelled, 'Everyone stay with your bike.'

Winnie asked what was up.

'Just a routine check.'

'Just routine, my fucking arse.'

The copper smiled. 'Call it what you want. Show me your licence.'

Winnie handed it over. The cop wrote down the particulars and handed it back. 'Any outstanding fines?'

'None.'

'We'll see.' The cop got on the radio to check. 'Why are you lot going to Newcastle? Not for trouble, are you?'

'For a ride, what's it look like?'

'We never know with you lot.'

Winnie ignored him and smiled at Swannie. After half an hour, they arrested one of Swannie's boys for an outstanding traffic ticket and took him away in a car. Kev took his colours from him as he entered the cop car. 'Our colours don't go in police cars, or any cars for that matter.'

After the cops had left, the boys stood around smoking joints and laughing and comparing stories. Except for the cops it was a nearly perfect day under sunny, clear skies. The boys set off for the Redbacks' clubhouse and a good time. Ocker directed them to the Hamilton Hotel and on his scanner picked up a conversation between the cops and their station. Turned out they were relieved to have had no trouble with the Miners.

Swannie was amazed. 'Sounds like they're going to knock off work and get pissed. It is Saturday, after all.'

It was the first time the clubs had got together and not all the blokes knew each other, but they soon got stuck into the ale. In their checked shirts and coal miners' singlets the Redbacks looked exactly like what they were: hard-bitten, tough cunts. Sorrow said most blokes worked for BHP but some were painters and dockers with the wharfies.

'We know a few wharfies in Balmain.'

'Well, they all know each other.'

'That's good to hear, Sorrow. You never know how we could help each other there.'

'The painters and dockers are notorious smugglers.' They shared a laugh.

The Redbacks had heard that the Miners had had a bit of trouble on the highway; they'd seen pigs in convoy a few hours before and knew they were lying in wait for something.

'What did the pigs say about us?' asked Sorrow.

'They wanted to know if we were coming to bash you Redbacks and I said we were and they said, good.'

Sorrow laughed.

'No problems, just a little bit of shit. They locked up one of Swannie's Southside boys; we're waiting to bail him, but first we want to find out what the score is for today.'

'The pub's ours for the night. We've got a band on out the back and we booked rooms upstairs. We've even lined up girls for the night.'

In their early days the Redbacks had about thirty-five members and a growing group of hang-arounds — there'd be no shortage of potential members in a blue-collar town.

'Much trouble up here, Sorrow?'

'Just a gang of fuckheads calling themselves the Nutters. They're everywhere. Fair dinkum, that's what they call themselves. A bunch of bikies on the north side, supposedly anti-clubs, but they ride together. We gave them a good flogging a couple of weeks ago and put about ten in hospital. They'll be back one day. Their spokesman is this old, grey-bearded cunt called Mad Charlie and they do whatever he asks without question; you'd think they were his kids.'

'How does he get them to do that?' Big Kev asked.

Sorrow said real quietly, 'Because they're fucking nutters, mate. We tried to have a little chat but it ended up in a brawl so we got into them properly last time. Tonight we've taken precautions.'

'I hope so, Sorrow,' Big Kev said.

Bikes arrived continuously and a fair crowd built up; most went to watch one of the early bands. A few girls strolled over and checked out the Miners. To the girls the Miners were big-city blokes, new blood, and the boys played their part and chatted them up and rolled them joints. Big Tony got out on bail without any hassle in less than an hour. He copped a $340 fine but said the cops were pretty good about it. He paid the money and walked out.

Winnie and Brian ordered some food from the kitchen and sat with Fred, an old Redback member, and had a quiet word about the Nutters.

'Are they as bad as Sorrow makes out, Fred?' Winnie knew loose cannons could make it really hard on everyone.

'Worse, mate. They're completely out of control. They might have it in for us after the dusting we gave 'em a few weeks back.'

Sorrow and Big Kev arrived back from their walk and Fred stood up. 'Gotta go, boys, we have a few things we have to check on. We'll catch up later, Winnie.'

When they'd gone, Winnie turned to Kev. 'What's their security like?'

'It's not too bad. They have a couple of armed blokes hidden away pretty good.'

'Let Swannie know what's going on and tell the boys to keep their eyes peeled.'

Sorrow and Fred, with arms folded, laughed and talked to some cops in a patrol car near the back entrance. The Redbacks charged ten dollars a head and a big crowd turned up, not all bikies. Inside the pub there was no room to swing a cat. Swannie and Brian walked past a table full of sheilas.

'G'day, girls, do you mind if we join your table?'

One of the girls replied, 'Not much room, boys, but you can have the table — we're on stage next.'

Brian started watching the football.

'Are you strippers?' asked Swannie.

'Do we look like strippers?'

Swannie smiled at the black-haired sheila sitting there, hands on hips, looking indignant. 'I guess you're not strippers then.'

The black-haired one said 'Fuck you', and downed her drink. 'Come on, girls, let's go.' The last girl, a pretty blonde, rubbed her arse roughly against Swannie's crotch as she made her way past him.

'What did I say?' Swannie asked as Winnie grabbed a chair and sat down.

'Don't worry about it, mate. Sit down. I reckon they're queer anyway, and who'd pay to see that black-haired bush Pig strip? They're in an all-girl band.'

'Well, I don't want to miss that. What do you reckon, Brian?'

Brian was pissed; he didn't have a clue. He turned his head and said, 'Parramatta's killing the other team and there's only a few minutes left.'

'I feel like a joint,' Swannie said aloud.

Winnie felt like one too. 'Just wait until Brian's game is over and we'll go up to our room and you can roll it up there.'

'Yes!' Brian shouted and punched his fist when the full-time hooter sounded.

'Come on, Brian, grab your beer. We're going up to the room to roll a joint.'

'Hold on a minute, Prez, I just want to make a phone call first.' Brian stood up and headed towards the pay phone.

'Who's he going to call at this time of night?'

'His missus. He has to check in, I guess,' said Winnie. 'I'll grab a few more beers to take up to the room.'

Winnie came back from the bar. Brian waited with Swannie, his happy excitement from the football win replaced by a dark frown for which his cunt wife Gina was likely responsible. She knew how to fuck with his head. Up in the room, Swannie rolled the joint and Brian sat on his bed and struggled to take off his boots for about five minutes before he succeeded. Swannie passed him the joint, Brian took one long toke, passed the joint to Winnie then dragged his bootless legs up and began snoring almost immediately.

'You know, Prez, some blokes just shouldn't drink,' Swannie said without sarcasm.

'And some blokes shouldn't get married,' Winnie said as he grabbed his drink and passed the joint. Winnie took the room key. 'Come on, Swannie, let's go and join the party.'

The bar area had emptied; everyone was out the back listening to the all-girl band play. Swannie wanted to see the little blonde bass player.

When he opened the door from the bar into the beer garden Winnie heard two muffled shots, the unmistakeable sound of a handgun. Then four more.

'That's gunfire, mate, let's go.' Winnie crouched and ran.

The shots appeared to be coming from a few different places. Some sounded further away and not so loud. Women screamed and men flattened themselves to the ground. Some ran off into the darkness. The band stopped suddenly and mayhem and chaos erupted. It was a madhouse. Winnie saw a bloke sprawled on the ground and blood everywhere. He spotted a bloke's head poking around the corner of the stage and a hand holding a pistol.

He yelled out, 'The shooter's behind the stage, get out of here!'

Some of the Redbacks ran towards the stage carrying baseball bats. Flashes lit the night as more shots rang out. Three people were down and motionless. One person trailing blood crawled into the darkness and collapsed. Someone with a baseball bat smashed some bloke on the back of his head with a healthy swing and kept pounding him until he lay still.

The shooters shot into the dispersing crowd. A grey-haired bearded bloke, illuminated by stage lights, waved a pistol around and squeezed off shot after shot and bodies tumbled. The cops must have been hiding, waiting for reinforcements, because they were invisible until the wail of sirens sounded. The shooting became sporadic. A young copper, white as a ghost, appeared out of the dark with gun drawn. 'What's going on?' He was trembling.

More shooting from behind the stage. The copper froze. Big Kev saw a cunt with a pump action shotgun shooting indiscriminately.

Big Kev yelled at the copper, 'Shoot the fucker before he kills anyone else!'

'I can't, I have to give him a warning first.'

'Fuck that, give the gun to me, I'll do it!' Kev shouted and tried to reef the gun out of the copper's hands.

The shooter pumped another round into the gun and fired at the stage, scattering screaming people everywhere. Then he pumped the shotgun and tried to shoot again but he'd run out of ammunition.

'Shoot the cunt!' Kev screamed at the copper.

The copper raised his gun and aimed with two hands towards the shooter but held fire. Three Redbacks jumped on the shooter, knocked him to the ground and kicked him mercilessly. The copper ran and aimed at the melee and threatened to shoot the next one to move. The shooter moaned horribly, and the Redbacks backed off until the cops handcuffed him and dragged him away. Wailing police sirens announced the arrival of three cop cars with blue and red lights flashing. The scene resembled a macabre discotheque.

There followed a deathly silence broken only by sobs. People called for help, and blood was spattered everywhere. Winnie made his way to the front of the stage, which was lit up like a Christmas tree. The blonde girl from the band lay unmoving, dead, her hair matted with blood.

The police turned their headlights on to high beam, lighting up a sea of terrified faces. A controlled voice blasted out over a loud hailer.

'Everyone stay where you are. This is the police. Stay where you are, ambulances are on their way. Please help your friends but don't move them.'

Voices cried out for a doctor.

A stream of ambulances pulled up and police and paramedics ran in all directions.

People huddled in small groups, hugging, crying; an evening with so much promise had turned to ashes in a few bloody minutes.

Winnie called out, 'Are all the Miners here?'

Everyone but Brian turned up; it would take more than a dozen gunshots to rouse him from his sleep. Winnie and Swannie sneaked off in the darkness to make sure Brian was okay. Although the night air was cold and heavy with the smell of gunpowder, sweat dripped from Winnie's brow. Faces appeared in the windows of the pub, trying to see what was going on outside. Suddenly two dark figures jumped out in front of Winnie and Swannie, the moonlight reflecting off drawn guns.

'Police! Stop! Put up your hands!'

'Do as they say, Swannie.'

'Get down on the ground!' the police shouted as they moved towards them. The tension in their voices was a warning. One cop trained his gun on them while the other moved towards them and patted them down. 'They're both clean.' A senior sergeant came out of the crowd and fronted Winnie.

'Did you blokes come looking for trouble?'

Winnie said dryly, 'Not us, mate, we're here for the party. All our members are over there; you'd better look for someone else.'

The Sergeant turned to the two cops and said, 'Stay with them. Get their names and write down what they say.'

'That won't take too long.'

'What do you mean by that?' The Sergeant walked up to Swannie and stuck his chin in Swannie's face.

'He means we saw nothing,' Winnie answered.

The Sergeant was fucked for words. He turned and headed back to his car. One cop had his notebook out.

Winnie asked, 'What do you think's going to happen next?'

The cop was young, and he had no idea. 'We've never had one of these before.'

After Winnie and Swannie gave their particulars they led the cops over to the Miners.

'I want everyone's particulars and statements on what you saw.'

No one saw a thing, that's what they told the cops.

Ocker had the scanner. The cops were too busy recording details to worry about it. Ocker kneeled and listened. 'Section three here, so far there are six dead, ten wounded, all gunshots.'

'Roger section three.' They were told to leave everything as it was until sunrise. Help was on its way from Sydney.

Pigs were everywhere and a cop told Winnie to keep the boys together until his boss arrived. He said that even if the Miners weren't involved, they would still have to answer questions, and then they could leave. Kev and Winnie stood apart and spoke quietly. 'Fuck, what a party. I wonder who's dead. Hope it wasn't Sorrow or Fred; they're both good blokes.'

'We'll find out soon enough, Kev.'

An ambulance pulled up before the stage as the sun rose. The cops herded some Redbacks into one area and some surviving Nutters into another. Police forensic photographers shot the entire stage area before the ambulance took the blonde girl's body away. In the early morning cool, sombre people huddled under blankets. It was one party no one would forget. Television trucks set up their equipment frantically; reporters, microphones in hand, couldn't wait to start broadcasting. The cops figured out who was involved and ignored the Miners. Most of the action had occurred at the front entrance and on the hill behind the pub, with a good view of the entrance, ideal for picking out the Nutters. Luckily Sorrow's boys were awake, because if the Nutters had entered, it could have been a lot worse.

The Miners walked into the pub and a sea of faces turned to watch. Most looked uncertain; they knew the Miners weren't involved but no one said a word. Winnie went upstairs to the room where Brian still slept.

'What's going on, mate?' Brian asked groggily.

'Don't worry, just get your boots on. There's been a real shit fight here last night between the Redbacks and those Nutters. Pigs are everywhere. The Nutters turned up and started shooting. Last count, there's seven dead.'

Brian pulled on his boots and vest. Winnie grabbed his saddle bags and hoisted them onto his shoulders and walked down and out of the pub. Brian followed a moment later but nothing could have prepared him for what the early morning sun revealed in the parking lot. Scattered, eerily motionless bodies lay covered in black plastic. Half a dozen cops stood guard over the Redbacks sitting on the grass while another group herded the Nutters into paddy wagons. A television cameraman got too close to the Redbacks, who responded by hurling rocks and abuse. He retreated before the pigs could calm them down. The area's top cop stood in a huddle with a couple of sergeants and detectives. They probably had no idea where to start with the many witnesses eager to talk. The Miners claimed they saw nothing and they stuck to it. The cops tried to get them to talk but no one said a word of any value.

Swannie spoke to some senior uniformed cops and then he walked over to Winnie and Brian.

'Prez, the Sergeant said we can leave when we want. I saw Sorrow. He took some shotgun slugs in the arm but he isn't too badly hurt. They took him to hospital and he said he'd catch up with you later.'

'That's good news, I hope the poor bastard's okay. Kevvie, I've had a gutful of this. Get everyone together and let's get the fuck out of here.'

The sound of fifty Harleys starting up and driving off shattered the early morning quiet. At the entrance the officer in charge and his sergeant waved them through. Kev rode up beside Winnie. 'I don't think we'll have to worry about any roadblocks on our way home.'

Television cameras recorded their departure and focused on the Miners patches. On the trip home the dark realisation of what belonging to an outlaw motorcycle club could mean hit home. At the Club grounds Swannie and the Southside Chapter left immediately. Everyone felt sick; the events had taken their toll, and they all just wanted to go home.

After the sound of fifty Harleys thundering out the gate diminished into the distance, Ocker turned up the volume on the police scanner and listened to reports from cops watching Swannie's Chapter heading south down Woodville Road.

'Roger … let them be, they've had enough this weekend.'

Everyone cheered and Ocker grinned like a kid.

Brian took a phone call from Gina. 'I'm off home. Gina said it's been all over the radio and telly. She's throwing a wobbly. They have footage of Miners on the news. The reporters said we were involved.'

Winnie knew the Miners were going to have to live down a lot of shit that had nothing to do with them.

Brian stared at the floor. 'Who really knows what's going on?' Then he got up and left.

'That Gina's got him cunt-struck,' said Big Kev.

'Aren't we all.' Ocker did a little tap dance and grinned some more.

'You are a dirty little man, Ocker.'

'That's me.' Ocker did a two-tap shuffle and the boys laughed.

The members began to leave; it had been a big night, a bad night and no one felt too good. The bar got a bit of a workout from the stayers, including the redeemed Nestor. He and Winnie stood with their backs against the bar and stared into space.

'A few blokes growing pot told me about another strain of pot with less leaf and more head. We could up production if we get some good seeds.'

'I always knew you had potential, Nestor.'

Eighteen months before, he didn't have two bob and now he offered to shout the bar and he was a better man for it. He lit up a huge joint and passed it to Kev, who sucked on it until the tip glowed brightly, then exhaled a long stream of smoke clouding the room.

'Pretty good shit, Nestor, for an old television thief.'

'Still hold that against me?'

'No, I like you, but you're a better farmer than you ever were a thief.' Kev laughed out loud.

Winnie called his mum and let her know that everything was cool even though she hadn't heard a thing. She spent a lot of time happily gardening. Then he rang Mimi. She wasn't at home, but she would have known all about last night.

Nestor said his goodbyes. 'A farmer's work is never done.'

'Nor is it as profitable,' added Kev. 'Seeya, Nestor.'

Nestor jumped onto his new Harley and kicked the motor into life, pulled on his helmet, gave the thumbs up and roared off.

Winnie headed into the bar where Ocker had a couple of nominees bailed up, giving them heaps in a loud voice.

'Do you want me to restock the bar while you two stand and watch me? Like fuck you will. I'll stand here and watch you two stock the bar and when you finish, sweep out the fucking clubhouse.' The nominees stood in a trance.

Big Kev walked in the door and roared out, 'You heard him!'

They both apologised, avoided eye contact with anyone except each other and got on with stocking the bar. Ocker came out from behind the bar, grinning. The boys made their way towards the old op-shop lounges and collapsed onto them. They'd always been uncomfortable, and when Big Kev lay back he felt a spring sticking into his back. He jumped up saying he'd had enough, pulled out his huge bowie knife, plunged it into the lounge and cut out a circle of upholstery, reached in, snapped the end of the steel spring off, shot it across the room, replaced the circle, sheathed his knife, brushed his hands together and said, 'That got the fucking thing.' He plonked down, swung his legs around and stretched out on the lounge in total comfort. Winnie and Ocker watched the performance silently and then applauded loudly.

Big Kev closed his eyes and his breathing slowed.

'He couldn't be sleeping already, could he, Prez?' Kev didn't stir.

When the nominees finished sweeping, Ocker called them over. 'Toothpick and Tim, isn't it?' The noms nodded, unsure of what was coming.

'There's a good sound to those names. Orright, you can fuck off now. Go home and see your sluts, whatever.'

'Thanks, Ocker.' They shook hands with Ocker and the Prez. The nominees moved over to Kev who didn't open his eyes, but simply put up his hand and waved.

Ocker said, 'Yeah, seeya, boys. Lock the front gate as you go.'

'Sure thing, Ocker.' They were gone in a heartbeat.

'I think Toothpick'll make it.' Ocker said. 'How long's he been a nominee?'

'About two months.'

'We'll see, then.' Big Kev spoke with his eyes shut. 'You know, Prez, I reckon we should put steel window shutters on the front of the clubhouse in case any smart cunt tries a drive-by shooting.'

'Yeah, that'd be a good move, Kevvie, considering what we saw last night.'

'Also I reckon we could build a brick wall out the front, a sort of a barricade. We've got a couple of brickies in the Club. I'll bring it up at the next Club meeting.'

A car horn sounded outside. It jolted them all. Ocker jumped up to see who it was.

'It's Mimi, Prez.'

Winnie jumped up. 'I'll let her in, mate.' He reached for his keys and went outside and unlocked the gate. Mimi drove in, parked, jumped out of the car and flung herself into his arms.

He gently pulled her head back with both of his hands, looking into her red eyes. He kissed her gently, then he kissed her eyes to make them better. He whispered, 'It's alright, baby.'

She sobbed, 'It's been all over the news and on television. What happened?'

'Come inside and I'll tell you all about it. Want a drink?'

Winnie locked the gate, went to the bar, poured Mimi's drink and they walked past Big Kev and Ocker spread out on the lounges. The boys both stood up as she passed.

'Hello, Mimi,' they said together.

'Hello, Kev, Ocker.'

Winnie took Mimi to a quiet corner. 'The way television showed it, there was a massacre up there.'

'Not too far off the mark.'

Winnie told her all. When he'd finished he said, 'And here we are, safe and sound.'

'God, it must have been horrible. That poor girl in the band.'

'It was awful, Mimi. What can I say?' They sat and stared into space.

Mimi looked into Winnie's eyes. She couldn't make out what he was thinking but saw he was in shock. She called out, 'Kev, did you call Sandy?'

'Not yet, it's a bit early in the day for her.'

'No, it's not, Kev. I spoke to her earlier, she's really worried.'

Big Kev walked away from the phone looking pretty sheepish. Sandy had given him an earful and he left soon after.

When Ocker followed a few minutes later Winnie called out that he was going to see John Baker in the morning and find out how they stood. Mimi lay on the lounge and without saying a word Winnie knelt beside her and kissed her, undid her dress, pulled himself on top of her and fucked her lovingly. Afterwards, she cradled his head in her arm, giggling and sobbing at the same time. He lived in a violent world; he made her happy but she never knew if she'd see him again. 'How long are you going to play at being a bikie?'

Winnie looked shocked. 'Mimi, this is not playing, this is my life, and if you want to be with me you just have to accept it. Otherwise, fuck off now. There's no halfway with this.'

'You're my man and I can live with what you are, but when I heard the news all I could think of was you lying dead on the ground.' Pulling him towards her, Mimi hugged him tightly. They lay together wordlessly. After a time Winnie whispered, 'We're going for a ride, baby. You'll look good in that dress on my bike.'

'No way, Peter, what's under there is only for you. I have my jeans in the car. I'll get them.'

Winnie grabbed a helmet for Mimi. She looked pretty terrific in jeans and stilettos. Winnie let out a long, slow whistle, 'You look like a real bikie's moll. We're off to Bells Line of Road.'

Mimi shook her head; she'd never heard of it. Winnie kicked up the side stand and took off, not too fast, not too slow, but he laid on the power smoothly. Mimi's arms tightened around him and that made them both feel better. They headed towards the Mount Kurrajong Hotel and the plateau on the ridge line between the vast canyons leading to Mount Victoria, a good fast ride with long, sweeping bends. There wasn't much traffic so Winnie throttled up while Mimi clung tightly. Mimi was a natural passenger; she leaned into the corners and they rode as one. They reached the village of Mount Victoria in no time.

Winnie could hear the rumble of an approaching pack of bikes: Twister and the Tigers on a run. They roared through the village and barely glanced sideways. Winnie moved his bike under some trees where they sat down on the grass and took in the panorama. He lit a joint, and offered it to Mimi.

'Do you know them?'

'Yeah, that was Twister, a bloke I grew up with, and his club, the Tigers.'

'Do you get on with them?'

'We have our moments.'

'Like what?' she asks.

Winnie just smiled. 'You ask too many questions.' He kissed her and they lay back and enjoyed the smoke. 'Remember our first ride to Little Bay when the cops chased a bloke and we took off?'

'Unforgettable, but what's that got to do with today, Peter?'

'Well, they're now in the Tigers.'

'Pretty ironic that today's nearly a copy of our first ride. Only better.' Mimi smiled.

Winnie jumped up and grabbed his helmet, reached down to pull her up. 'Come on, we can stop at the Mount Kurrajong pub for a beer.'

'Have they got rooms there?

'Yeah, I think so.'

'Do you want to stay the night?'

Winnie smiled at her. 'Why not?'

The thought of spending another night with her excited him. He couldn't get enough of her. He buckled up her helmet, kissed her and the thought passed through his mind, This must be love. He'd never shown this much emotion to anyone, even his mother. He liked it deep down, and that thought stayed with him as they rode back to Mount Kurrajong, taking it nice and easy, with Mimi enjoying the beautiful view. When they reached the hotel he slowed down in the rough driveway at the front entrance and cruised slowly around to the car park, which was filled with the Tigers' bikes. A few of the Tigers were standing beside them. He hoped they didn't want to get smart. Even though he was alone, he never thought of driving straight through. While he parked he noticed that one of the Tigers raced inside to let the Twister know that Winnie had pulled in. By the time Winnie and Mimi took off their helmets he saw Twister and Kero Ken walking out onto the veranda.

Winnie told Mimi to stay close and they walked towards the pub arm in arm. 'Will there be any trouble?' she asked.

'No, but they might get a bit smart.' As they headed towards the hotel a couple of Tigers stood on the bottom steps as if to block the way.

Kero Ken shouted to them, 'Oi, you blokes! Get out of it!' He waved them away.

Twister shook hands with Winnie. 'I heard you were caught up in a bit of shit, Winnie.'

'Not us, Twister. You can't believe everything you hear.'

Twister asked, 'And who's the lovely lady?'

Winnie just stared at Twister, who laughed nervously. Mimi and Winnie made their way into the hotel. Twister and the Tigers mounted up and rode off. Winnie organised a room at the front desk as the patrons walked out to the veranda to watch the Tigers leave. The Mount Kurrajong Hotel had long been a bikies' beer stop, but the new bikies and their Harleys were different, a little more organised and a little more threatening, and everyone wanted to take a look. The owner handed Winnie the key to his room. 'Upstairs and to your left.'

'Thanks, mate.'

The owner stared at Winnie's Miners patch. He'd obviously seen the news and didn't seem too happy about giving them a room. Winnie grabbed Mimi's hand and they walked upstairs. He opened the door.

'It's not very big, babe. Just enough room for a double bed.'

Mimi jumped on the bed. 'This is all we need, Peter,' she said, and patted the bed.

Winnie tossed her the key. 'I'm going to put my bike away, then we can have dinner. I want to watch the news on television to see what everyone is on about.'

'Okay, I'll just freshen up.' Mimi grabbed a towel and disappeared into the bathroom.

Winnie went downstairs and talked to the owner about garaging the bike for the night. The pub's handyman showed Winnie an empty lock-up. When Winnie was satisfied with the security he went back to the room and knocked on the door. Mimi opened up. 'Fuck, you look beautiful, Mimi.'

'It's marvellous what a girl can do with some lipstick and a hairbrush.'

Winnie washed off the road grime and wet his hair. When he turned to get his towel, Mimi stood there holding it.

This girl is for me, Winnie thought. But he was in a bit of a hurry, he didn't want to miss the news, and he dried quickly, grabbed the room key, slipped off his Miners patch and laid it on the bed. 'Let's go.'

They made their way downstairs to the bar and found a table where they could watch the news.

Winnie ordered dinner and beers and sat down in time to catch the news. 'It has been confirmed that six bikies and one innocent girl died in a vicious shoot-out between rival motorcycle gangs in Newcastle on Saturday night.' The footage showed a line of Miners riding out, giving the impression that they were involved. 'Senior police were horrified by what they described as a massacre. Few details have been released, but it is believed the shoot-out was between the Redbacks outlaw motorcycle club and members of a rival Newcastle gang.'

The news continued and the drinkers moved back to the bar in silence. Winnie heard the publican saying, 'If they want to shoot each other why don't they go out into the bush and do it instead of in a pub?'

Mimi looked at Winnie. 'What do you think, Peter?'

'I agree it shouldn't be done in public.'

'So it's alright to shoot someone, but not in public?'

It was the kind of question Winnie hated; there was no easy answer. 'It might be the only way sometimes.'

Mimi was about to pursue it but had the grace not to. The waiter brought their food to the table and Winnie ate quickly.

'I didn't realise I was so hungry.' He hadn't eaten a thing for over a day.

Mimi did not quite finish hers. Winnie asked if she felt okay.

She touched his hand. 'Yes,' she smiled warmly. 'I want an early night. I think we've both had enough for one day.' Winnie led her back up to the room.

He pulled off his clothes and jumped under the covers. Mimi went into the bathroom and when she came out a few minutes later Winnie was asleep. She turned off the light and slipped into bed and stared at his face, which was illuminated by moonlight. She saw a young boy's face and wondered at how quickly he had changed her life. She snuggled up to him and drifted into a secure sleep.

The thump of Winnie's bike echoed as he warmed it up while waiting for Mimi to come out of the pub. She walked down the stairs, her blonde hair shining in the sunlight, and Winnie helped her with her helmet. He headed back to the Miners clubhouse at an easy pace, slow enough to stay out of trouble, but fast enough to enjoy the ride.

Mimi handed Winnie her helmet. 'Thanks, that was a wonderful ride. When will I see you again?'

'Soon.'

'Don't make it too long, Peter.' He kissed Mimi through the open window and watched her drive off.

Chapter 13

Winnie pulled into the back of the shop, where the boys sat around on chairs enjoying the sunshine and eating takeaways. Big Kev looked half asleep. Ocker stood, announced 'I've got work to do', and headed towards his spray booth.

Brian leaned in to Winnie. 'Prez, got a minute? We're getting low on hash. We've got a good market but if we have nothing, the punters'll go elsewhere. We're really cashed up and I heard some street talk about the Tigers having a hash shipment coming in. They claim it's wrapped in gold cellophane. It is not supposed to be as good as ours but if that's all there is ... you'd better see the Pig. It's easy to lose customers and fucking hard to get 'em back.'

The Pig rang a few hours later. 'How about Fritz's at eight?'

'Good,' Winnie replied and hung up.

He grabbed a cloth and started cleaning the six second-hand bikes they had on sale. He wanted new bikes on the floor, to attract new, up-market customers with more money; he wanted Harleys. Winnie was miles away, deep in thought.

Brian wandered over. 'What are you thinking about, Prez?'

Winnie stopped polishing and looked at Brian. 'Well, mate, we don't have many bikes people with money want, just these old British bikes. Maybe we should become a Harley dealer. What do you reckon?'

'Well, it's either Japanese or Harley and the way Harley's going I reckon that's the go. I heard Fraser's in Newcastle bought the Burling & Simmons New South Wales Harley import licence and they're opening up in Homebush. Why don't we set up a meeting with them? I'll talk to Kev and Ocker about it. We're all cashed up from the hash. Any outstanding debts?'

Only Smouch owed money. He was always short and word got back to Winnie that he was forcing some of the nominees to sell hash for him.

Kero Ken said he was hanging out with the Tigers from time to time — not a hanging crime, but not good form either.

'What does Smouch do with his money?' Winnie asked.

'He's always buying drinks for anyone and last week he took a couple of the nominees to a brothel, shouted them the night and bragged about being a Miner in front of the sluts.'

'Yeah, who's paying for it?'

'Dunno, but he's been mumbling about us taking the lion's share of the money and him doing all the work.'

'Is that right? Our members get hash cheaper than anybody else and they all make a good earn. Smouch wouldn't have two bob if he wasn't in the Club.' Winnie turned to Kev. 'Have you heard about Smouch mouthing off about our business?'

'Yeah, Prez, I heard that from Kero Ken. I meant to tell you about it but with so much going on I forgot. I like the bloke and wanted to talk with him first. It's true.'

'Fuck him.' Winnie said it in his scariest voice. 'Fuck him.'

No one had to sell hash if they didn't want to and Smouch was using his members and middling the profit. He probably thought he could take none of the risks and make all the money. Winnie didn't like bullying. He thought of Nestor two years before, at the point of expulsion, but he'd come good, for the common good. Maybe he'd still be on his couch between break-ins if not for one great chance; now he had respect for himself and for the Club. Smouch was in it for what he could get for himself. The more Winnie thought about it the madder he got. The whole point of the Miners was to look after each other; one weak link and the whole thing could tumble into shit. Winnie wasn't wearing it; he was going to do something about it, teach him a lesson and front him at the next meeting.

'He also told Kero he'd make a good president one day.'

'Did he? Well, we'll see about that. Just be prepared on Friday night, Kev. Keep it to yourself. I don't want to tip the cunt off. No second chances here, mate, you know the score.'

'I know, Prez.'

'Have you got today's newspaper, Brian?'

'Yeah, Prez, do you want to read about the shoot-out?'

'No, fuck that, mate. I'm vacating Mum's place and handing it back to the Housing Commission. I want to look in the real estate section and start hunting for my own house. I'm damn near homeless.' Winnie thought about what he'd just said and laughed loudly. 'I just want a unit, something nice and simple with a lock-up garage. I don't need to mow lawns.' He stuck the newspaper in his back pocket and pulled on his leather jacket for his meeting with the Pig.

The Sergeant sat down across the table and gave Winnie a broad smile.

Winnie moved his glass, planted his elbows on the table and leaned forward to the Sergeant. 'What the fuck is going on with the hash? We're ready to go, the punters are lined up around the block, we look like eggs. I've delivered, got the cash and your blokes are happy. Introduce me to your man. Show some faith.'

'He won't be in that, Winnie.'

'It's about business. You tell them if they don't, I'll have to work for someone else. I've done enough for them, I deserve it.'

The Sergeant sat for a moment. There was something in Winnie's look that made him think a second or two.

'I'll be right back. Enjoy your beer.' He stood up and walked over to Tony and they had a little whispered conversation. Tony pulled the curtain aside and the Sergeant disappeared. Winnie had been watching him and thinking to himself that these cunts are no different from anybody else: it's all in the way you speak to them. As long as they don't think you're bullshitting them. He'd go over to the opposition if he knew who they were. Winnie was surprised at his own disregard for authority; he knew he had it in him, but this time he felt comfortable with it. These arranged dinners and the pretence were beginning to get to him. The Sergeant returned after about five minutes and sat down, looking straight at Winnie.

'Alright, have it your way. He'll meet you later tonight.'

'Good.' Winnie was somewhat surprised. It had worked; the Sergeant had blinked first.

'Now, look, Winnie, this bloke is real connected. Don't get smart with him.'

Leaning over, Winnie said he couldn't be that connected if he had to get the Miners to look after the Bosinjaks for him.

'No, politically connected — he and the Police Commissioner play golf and he knows most of the politicians who matter. It's blokes like you and me who carry the can if any shit comes down.'

'Well, we'd better see that no shit does come down. Your mate — when do I get to talk with him?'

The Sergeant glanced at his watch. 'I'll be back in a minute, Winnie.'

He left the table and reappeared a couple of minutes later, beckoning Winnie to follow him through the kitchen. They walked out the back door to a parked Jaguar in the darkened lane. The Sergeant opened the back door and held it open for Winnie to climb in. There was a solitary person in the back seat. The Sergeant shut the door and got into the front passenger seat; he turned around and said simply, 'Winnie, meet Karmal.'

Karmal reached out a hand and Winnie gave it a firm shake. 'Mr Winnie, Sergeant tells me you can be trusted but he also says you have a few concerns.'

'You should know I want to hear it from the horse's mouth instead of the messenger.'

'Don't you trust the messenger?'

'He's only the messenger.'

'True, Winnie. Tell me what your concerns are.'

'Reliability of supply. We don't want to lose our market and if you can't supply we'll have to go elsewhere. We heard about a new supplier. A shipment is supposed to be here next week.'

'You are talking about the new shipment; I can assure you it will not hit the street. Am I right, Sergeant?'

The Pig nodded.

'The problem is Afghanistan — there are some freelancers about who sell to anyone. I have been assured that it will not happen again. My shipment is already on its way; you shall have it within the next fortnight. Is that your only concern?'

'No, we also want it cheaper.'

'Are you getting greedy, Winnie?'

'No, but I know how important we are to your business. Also I know that we're paying top dollar, so it's up to you to show how you value us and drop the price.'

'A politician in the making, don't you think, Sergeant Burrows?'

'Quite audacious,' the Sergeant replied, almost laughing.

'And what's to stop us from just getting rid of you, Winnie?'

'We're reliable, we always pay cash up front and we're secure.'

'But so are many people, Winnie.' With that the Sergeant pulled out his snub-nosed service revolver and pointed it at Winnie's head. 'What's to stop us from just shooting you and dumping you in a back alley? You're just a bikie from the western suburbs. Do you think anyone will care?'

Winnie looked straight at the Sergeant. 'Fuck knows who'd care, but the Miners know I have this meeting tonight and it doesn't matter a fuck how connected you are, they'll come after you. They won't worry about your bullshit justice. They'll just wipe you out.'

Karmal smiled. 'It is just business. Put that gun away, Sergeant.' The pistol went back into the shoulder holster. 'Now, how much cheaper do you think it should be?'

Winnie looked straight into his eyes. 'A thousand a kilo cheaper.'

'That's a nice round figure, Winnie.' He thought for a few seconds and agreed to $4000 a kilo. 'I want you to forget me from now on and continue to deal with Sergeant Burrows.'

'A deal,' Winnie said and reached his hand out.

'Sergeant, tell Fritz tonight's tab is on me. Now I have to go.'

The meeting was over. Karmal got out of the back seat, opened the driver's door and slid behind the wheel. Winnie and the Sergeant stood in the lane and watched him drive off.

The Pig looked at Winnie. 'Sorry about the gun, Winnie. I'm just playing the game, is that clear?'

'We're all playing our own game. We all have our own part. Now come on and let's get on the piss.'

The Sergeant picked up his glass. 'Here's to you, Winnie. You did alright tonight.'

Winnie picked up his glass and took a big sip. 'What's going on with the gold cellophane hash shipment?'

'Well, the stupid cunts bringing it in are amateurs. They never did it before so even before they got it into the country they tried to break into the local market, promising to sell it cheap. Therefore every cunt and his dog knows it's coming. We've known about it for two months. We have tails on the main operators. They'll lead us to it. We'll bust them and the police department will get good press.' The Sergeant looked smug for an instant.

Winnie said, 'How did you get so bent — not that I'm complaining.'

'In this job, Winnie,' the Sergeant refilled their glasses, 'the pay is steady, but small. I have kids and I want them to have a better start in life than I had. We're both on the same side.'

Winnie gave that idea some thought. Poor bastard, he thought, four kids and the world could come crashing down in an instant. Same shit, same side — no, not on the same side, but same shit nonetheless.

'You heard what happened to the Redbacks up in Newcastle? Will there be charges?'

'Too right there'll be charges. You can't have a fucking massacre like that and not expect to have charges. A word to the wise, Winnie: there's going to be a crackdown on bike clubs after that little caper, I can tell you. The word came from the top.'

'We had nothing to do with it,' Winnie replied.

'Just tell your members not to carry anything on them while they're riding. The whole force is on the lookout.' The Sergeant opened his coat and pulled out two cigars. 'Want one of these?'

'Why not?'

Winnie pulled up outside the shop before six, opened the roller doors, let in the sunlight and made coffee. Ocker walked in carrying a bowling bag and looking like a kid with a new toy. 'What have you got there?'

'A mobile phone — the future, Prez. Have a look.'

Winnie peered in. 'Does it work?'

'I'll show you.' Ocker dialled on the shop phone. The mobile phone rang. Winnie picked up.

'Can you hear me?'

'As clear as day.'

Ocker hung up. 'Could be handy selling product. Everyone will want one. I had a talk with our investment bankers. They know people trying to raise some cash to license sales for Motorola phones. They needed investors and I had some money. It may not pay for the first couple of years, but who knows?' Ocker hugged his mug of coffee.

Winnie's thoughts raced. Mobile phones could make things a lot easier for business.

Ocker had an idea. 'Just imagine running prostitutes. I could line them up on the go, keep 'em busy.'

'Have you got a few girls, Ocker?'

'I look after the high rollers with special escorts. They look like models and fuck like sluts … for a good price. Three are off to university with the money they've made. A mate at the Hilton Hotel moves hash for me and talks to visiting businessmen. They all want an escort for dinner and maybe a little hanky-panky afterwards. His girls were a little over the hill so my girls filled the bill.'

'Do you have any trouble?'

'One bloke wanted me to pay him. I was offering a service, he should have paid me.'

'So what did you do?'

'Well, I got Kev to come with me to see him. He didn't say a word. He just nodded.'

By now Winnie was laughing. 'That's the way, mate.'

'Here's Big Kev now,' Ocker said. Winnie cocked an ear, hearing the faint rumble of a Harley approaching.

Kev roared into the workshop and killed the motor. 'Morning, boys, what's new?'

'Ocker's been telling me about his new girlie business.'

'Yeah, the dirty little cunt, he keeps the good ones for himself.'

'That's the deal, Kev,' Ocker replied.

'I didn't tell you yet, Ocker, but the word on the street is that the state government is legalising brothels soon. Sandy and I plan on opening up five out in the suburbs and I'm going to need a lot more girls than you can supply. Know what we're going to do?'

'No, mate.'

'Me and Sandy are going to import slope-heads to work in the brothels. Sandy knows a Chinaman who'll bring them in for us. Have you ever been fucked by a slope-head, Ocker? Well, they can do the most amazing things.'

'You will have to lend me one for a week, Kev,' Ocker said with a big grin.

'We'll see, my little mate.' Big Kev grabbed Ocker in a playful headlock and then let him go.

Ocker wanted to know how come Kev knew so much about slope-heads.

'Vietnam.'

Brian made his way into the workshop and caught the end of the conversation. 'G'day, mate. How'd you go last night?'

'Sit down, Brian. Now you're here I'll tell you all about the Hash King. He brings it in directly from Afghanistan; he's the buyer, the importer and reseller. No middlemen involved, so what he says goes. It's some tribal thing. The blokes bringing in this new shipment are his opposition. They planned to sell it cheaper and undercut us but the Hash King knows exactly what ship it's on and the cops are going to nab the lot. The cops'll get big headlines, the politicians'll be happy, but the blokes bringing it in will be very unhappy. I heard it from the horse's mouth last night. I also got the Hash King to drop his wholesale price by a thousand a kilo. Twenty per cent.'

'Where does the Pig fit in, Prez?' Big Kev asked.

'He's the go-between. I don't know his deal, that's between him and the Hash King, but I reckon he's doing alright. Everyone is using each other — that's business. So we should have our new supply in a couple of weeks, but just keep it to ourselves until it arrives.'

The air cleared, the boys sat back; the full importance of what Winnie had said began to sink in.

Ocker said he'd heard that the Tigers were pretty close to some blokes bringing in the new supply of hash.

'It'd be a real shame if the Tigers went down with the importers,' Brian laughed.

Winnie had the last word. 'We're going to put up the price on ours as well.'

Winnie talked to Kev about giving it to Smouch, to show members it was no game — loyalty above all. Kev's eyes narrowed as he mulled it over. One day you love them; the next day they're nobody. Once it was done, Smouch'd likely fuck off interstate — when he'd mended, that is. Kev knew what had to be done. His blank face said it all.

'Have you seen Ocker's latest toy, Kev?'

'Yeah, he's becoming a real gadget man.' Kev managed a smile.

'You wait and see what happens in the future — I'm going to make a nice little earn out of them.'

Big Kev reckoned he was going to stick with what he knew, bikes and brothels.

Brian wanted more Harleys on the showroom floor. There were no second-hand ones around so a couple of Swannie's boys planned a trip to the States to buy some and ship them back in a container. The Miners were promised first pick. The spare parts went off, more every week, mostly for Harleys, no more Triumph stuff.

Winnie went off to spend some of his money on a townhouse in Stanmore. He'd looked at a few and had started to like the idea of being close to the city and not far from the shop, and settled on the Stanmore area, about halfway between. When he decided on a place and announced he was off to buy it, Brian's ears perked up.

'Are you moving Mimi in?'

'I haven't thought about it, mate, I've only thought about getting out of Mum's place. I don't think I'll ask Mimi; not yet, anyway. She has her own place.'

'Reckon she'll knock you back?'

Winnie smiled and dialled her number. Her voice aroused him, his cock ached. 'I'm off to make an offer on a townhouse today and I wondered if you could organise a deposit for me. I'll get our solicitor John Baker to call you and you two can work out the paperwork for me.'

'There shouldn't be a problem.'

He asked her to help him pick out furniture for it and Mimi relaxed; she liked the idea of being involved.

'Just let me know the amount, and who to make the cheque out to. I'd better go, I have a meeting in two minutes. I love you, Peter.'

He wanted to say something to that but in the shop he kept his thoughts to himself. He loved the way she switched straight to business; he found it professional, sexy. He would have loved to see her that night.

He called John Baker. 'John, I want to buy a townhouse in Stanmore and I want you to look after the paperwork with Gregson & Gregson Futures' Traders. Speak to Mimi Gregson.'

'I know them; you're not playing with Mimi, are you?'

'She could do worse, John. I'll bring the paperwork over to your office this afternoon if I get a commitment and we can have that talk about the strike force the cops want to set up for bikie gangs.'

'What time?'

'About five o'clock.'

'That'll be good, Winnie. See you then.'

Winnie hung up and watched Brian doing his spare parts order. 'Did you hear about the police task force?'

'Don't worry about it, Winnie. It'll be years away.'

'Good to know what's going on. You know the old scouts motto: "Be prepared".' That gave them a big laugh.

'Who's having all the fun?' Swannie called out. 'I need a new battery for my bike and I'm wondering how long before the hash comes in. People are screaming for it. It's hard to do business without a steady supply.'

161

'Don't worry, in about two weeks we'll be set. But just keep that to yourself. There's been a problem but that'll be sorted out next week, then we're on.'

'Smouch has turned into a cunt, hey?'

'How do you know?'

'I spoke to Kev. Would you like me to come over on Friday night?'

'No, mate, he's our Chapter's problem. We'll look after it.'

Winnie grabbed his vest and slipped into it. 'Well, I'm out of here. I'll see you later, boys.'

'Don't forget, Prez, if you see Mimi tell her about the barbecue on Sunday week. Gina keeps nagging me about it.'

'I won't forget, mate. Seeya, Swannie.'

Turning off at Stanmore Road, Winnie pulled up near the railway station and parked his bike outside the real estate agent's.

'Hello, my name's Jim Howarth.'

'G'day, Peter Winifred.' They shook. 'I want to buy …' Winnie pointed to the display of townhouses on a board, 'one of those and I want to move in next week.'

'Mr Winifred, it'll take a couple of weeks to organise the paperwork and for you to get your loan through. The townhouses are all ready, you just need to get the paperwork organised.'

'I'll be ready to settle next week, if there are no problems.'

'Please take a seat while we get the sale contract drawn up. If you can get your legal people to look it over and get it back early next week there shouldn't be a problem.'

Winnie marvelled at the difference money made. He sat down to wait.

The boss came back with the contract in his hand. 'Here you are, Mr Winifred.'

Winnie saw him in a different light. He took the contract and shook hands.

At John Baker's office Winnie parked his bike in the underground garage. Lindy sat behind the counter, smiling as he opened the door.

'When are you going to come to our clubhouse, Lindy?'

'My boyfriend would kill me if he knew I went.'

'Nothing would happen, you know.'

'Try and tell him that.'

'Get rid of him. I have a few good young fellas who'd give you a good time.'

'One day, maybe, Winnie.'

Baker opened his office door and ushered out his client. Winnie passed the contract to him.

'I want to move in next week.'

'I'll rush it through, Winnie.'

'Good-oh, John.'

'I heard the police think the shoot-out was over drugs.'

'What a load of shit, John. They just didn't like each other. The mad cunt in charge of the Nutters had it in for the Redbacks. He was against anyone dealing drugs on his turf and that's why they were at war. Anyway, it's good the old Nutter cunt is dead.'

'So that's what it was all about.'

'Fucken oath, John. Fiction is stranger than the truth. What about this taskforce? How does it operate?'

'Only talk now. I imagine they'll set up guidelines designed to stop criminals consorting.'

'How often will the pigs abuse that?'

'Often, Winnie. They're talking about this only for New South Wales, Squizzy Taylor told me. He's working full time in Parliament House. He might be able to find out more for you. No matter what the police want, the politicians have to give the green light. If he doesn't know, it wouldn't take him long to find out.'

'You'll keep me informed if there are any problems with the townhouse, John?'

Winnie walked out and rode to the Friday night Club meeting and headed for the bar for two fingers of Jack Daniels. Smouch held forth at the end of the bar, the centre of attention. He spotted Winnie and waved. It looked as if he'd been on the piss all afternoon.

He raised his glass and shouted in a disparaging tone, 'Here's to ya, Prez.'

Winnie smiled, raised his glass in response. He'd let the original members know about Smouch before the meeting. Smouch was oblivious to what was going on and continued bullshitting.

Kev turned to Winnie. 'I wish I was that good, Prez.'

Nestor turned up on his new Harley, a beautiful, dark green but for the chrome. He'd chosen green to match his pot. Kev told Nestor about Smouch, then called the meeting to order.

Winnie's eyes burned black, emotionless. 'Right, first thing to discuss is outstanding warrants. If anyone has any they have to sort them out tomorrow or they can't go on Club runs. You saw what happened on the way to Newcastle, one of Swannie's boys got done. It puts everyone out while we go and bail him. Do you all get that?'

A chorus of assent echoed around the room. 'Next, there's no doubt the pigs'll want to interview every one of us about the shoot-out at Newcastle. They're going to want statements from us. I have this simple advice for you: you saw nothing. The last thing we want is to be involved in a long court case. If anyone wants to get some free government money for stress or whatever over it, I have a pamphlet here that tells you how to go about applying for it. I'll show it to you after the meeting. It's money for jam.' A few of the boys laughed. 'Next …' Winnie's voice changed, 'Smouch, you're not happy in the Club, are you?'

The coward in Smouch sensed something was up, though he had no idea what was to come. 'Why's that, Prez?'

'I hear you're not happy being a Miner. We gave you the opportunity to make an earn and you haven't been paying for it. You badmouthed me and some other blokes — you said we made all the money and you got fuck-all.' Winnie started moving as he talked. 'You think you can do a better job as President?'

'No, I don't,' Smouch stammered.

'Well, why have you been telling that to anyone who'd listen?' Smouch fought for words that would not come. He stammered a bit and then shut up.

'You fucking have been!' Kev shouted in Smouch's ear.

The members in the know just stared at Smouch and the new ones looked at each other nervously; it was all new to them.

Winnie started again. 'I could handle most of that and put it down as piss talk, but what I can't handle is your disloyalty to the Club. You told the Tigers you were going to take over the Miners and affiliate with them.' It was a bombshell Winnie had kept to himself. The members were shocked. Someone called Smouch a rat.

Smouch, near to tears, stared at the floor. 'They made me do it, Prez.'

'Nobody can make you do anything. You were told to keep away from them and not to party at their clubhouse,' Winnie roared. He whacked Smouch on the shoulder with a length of pipe and Smouch fell off his chair.

'Take off his colours.' Someone pulled off Smouch's vest then delivered a solid boot in the guts. A few other members joined in while the rest stood back. Winnie bent down and pulled Smouch's head off the floor. Smouch offered no resistance. 'You're a dog cunt. What are you?'

'A dog cunt,' Smouch whispered. Winnie stood back and kicked him again. Everyone heard the sound of bones breaking. It stopped the blubbering.

'Get him the fuck out of here. Get the noms to drop him off at a railway station.'

'Smouch had been told not to hang out with the Tigers, the cunt, but he was weak enough to let Twister put all those ideas in his head. Twister knew he couldn't fuck with the Miners from the outside so he tried from the inside. But it was Smouch's fault for being piss-weak.' The room went deathly silent.

'What if he tries to join the Tigers, Prez?' Brian asked.

'We'll have a meeting with them and if they have him, it means war. No one joins another Club after they've been a Miner, clear?'

The members nodded as one.

'What's next?'

'Toothpick is due for his colours. Anybody have any objection?'

Nestor piped up. 'He was pretty close to Smouch.'

'That doesn't mean he's like Smouch. Let's see what he has to say about Smouch.'

'I'll get him,' Big Kev said.

'If we like what Toothpick says we give him his colours, okay?'

The members agreed.

Big Kev came back in, followed by Toothpick. He knew what had happened to Smouch, but he didn't know why. Toothpick stood in front of the members.

'Do you still want to be a Miner, even after what we did to Smouch?'

'Smouch was a big mouth,' Toothpick replied. 'Tiger-loving cunt, Prez.'

Winnie smiled and looked at the approving boys. Winnie shook hands with Toothpick and passed him his colours. 'Congratulations, mate, wear them with pride.'

The boys crowded around the new member, patted him on the back and welcomed him to the Club. 'You'll look good in our colours,' said Winnie. 'You know what our rules are, they're simple: be a man, don't be a cunt to the Club or Club members and you'll be right. Right?'

Toothpick grinned, 'Yeah, Prez.'

'Okay, meeting's over. Let's have a drink with our new member.'

They burned Smouch's colours and then Ocker went behind the bar and organised the Miners' toast to Toothpick. He set up shot glasses, filled them with bourbon and they skolled the first of many.

In walked Squizzy, disguised in chalk-striped business suit. Wolf whistles and catcalls greeted him from members who recognised him. He ordered beer for everyone. Squizz had married Michele, a nice girl from Lismore, and they were expecting a baby. She'd gone home for the week, giving Squizz a night out. He worked at State Parliament House in the public service, advising the justice department and learning something new every day — mostly scuttlebutt, but from time to time he mined good stuff. Tonight, he said, he had something new.

He told them all he knew about two coppers who'd spent six months in the States working with the FBI and had returned with some new ideas on how to combat organised crime. They planned on stopping clubs before they became too organised, reckoning, rightly, that bikies were the future of organised crime in Australia. There was a lot of talk after the Newcastle shoot-out and they'd begun creating a profile of each club: its members, where they worked and lived and so on. He told them to be vigilant on runs: the cops were onto anything that moved. He'd got copies of their reports and passed on the news. In his opinion, the cops wouldn't easily succeed at State level, but if they set up a Federal force, recruiting police from the State forces, it could get grim. He told them to hide their assets by transferring titles. He knew that Mimi's father was a skilful man with assets and would show them the ropes.

'Squizzy, it looks as if you've gone a long way. Instead of joining our Club, you have yours; it just runs a different way.'

'You got it, Prez.'

'It's party time,' said Kev.

They went out to the bar and got stuck into the grog. Winnie reckoned Squizzy had earned a few quid with that information; a small investment might pay big dividends. He got Brian to loosen up a thousand, then handed it to Squizz, hoping it was a fair price. Squizz looked shaken, but Winnie pointed out that the information was valuable to them. How valuable exactly? One thousand dollars' worth. Squizzy had a baby on the way. Cash would come in handy, so he slipped it into his breast pocket.

Long after the pubs shut, the Miners stayed open. The trick was to try and keep the idiots out, but some always got through. Winnie and Kev played eight-ball until some drunken egg put a coin on the table and challenged the winner. Kev and Winnie smiled at each other and ignored him. Kev ran the table. When the game was done, they shook hands. The challenger sauntered over and slotted the money into the table and the balls spilled out.

'I'm playing the big fella.'

Kev looked him over. 'Set them up, then.'

The egg's friends came over to watch. He thought he was pretty sharp. Winnie stood back and watched in amusement while Big Kev cleared the table without giving the bloke a shot. He and his friends watched in amazement. Big Kev replaced his cue and was walking over to Winnie when the bloke called out, 'Do you want another game, big fella?'

Big Kev turned and gave him a look. 'Don't call me big fella, cunt face. You can have the table.' Kev turned away.

'A bit scared to play me again, big fella?'

Big Kev turned and took three giant steps over to the big mouth. His friends jumped back as if to say, 'You're on your own.' Kevvie grabbed him by the throat, lifted him off the floor until the bloke's eyes bulged. 'I told you not to call me big fella.'

The music was so loud in the clubhouse that few people heard what happened. 'Listen to me, cunt. I don't want to play pool with you and you don't come into our clubhouse with your big mouth trying to impress your friends.' Still gripping him by the throat, Kev walked him to the front gate, dropped him like a bag of shit, kicked him up the arse and told him, 'I never want to see your face here ever again.'

The poor cunt's face was white. He trembled.

'Now get the fuck out of here.'

Big mouth got to his feet and ran up the road. Big Kev walked back into the clubhouse and asked big mouth's friends if there was anyone else who wanted trouble like their mate.

One of the blokes replied, 'He's not our mate, we're just here to have a good time.'

'That's good,' Big Kev said smiling.

Winnie looked at him and said, 'I think you have an admirer over there.'

Kevvie turned and looked. A girl in a short black dress gave him a big smile. Kevvie smiled and waved. She gave him a you-can-fuck-me-anytime look, then turned back to her friends, glancing occasionally in Kev's direction.

'Okay, Kev, let's get the slut in the black dress to come out the back with us. I'll go and chat her up while you get the drinks.'

Winnie caught the girl's attention and motioned her to come over. Winnie watched her walking towards him; she was a sexy thing.

'Hello, I'm Adele. Nice to meet you.'

'Pretty name. Would you like to come out the back with my mate and share a joint?'

'I'd love to,' Adele said.

'Come with me, I'll roll you the finest joint you ever had.' They walked out the back. Winnie stared at her black dress, which rode up high on her thighs. It was pretty obvious she wasn't wearing panties.

Big Kev lifted up the hem of her dress.

'Are we are going to have some fun tonight, Adele?'

'Too right we are.'

Big Kev fired up the joint.

Adele was a local girl, a real classy dresser. She leaned back and her dress inched up some more.

She looked at Big Kev then at Winnie, 'I like to fuck and I like to suck. Who's first?'

'Our type of girl.' Big Kev took a long hit on the joint, leaned back in his chair and blew a thin stream of smoke, passing the joint to Winnie. His hands free, he lifted up Adele's dress and exposed her bush. Adele smoked the joint and opened her legs. Big Kev slowly rubbed his fingers up and down her slit. She moaned and pulled out his cock.

'You're right, this is the best joint I ever had.' She rolled her hips around Big Kev's fingers inside her. 'Fuck me, Kev.'

He didn't have to be asked twice. He placed one hand under each cheek and lowered her onto his rock-hard cock. Winnie dropped his jeans and Adele took his cock in her mouth and rolled her tongue around and massaged his balls. She rocked against Big Kev and moaned loudly. Winnie blew into her mouth, Big Kev blew in her bush and she nearly collapsed from her orgasm. The three gasped for air. Winnie pulled on his jeans, reached for the ashtray and lit the joint.

'Isn't that the finest joint you ever had, Adele?'

'The finest.' She smiled warmly.

Winnie passed her a drink. 'Here, wash it down with that.'

Winnie walked out. Ocker saw the look on his face. 'What have you been up to, Prez?'

'Having fun, the big fella too.'

'Any room for me, Prez?'

'Just take these drinks out and see what happens, mate.'

The scanner crackled away behind the bar. 'Anything going on?' Winnie leaned in to the scanner.

'Yeah, Prez, they pulled over some Tigers running red lights on Parramatta Road.'

'What a shame.' Winnie surveyed the clubhouse. He was glad to see most of the members. They needed a good get-together after the Smouch episode.

'You sure it's alright to go out the back?' Ocker wasn't convinced.

'Come on, mate, would I bullshit to you?' Winnie tried to look non-committal. 'Just take the drinks out and see what happens.'

'Where have you been, Prez?' Brian asked with a leer.

'Entertaining with Big Kev.'

'You blokes still get the girls,' Squizzy laughed.

'Yeah, it's a lot different with girls these days, Squizz. Instead of lining up on the wet grass under the Harbour Bridge with some bush pig, tonight we have a sheila that looks like a model sitting out the back with no pants on and we're all in here talking and having a beer. All she wants to do is fuck Miners. We do it with more class and in comfort these days.'

The group cracked up.

'How about you, Toothpick? Would you like to go out and be entertained? It's our welcome present.'

'Fucken oath, Prez, I'm in the mood for a bit of entertainment.'

'Off you go, then. Just go gently with her.'

Toothpick grabbed his drink and headed out the back. He was back in a minute. 'You didn't muck around, mate.'

'Ocker wouldn't let me in, told me to fuck off and come back later.'

Winnie and Brian pissed themselves laughing. 'That's what you'll learn about Ocker — if he has a woman to himself, he's a sick little puppy and does all these little tricks with them; he could be in there all night.'

'What sort of tricks, Prez?'

'I don't know, but the only time that door will open will be when he goes for more drinks. You might have to wait for hours. I wouldn't be surprised if she's not working for Ocker in one of his businesses by the time she leaves here. Ocker has the gift of the gab. Just hang around, mate, you'll be right.'

Squizz had something else to tell them. The police were going to interview everyone again about Newcastle. They'd already started in

Newcastle and would soon move down to Sydney. They knew they'd get no new answers because it had been too dark to see and there was lots of confusion, fear and panic, but they were trying it on anyway.

The phone rang. It was someone called Monica calling from the Emergency Ward at Liverpool Hospital. One of the members, Phillip Jones, had been involved in a traffic accident. He was in a pretty bad way and they'd sent for his parents.

Winnie turned off the music, made the announcement and sent all the visitors home.

Everyone was sorry to hear about Jonesy, who was known as a great bloke.

Ocker stepped out from behind the door, stark naked except for one sock. Winnie told him the bad news.

'How is he?'

'Pretty bad. It doesn't look real good; they sent for his parents. Where's the girl, mate?'

'She's having a nap. I didn't have the heart to wake her up.'

Winnie took off his colours and handed them to Brian. 'Look after these for me, mate.' He and Big Kev rode wordlessly to Emergency. When they entered they saw police standing with an elderly couple who looked devastated. The parents had just given permission to turn his life support off. Someone ran a red light, no witnesses yet; the cops were trying to file a report.

Winnie spoke to Jonesy's parents, telling them that Jonesy was liked and respected in and out of the Club. He introduced Kev.

'Phillip always spoke highly of you,' his mother said between sobs.

'Look, don't worry about anything, Mr and Mrs Jones, the Club will organise everything. If it's alright, we'd like to come to your place tomorrow and talk about the arrangements for the funeral.'

With that, the realisation of Jonesy's death hit his mother again. She began weeping uncontrollably. The old man nodded and led Jonesy's mother out of the hospital; both looked utterly drained. Big Kev and Winnie stood together watching, then a nurse walked up to them. She'd been crying.

'Hello, I'm Monica. I rang you at your clubhouse.' She gave Winnie a parcel.

'Oh, g'day, Monica, I'm Winnie. This is Kev. Thanks for doing that for us.'

She looked at the parcel. 'It's his colours. I know the Club would want them.'

'Did you know Jonesy?' Big Kev asked.

Tears welled in Monica's eyes. 'Yes, we were in high school together. I'd better go now.'

'Thanks again.' Winnie said. 'Come on, Kev, there's nothing else for us to do here.' They left the Emergency Ward and rode back to the clubhouse compound, which was filled with bikes.

Winnie announced Jonesy's death. 'A good bloke, a great member.' The news slowly sank in. 'He was a good mate. The funeral will be next week.' Winnie paused for a second. 'Death's never far away when you ride a motorcycle. Here's to Jonesy and here's to the Miners.' The boys raised their glasses. 'Ride to live and live to ride.'

'To Jonesy!' they yelled. One of the boys had an uncle with a funeral parlour and they arranged for him to handle the funeral. It was a few days until the body was released but the plan was to hold the funeral on Thursday.

Jonesy's bike turned up on the back of a truck. The bike was crushed on the left hand side, proving it had been a big hit, couldn't have been much worse. They planned to fix it and sell it and give the proceeds to the parents for a holiday. They could use one.

Inside the bar Ocker was telling Toothpick how the girl in the black dress gave him the best head job he'd ever had, and what he missed out on.

'Stop it.' Toothpick was rubbing his crotch. 'I'll have to have a wank if you don't.'

Ocker pulled on a serious face. 'Hey, just remember, Toothpick, you're only a new member.' Toothpick didn't know how to react. Ocker grinned. 'Tell you what, mate, I'm seeing her tonight. You can come too.'

Toothpick grinned broadly. 'They said you were a good bloke.'

Everyone laughed. It helped to change the sombre mood.

Winnie dialled Mimi. Before she could answer two Harleys rode slowly past the clubhouse. The riders looked in, then accelerated away, Tigers patches clearly visible.

'I wonder what those queer cunts are up to,' Big Kev said to no one in particular.

'Ocker, go and make sure the shotgun is loaded. I don't trust them.'

Ocker pulled out the sawn-off pump action shotgun. He checked to see it was loaded and laid it on top of the safe. He was about to tell the nominee not to touch it when they heard the sound of Harleys coming down the street and swinging into the Club compound.

Twister got off his bike and shook hands with Winnie and Big Kev. 'I hope you don't mind us dropping in, Winnie. We just wanted to have a drink with you for Jonesy. We heard the news — a good bloke, sad news.'

'How come you knew him so well?' Big Kev asked.

'He was my cousin.'

Ocker replaced the gun in its hole.

'It's cool, Twister,' Winnie said. 'It's been a long time between drinks for us. Why don't we go outside and sit in the sun. It's been a long night. We lost another member as well.'

'What, dead?' Twister looked surprised.

'No, not dead, Twister. Smouch's in hospital.'

'Yeah, I know him,' Twister said with a cool smile. 'He had a lot to say. Went on about how he was going to become President and take over your business. He was off with the fairies. Good for a laugh.'

'Well, he's gone now.'

'I knew Smouch wasn't going to be around for long, the way he talked himself up.'

'Just don't let him join your club — we won't like that.'

'Wait until I get my hands on him. I hope he does come back to our clubhouse.' Twister was incensed.

He raised his drink and toasted the just departed. 'To Jonesy.'

'How did you find out about him being in an accident so quick, Twister?'

'His father called my mother. He was an only child. They're real battlers, too.'

'Yeah, I saw that,' Winnie answered thoughtfully.

'You believe me, Winnie, about Smouch?' Twister looked up at Winnie.

'I believe you, Twister.'

'I just didn't want to interfere in your Club business, that's why I never said anything.'

Twister talked a bit about his trucking business and how he was moving rigs interstate. Life was pretty good. He finished his drink and walked out with his boys.

'The funeral is probably Thursday,' Winnie called after him. 'You're welcome, but no trouble, alright?'

* * *

One of the Tigers had bragged about getting their shipment of hash in a week and had offered Ocker some. Ocker remembered Winnie and his night in the laneway behind Fritz's with the Hash King and the Sergeant. If the Tigers were involved in the new shipment, it'd be a shame, but they wouldn't be getting a solitary ounce. Ocker said fuck-all; it was none of his business what the Tigers got up to.

Ocker got off the phone and grinned. The girl in the little black dress was coming back for more.

Big Kev grabbed Ocker around the neck. 'You are a dirty, filthy little man. What's mine is yours and what's yours is yours — that is the way it is, isn't it?'

'So you're saying I'm a sheriff.'

Both Winnie and Big Kev pissed themselves. 'That's it, mate.'

'I'll see you at the shop on Monday, boys. Ring me at Mimi's only in an emergency.' Winnie shook Toothpick's hand, 'Welcome to the Club, mate. It's been quite a start for you. You'll make a good member. Ooroo.'

Big Kev said his goodbyes and followed Winnie through Liverpool to the intersection where Jonesy had been fatally hit. They sat wordlessly. After a few minutes they took off for the Cross, where Kev peeled off and Winnie headed for Mimi's. She bounded down the stairs, threw herself into his arms and kissed him.

Chapter 14

The parents were inside sitting with Jonesy. Winnie sat next to the grief-stricken father.

'Both of us thank you, Peter.'

Winnie kissed a quietly sobbing mother then went to the open coffin and looked at Jonesy at peace. The undertaker had done a good job dressing him in his colours. The sound of bikes arriving disturbed his thoughts.

He was surprised when he walked outside and saw how many people had turned up, including Twister and his Tigers, the Commandos, the Redbacks and even the God Squad motorcycle clubs. At eleven o'clock the undertaker instructed the pallbearers from the Club on carrying the coffin and they followed him out to the waiting hearse. He closed the back and it pulled away slowly, followed by the formation of bikes.

At the cemetery, a crowd stood around the wreath-strewn grave. Club women huddled, crying.

The awful truth of the grave was all too much for Jonesy's mother, who put on a bit of a turn. The celebrant read Jonesy's eulogy, said his piece and signalled someone to lower the coffin. Shovels appeared and each Miner contributed until the grave was filled; even Twister walked over and tossed in a handful of dirt. When all was said and done, they rode back to the clubhouse; the women were driven in a stretch limo. Jonesy's parents didn't come — the old man reckoned it would be too much for his wife.

'Look what I found,' Big Kev said as Sorrow and Fred walked into the Club; Sorrow had survived the massacre but his arm was in a sling.

'G'day, Sorrow, Fred, glad you're alright.'

'Yeah, Winnie, that goes for me too, but we're going to get charged with god knows what. No one's made a statement yet, so they're up a blind alley and they can't make out what happened.'

'The Nutters aren't making statements either?'

'No, Winnie, I'll give them this much, they're staunch. The old Nutter had been using them; it wasn't about us wearing colours in their territory, it was all about him selling drugs on the north side and he thought we were moving in. The funny thing is, we weren't, but we will now.' He grinned. 'And some of those Northsiders will make good Redbacks. It's a good thing the old cunt is dead, even if someone had to pay for it.'

'How bad is your mate?' Big Kev wanted to know.

'Not too bad, the bullet went straight through and chipped the shoulder bone on the way. The old cunt couldn't shoot straight but he wasn't far off. We're real sorry to hear about Jonesy, Winnie. I never knew him but a few of the boys did. They were going to do a bit of business together. Do you reckon someone else can look after them?'

Winnie smiled. 'I'm sure Jonesy would like that. Ocker, look after it, yes?'

'Sure thing, Prez.'

'Come on, boys, let's go inside and have a drink to our dead mate.'

Brian welcomed each car load of mourners to the clubhouse. Jonesy's uncles and cousins and a few aunties and nieces turned up and got stuck into the open bar for a couple of hours, and the Club paid.

Winnie noticed Rastus and Spike across the room and raised his glass. Rastus nodded towards the back of the clubhouse, and Winnie moved to meet him there. 'What's up, mate?'

'I have a little speed. Want some? One snort revs you up and you can drink piss and party all night!'

'That sounds alright, Rastus!'

Rastus got out some white powder and handed Winnie a rolled-up banknote.

'Here goes!' Winnie put the note up his nose and inhaled the powder.

'Holy shit, that burns!' Winnie exclaimed and handed the note back to Rastus. His eyes watered and he felt tingly all over. He announced that he was off to see if it worked.

The night went quickly, in a blur; he could hardly believe it.

Rastus reappeared. 'How'd you go with the speed, Winnie?'

'Now I know why they call it speed, mate. Reckon it could become popular. Is there much of it about?'

'I'll find out for you, Winnie. I want to know myself.'

'We should get some. There might be an earn in it for us.'

Winnie rounded up Kev, Brian and Ocker and told them about what Rastus had given him. He got Rastus to open his little stash of speed and show them what it was all about. Rastus looked a sight with his missing teeth, a dirty, greasy beanie pulled down near his eyes and a cigar hanging out of his mouth. He poured the contents onto a mirror, pulled out a knife and made six lines in front of him.

'Will I like it?' asked Brian.

'Too right you will.' Rastus rolled a note into a straw.

'Never done this before,' said Brian after he'd snorted.

'Yeah, it sure looks like it,' Sorrow said with a laugh. Brian handed the note to Ocker, who snorted it up like a vacuum cleaner. He pulled his head back, wiped his nose with the back of his hand and passed the note to Big Kev.

'You want to start cooking your own speed, Winnie?' Rastus wiped what speed was left on the mirror with his finger and licked it. 'Yum, not too bad if I say so myself.'

Winnie nodded. He liked the vertical nature of a business where you made your own product, distributed it and copped the profit.

'You need chemicals we can supply,' Rastus continued. 'Glassware from laboratory supply shops and a cook who knows what he's doing. That's the hard part. You need someone you can trust. Once we teach you how to do it, you're set. But it's dangerous — you have to do it properly, otherwise you can blow yourself up. Your chemicals are normally worth about forty grand a pop, so you don't want just any cunt experimenting.'

'Well, supposing we wanted to cook our own, how soon could we get the chemicals, Rastus?'

'As soon as you're ready, Winnie. It isn't cheap to start up. The most expensive part is the pseudoephedrine — it'll cost you twenty grand for twenty litres — but your returns are about a quarter of a million, when it's pure. You can cut it, it depends on what quality you want. I normally cut it about five times. That's what you had before. How was it?'

Winnie could feel his scalp tingling from his line. 'Yeah, alright.'

'You're best to set up your lab in the countryside because it gives off a pretty weird smell. Don't have too many people coming and going. The locals will notice bikies, so use cars and only go at night.'

'Why share all your information with us?' Brian normally never said a word. It was a fair question.

Rastus looked up. 'I supply most of Melbourne, I'm not worried about Sydney. My business is supplying the chemicals, but if you boys don't want it, there are other people who'll jump at the chance.'

'We're just amazed at how you're helping us,' said Brian. 'It's like you're a Tupperware salesman.'

'To the Tupperware party!' Rastus said, raising his drink, and they all burst out laughing. It broke the tension. 'We'll get onto setting it up this week, Rastus. You'd better give me a list.'

'It has to be cash up-front for the chemicals.'

Winnie looked at Brian, who smiled at Rastus. 'Not a problem.'

'I always knew I was going to like you Commandos,' Big Kev announced loudly.

Rastus said, 'Same, mate,' then lit his cigar and filled the room with smoke.

Winnie saw a couple of plain-clothes pigs around the clubhouse, blatantly eavesdropping. 'Come on, Kev. Let's have a little chat.'

Winnie strode over and stood behind them, and spoke just loudly enough to be heard. 'Who invited you two to this private wake?' It startled the coppers, and neither knew what to say. 'I'd advise you both to piss off now, otherwise I won't be responsible for what might happen.'

They looked around and saw they were surrounded by Miners, and left the Club grounds quick smart.

Winnie thanked Rastus for giving them the opportunity to do the speed in Sydney. He was in a mood to party. A group of Jonesy's relatives and his Aunt Bess entertained a few members with funny stories about the young Jonesy. Then the Rat turned up. He'd been gone a year or so; no one knew where he'd gone. His hair was longer than it had ever been and was bleached white from the sun — he looked like a real surfie.

'So where have you been, Rat?' Winnie was curious.

'I started using heroin again, Winnie. I had to get away from the peninsula scene so I loaded my car and camped at this uninhabited beach for three months. It was tough going cold turkey at the start but after a while I went back surfing and got my body back in shape. I already had my soul under control. I lived on fish and tinned food and almost beat the habit. But I had a bit of money, so I headed up the coast surfing and meeting locals. I put myself to the test, partied with them and was offered but declined — until I gave in. That's when I knew I was in trouble. So I kept heading north and worked on a prawn trawler in the Gulf and stayed on it for a year and kicked the habit. The Skipper said he trusted me and asked if I'd go on a special trip as a deckie. He told me I'd make three grand for a few days' work. I didn't twig until one night we met another ship at sea, loaded about five tons of Buddha sticks into our hold and smuggled it back, no Customs, no worries. He's an old pro, I admire him. He even adjusted our ballast so we floated right.'

The Rat didn't know where the dope had gone to. One night two trucks arrived, loaded the dope and off they went. The Skipper came from a long line of smugglers who had supplied rum to the early settlers. It was in his blood. Until the drug business started, he fished eight months of the year. He still did both; he liked fishing, and trawling was a good cover.

'I'm on good terms, and we might need him one day. Look, I'm clean now and I need to earn a quid and start business again. I have a market for hash and grass. When can we start?'

'In a couple of weeks, Rat. There's grass available now. You can work it out with Ocker, he does it. I'll catch up with you later.'

'Good to be back, Prez.'

Brian and Kevvie sat with the women outside. Ocker showed off his new mobile phone to Aunt Bess. She was plumpish, big-titted and in her mid fifties, with a few stiff drinks inside her. 'That Ocker has no shame.' Rastus licked his lips, pulled on his cigar and smiled toothlessly. Winnie couldn't believe it.

'You wouldn't, would you?'

'Watch me.' Rastus got up. 'Besides, I want to check out his mobile phone.'

Aunt Bess waddled out the back flanked by Ocker and Rastus. Winnie wondered if she knew what she was in for. It would make a good blue movie. He hoped the women didn't hear about it; they could get jealous over Aunt Bess. She was old enough to be their mother and there she was in the back room with Ocker and Rastus, doing god knows what. No one talked but it was something that made her groan a lot.

When they re-emerged, Kev said to Ocker, 'Come on, don't leave us in the lurch.'

'You don't want to know,' said Rastus with a leer, 'but she sure taught me a few things.'

Aunt Bess waddled back from the ladies. 'Hello, boys.' She pinched Brian on the arse and sat down with Rastus and Ocker.

People left until only Club members and the Rat sat in the marijuana-smoke-filled room. The unsmiling Rat came over and sat down with Kev and Winnie.

'The Prez told you, Kev? What can I say, except I'm clean now.'

Big Kev tapped Rat on the chest. 'I admire that you came out and told us. We love you like a brother, but if you ever touch that shit again you'll have me to worry about.'

'Kevvie, I swear I won't. Been there, not going back. I have my old market back and now I just need the goods. I'll buy something up the coast when I'm cashed up. Met this little surfie chick up north and she's moving down in a couple of months.' Now it was the Rat's turn to need the boys, and they all remembered that he'd helped them in the beginning of their pot days.

Mimi phoned. 'Hello, Mr Winifred, it's Mimi Gregson. Good news — you are now the proud owner of a townhouse. We exchanged contracts today.'

Winnie thanked her and asked when they could choose furniture.

'That would be my pleasure, Mr Winifred.' Then she whispered, 'I'm looking forward to it.'

'Okay, call you Saturday.'

Chapter 15

Rose Tattoo were playing in Parramatta and the boys felt like going. It was still early, and people were lined up down the block. On the door were two burly blokes, the Mario twins. Winnie hadn't seen them since school. They spotted Winnie and Kev and waved them in. Tony and Bruno Mario had migrated with their parents from Italy but no one ever called them wogs — they were too big, and too tough as well. Few could tell them apart so everyone called them both Mario. The Marios knew about the Miners and their clubhouse and had always meant to come, but they worked seven nights a week.

'Any time you like, boys, come over for a drink,' Big Kev said. 'How long have you been bouncing, Mario?'

Both started to answer simultaneously, and everyone laughed. Tony Mario joined them at a table and told them that after they left school they'd worked with their old man at the fruit markets, but it wasn't what they wanted. When he retired and moved back to Italy he left them the family home. They wanted to open nightclubs; the only thing they knew was markets or fighting so they chose the fighting.

'Do you get much trouble?'

'Only when you aren't around, Kev.' Mario laughed. He was a big, easygoing bloke until you pissed him off. Then he could turn. His twin was the same, only meaner.

'I'll have a talk with you, Mario, about your nightclub, if you like.' Winnie said.

'Okay, see you later, work to do.' He went to look after the front door.

'The Mario brothers haven't changed much, Prez, except they've got bigger.'

Later, Tony headed back to the table. 'You intrigued me, Winnie. What do you want to talk about?'

'Well, Mario, if you had someone willing to put up the money for a nightclub, would you take it?'

'All depends on how much say they want in running it.'

'I'd put up the money and want nothing except that it's run properly and I make a decent earn. I know you two blokes would make it a big success.'

'Winnie, the nightclub was going to be just a start for us. We want to run big rock shows and some Broadway shows as well. From rock to opera. The nightclub is the first step to establish ourselves in the entertainment industry. There are plenty of rip-offs but if we book popular acts and pay well, we get a good name.'

'You have big ambitions, Mario, and I want to invest. I have cash, you need some, so let me talk to my banker about it.'

'You must be doing alright, Winnie.'

'Give me your number and I'll call next week.'

'Okay, Winnie, you're on. I'd better go now, we're expecting a big crowd tonight.'

A couple of drunk sluts made their way to the table. 'We love bikies. Can we sit here?'

No one paid them any attention until they tried to sit.

'Don't sit there,' Winnie said quietly.

'Why, do you think you're too good for us?'

Her friend tried to pull the mouthy one away. 'Come on, Jenna, leave it.'

'You fucking Miner cunts,' the mouthy one said, then she threw her drink at Winnie.

Big Kev stood in one motion and head-butted the mouthy one into a chair. Her girlfriend looked stunned and wordlessly followed Big Kev as he dragged her mate's chair into a corner. 'When she wakes up, take her out of here. I don't want any more bother.' Kev made his way back to the table.

'Do you know those sluts, Kev?'

'Never seen them before.' The slut was coming to, focusing on her girlfriend, trying to figure out where she was. She turned and mouthed more obscenities. Her girlfriend grabbed her by the hair on either side of her head and spoke to her. Big Kev just stared. The slut's eyes wobbled back and forth.

'I think she's used to getting her own way,' Kevvie said and that got him a big laugh. It only worked her up. She started screaming over her shoulder as her girlfriend walked her outside.

'Thank fuck they're gone,' said Kev. 'Now we can watch the band. It should be starting soon, I saw Angry Anderson's bald head bobbing around before.'

'Who's he?' Brian asked.

'You should go out more, mate. The lead singer of Rose Tattoo, even I know that,' Winnie said.

'You're single, Prez. Wait until you get married and have kids, you'll want to stay home too.'

One of the Mario brothers came over to the table looking concerned. 'Did you blokes have problems with a couple of girls?'

'They're gone now, Mario. It's alright, mate, it was nothing.'

'Maybe not, Winnie. Those two run with some mad cunts and if you stirred them up enough there's a good chance they'll be back with them.'

'How far do they have to go, Mario?'

'Back of Penrith. If they come back, they'll have numbers. We won't be able to help if you're still here.'

'We're not going anywhere, Mario,' said Big Kev. 'We're here to watch the band.'

'If they come, how long will it take for them to get there?' asked Winnie.

'About an hour to an hour and a half.'

'Tell you what we'll do. There are nine of our members plus Rastus and two of his boys at the clubhouse. Have you got any bats, Mario?'

'Yeah, Winnie.'

Mario number two announced, 'They're coming back, the slut just rang. She's as mad as hell.'

'They might be bullshitting,' said Kev.

'No, no,' the Mario brothers answered together. 'They'll come.'

'Well, you have a choice, boys — call the pigs, or do it our way.'

They turned to Winnie. 'Your way, mate, as long as we can keep it outside.'

'Brian, ring Ocker. Tell him to bring the boys from the clubhouse and park over the road. They'll know when the queer cunts arrive. Tell him not to be late.'

'Okay, Prez.'

'Mario, let them into the foyer and we'll meet them with the bats. Then Ocker and the boys can get them from behind. No knives.'

'But Winnie ...'

'Don't worry, Mario, we know the score.'

Mario showed Kev where they stored the bats.

'Still glad you're a member?' Winnie asked Toothpick.

'It's not a problem, Prez.'

'That's the way. We'll flog the bastards.'

The band struck up loudly and drowned out the packed house. Winnie, Big Kev and Brian stuck together but it was pretty hard for the boys to enjoy the show.

Ocker appeared and Winnie explained the plan. 'As soon as they enter, bring the boys over. Tell them not to get the bouncers, they're with us. After we finish with the pricks, you and the boys go back to the clubhouse so when the pigs come they'll only find victims. The bouncers can explain it to the pigs. If these pricks are as bad as the Mario brothers say, the pigs might be glad we did it.'

Within fifteen minutes, Mario number one waved Winnie and the boys over. They grabbed bats and headed for the foyer, where Mario number two stood barring the door. The two sluts, surrounded by a wall of about fifteen bikies, shouted abuse. Mario and his brother tried talking quietly but the shouting and swearing got louder and more threatening.

'Prez, this is going to be a piece of piss.'

'Right, Kev, you and Brian go to the left.'

'Come on, Toothpick, follow me.' Winnie walked up behind the Marios.

The slut shouted, 'There they are, the cunts!'

The blokes looked as if they'd been in the bush for a month and were eager to fight. Winnie and the boys began giving it to them. They had no alternative but to run Ocker's gauntlet, where his boys belted them as they passed. The two sluts screamed at them as they ran from the torrent of blows, then, bruised and bloodied, got on their bikes and fucked off.

'That was a good result, boys,' one Mario said. The other one just grinned.

Kev and Toothpick handed the bats back to the Marios. The sluts glared at Winnie.

Ocker gave them the once over. 'They don't look too bad, Prez.'

'What have you got in mind, Ocker?'

'Spoils of war.' Ocker talked to them and a minute or two later the sluts and the boys headed back to the Miners clubhouse.

'What do we do, Prez, stay or go?'

'I reckon we've had enough for one day. Toothpick, get the car.'

They jumped in the Ford and took off. 'Where to, Prez?'

Winnie turned his head around to the back seat and said, 'What do you reckon, boys, a brothel?'

'Count me in,' Big Kev shouted. 'Whoopee!'

'I'll come,' said Brian, 'but I'm not performing.'

The Prez and Big Kev laughed. 'Yeah, yeah, we know, you've got Gina at home.'

'Won't your missus care, Kevvie?'

'Just as long as I don't fuck her mates. Anyway, we're a long way from town. We don't know many operators out here.'

'What about you, Toothpick?'

'Yeah, I'm in, Prez.'

'Do you know where to go, Toothpick?'

'There's a new one at Prospect with some good girls in it, but it's expensive. Do you want to try it out, Prez?'

'Whaddya reckon, Kev?'

'That'll do, Prez.'

'You heard the man, Toothpick.'

'Prospect it is, Prez.'

Brian fired up a joint before passing it to Big Kev, who urged Toothpick to 'get up it'.

Winnie looked over at Toothpick. 'You just stick to the speed limit, mate.'

Toothpick pulled into the brothel and parked around the back. A single light burned above the door.

'It doesn't look much,' Big Kev said, 'and it certainly doesn't look busy.'

'Come on, let's see what they have.'

Kev pressed the button on the intercom.

A voice asked, 'How many of you?'

'Four,' Winnie said in a strong voice.

The door clicked open and revealed the madam in a black caftan.

'This way, gentlemen.' Her accent was strongly European. 'Would you like drinks or do you want to see the girls?'

'We're in no hurry,' Winnie said. 'Let's have a drink.'

'Speak for yourself, mate, I want a girl now.' Big Kev was keen.

'That can be arranged,' the madam said. 'How long would you like to spend? It's a hundred dollars an hour.'

Big Kev pulled out his wallet and handed her two hundred dollars. The madam pulled open a curtain revealing four girls behind a one-way window, totally oblivious to the boys. They all wore up-market underwear. One looked African, her skin almost blue-black.

'I'm having her,' Big Kev grinned.

'No wonder they charge a hundred an hour, Kev. Compared to yours, these are princesses.'

'Yeah, I know, mate, but at our place you only pay thirty bucks.'

'They don't look too bad at all, do they?' Brian noticed. 'But not for me. I'll wait in the bar. Have fun.'

'Oh, we will,' Kevvie said. 'I'm ready.'

'Her name is Sabrina. I will show you the room then get her for you.'

Big Kev disappeared up a hallway. Winnie and Toothpick stared at the girls.

'Which one do you fancy, Toothpick?'

'Your choice first, Prez.'

'I'll have the blonde. Have you got enough money?'

'Yeah, I'm right thanks, Prez. I think I'm going to put it on the madam.'

'I don't blame you, mate.'

They watched the madam enter the room and walk over to the African pro. 'She must be six foot tall,' Winnie said. She looked alright, dressed in all white. The madam led her out of the room.

'You were right about this being high class, Toothpick. I bet they do alright. They must have some good protection to invest so much out this way. They wouldn't do it otherwise.'

Just then the madam returned. 'Are you gentlemen right?'

Winnie turned to her. 'My little mate here wants to know if he can have you.'

'No, not possible. You will enjoy the younger girls.'

'What's your name?' Winnie asked.

'It is Ava, darling. And yours?'

'I'm Winnie and this is Toothpick.'

'Pleased to meet you both. And your other friend?'

'Brian,' Winnie replied. 'He went to the lounge. He's not a customer.'

'This is okay. Franz is out there, he will look after him. Have you decided on a girl, or would you like a drink first?'

'I think I'll have that one.' Toothpick pointed to a small Italian-looking girl.

'Be gentle with her,' Ava said to Toothpick, 'she just started working. Her name is Milena.'

'I'm gentle with all of them,' he replied, and followed her out.

Brian sat in the lounge chair, drink in hand. One of the biggest men Winnie had ever seen stood talking to him.

'This is Franz, Winnie,' Brian said.

'Would you like a drink, sir?' He shared the European accent of the madam.

'I'll have the same as him,' Winnie replied.

'Are you going to see one of the girls?'

'That's what I'm here for.'

'Then there is no charge for the drink,' Franz replied.

Winnie walked around the room looking at exotic drawings.

'That is Ava's work.' Franz watched Winnie carefully, he wasn't taking any chances. Just then Ava entered.

'I was just admiring your artwork, it's very good. I'm ready now. I'll go with the blonde.'

'Just one hour, Mr Winnie?'

'That's all I need.' Ava took him by the hand and led him to the room. 'You've chosen Julie, she's a good girl. '

'I wouldn't mind you either.' He gave her a big smile.

'No, Mr Winnie. I only do it for love. This is just a business for Franz and me. One day we might meet, and we'll see.' She opened a door, revealing a double bed and a mirrored ceiling.

'This'll do,' said Winnie.

'You may have a shower first if you like.'

The door opened and Julie entered.

Brian looked up at Franz. 'Do you mind if I smoke some pot?'

'Not in here,' replied Franz, 'we want to keep this place drug-free. We never know exactly who'll be coming through that door next.'

'How long do you stay open, Franz?'

'We're flexible. We try to close about six.'

'How long have you been open?'

Ava the madam walked in. 'You ask a lot of questions.'

Brian was caught off guard. 'Just making conversation. Don't worry, we're not the police.'

'Oh, I know that.' Ava added, 'You're the bikies. Why do you come to my house? Don't you run your own?'

'Not me. Some of the other boys do. It's not my go, we have a motorcycle shop.'

'What else do you boys get up to?'

'Now who's asking too many questions?' Brian said.

Ava laughed. 'Let me get you a drink. It's on the house.'

'Sounds alright to me!'

'Who is Mr Winnie?'

'He's the President of our Club and a partner in the motorcycle shop with me.'

'Is he married?'

'He's not the marrying type. Winnie's different.'

'In what way?'

'You'd have to get to know him. He's special.'

'Oh, I can see that,' Ava said, just as Winnie walked in.

'That didn't take long, Prez?'

'No, it's just what I needed, though.'

The buzzer sounded and Ava left to care for her new customers.

Big Kev strutted back smiling. 'That's the best root I've ever had!'

'You don't want Sandy to hear you saying that, mate,' Brian said.

'As long as you don't say anything to your missus, Brian, she won't find out.'

'Gina wouldn't say anything, Kev.'

In a stern voice Winnie added, 'Just don't say anything to her.'

'I won't, Prez.' They waited for Toothpick, who took his time.

'C'mon, let's go,' said Brian. 'I'll see you again, Franz.' Franz smiled; it almost looked warm. Ava spoke to some new customers of Middle Eastern appearance who were staring into the one-way window. Winnie winked at her as he walked out.

'Thank you for coming, gentlemen. You must come again.'

'It was our pleasure, Ava. You run a good joint here.'

'Thank you, Winnie. The door will close behind you.'

'You see, Kev, what sort of market is out there, mate? You should look at starting up out here too.'

'We've all been looking around. It's just convincing Sandy — she loves the Cross.'

'You don't have to move.'

'I know, Prez. Me and Ocker formed a company, so when they legalise it, we'll be ready.'

'They might take a few years before they do.'

'That's okay. We'll just carry on, and eventually instead of the pigs getting our tax, the government will. That's what I wanted you to see the Sergeant about. I'll talk to you about it later.'

The passengers piled in, Toothpick started up and they took off into the night.

'Get the heater on!' Big Kev yelled.

'You're just a big sheila, Kev,' said Winnie.

'And you've never had malaria.'

'Oh right, Kev.' Winnie had no idea how bad malaria could be.

'And neither have I, Prez.'

Winnie just glanced back and said dryly, 'You're a queer cunt!'

Toothpick turned on the fan full bore until the car warmed up and they drove back to the clubhouse in toasty warmth.

'We went to a new whorehouse in Prospect, Ocker,' said Kev.

'Any good?'

'Good girls and well set up. I didn't think there'd be a market but they had four girls, so it can't be too bad. They charge a good price, too. We should talk to Sandy about looking for sites out here, instead of concentrating on the city area. You know, spread it out a bit.'

'Who else is out the back, Ocker?'

'Just the Rat, Prez.'

'We need to talk. Let the nominees finish their game of pool, get them to clean up, then let them go. I'll go and wake up the Rat.'

Winnie opened the door to the back room and switched on the light. The Rat's eyes opened. He blinked furiously; you could almost hear his brain ticking over while he tried to figure out where he was. He stared at Winnie for a moment.

'G'day, Prez. I can't drink like I used to.'

'That's what heroin does to your liver, mate.'

'Prez, do me a favour, mate, will you? Don't mention that part of my life too much. I'm not proud of it.'

'It's a deal, Rat, as long as you don't tell anyone else about your fisherman mate. He could come in handy one day.'

'You're the only person I'd trust with the story, Prez.'

'Good, mate. Now, you've spoken with Ocker about starting up business again.'

'I have, Prez, but I haven't got enough for cash up-front.'

'You'll be right, we'll look after you. But you'll have to leave now, mate, we're locking up.'

'See you, Prez, and thanks for a good night. I love you blokes. See ya next week.'

'Right, first cab off the rank is the hash, Brian. How's it going?'

'None left, Prez. There hasn't been for a couple of weeks and I don't know how good the information is from the Sergeant, because Twister was telling me their hash is here, and we can buy off them this weekend. He was pretty positive that they'd be unloading it in the next couple of days.'

'The only thing I can say, Brian, is that the Sergeant has never been wrong. You know what he said — it might get here, but it won't hit the streets.'

'But Prez, if it does, we'll have no option but to buy from them, otherwise we'll lose our markets, and we don't want that. Our take might shrink a bit, but at least we'll keep our customers.'

'It's obvious they don't have it yet, so we'll just have to be patient. If they get it, we'll consider buying it from them.' The Prez paused in thoughtful silence. 'We've been paid our share of the hash money. Are you blokes happy with Brian as treasurer? I know I am.'

Ocker and Kev nodded approvingly.

'I hope you don't keep too many books, Brian?'

'No, Prez, I use a different book for each shipment and when we sell out I destroy it. I'm doing exactly what you wanted — Gina pays your share into your account at Mimi's father's bank.'

'Yeah, I know, Mimi paid almost eighty thousand from my account yesterday for my unit.'

'It's a good feeling, Prez. You'll know how I feel about my new home after you move into yours. When are you moving in?'

'Soon, I hope. Do we still have some grass left, Ocker?'

'About thirty pounds. Nestor's going good, Prez.'

'I hope he's doing the right thing by us?'

'He is, Prez. It all goes to Club members and they have no trouble moving it. He grows good pot, no seed or stem. A few members help him harvest.'

'Okay, next we have to learn how to cook speed and find a good spot to do it. I think we should take the advice Rastus gave us, rent something rural. We'll take the lease out under a bodgie name. Maybe Brian can take Gina and Kitty along with him so the real estate people think they're renting to a family.

'Now we're going to need a reliable cook, someone who can teach us how to do it. Ocker, can you get onto that?'

'I've been thinking, Prez … one of the girls from the escort business is finishing a degree in industrial chemistry. I'll have a quiet word.'

'Make sure you can trust her before you say too much.'

'I know, Prez. She comes from a good family and I have some photos of her I'm sure she wouldn't like her family to see.'

'That's the way, Ocker.'

'It was good to see the Rat. He used to move a lot of gear for us on the northern beaches. Do we give him credit, Prez?'

'He spoke to me about that, Ocker. What do you think?'

Big Kev stood. 'He gave us credit when we first started.'

'What do you say I give him six months' credit?' said Winnie. 'By then he should have a bank.'

'Yeah, that sounds fair enough,' Ocker said. 'Should I let him know, Prez? He's coming to see me for some grass next week.'

'Yeah, tell him he's got credit until he's cashed up.'

'I also told him that in the near future we'll have speed for sale. We'll just about have Sydney sewn up, with us out here in the west, Swannie on the Southside and Rat doing the Northside. If we have good quality, supply and price, our products will do the rest. If the Sergeant finds out about the speed, he'll want a bigger sling every month.'

Big Kev added, 'He'll find out and he's a greedy cunt.'

'It'd be better if we got in first and offered him extra. It makes sense if we tell him what we're up to. That way he knows to keep an ear open; it'll be cheaper in the long run.'

Brian made a mental note. 'How much will we offer him, Prez?'

'Let's wait and see how we go with the speed first of all — that's our priority. This is going to take a bit of cash to start up, for the chemicals, lab equipment and whatever else. We'll keep separate speed and pot books and use our own money to get it started.'

'How much, Prez?'

'I'm not too sure, maybe twenty-five grand each. You should all be cashed up.'

'I'm not travelling that good at the moment, Prez.'

'How come, Brian?' `

'Well, with the new home, I'm just about broke at the moment. That's why I want to know when the hash is coming, so I can make an earn.'

'That's okay, Brian, I'll put in for you.'

'Thanks, Ocker.'

'Don't worry, Brian, I'll just take it out of the first batch.'

'Your portable phone business must be going okay, Ocker?'

'To be honest with you, Prez, it's costing me at the moment. They're too big and don't work in a lot of places.'

'I told you that, you silly little cunt! You need a line for a phone to work.'

'I'm too far into it to pull out now.'

'How come?'

'I bought shares in the phone company. You're not Mimi's only customer, you know.'

'Okay,' said Winnie, getting back to business, 'everyone knows what they have to do, so let's get onto it. I'd like to have the lab set up and running within a month.'

'I don't know where Brian spends all his money, Kev,' Winnie said later. 'His house couldn't have cost him all his profits.'

'It's Gina, Prez. Her gambling habit. She pisses it away as soon as he makes it.'

'It's got fuck-all to do with us, Kev.'

Chapter 16

Brian wanted to expand. He'd heard the Harley family had bought the company back from AMF and had developed a new, reliable motor.

'Do we want to sell new bikes,' he asked, 'or keep doing custom bikes and parts?'

Selling custom work only meant money if they could get distribution rights for parts in Australia. Then they'd need to move into a highly visible location somewhere.

'Do we keep going the way we are, or do we go big?'

There were big dollars involved; everyone gave it due thought.

'I've never seen you so passionate about anything like this before, Brian.'

'It's just a great opportunity, Prez.'

'How do you expect to do it?'

'I have a list of suppliers in the States; I worked out who can supply the best quality parts to build a custom bike. Instead of doing repairs on bikes we'd be building custom bikes to order.'

'That'd be the go, Brian!' Big Kev liked the idea.

'And I can paint 'em,' said Ocker.

'That's the go, boys!' Brian was ecstatic.

'It sounds good, Brian, but you haven't told us how we're going to do it.'

'I'll go to the States, see the suppliers, sign contracts and get distribution rights, and if you blokes want to be in it we should set up a company. I'll do all the work. Trust me, if we only become a Harley Davidson dealer they'll tell us how to run our shop and we'd have to pay plenty to get the dealership. This way we only sell after-market parts. Everyone in?'

'Yes, Brian,' they chorused.

'Okay, Brian, see Johnnie Baker and get him to organise the paperwork,' said Winnie.

'How about we call it High Speed Custom Imports?'

'Yeah, that sounds good, Brian.'

The phone rang. Kev listened for a minute wordlessly then put down the phone.

'That was Sandy. The Tigers got busted with their hash! It's all over the front page of today's newspaper.'

The front page told the story in one big, black headline: 'Sydney Bike Gang Members Arrested in Major Narcotics Operation'. The report continued:

Three members of the Tigers motorcycle gang have been charged with possession of a large shipment of hashish. Police spokesman said of the haul: 'The arrest followed a combined Customs and New South Wales Police operation. Police followed the shipment from a cargo vessel in Darling Harbour to a warehouse at Mascot where police arrested three men for further questioning. Police expect more arrests.'

'Who'd they get, Kev?'

'No names yet, Prez. The Pig's information was spot on. I hope Customs missed our hash.'

Ocker called the Tigers clubhouse and Twister answered.

'Did you ring up to gloat? Well, you can get fucked!'

'Hold on a minute, mate!' Ocker said. 'I don't know what you're talking about, Twister. I've just rung to say thanks for coming to Jonesy's funeral. What are you on about?'

'Haven't you heard? They got Kero Ken and a couple of our members yesterday with a pile of hash. You can read about it in today's paper!'

Nearly pissing himself laughing, Ocker controlled himself enough to tell Twister, 'Fuck, I'm sorry to hear that, Twister. I'll talk to you soon.'

'Who'd they get?' Winnie asked.

'Kero Ken and some others.'

'Poor old Kero, hey? He has all the luck. Unless they give someone up, they'll be doing big time.'

'Kero won't give anyone up,' Big Kev said.

'The Hash King's behind this. I hope he doesn't do the same to us.' Big Kev sounded worried; they'd entered the big time now.

'Do you think Kero will get bail, Prez?'

'I can't imagine it, Kev. They got caught with a fair amount.'

'Why are you worried about him, Kev?'

'I remember the night he helped us up the Cross.'

'He's not a bad bloke. It's just a pity he's related to Twister.'

It was time for Winnie to go. He primed the motor, pushed the choke down a little and let it idle.

'What a night, mate. Can you believe the last twenty-four hours?'

'No, mate. I've got to think about it for a couple of days.'

Winnie engaged the clutch, kicked the bike into first gear, let off the clutch and roared to his mother's place for the last time. His brother Warren was watching men loading a small rental truck.

They shook hands; it had been a while. Warren had put on a few extra pounds, Winnie noticed.

'How're you going, brother?'

'Not too bad, Peter. I never thought I'd see this day. It was a good thing you bought that place up the coast for Mum. I thought she'd end up dying here.'

'She's got a lot of living to do yet, mate.'

'I know, Peter, but who'd have ever expected us to have enough money to do it? Your motorcycle shop must be doing alright!' Warren smiled at Winnie wryly. 'You're not doing drugs are you, mate?'

Winnie admitted to a bit of marijuana. He didn't want to supply too much information. He knew all too well what Warren was like. You couldn't tell him anything; he'd always tell the world.

'I just sell a few ounces, that's all, mate. I had to take out a loan to get Mum's place.'

'I wish I could do more to help her, Peter, but with three kids and one wage, it's hard.'

Winnie patted him on the shoulder. 'I know, Warren. Why don't you get your missus a job too?'

Winnie knew that suggestion would be fruitless; the lazy slut wouldn't get off her fat arse from watching the box unless she had to go to the fridge.

'Well, maybe it's not that bad, but close to it. It's too hard for her with the three kids — who never get to see their uncle, I might add. I'm going to save our bedroom furniture for my two boys. Their room will be like ours.'

'I don't think so,' Winnie said smiling. He remembered Warren's asthmatic wheezing. In the hot months, Winnie waved a towel to keep him cool until their father bought him an electric fan.

'Someone from the bank rang. Someone called Mimi? The way Mum told it, you were friends.'

'We are. Her old man owns a futures' traders. You go to an office and give them cash and they invest it in new ventures. Better returns.'

'It sounds high class to me, but if it works, why not?'

'I'm going inside to grab a few things, Warren.'

'Okay, Peter, I'll help these blokes load up.'

Winnie stuffed his clothes in his saddlebags and pulled out the cash hidden beneath his wardrobe, his emergency money, about ten thousand. He counted out five hundred dollars and put it in his pocket, grabbed his bags and walked out without looking back. He pulled out the five hundred. 'Here, take this, Warren.'

'I can't take this, Peter, you've done enough already.'

'Take it, mate; it's for your family. Give them a treat. I'm doing alright. I forgot I had it in my sock drawer!'

Warren pocketed the cash.

'Here, take this too.' Winnie passed over a bag of pot.

'I don't smoke that shit, Peter.'

'Try it one day when your missus is having a bad day. Go down the backyard and roll yourself a joint and see how you handle it. It's better than beer, plus it's good for your asthma. It helps clear your air passages. Fair dinkum! Would I lie to you, brother?'

'I've never understood you, Peter.'

'Don't try, mate.'

'Peter, how about making an effort to visit the wife and kids?'

'I will, mate, I promise.' Winnie shook hands then threw a leg over his bike and started it up.

'The boys want to see your Harley. They're Harley mad!'

'Seeya, mate!' Winnie rode down the road, his old street, for the last time. He thought they should keep some of these identical houses for future generations before they were bulldozed. Warren watched him ride up the street. One of the blokes helping load the furniture said he'd heard the Miners were bad bastards.

Warren replied firmly, 'They're only bad if people deserve it. Now let's finish loading and not another word, okay?' The bloke looked crestfallen.

Winnie rode to Stanmore and parked outside the real estate office. The owner's son walked out to greet him. 'I love your bike, Mr Winifred. I guess you're here to pick up the keys to your new place? Everything's ready. Come into the office and sign the paperwork and it's all yours. You can have the keys now.'

Winnie signed the contracts.

'I'll send these deeds to your solicitor.'

Winnie shook the young bloke's hand. 'Nice doing business with you.'

He picked up the keys, mounted his bike and headed for his new home on a quiet cul-de-sac lined with brick Federation-era homes. He pulled up outside his townhouse and unlocked the garage door. He rode in and locked up, then walked to the front door and pulled out the front door key. He was very conscious of entering his home for the first time and wasn't sure what he'd find. The last time he'd seen it the rooms were starkly empty. He opened the door and saw it was furnished. He and Mimi had spent a morning selecting things and somehow she'd managed to get it delivered and arranged in a few days. He pulled open the curtains at one of the front windows and noticed somebody peering at him from the house opposite.

He inspected each room. In the kitchen a vase of roses with a card sat on the bench. He hadn't seen a bunch of red roses for a long time; they made him think of Mrs Wright. He read the card.

Dear Peter, I took the liberty of having everything delivered yesterday and with the help of the delivery men, it was easy. Hope you like the flowers! See you tonight. Love, Mimi.

He opened the fridge; she'd stocked it with food and beer. What a little house mouse!

The previous day and night of partying began to catch up with Winnie. He stripped, turned on the shower and stood for ten minutes under the hot water. The memory of the whore the night before gave him a slight guilty pang. He thought about Mimi's unconditional love; he thought he would have to show her more respect, and promised himself he wasn't going to stray again. Mimi had put new linen on the bed and Winnie slept instantly. He awoke to the smell of frying bacon. In the kitchen Mimi held a spatula in one hand and shook the frying pan with the other. He grabbed her waist and kissed her neck.

'I love you, Mimi.' He'd said it without a second thought. He hadn't said that to anyone before.

She said nothing, showed no emotion apart from a raised eyebrow. She elbowed him aside. 'Come on, out of the way! Breakfast is ready. Sit down.' Her tone changed. 'There's only one thing I ask of you, Peter. If I move in, you'll have to promise me that I'm the only woman in your life. I don't want marriage or a ring; I just want you to be faithful.'

Winnie wondered how much she knew.

'I don't want any bullshit, just that commitment.'

'You've got it, Mimi. Just don't try to change me. You know what I am.'

'That's what I love about you, Peter.'

Food was the last thing on his mind. He turned off the stove, reached for her hand and led her into the bedroom. It was in the days of 'couldn't keep their hands off each other'. They lay on their backs gasping for breath after an athletic romp. He lit up a cigarette, then passed it to her.

'How'd you get in last night?'

'The real estate agent gave me a key. I explained what I was doing. The young real estate guy really liked you, Peter. You touch a lot of people. It's the good in you.'

'Don't make me blush.' He thought about the whore he was with last night. Mimi must be psychic.

He went to the window and pulled back the curtains and looked at the house across the street where he'd seen the curtains move the night before. An elderly woman watered her garden and every so often glanced at Mimi's Mercedes sports car.

'She must be the street gossip. I bet she'd love to know the score with us.' He watched the woman for a moment or two — she looked happy, so maybe she wasn't the street gossip after all.

'I've been looking forward to a ride today, Peter.'

'Come on, then, let's get ready. We can go up and visit my mother in Woy Woy.'

Winnie threw his saddlebags on the bed.

'Peter, look!' Mimi pointed at the new quilt and Winnie saw oil from his chain cover.

'Oh Jesus, Mimi, sorry.'

'You're hopeless!'

'I suppose most girls would go off their head.'

He dressed and pulled on his colours. Mimi looked drop-dead gorgeous in a red silk scarf and new black leather jacket and jeans with knee-length Italian boots. 'You look great. Been shopping?'

'I do it for you, Peter.'

He kissed her and sneaked in a pat on her backside.

Winnie rolled his bike out of the garage and Mimi drove her car in. While he waited he caught the eye of the lady living opposite. The woman waved and Winnie waved back.

Mimi held out a thick package. 'Can you carry this for me, please?'

'What is it?'

'Chocolates for your mother.'

Mimi waved to the woman and the woman waved back. They headed up the tollway to the Central Coast with Mimi looking as if she'd stepped off the runway at a fashion show. Winnie headed toward the bowls club where his mother played bingo. He pulled up outside. 'She should be finished soon.'

He gave Mimi the chocolates and they entered the club and signed the visitors' book.

Winnie asked, 'What's my new address?'

'12 Coopers Crescent, Stanmore.'

Winnie passed Mimi the pen.

'What's my address?' she asked him with a big grin.

'12 Coopers Crescent, Stanmore.' Mimi wrote it down and Winnie took her by the hand and headed towards his mother. He sat behind her until she noticed him and shouted out his name. The bingo caller thought he had a winner. All eyes went to his mother.

'Sorry,' she said. All eyes went back down to the cards, until a lady shouted 'Bingo!' His mother threw in her ticket and Winnie kissed and hugged her.

'You remember Mimi, Mum?'

'How can I forget her?'

Mimi embraced her and handed her the chocolates. His mother's friends watched admiringly as she unwrapped the hand-made Belgian chocolates and immediately popped one into her mouth. Mimi politely declined when offered.

'How have you been, Peter? You're looking healthy and happy.'

'I saw Warren at the house yesterday.'

'Yes, he told me last night on the phone. You're a good brother to him. You should try and see more of him and his family. That's all the family you have.'

'I've got the Club too, Mum.'

His mother patted him on the knee. Looking at Mimi she said, 'Don't worry, love, he'll grow out of it.'

Winnie smiled at Mimi and she beamed back at him.

While waiting at the bar for drinks, he watched his mother and Mimi talking. As he approached the table the women stopped talking.

'I'm not interrupting anything, am I?' He put the drinks down.

'Not at all, Peter.' Mimi stifled a laugh. She looked like the cat that had swallowed the canary.

After lunch they said their goodbyes.

'Now, don't forget about Warren.'

'I won't, Mum.'

They walked out to the bike. Mimi asked, 'Why don't you see more of your brother?'

'Not you too! It's simple: we don't have much in common and, if you must know, I just don't like his missus.' He'd never addressed her so abruptly. On the ride back to Sydney he felt bad about it and when they got home he took her in his arms and whispered, 'I love you.'

The next morning in bed he turned to Mimi. 'Is it okay if we go to Brian and Gina's party today in your Mercedes?'

'What's mine is yours, Peter. You can drive if you like.'

Driving the Mercedes proved a real luxury. It felt as if the car was flying, and he almost missed the turn-off to Brian's new home near the top of Snow's Mountain. The area was almost unrecognisable after being covered with dream homes. Brian's place was a huge brick pile and Winnie suddenly understood why Brian had no money. Winnie parked and passed the keys to Mimi. 'Just in case I have a few drinks too many.'

Mimi went to the boot and lifted out a wrapped gift. 'Just a little something for their new home.'

'You're unreal.' Winnie relieved her of the box.

Little Kitty ran out. 'Uncle Peter!' He scooped her up with his free arm while she wrapped her arms around his neck, kissed him and then looked around at Mimi. 'Is this your girlfriend?'

'Yes, Kitty, this is Mimi. But you're still my girlfriend too.'

Kitty held Mimi and Winnie's hands and led them out to the thirty or so people gathered around the barbecue.

'I'm so glad you were able to come, Mimi!' Gina hugged Mimi, who handed her the present.

'A little house-warming gift for your home.'

'Thanks! Come and have a look around.' Gina smiled proudly. 'Brian, can you introduce Peter around?' The women headed into the house and young Kitty followed.

The distinctive sound of approaching Harleys rumbled in the distance. 'That'll be Kevvie and Ocker.'

Brian introduced Winnie to Gina's cousin from Brisbane as the bikes pulled in.

Brian rushed off. 'I'll be back in a minute, Prez. I don't want them to park in the driveway. They'll drip oil!'

Winnie made small talk with the cousin until Brian came back.

'Look at this!' Brian turned towards a setting sun that backlit the distant ranges and coloured the sky gold. 'But if you look east it's a terracotta valley.' Winnie had played in that valley as a kid but he couldn't remember exactly where. They stood and stared until Big Kev, Sandy and Ocker arrived.

'Hello, sexy!' Sandy kissed Winnie.

'How're you going, madam?'

'You're a cheeky bastard.' They hugged, and she whispered, 'I hear you were out lately. Now where was it? Um, yes, that's right! Over at Prospect, a place run by Ava.' She paused for. effect, then reassured him, 'My lips are sealed.'

'I know, Sandy.' He thought about the R and R Yanks she'd seen while Kevvie was in Vietnam. He put his arm around her and walked her to the boys.

'Come on, Sandy, let's have a trip down memory lane. We're trying to work out where our track was.'

'What track?' Sandy stared at the sea of terracotta roofing tiles.

'That's where we raced our motorbikes when we were kids, the four originals.'

'Is this the first time you've been back? How do you feel seeing the valley covered in houses?

Kev just stared.

Brian broke it up. 'Come on, don't get all sentimental on us. What about a drink?' The consensus was that a drink was a fine idea.

That Sandy knew about their night at the whorehouse in Prospect amazed them; they had no idea how she'd found out.

'Fuck, I think it's better we don't tell Brian. He'll shit himself!' Kev said.

Ocker added, 'You know he made us move our bikes from the driveway onto the street. I reckon before we're allowed in the house he'll make us take our boots off. He might not even let us in.' He cackled at the thought.

Brian urged them to meet the other guests and Gina's parents and they exchanged pleasantries. Brian's mother and father had never liked Winnie and had always blamed him for whatever trouble he and Brian got up to.

Big Kev, Winnie and Ocker ended up talking to Gina's cousin, Bobby. 'I've heard so much about you boys from Gina.'

'All good, I hope?' Winnie winked.

'All good. Your Club has a pretty good reputation up our way. I'm in a club in Brisbane, the Sharks. We started six months ago in the Moreton Bay area.'

'Any trouble from other clubs?'

'The Tigers from Sydney just started a Chapter and we had a few problems, but it's all sorted now. Their President, Twister, came up and we talked.'

'We know Twister,' Big Kev said. 'If you stand up to him he'll back down. Was a big bloke called Kero Ken with him?'

'He was.'

'Well, you won't see him for a bit, he just got busted with a huge load of hash. Customs and the pigs are making a big deal out of it.'

Bobby joined the boys in Brian's garage. It was immaculate, with all Brian's tools neatly arranged and everything in its place. His Harley sat under a dust cover. Another bike in the corner was also covered neatly with a sheet: his original BSA 125 cc Bantam. They lifted the cover and revealed the fully restored bike, its tyres fresh, its chrome glistening. At that moment Winnie wished he had kept his too.

Brian divvied up speed on a small mirror. 'Here, you go first, Bobby.' He held out a rolled-up note.

'I haven't had this before,' Bobby said, with a hint of apprehension. 'What's it like?'

'It gets you cranking!' Brian quoted from experience.

Bobby stuck the tube up his nose and snorted the line in one. His eyes watered almost immediately. 'Whoa! That's the go.'

The boys all had their line and walked around the garage and gawked at the posters of long-ago bike races.

'Do you do any business in Brisbane, Bobby?' Winnie's mind was always on the job.

'A fair bit of pot, but not much else. There isn't much of anything up our way.'

'We'll be able to look after you in a week or two and you'll get a good deal.'

'How many members do you have?'

'Fifteen. We don't want to get too big, just tight.'

'That's the way,' Big Kev said.

The smell of the barbecue drew them to the table where Mimi and Sandy met the boys with empty plates.

Kitty asked Winnie, 'Can I sit with you, Uncle Peter?'

Winnie looked at Gina. 'Of course you can,' Gina answered for him.

Kitty looked up at them confidently. 'I like Mimi, Uncle Peter.'

'So do I, Kitty.' He squeezed Mimi's free hand.

After dinner Winnie went and located the trotting track where it had all started. The track had more stalls, floodlight towers and new grandstands; it was a far cry from the old country track he'd known. He wondered who collected the horseshit. He tried to work out the delivery route they'd taken as kids. The roads looked the same, just with a lot more houses. He could still make out some landmarks quite easily and was sure it was still a long push up the hill. He wondered if Mrs Wright and her roses were still alive. He found Joe the Ukrainian's house. If he'd been a concentration camp guard, he'd likely gotten away with it. Winnie had never heard of one being caught out there. The Housing Commission estate was intact. He'd only ever had a few customers for horseshit in there: they were all too poor. Practically the whole neighbourhood had given him a hard time, but Winnie'd always remembered someone's advice: 'Where there's muck, there's money.' He and Brian must have looked funny pulling a billycart stacked with sugar bags full of wet horseshit. He remembered the smell and tried to place where he'd smelled it recently. Then it came to him: the smell of the cigars Rastus smoked!

Mimi walked up behind him. 'Memories?'

'Good ones. They shaped my life. I was thinking of Mrs Wright and her roses.'

Big Kev and Ocker started laughing.

'What are you laughing at?' Winnie asked.

'Running Twister off into the bushes,' said Kev. 'We just found the spot!'

* * *

The visitors touring the house resembled a conga line. Brian stood at the door and asked the boys to take off their boots. Ocker said nothing but looked as if he wanted to. Brian got no opposition from the boys. He gave them a running commentary, walking from room to room. The tour lasted a little too long so Ocker and Winnie hung back and darted down a hall leading outdoors. They grabbed beers and sat down on lawn chairs.

'Prez, while I have a quiet minute, I want to tell you I found a final year chemistry student who reckons he could cook for us. He lives with one of my university girls, the one I have the naughty photos of. I saw him last night. He reckons it'll be a piece of piss for him. He wants to make enough to go overseas and it's easier than driving taxis. He's prepared to show you how to do it as part of the deal. Whaddya reckon?'

'How much does he want?'

'Ten grand a cook.'

'Do you reckon it's worth that much?'

'Fucking oath, Prez! We could make twenty times that with every batch.'

'Tell him we have to meet; if he checks out, he's got the job. Get him to give you a list of everything we need.'

'He's working on that now.'

'Well done, Ocker.'

Brian came out of the house. 'I won't be at the shop tomorrow, Prez. Gina and I are going to look for a lab.'

'Ocker found a cook, so it looks like we're into a new business, mate.'

Winnie and Mimi said their goodbyes, and little Kitty ran over with a final request. 'Can I come and stay at your place one night?'

Mimi bent over to her. 'Come and stay for the weekend, when your parents are in America. If that's all right with you, Brian?'

'Kitty's staying with my parents. I'm sure it wouldn't be a problem.'

Mimi drove while Winnie relaxed. 'Gina told me you're changing the direction of the bike shop.'

'It was Brian's idea to get distribution rights for custom parts. I suppose you told her that you convinced Brian to diversify?'

'I didn't want to spoil her party, Peter.'

'She won't find it a picnic waiting around in hotel rooms while he's in meetings.'

'Oh no, she's not doing that! She told me that she's going to Las Vegas while he works.'

'That could be a problem.'

'Why's that, Peter?'

'She has a gambling problem.'

Mimi couldn't imagine what Winnie meant and let it go.

Before Brian and Gina left for the States they found a perfect house to set up their lab, an hour out of the city. Gina hung nice curtains and made it look homey. Winnie, Kev and Ocker went out to see it at night. Ocker brought the lab equipment and everything except for the hard-to-get pseudoephedrine. Rastus had that end covered — it would be here in a few days.

'When can the cook start work?' asked Winnie.

'As soon as we need him,' said Ocker.

'Well, line it up for the weekend. You and Big Kev bring him out, and blindfold him so he doesn't know where he's going. He's not to leave. You stay here with him, so he can teach you how to do the cooking. Bring him out on Saturday night and I'll make sure I'm here, so I can have a talk with him.'

'You haven't heard from the Pig yet, Prez?'

'You know what he's like. He only meets me when he has something. Don't worry, he'll ring.'

'I see Kero Ken is going to wear the importation charge, Prez,' said Kev. 'I knew he wouldn't give anyone up.'

'Yeah, Kev, he's a good man. Twister's lucky to have him. I hope he looks after him.'

'Twister only ever looks after himself,' Big Kev replied with a sneer.

The Saturday newspapers reported that Sorrow and his boys had been committed to stand trial for murder. Bail was refused. The police were worried they'd intimidate any witnesses but there were no witnesses the cops could find. Winnie wondered if they'd get off.

Ocker brought the blindfolded student cook out to the house on the Saturday night. Winnie removed the blindfold. The kid tried to focus in the light. He held up a hand to shade his eyes and found himself staring into Winnie's cold eyes.

'Look at me closely, Mr Cook. If you ever say one word about this to anyone, my eyes will be the last thing you'll ever see.' Winnie pulled out a

.38 Special from his back pocket, pointed it at the kid's head and mouthed 'BOOM!' before putting it away.

Big Kev broke the silence. 'This is Steve, Prez.'

Winnie smiled and reached out his hand to Steve, who shook it firmly. 'I don't want to scare you too much, mate, but security is number one.'

'I understand. I'm only in it for the money. This is my final year. Doing this will finance my dream of touring the world.'

Big Kev and Ocker brought in the supplies.

'What about your degree?'

'I'm almost finished.'

Winnie met Ocker carrying in cases of beer and two bottles of bourbon.

'No piss in here, put it back in the car.'

'Come on, Prez, I'll be here all week!'

'I don't want any accidents.'

Ocker turned to Big Kev. 'He won't let me have any piss.'

Big Kev laughed and put down the groceries.

'Come on, Steve, let's make sure you have everything you need.' Winnie pulled out a piece of paper and ticked each item off. 'Yes, it's all there. Good, let's go and check the glassware.'

Steve unpacked the burners, full gas bottles and tubing and told Winnie they'd have as good a lab as at the university.

'I'll drink to that!' Ocker said.

Winnie clapped Ocker on the shoulder. 'You've done a real good job here, mate. Top quality everything!'

'When are you going to start, Steve?'

'The quicker the better, Prez. We can set up in the morning.'

'That's what I like to see — progress. How long will it take for the first batch to be ready?'

'The first one will be a little slow, but if you come back on Wednesday I'll have five pounds for you. If you cut that five times, you'll have thirty pounds.'

'Then we'll be counting the money!' Ocker smiled at the thought.

'Not too soon, mate. The cooking is one thing. Then we have to find a market.'

'You won't find that hard, Prez,' Steve said. 'The university runs on it.'

'No, we have our own people and you're not to take any product and sell it. You can have some personal, but you can't be known. We're paying you enough. We'll see you on Wednesday.' Winnie and Kev walked out to the car.

'That was pretty heavy with the cook in there, Prez.'

'He has to know that he's not playing with boy scouts, Kev.'

'Yeah, I know, Prez. How often do you think he'll have to do a cook?'

'I don't know, Kev. It'll all depend on how long it takes to get rid of it. We have everyone waiting for it. I'm going home now, I'll see you on Monday. With Brian in the States and Ocker out at the lab, it's important that you and I keep the shop looking busy.'

Winnie opened for business on Monday morning and worked at the front desk. A steady flow of customers ordered parts or picked them up. He enjoyed the contact. The business had increased by almost fifty per cent over their first year and Harleys were becoming popular; if Brian's plan to specialise in custom bikes came off they'd need bigger premises. Everything would be legal; no more stolen bikes. Swannie turned up late in the afternoon with his girl. She was gorgeous, a stunner. Winnie walked out to greet them.

'This is my girl, Kim. We've just been for a ride. We thought we'd drop in and say hello.'

'Hello Kim, call me Winnie.'

Swannie asked Kim to buy him a packet of cigarettes at the shop on the corner.

As soon as Kim was out of earshot Swannie got down to business. 'Any news on the hash?'

'Still heard nothing as yet. It shouldn't be too long but we're going to have the speed ready this week, mate. It'll be here all the time. We won't have to rely on anyone when we have production in full swing.'

'When can I pick it up?'

'Thursday. It's already going to be cut, just don't jump on it and you'll do all right.'

'How much is it?' asked Swannie.

'Ten grand a pound. That's a fair price. There's enough in it for everyone to make an earn. If you sell it in ounces for a thousand per ounce you'll make six grand a pound.'

'You've got it all worked out, Prez.'

'It's business, Swannie; that way your boys can make a quid.'

Swannie's new girl bounced back carrying the cigarettes. Winnie couldn't resist.

'Not a bad set of titties, Swannie!'

'Yeah, they're not bad, Prez.'

Kim handed Swannie his cigarettes then wandered around the shop and pulled out a t-shirt from a display. 'How does this look, babe?' she asked.

'Great, would you like it?

'Yes, please.'

'Looks like you have a sale!'

Winnie folded it and bagged it and gave it to Kim, and Swannie paid.

'We're going to sell after-market parts and build choppers,' said Winnie. 'No more working on old bikes. Brian is in the States nailing down distribution rights for suppliers like Sands, Paughco, Jammer frames and whatever else he can organise. Maybe we'll do tyres, too. We're already looking for a bigger shop.'

A sly grin appeared on Swannie's face. 'We're off now, Winnie. I'm getting a present from Kimmie when we get home.'

'You're a horny bastard!'

'Aren't we all?'

Winnie waved Swannie off, his balls tingling in anticipation of getting home to collect his own special present.

On the Wednesday night Winnie and Big Kev drove out to the lab. They discussed how they would sell the speed, in ounces or pounds.

'It all depends, Kev. With our boys I think we should just do ounces. If the Redbacks still want it, we'll sell it to them and Gina's cousin in pounds. I told Swannie ten grand a pound. Any other clubs it'll be twelve. It's going to be good quality, so they'll still do alright.'

'I don't know about the Redbacks,' said Kev. 'Ocker already arranged it with them, but most of them are in jail. '

'They'll beat the charges. They're just trying to break them up, with all the bullshit charges.'

'Have you got the money for the cook?'

'Yeah, it's in the glove box.'

They arrived at the house and Ocker met them eagerly. 'Am I glad to see you! I haven't slept for two days, I've got to get out of here! It's sending me mad! It's the fumes. I should have worn a mask like Steve. I won't make that mistake again!'

Winnie coughed immediately. 'Fuck! Leave the front door open. I see what you mean!'

'Did you bring the piss back, Prez?'

'No, I don't have it. Where'd you put it?'

'In my van.'

'Well, it's still there.'

'Fuck, I'm a silly cunt!' Ocker returned with a bottle of bourbon. 'Anyone want a drink?'

'No, you have one, mate. It looks like you deserve one!'

'Thanks, Prez.' Ocker took a long slug. 'Ah, that's slowed me down a bit.' The boys laughed.

'And where's Steve?'

'He's just packing everything away. How often will we need him, anyway?'

'We'll see how long it takes to move it. Do you think you can make it yet?'

'No, it's very technical. I'll need to do a few more cooks with him before I'm confident of giving it a go myself.'

Winnie and Kev headed to the kitchen where Steve was cleaning the equipment. He wore a mask, a lab coat and rubber gloves and looked the part. He nodded and mumbled something under his mask.

'Ocker tells me you're finished.'

Steve pointed at the speed in a large glass flask.

Kev set the scales down on the table. 'It doesn't look like speed.' The beige crystal appeared moist.

'You probably haven't seen it before it's been cut. This is pure shit. Number one.'

Winnie took over and weighed the result. 'There's just over five pounds.'

He grabbed a spoon and adjusted the weight to five pounds. The extra quarter of an ounce he bagged and handed to Steve.

'That's your personal stash. Don't sell it.'

Ocker made some lines. 'Do you want to try some, Prez?'

'Why not?'

'You can't snort it yet, it needs to dry out. You'll have to eat it.'

They took turns in tasting the crystal.

'Fuck! That tastes like shit! Give me the bourbon!'

'Do you want some, Kev?'

'Fucken oath! Anything that tastes that bad must be good for you.' Kevvie aped Winnie's facial expressions; it was bitter and its effects were almost immediate.

Winnie gave the ten grand to Steve. 'Best to count it in front of us, that way there's no problems.'

Steve counted into thousand lots until he had ten piles laid out.

'A pleasure doing business with you.'

'Now, Steve. What's the best way of cutting this?'

'Get a big blender. It's best to go with an industrial one, they're pretty cheap. Go with this ratio: one pound of base to five pounds of glucose. Mix it up properly and bingo, six pounds of good quality street speed. You'll end up with thirty pounds, that should give you a good return.'

'Yeah, and we take the risk. Now, Steve, when we need you again, are you up for it?'

'I'll do it as many times as you need until the end of the year.'

'Ocker will be right by then, anyway. He's a quick learner, so you better be a good teacher. And Ocker, don't forget to blindfold Steve when you leave, as a precaution.'

Big Kev was revving off his head. 'I've never had pure speed before. Shit, I feel like I'm going to have a heart attack!'

'You'll be right, Kev. Have a Valium when we get home. At least we know how good it is.'

'How are you feeling, Prez?'

'Just like you, mate. We'll stash this in a lock-up near the shop and I want only us to know about it. I'll bring my blender from home and we'll mix it up there tomorrow because I want to move it soon. I'll pick up some glucose on the way in tomorrow.'

In three weeks they moved thirty pounds. It was easy getting money; the hard part was making the money clean and legal. It was good having the Gregson bank on their side, but the banking laws were changing and in future they'd have to be more creative. It was a good thing they had Mimi's early advice, but hiding hundreds of thousands in bundles of twenties and fifties proved harder.

Brian had good news the morning he got back. It was the longest Brian and Winnie had ever been apart except for their time in different reform schools. 'How'd you go on the business side?'

'I got distribution rights from enough suppliers to build a complete bike, except for the motor, which we can get here through Fraser's. I also had a look at a few chopper shops and that gave me some good ideas for the new shop.'

'Did you go to Disneyland?' Big Kev asked with a cheesy grin.

'I'll show you the photos, Kev. I haven't told you everything yet, though. This is the bonus from our trip — Gina had a big win at a casino in Las Vegas.'

'How big?'

'A hundred and eighty thousand American dollars!' The boys whistled. They were rolling in it. 'Gina's at the bank now converting the casino cheque to Australian. I reckon she'll get $220,000. Did you get the lab up yet, Winnie?'

'Too right, and we sold the first batch already and Ocker's off tonight again with the cook.'

'Now that we're all together,' Winnie got their attention, 'I saw the owner of the building where our shop is. He owns three buildings adjoining ours and he's prepared to sell to us. I reckon we should buy them all, gut 'em and turn 'em into one big shop. It'll be just the right size for what Brian proposes we do. What do you boys think? We wouldn't have to change our address.'

The boys nodded; it all made sense, and having cash helped. 'I was going to see Mimi and get her to organise a loan for us, but I have a better idea. What do you reckon, Brian? We use Gina's windfall to buy it in all our names and we pay her cash from our drug money.'

Brian looked worried. 'I'll have to ask her, Prez.'

'It was your money that won it, don't forget. Just tell her that the money's going into something you really want. It just makes it simpler for us to buy an asset using clean money.'

'I know, I know,' Brian replied. 'I'll talk to her tonight.'

Ocker left to pick up the cook. He waved goodbye and disappeared, carrying a huge box with supplies for the week.

Brian laid out papers all over his desk. 'I've got all the documents that I've signed with all our new suppliers from the States. I've also got an appointment with Johnny Baker this afternoon. I want him to have a look at them for us, make sure they're all legally binding.'

'Good idea, Brian. Anyway, we don't need you here. I like playing shopkeeper.' Winnie smiled.

Brian left, and as the roar of his bike faded Big Kev and Winnie chatted.

'That'll work out good, Prez, if Gina can put up the cash. If she only ever does one good thing for him, I hope this is it.'

'He might just put his foot down with her. He really wants a chopper shop. He can get what he wants, if he wants it enough. I've seen it all his life. He just lets her run the ship. He likes it that way.'

'I suppose you're right, Prez. I guess she was lucky enough to win it.'

'If you win big, Kev, you eventually have to lose big. I just hope Brian can afford it when she does.'

'Well, this isn't getting any work done. I'm going to pick up the tools.'

Winnie tried to envisage the layout with the adjoining shop space. Big ideas flashed though his mind until he heard the phone ringing.

'Is that you, Peter?' Winnie recognised the Sergeant's voice. 'How about dinner tonight? Eight o'clock, same place.'

The hash must have landed. Winnie whispered to Kev, 'The Pig just called. I'll meet him tonight. He sounded cheerful.'

Chapter 17

The Pig sat at their usual table at Fritz's, which afforded a clear view of the entrance. They exchanged pleasantries.

'So, I hear your opposition got involved in that hash importation business and they're going down for a while.'

'But you knew about that all along. It was a set-up.'

'No, they were just stupid and they dealt with the wrong people.'

'Why didn't you tell me that the Tigers were involved? Didn't you trust me?'

'It wasn't your Club,' said the Pig. 'That's our deal. It wouldn't have made any difference, would it? You wouldn't have told them, would you?'

'No.'

'Well, don't worry about it. That's business. It had to happen the way it did and now you're back in business again.'

'Are you ready to order, gentlemen? I recommend the special this evening.' It sounded good in Italian so they both ordered it and Tony left them.

'When can we pick the hash up? People are screaming for it.'

'Soon, but I don't know how much longer we can bring it in, Winnie. Customs is toughening up and they're not telling the New South Wales coppers much.'

'Don't they trust you, Sarge?'

The Pig just looked at Winnie and gave him a knowing smile.

'I just might be able to help you there, Sarge. I have a mate who has a mate.'

'Yeah, yeah, Winnie. Everyone has a mate.'

'No, this is fair dinkum, if you're interested.'

'Go on, Winnie.'

'This bloke owns a trawler and has done a few loads of Buddha sticks.'

A light went on in the Sergeant's eyes. 'So that's how it's coming in!' The Sergeant had heard of the Buddha sticks; Sydney had been swamped with them for a few months, and kids all over the city went off their heads on the strongest dope ever.

'Anyway, he knows the drill, he has the boat and he can do the job. Worth a thought?'

Tony placed their meals before them, ground pepper onto the pasta and took off. The Sergeant waited for Tony to leave then he poured a line of salt on the table. Winnie wondered just what the fuck he was up to.

'I knew a bloke who snorted a line of salt like this. Had a headache for a week. They told him it was speed. He reckoned it was the best speed he'd ever had. We called him "Salty" after that. The point is, Winnie, if you manufacture and distribute speed, I have to know.'

Winnie's eyes narrowed and he stared at Burrows. 'I don't have to ask your permission to do anything.'

'No. You're quite right, there. You don't, but when you're doing powder you get attention. They're bringing younger men into the squad, a bunch of bible-bashing zealots. You'd be advised never to give them a brown envelope, 'cos the little turds would go straight to Internal Affairs and dob on ya. I have a mate in there, and he keeps me informed.' He looked pretty satisfied with that. 'I'm still in charge, but you have to be careful. I know you're making a good whack out of speed, so let's say we put my retainer up to five grand a week.' He blew the line of salt off the table. 'Your business could go like that if you don't use your head. That's why you'll pay me. It's business, Winnie. I have to pay my mate in Internal Affairs and sling some of the boys in the squad. It's not all for me.' Winnie went back to his dinner, thinking that Burrows was not as tough as he thought he was.

'What do you know about the Redbacks' case?'

'They've all been committed to stand trial for affray and some for murder.'

Winnie, frustrated, snapped. 'I know that! What about the case itself? Have they got much to go on?'

'Fuck-all, Winnie. Most will walk; it's just become too political. The government wants to look tough on crime. In a year's time, it'll all be over. They're on remand now. Like I said, they'll all walk; there's just no evidence that'll stand up in court.'

'That's good to hear.'

'What are they to you, anyway, Winnie? Are they aligned to your club?'

'We align with nobody, they're just mates. Have you heard anything more on that task force investigating bikies?'

'No, those blokes went to the Federal Police force. I have a mate in there who told me that bikies are not their targets yet. You'll have to expect it one day though. You'll have to pay extra for that info — it's a Federal issue and they don't miss a trick.'

Winnie leaned forward. 'It's like a little club, the Bent Coppers' Club.' Then he changed the topic. 'How come you said you knew we were manufacturing speed before?'

'Just a guess, Winnie. Your blokes started selling it, therefore I assumed you were. It's just a copper's way of thinking. That's all. I don't care if you are or not. The hash should be available in a day or two. We'll use similar arrangements for the pick-up, okay? I'll call you with a place and time.'

'Ocker knows the drill.'

'Good.' The Pig finished and glanced at his wristwatch. 'I've got to go now. We've got a job on tonight. It's your shout for the meal. I'll talk to you soon.' He waved to Tony as he left the restaurant.

At the Friday night meeting at the Club — affectionately called 'church' — all the members turned up. They included truck drivers, handy for interstate deliveries, a solicitor not used for Club business and a catering manager. Nestor was back from his marijuana cultivation mission and looked sharp.

Ocker, back from the most recent cook, delighted in showing Winnie and Brian his newest mobile telephone. Everyone was animated and the music blared so Ocker spoke louder to be heard. 'This is the new model I picked up today, Winnie.' He held out his mobile phone for inspection. 'It's a Nokia, smaller than my other one, but it's still a brick! Next time I go out to the lab, try calling me in the taxi and then you'll see how convenient they can be.'

Ocker wrote the number on a card and handed it to Winnie, who had no interest in gadgets or mobile phones. Winnie winked at Kev and pulled him aside for a quiet word.

'Kev, Rastus is moving back to Melbourne. Whatever trouble he had down there has been sorted. They're going to reopen their clubhouse and we talked about taking a Club run down there while we're fitting out the new chopper shop. He wants us to attend the reopening. There's just one thing: Spike's not going back. He likes Sydney too much. That's not going to cause any problems for you, is it, Kev?'

Kev said no. Spike had turned out to be a good, knowledgeable asset to the shop.

'He'll still be a Commando but he likes building choppers, so he can still work for us. Anyway, that's not the main reason he's staying — he found a girl.'

Kev knew about the girl; he was glad Spike had decided to stay.

Brian weighed in. 'Spike has some great ideas on building choppers. Our custom parts side could make us the number one chopper shop in Australia.'

Winnie spoke to Brian. 'You'll have to build me number one and I'll design it.'

'Sure, Prez, mate's rates for you.'

'I just heard from the Mario brothers. They're coming around later for a drink. It'll be good to repay them for helping us out at the nightclub.'

'Yeah, I liked those blokes, even if they are wogs,' Big Kev said.

'We should put it to the boys at the meeting about going to Melbourne, Prez,' said Brian.

'I intend to.'

Big Kev boomed out, 'Meeting starts in five minutes!'

Brian collected fees. Winnie took the floor. 'You know how close we've become to the Commandos. They're moving back to Melbourne and they've invited us to the reopening of their clubhouse next month. I thought it would be a good idea to have a Club run to attend the celebrations. What say you?'

Most of the boys were pretty excited. Some had never been out of Sydney.

It was agreed unanimously: they'd go.

'I'll let Swannie and his boys know,' said Winnie. 'The next item on the agenda's pretty important. Now we're selling the speed, everybody has to be much more careful. The pigs are getting even heavier on the powder, much more than the green. You can't just sit around in the pub, selling grams, as some of you do. I'm aware of what you're doing, and if you keep carrying on like that you're going to attract attention. Benny's one of them.'

All eyes turned to Benny. 'Don't worry, Benny. You're not in the shit. You just have to change your ways. Everyone does. No more selling drugs — and I mean *any* drugs — while wearing your colours. No selling to people you don't know. Form your own circle of dealers and don't stray. Only sell ounces. If anyone enters your circle and wants a pound, fuck him off straight away. I bet you he'd turn out to be a narc. We don't need the Club name involved; we still have a lot of members who don't do the biz. If you happen to get done wearing Club gear to the lock-up we're all fucked. Does anyone have a problem with that?'

Kev boomed out, 'If I find out anyone's still doing it, they'll have me to deal with! Is that clear, Benny?'

'Yes, Sarge.'

Benny had been a member for a few short months and hadn't yet seen Big Kev go off, but he'd heard about it. He shrank into his seat.

'And that's all for tonight. Meeting closed.'

It was a full moon with a good feel to it. Boys laughed and bullshitted each other around the bar.

'Ocker, how are you going with the cooking, mate?'

'Well, Steve reckons I'm ready to do it by myself. Just in case, he's prepared to come while I'm doing it, but I need a couple of assistants.'

'Do you have anyone in mind, Ocker?'

'Toothpick?'

'I'll talk with Kevvie and Brian first. There shouldn't be any problem. He's done the right thing so far. We might have to pay him a bit more than the uni student because he knows how much we make out of it. We'll give him twenty a cook, and we'll do about twenty a year.'

'What if he gets greedy, Prez?'

'Let's not think like that. We'll try trusting him first. I'll put it to him later. Have you been looking after the Rat?'

'Yeah, he's right, Prez. He's putting together a new network and doing about four or five ounces of speed a week and a few pounds of the green. He's just waiting on the hash.'

'Well, it's here, mate. I saw Burrows the other night and told him about Rat's mate with the trawler up north. I need to speak with Rat about it. Let's see if he's been bullshitting us or not because there might be a good job for the bloke to bring in some hash. According to the Pig, things are starting to tighten up on the docks with Customs.'

'When do we take delivery, Prez?'

'Same deal as last time. I'll let you know where and when; we give them the money and you pick up the truck. If you think it's off, don't go near it.'

'Don't worry, Prez. I won't.'

* * *

The Mario Brothers turned up. They were not easy to miss: two massive Italian boys dressed in white shirts and black pants and shoulders a pick handle wide.

'You've got a great clubhouse here, Winnie.' They followed Winnie past a glass case displaying a picture of Jonesy doing a burnout.

'That's one of our mates, killed by a red light runner a few months ago.'

The Mario Brothers stopped and checked out the commemoration, and a board covered with pictures of people having fun at past parties.

Winnie turned to the Marios. 'This Club is where the money is, with people drinking and having fun, and it's even better if you own the bar.'

'Then you're in the money!' Mario one said.

'What have you got in mind, boys?'

'The breweries are selling off pubs. There's a few that aren't worth much; we'd be looking to transfer the licences to other pubs. But we need investors.'

'Do you have money?'

'What bank would lend two wogs with no assets the money to buy a pub? We can't even get a proper interview! We were hoping you'd be the bank. We don't want to buy one pub — we want three, and we know which ones we want. We're hoping to get them at a good price. You'd be the investor and we'd give you an equal share. We'll run the pub and nightclub side of it. We've got enough cash to buy one now but you'd have to fund the other two, and maybe some of the refurbishment work. We estimate two hundred grand.'

'Where are they?'

'Oxford Street in the city and one in Balmain.'

'They're not great areas.'

'Not yet, Winnie, but they will be soon. Sydney's changing; everything is changing. Look at you, Winnie. We knew you'd get on; we remember Brother Michael dragging you around by the neck and banging your head against the blackboard and trying to humiliate you by hanging you on the hat peg. He expected you to start howling and crying but you never did. It was funny but you were tougher than he was!'

'You blokes remember that?'

They nodded.

'Now, if I'm getting this right I'll have no say in the joints, but I'm still an equal partner?'

'All depends on what you want to have a say in, Winnie. This is our passion. Come with us; we know what we're doing.'

'Okay, boys.' Winnie raised his hands in mock surrender. 'I'm not saying I want a say, I'd just like to reserve my right to, if I think it's needed.'

'We won't give you the need, Winnie.'

'When do you need the money?'

'Not for a few months, though I'll tell you now that we have a second cousin working at the Tender Office; we can't lose, but we still have to pay a fair price.'

'Give me a month's notice so I can get a solicitor to draw up the papers. I use John Baker in Parramatta and you can use him too if you like. He'll be acting for all of us. The money will come from Gregson & Gregson, they're futures' traders.'

'We don't like banks, Winnie.'

'This one you'll like. I'll introduce you to them one day. It's just a small company with one office and plenty of money.'

'Then it's a deal, Winnie?' said Mario one.

Winnie nodded.

'Good on you, Winnie.' Mario two shook his hand. 'What do you want to call the company, Winnie?'

'The Mario Brothers. What do you guys reckon?'

Both brothers laughed. 'Why not, Winnie? This is just the start. You'll be hearing from us soon.' They shook hands cordially and left.

'What did the Mario Brothers want, Winnie?'

'I'm going into business with them, Kev, into pubs.'

'What else are you getting into, Prez?'

'Who knows, Kev? We'll just have to wait and see.'

'I'll drink to that, Prez.' Big Kev downed his drink.

'You're not on a mission tonight, are you, Kev?'

'Why do you say that, Prez?'

'I've known you too long, Kev. What's up, mate?'

Big Kev looked sad.

'You can talk to me, mate. What's up?'

'It's Sandy. She was pregnant. I didn't want to tell anyone yet but she lost it last night.'

'How is she?'

'Not too bad. Her mother came down and she's with her now. I think she's more sorry for me, but as long as she's all right I don't care that much.

This isn't the first time, Prez. I didn't want her to try again, but she insisted. There'll be no more now, they're going to operate.'

'Where is she, mate?'

'In the Crown Street Women's Hospital.'

'She needs her friends' support,' said Winnie. 'I'll give Mimi a ring.'

The Women's Hospital was lit up like a Christmas tree. The parking attendant offered them the spot next to his box and introduced himself as Eddie.

'One of you guys a new father, eh?'

'Something like that,' Big Kev replied. 'My name's Kev. Look after these bikes and make sure they're there when we get back.'

'With my life,' Eddie said, as Kev moved off.

'My name's Winnie.'

'I'm pleased to meet you, Winnie. Is your mate alright?'

'He'll be right. Thanks for the spot.'

At eight at night the maternity ward swelled with beaming couples staring at their newborns through the observation window. The smell: a cross between shit and antiseptic. The boys stood out in their colours and riding gear and windswept hair. When Mimi joined them she looked prim and proper in her banker's suit. They ignored the looks from staff and patients alike. Sandy was in room 420.

Mimi and Winnie ran headlong into a bloke with his arms stuffed full of women's clothes. His wife had collapsed to her knees and was clutching her stomach in pain and screaming loudly. The husband panicked and called for help. Nurses rushed towards her. 'Get her to the delivery room!' An orderly arrived with a wheelchair. Suddenly a woman screamed from a room somewhere.

'Kev, you go and see Sandy, we'll come up later.'

'Come on, Peter.' Mimi knew it was only a matter of time before Winnie bolted for the door and into the night. She grabbed his arm and they headed outside. 'There'll be shops open down the road.'

They walked out into the night and the smell of the city hit them. 'That's better!' Winnie took a deep breath. 'It's like an abattoir in there. How's Sandy?'

'The doctor said she came really close to dying from blood poisoning. She's going to be okay but she won't be able to bear children. They gave her a hysterectomy.'

Kev felt mixed emotions welling up. Determined not to start blubbering in front of Sandy, he rode up and down a few times in the lift, composing himself. When the door opened, the silence hit him. He found himself whispering to the nurse on duty, 'Where's room 420?'

In an equally quiet voice, she directed him. 'Third room on your right.'

She appeared oblivious to his colours; maybe bikers came in all the time. He paused briefly in front of Sandy's door before entering. Sandy lay asleep in bed with a drip attached to one arm and a bank of machines monitoring her condition. Her red hair contrasted starkly with the white room. She looked peaceful. Kev's eyes filled with tears and a few escaped down his cheeks. He raised his forearm and wiped it across his eyes. He didn't want to disturb her and turned to leave the room, then he heard her voice.

'What are you doing here, boofhead?'

He walked to her bedside and she reached out with her free hand. He lost control and sobbed and kissed her gently and laid his head on her breast.

Sandy rubbed his head reassuringly. 'Everything's going to be fine, you big baby.'

In between sobs, Kevvie whispered, 'I thought I was going to lose you and I never told you how much I love you.'

'Keep going.'

He kissed her and hoped that said enough. 'Tell me the truth, babe. What did the doctor say?'

'I just need to rest up for a while, but there's no chance of us ever having a baby.' She wept. 'I know how much you've wanted to be a father. I'm sorry, Kevvie, but it's not on the cards now.'

Kev held her tightly and they cried together and said nothing much. Nurses popped in every few minutes and adjusted things and checked vital signs and Kev was up and down and in and out of the room while the professionals took charge. He walked the halls and watched the women walking to and fro and when the last of the nurses left he went back in.

'It's okay if you want to go and find yourself another girl.' Sandy let out her grief in a wail from the bottom of her being.

Kev looked directly into her eyes. 'You're a silly bitch! Where would I find anyone crazy enough to put up with me?'

Sandy pulled his face towards her and kissed him. A knock at the door interrupted them. Winnie entered and held the door open for Mimi. She carried a huge bunch of flowers in one hand and a plate of small cakes in the other.

'Everything looks alright in here!' Winnie quipped with a smile as Kev and Sandy beamed back. Winnie embraced Sandy.

'Everything's just fine, Prez. Just fine.' She squeezed Winnie's hand.

Mimi kissed her. 'Hello, darling.' Sandy wasn't used to women showing her much affection — even her own mother never found the time — but she liked it when they did.

'I brought you some cakes,' Mimi said. 'I hope you can eat.' She tried to hide her tears from Sandy, but with no success.

Sandy took Mimi's hand in hers. 'It's okay, Mimi. Don't cry or you'll start me off again.'

'Can you find a vase for the flowers, Peter?' Kev mimicked Mimi and got a big laugh. Winnie shook his head on the way out the door to find one.

Mimi watched Kev and Sandy and noticed how they'd discovered each other.

Winnie entered clutching a vase. 'Hey, Kev! There are some good-looking nurses here; you should've seen the one that got the vase for me! It was up on the top shelf and she had to reach up for it. Nice set of ham 'n' eggs.'

'You're such a tart, Prez!' Sandy said.

Mimi picked up the flowers. 'Here, give me that vase so I can clonk you with it!'

Winnie winked at Mimi and she headed to the bathroom to get water while Winnie held the door open.

'Is this some competition to see who can be the biggest gentleman? We know what you're both like,' Sandy said.

'Anybody like a cup of tea?' Kev asked.

'Yes, I'll have one,' Sandy said.

Winnie and Kev went out to wander the halls in search of some tea.

Mimi called out to them, 'Watch out for those nurses!'

Two nurses watched the boys make tea.

'What do you reckon, Kev?'

Winnie looked over his shoulder and slipped across the room to the nurses. 'What time do you knock off, girls?'

'Why's that?' the not-so-pretty one asked.

The prettier one shot her a 'shut your mouth' look. 'We're off duty now.'

'Do you want to go for a ride?' Not waiting for an answer, Winnie said, 'We'll meet you outside the parking booth in half an hour.'

'You live dangerously, Prez.'

'No danger, Kev. We'll be long gone before Mimi leaves. There's no use in just hanging around. Give them some time to have a good talk.'

'Sandy and Mimi are good friends, Prez. It's what they both need.'

Winnie took another peek at the nurses. 'You can have the ugly one, Kev.'

'I don't care, Prez. I just want an empty.'

Winnie backed into the room.

'What have you boys been up to?' Sandy missed nothing.

'Well, we were just saying how good you're looking, considering what you've been through, and Kev doesn't want to go home to an empty flat, so ...'

Sandy picked up where Winnie'd left off. 'You're going back to the clubhouse.'

'Now, how would you guess that?' Mimi quipped. 'Go and look after Kev.'

Winnie whispered, 'I could take you home right now.'

'Do you think I'm that easy?' Mimi said in mock indignation. 'No, you go with Kevvie.'

Kevvie leant over Sandy and whispered, 'See you tomorrow, babe.'

The girls watched the boys leave.

On the ground floor they ran for the exit. 'Let's get out of here, mate!'

'Yeah, I need some fresh air,' Kevvie said.

'I think we're going to have some fresh pussy.' Winnie looked across the road. Kev followed his gaze and saw the two nurses from the fourth floor waiting by the parking attendant's booth.

The little smart arse offsider piped up, 'So where are your bikes?'

Big Kev put his arm around her shoulders and steered her to the cashier's station and the waiting Harleys. 'Come with us, Florence Nightingale.'

'Is she always like this?' Winnie asked the good-looking half of the duo.

'Wait till she has her first drink. It changes her. Where are we going?'

'I'll take you for a good ride to our clubhouse; you can have a drink there.'

'We'll be safe there, won't we?' She looked at him for reassurance.

'Nothing will happen that you don't want at our clubhouse, except maybe losing a game of pool.' They walked up to the Harleys.

'Harleys! I love Harleys,' the ugly nurse said as she walked over to the bikes.

Eddie came out of his office. Winnie reached for his wallet.

'How much do we owe you, mate?'

'No charge, boys, it's on the house.'

'Thanks, Eddie. We'll catch you around the traps one day and buy you a beer.'

'No problems, boys.'

Winnie asked his nurse her name. 'Leslie.'

'Have you been on the back of a bike before?'

'My father had a Triumph. I used to go for rides with him.'

'Get on, then.' He wheeled the thumping Harley out of the parking bay.

Eddie raised the boom gate while up in Sandy's room the nurses changed her bandages.

Mimi stood by the windows and looked over a darkened city. When she glanced down, she saw both Winnie and Kev had females on the backs of their bikes. She stared, not wanting to believe it.

'You bastard,' she whispered as they roared up the street. Tears flooded her eyes as she bit her lip and decided not to say anything just yet. 'You just wait, Mr Prez,' she said under her breath, utterly betrayed.

Waiting for the lights to change, the nurse leaned forward to talk to Winnie.

'Hey, Prez, is that your missus back there? I don't fuck other women's men.'

Winnie shrugged, the lights turned green and they left the cars far behind. At the next set of traffic lights, the nurse said, 'You don't care if I don't want to fuck you? I'm only coming because my mate wanted to.'

Winnie turned his head around and eyed her titties straining to get out of her jacket. 'Kev needs a woman tonight.'

'And what about you?'

'I need a woman every night!'

Winnie immediately dropped his clutch and brought the front wheel up and did a wheel stand across the intersection. The nurse held on for dear life, then freed her fingers from his ribcage. 'Fuck' is all she said, and then she grabbed his cock.

'You don't fuck other women's men?' Winnie chuckled to himself. They pulled into the clubhouse, parked and dismounted.

'You girls should've worn your uniforms!' Kev was in a mood.

'Yeah, right,' the little ugly one said and both girls erupted laughing. 'Are we going to be safe here?'

Big Kev put his arm around her shoulders. 'Just come with me.' When they were at the bar, he said, 'Now, what do you drink?'

'Rum and coke, please.'

'How's Sandy, mate?' Brian was concerned.

'She's good, boys, real good, and over the worst of it.'

'And who have you got there?'

'Nancy,' she said in a tiny, demure voice then took a long gulp of her drink. She wasn't a beauty but she was alright.

Ocker got his nose in early. 'That's a pretty name.'

'You keep away from her, you dirty little man!' Kev was onto Ocker. 'Nancy's a nurse, she looked after Sandy. Now I'm going to look after her.' He stroked her hair while she finished her drink.

'Same again, please.'

'That was quick!' Kev said. Other members inquired about Sandy's health, and Kev was touched.

Winnie lit a cigarette. Leslie rubbed one finger lightly over his nose.

'You think you're so cool.' Winnie drew on his cigarette then slipped his hand into her crotch. She removed the cigarette, covered his mouth with hers and stuck her tongue down his throat. He blew smoke out through his nostrils then pushed her away and coughed.

'Are you trying to kill me?'

'Well, don't grab my cunt!'

Winnie laughed. 'I love your tits.'

'You're up yourself.'

She leaned over and kissed him and rubbed her crotch against him.

'Can I get a drink?' Leslie asked.

'You're getting me all hot.'

'That's the idea, but don't get your hopes up.'

'Did I miss something, or was someone else just rubbing their cunt all over me?'

She put one finger up to her lips. 'I'm such a tease, aren't I?'

With that, Winnie laughed and shook his head. 'Yes, that's what you are. Now, would you like a line of speed?'

'Right now, that's just what I need. We've just finished a twelve-hour, five-day week.'

'Do you like being a nurse?'

'There's a lot of shit and the hours are awkward, but it's all worth it when you see results, like Big Kev's girl. She was close to death, you know.' She paused, deep in thought. 'Just seeing her face change in the space of half an hour is rewarding.' She smiled, satisfied. 'Just to know I've helped in her recovery is why I do it, and now I sound like Mother Teresa!'

'Who?' Winnie asked.

'Don't worry. Come on, where's my beer?'

She smiled, downed her stubby in a few long swigs then belched loudly. 'Ah, that's better!' She grinned at the boys.

'What a girl!' someone remarked.

'As dry as a nun's cunt,' she said and moved closer to Winnie. 'Where's that line you promised me? I don't want to have it in front of the boys.'

Winnie was stunned. 'I've never heard a woman speak dirty like you do, ever. Are you like it all the time?'

'It's terrible, isn't it, Prez? Now come on, where can we go?'

'Follow me,' he said. They made their way into the back room.

He flicked on the light. 'Good, no sleeping bodies.'

Winnie pulled out a bag of powder, poured some onto the table and chopped up two lines.

'You've had this before, have you?'

'Come on, Prez. I'm a nurse.'

'Here you are.' Winnie held out a rolled note for her. She pulled aside her tumbling blond hair, bent forward and snorted half the line, paused and then vacuumed up the rest. Her eyes watered, and she passed the note to Winnie. She stuck her finger tip into her stubby, moistened it, put her finger to her nose, snorted the beer to flush out her nasal passage, then tilted her head and let the rest of the amphetamine run down her throat.

Winnie looked on in awe. 'What are you doing?'

'I've seen the noses of users. Particles of powder get caught in the membrane and eventually it eats its way through to the other nostril. They have to put a plastic one in. The doctors talk about it when they're doing the operation.'

Winnie snorted his line. 'Can I borrow your beer?' he asked.

'You're not sticking your fingers into my beer. I don't know where they've been! Here, stick them out.'

She poured a little beer over them and he did what she'd done, then threw his head back.

'I'll have to teach this to the boys. You can't help but do good, can you, Nursie?'

She tapped the stubbie's neck on her bottom lip.

'You're a sexy bitch.' Winnie reached across and rubbed her crotch.

She leaned back and looked him straight in the eye. 'Can I just suck you off?'

He undid his belt buckle and let his jeans fall to the floor. He pulled out his stiffening cock.

Nursie put down her beer and grabbed his cock and started doing her stuff, and Winnie leaned on the wall for support. She had great technique and when he blew his load she didn't miss a drop and continued to suck on his deflated cock. She collapsed for a few minutes, breathing heavily, as if she'd run a marathon.

Leslie swilled down the rest of her beer in one hit. Winnie pulled his jeans up and squared himself away.

'Won't fuck, will suck — suits me. Would you like another beer?'

She pinched him on the arse. 'Yes, please. I want to meet your mates.'

'Let's go and meet them.'

Big Kev stood with a pool cue in his hand watching Nancy play her shot at the table. She looked better and better as the night progressed.

'How's she going, mate?'

'She's right now. It only took one drink.'

'Do you think you'll get an empty?'

'She's like a moth to the flame, mate!'

'I missed!' she said and sidled up to Big Kev.

'Oh, no, you haven't!' Big Kev grabbed her on the arse.

'Hello, Prez.' She sounded slightly tipsy. 'Hi, Leslie! Where've you been? Or shouldn't I ask?'

Leslie just smiled.

The next moment Winnie turned his head to see how Ocker was going with Leslie. He stopped dead — no Leslie, and no Ocker either!

'I suppose that's the end of her for the night. She said she wanted to meet a few of my mates.'

Winnie was dead tired and decided to call it a night.

'Feeling guilty, Prez?'

'No, mate. She's a strange one. Anyway, eating isn't cheating.'

'In what way?'

Winnie leaned over, so the not-so-ugly one couldn't hear. 'Won't fuck, will suck. She gets off on sucking cock! I won't be surprised if she does everyone here.'

Kevvie looked around the room. 'I reckon there are a couple of litres of come in here for her!'

Winnie just laughed and said, 'Make sure she gets home alright, and if she doesn't want to fuck, leave it at that. You have a good night tonight, Kev.' Winnie clapped Kev on the shoulder. 'I'm off.'

Winnie walked to the door and ran into the Rat and Rastus having a joint outside. 'Hey, Rat, did you catch up with the Skipper yet?'

'Last week. He'd like to discuss it with you, but he won't come down. You'll have to go up there, he doesn't like cities.'

'How long a drive?'

'A couple of days, or you could fly in a few hours.'

'I've always wanted to have a look around, I'll drive.'

'Let me know when you're going because he goes to sea for weeks; there's no use going then.'

'I'll let you know, Rat. What are you two up to, anyway?'

'A bit of this and a bit of that.' Rastus said, with a toothless grin.

'I'm going to piss off now. If you boys are interested, Ocker's got a hot chick inside and she seems to want all the Miners. He's sheriffing her so you should introduce yourself and the boys real soon.'

Winnie noticed Leslie's purse on his seat and handed it to one of the boys. 'When you see her, give her this.'

He rode home and when he turned into his street he slowly idled his bike into his garage and chained it up. He opened the door quietly and made his way to the bathroom for a hot shower. When he entered the bedroom Mimi was asleep and he noticed it was 3.15. He was still revving hard from the speed. His thoughts turned to Leslie and he found himself getting aroused. He tried to get close to Mimi, who tensed up and moved away.

'Don't touch me!' she said venomously.

'What's up, baby?'

She tossed off the blankets and stood up. The sight of her standing, taut breasts straining against her nightie, only served to arouse him even more.

'I saw you with those nurses on the back of your bikes. Kev I can understand, but you?' she sobbed.

'You're right, there was a girl on the back of my bike. Those girls just finished twelve-hour shifts. They wanted a place to party and we took them to the clubhouse, where they are now. They looked after Sandy and we wanted to thank them. That's all there is to it. If I was interested in them, do you think I'd be home now?'

'Why are you home now?' Mimi asked in a small voice.

He held her face in both hands. 'Because I wanted to be with you.'

For once that wasn't a lie. She appeared satisfied with that and kissed him.

He tasted the salty tears on her cheeks and almost felt a pang of guilt when he took her in his arms. He whispered, 'I'm not worthy of you. If I thought you seeing another girl on the back of my bike would upset you so much, I wouldn't have done it.'

He knew he'd sailed a bit too close to the wind. He pulled her into the warmth under the sheets.

'Would you have told me?'

'Most probably not.'

'What do you mean by that?

He gently rubbed her back and felt her nipples jutting against his bare chest. Luckily he hadn't fucked Leslie the nurse, so he felt no guilt. He slid her nightie up her back.

In the morning he lay in bed while Mimi made coffee. The aroma wafted into the bedroom. He looked out the window at the skyline of Sydney, roof tiles and television antennas in the short view and the Harbour Bridge in the distance. The security grilles on the windows made it seem like a jail cell. The Saturday traffic noise in the distance was tolerable, but one day he wanted to get out and never come back. One day, he thought to himself, one day.

Mimi brought in a tray with cups of hot coffee and the Saturday newspapers.

She flopped onto the bed, bit into a piece of toast and read the finance section.

He pulled the travel section out of the pile and read about Tuscany. He asked suddenly if she was ready for a holiday, and her eyes lit up. 'I thought we could go for a drive up to Bundaberg.'

She was secretly disappointed — she'd had visions of Tuscany. 'That'll be nice, Peter. I've never been up there.'

'I thought we could go up in your car in a couple of weeks. Maybe we can stop at Byron Bay on the way. It's beautiful up there. I'm planning the trip for when I get back from the opening of the Commandos' new Melbourne clubhouse.'

Mimi and John Baker had a busy week ahead converting Gina's Las Vegas winnings into a large payment for the shop; when it was all over it wouldn't cost Gina a penny and the proceeds from all the grass and hash sales would sink from view. Mimi read the business section while Winnie stared at the headline on the front page: 'Outlaw Motorcycle Club Members Nabbed in Huge Hash Haul'. He scanned the report:

The three men charged with possession of almost three thousand kilos of hashish have direct links to the Tigers outlaw motorcycle club. They pleaded not guilty to importation charges and will face trial next week.

The article was accompanied by a picture of the accused. Winnie stared at it: not a bad photo of Kero Ken. Twister, the dickhead, was nowhere to be seen, always in the right place at the right time.

Mimi read that Ocker's Nokia shares had soared. 'They're going to make him a lot of money one day.'

'Speaking of making money, I've gone into business with the Mario brothers. They're looking out for some city pubs and I'll be a silent partner.'

'Do they know anything about running pubs?'

'They think they do and that's all that matters. They'll be coming to see you with the paperwork. I'd like you to give them whatever they want from my account. John Baker is looking after the leases and contracts.'

'You never cease to amaze me, Peter.'

'The opportunity came up, I had money, they needed some, I offered and they accepted. Easy-peasy. It'll be a good earner in a year or two and I trust them. They're old mates from school.' Mimi shook her head and went back to the financial pages.

Chapter 18

Winnie called the clubhouse and Kev answered. 'What happened to the nurses?'

'Ocker sent them home in a cab. Everything's fine. I'm off to see Sandy now.'

'Mimi knew about us taking the nurses there last night.' There was a long pause. 'I couldn't deny it. I just said that they wanted to party after their shift and we offered to take them to the clubhouse. I'm glad I went home early. I just wanted to let you know. Say hello to Sandy. I'll see you Monday.'

Winnie opened a bottle of Krug champagne and filled up two flutes. He had no idea the Krug was a present from one of Mimi's clients, or that it ran to over $100 a bottle — he couldn't have cared less. All he knew for sure was that his life was better since she'd come into it. He handed her a glass. 'You're beautiful, Mimi.'

'When we go to Bundaberg, can we go on the Harley? I'd love to go on a really long ride.'

'Believe me, babe, our arses wouldn't handle it, not on my bike anyway. Also, I don't want to attract any attention, because I have meetings with a few business associates.'

Mimi wanted to know more but she knew the rules. No questions.

She stretched out on the lounge and closed her eyes. 'I'm tired. Had a hard week with a Hong Kong client. That's where the champagne came from. Nice, isn't it?'

'Is he loaded? What's his name?' He looked at her then held up his hands. 'Yes, I know, no questions. Want a line of speed?'

'Oh, come on, Peter. I'm an Eastern Suburbs girl, of course I do.'

He pulled out the bag he'd shared the night before with the nurse, flicked open his knife and covered the tip with powder. 'Open up.' He tipped the contents into her mouth.

'Oh, that tastes terrible!' She took a gulp of champagne to wash it down and he followed suit. She felt a tingling sensation across the top of her head. 'I'll be up all night.'

Winnie topped up their glasses and they sat back and relaxed.

'Have you ever thought of living in the country?'

'What in the world makes you ask that?'

'I've just been thinking that it'd be good to have some space around.'

'I've never thought about it. I like living in Sydney, Peter.'

'I don't mean the bush, just somewhere quiet with a few acres. It's something to think about.' He stood up and headed for the shower.

He pulled on the new shirt Mimi had bought him, and admired his reflection in the mirror while Mimi leant against the doorway. 'Not bad.'

'It's your good taste! You can buy clothes for me anytime.'

'I think we should call a cab tonight,' she said. She walked in and stood behind him then wrapped her arms around him.

Mimi unzipped him and pulled out his dick. He shuddered at the touch of her cold hand, and their eyes met in the mirror.

'Has the champagne gone to your head?'

'Can't a woman please her man?' She stroked his cock until it lay erect in her hand.

'You can do whatever you like.'

Mimi unbuckled his belt and dropped his jeans, positioned herself so her head was right in front of his prick and took him in her mouth. He massaged the back of her head and watched their reflection in the mirror. She bobbed her head up and down and they started moving as if dancing slowly. Mimi squeezed his balls and nearly choked trying to take too much down her throat. Winnie started to come and attempted to pull out but she moved his hand away and swallowed.

When his dick went limp she fondled his balls and gazed into his eyes. 'I love you.'

He bent down to pull up his jeans and got a sudden sense of déjà vu. He'd done exactly the same thing the night before with the nurse. He tried to put her out of his mind. Tonight was Mimi's night.

Winnie held the door open for her then followed her into Punchinello's, one of the top restaurants in town. A few heads turned as they walked in.

Mimi headed for the bar over to the side and Winnie followed her lead because she seemed to know what she was doing. The manager, Gino, looked up and spotted Mimi. He bunged on the charm.

'Miss Mimi!' He walked over and embraced her and kissed her on both cheeks then led them to a corner table.

Gino flapped open the napkins expertly and laid them out on their laps. He handed them each a menu and placed the wine list before Winnie. 'I'll be back soon, Miss Mimi.'

One of the suits at a table nearby shouted, 'Gino!'

Winnie was shocked. 'I thought this was a classy place?'

People stared at the suit.

'What are you looking at?' the suit shouted at the guests at another table.

Gino hurried over. Winnie recognised the Gibbs brothers from Balmain. Infamous standover men. He saw Gino jump at their every request.

Gino came over to Winnie's table. 'Are you ready to order wine, Miss Mimi?'

Mimi scanned the wine list and pointed to the reds. 'We'll just have a bottle of the Clare Valley shiraz, Gino, and the veal parmigiana.'

Gino nodded and smiled. 'Excellent choice, Mimi.'

He gathered their menus and the wine list. Again the loud voice shattered the ambience in the restaurant. 'Let's go to the red-hots!'

'Oh, I hope so,' Gino muttered under his breath and hurried into the kitchen.

Winnie looked at Mimi. 'Do you know what they're talking about?'

'I'm not that naive: the trots at Harold Park.'

'Good girl.' He smiled.

'Gino!' The voice hollered out again, and then, without waiting for a response, 'Bring me the fucking bill!'

Gino added up their bill on the register and took it over to the Gibbs's table. They got up, knocked over a chair in their wake and just left it there. Gino handed the bill to the loud one. He tried to read it but the alcohol had worked its magic and he had a hard time focusing. He pushed it back at Gino.

'How much, you little wog?'

Gino let the insult slide and punched up the amount on the register. All the patrons watched as one of the Gibbs brothers pulled out a fat wallet and thrust some hundred dollar bills at Gino before following the other suits out the door.

'You can't buy good manners,' Mimi said, as Winnie watched them leave.

Gino picked up the toppled chair and a kitchen hand helped him clean the table. Gino looked relieved and poured Mimi a taste of the shiraz. After the champagne at home and a line of pure speed, Mimi was in an upbeat mood, and a sassy one at that.

'Come on, Gino. Just pour the wine.' She waved her hand over the glass.

He filled their glasses while Winnie watched, amused at her antics.

Mimi took a sip. 'You know what, Gino, you're born to die, but you live to suffer.'

'Sometimes I think so, Miss Mimi.'

'Where did you get that?' Winnie asked, a little miffed at the remark.

'I don't know, Peter, it just came out. But I hope it's not true.' She took his hand and kissed it.

People seemed much more relaxed now that the Gibbs brothers had gone. They became more animated; the atmosphere lightened up.

'That's what it's like when you and your mates go anywhere — people are scared.'

'We don't carry on like those pricks.'

'You don't have to.'

'Well, that's their problem. They're scared of the unknown. Most people who know us are okay with us. Look at you.'

'Oh, yeah. I'm scared of you,' she said with a cheeky grin.

Winnie leaned over and kissed her and Mimi rubbed his leg under the table.

Gino delivered their meals and smiled broadly at Mimi. She blushed like a little girl.

'Buon appetito!' he said as he held the pepper mill over Mimi's plate.

'Thank you, Gino.'

Winnie tucked into his meal with vigour. 'This is nice,' he said, devouring it in record time.

'Are you all right, babe?' he asked, as he noticed Mimi frozen and holding her knife and fork above her plate but eating nothing.

'I don't think I should've mixed my drinks.' Winnie couldn't remember ever seeing her pissed before. She headed off quickly to the ladies' room.

Gino approached. 'Is everything all right, Mr Peter?'

'It's okay, mate, she's had too much to drink. You'd better call us a cab and bring me the bill.'

'Not tonight, it's my shout.'

'Okay,' Winnie said, shrugging his shoulders. 'Your shout.'

Mimi returned looking graceful, but smiling weakly. She sat down slowly. 'I'm sorry, Peter, but can we go home?'

'I've got a cab on the way.'

'Oh, you're a darling.'

Winnie took Mimi's hand, helped her stand and walked her to the door. She spoke Italian to Gino as she passed and they hugged and kissed like family. They glanced at Winnie a few times and then Gino extended his hand.

'Good night, Mr Prez.'

'Yeah, good night, Gino, and thanks.'

Gino walked them to the waiting taxi and waved goodbye.

Chapter 19

The boys changed the shop's name from Snow's Custom & Mechanical to Western Choppers on the Monday morning. The newly painted sign was hung outside. Brian put on a sale of the old British spare parts and blokes lined up to get bargains.

Kev and Spike serviced the members' bikes before the Club run to Melbourne. Most members were doing business and, for them, cash was no longer a problem.

Brian was ecstatic; his plan was coming to life. 'I can't wait to get the new shop going! I can see it now. Over to the side there'll be glass cabinets displaying custom parts and jewellery, clothes and boots.'

'You've got it pretty much worked out, mate.'

'Don't you like it, Prez?'

'Looks good to me, you silly cunt! Where's Kev?'

'Out the back.'

Winnie had no specific role in the shop; he just filled in when required. The shop buzzed. Even Ocker worked on bikes — there was no time for spray-painting.

'Is there anything I can do to help, mate?'

'That Low Rider needs a new chain and a set of front brake pads. If you want to look after it, that'd be a bonus, Prez.'

'No worries, Kev.' Winnie got straight on with the task.

'How's Sandy, mate?'

'She's going home with her mother for a couple of weeks. Works out fine, Prez, with the run and us busy doing the new shop. Brian's pretty excited by it all. Did he tell you he wants to bring Gina in to run the clothes side of it?'

Winnie stopped what he was doing and smiled at Kev. 'No, he hasn't mentioned it. What does he want, for her to be here every day?'

'No, he never said that.' Big Kev chortled at the expression on Winnie's face.

'Does Ocker know this?'

'I think so.'

'We'd better have a talk to Brian,' said Winnie. 'I wonder if that's the price we have to pay for getting her money.'

'It could be, Prez.'

Spike brought a bike back from a test run and parked it. 'Another one done.'

He picked up the job card and stuck it on the seat and wheeled the bike out to the front, ready for collection.

'Are you coming to Melbourne, Spike?'

'Yeah, Prez, I'm flying. I just don't want to ride down with you blokes, it wouldn't feel right.'

'I understand, Spike, I wouldn't ride with your club either.'

Ocker joined them. 'Getting your hands dirty, Prez?'

'Get fucked.'

'Kevvie tells me Mimi sprung you with the nurses.'

Winnie gave Kev a look.

'I had to, Prez. When Sandy was really crook we said a few things to each other.' Big Kev almost blushed.

'Said what?' Winnie quizzed.

'Oh, nothing.' Kev turned away and headed back to the workbench.

Ocker whistled 'Here comes the bride' and everyone but Winnie joined in. Kev continued to tinker around the workbench and everybody laughed. Kev turned a carburettor in both hands, bent down and fitted it onto the motor.

'Ocker — or should I call you the sheriff — did Leslie get her purse that she'd left on my bike?'

'Yeah, the boys gave it to me. It's okay, Prez, 'cos you know what?' he asked matter-of-factly, then answered his own query, 'I *am* going to sheriff Leslie. We get on real good together and I might see her again.'

'What's going on around here? Not you too, Ocker? Are you sick of the sluts?'

'No, but I like Leslie.'

'She's not a bad head job, is she?'

Nobody had ever seen Ocker get so shitty so fast. 'Don't say that again, Prez!'

Winnie realised he was fair dinkum. 'Okay, mate, I won't.' He knew how much it might affect a bloke if you told him his missus gave a bloody good head job.

Spike looked at Winnie and shrugged his shoulders. They smiled at each other and got on with their work.

At the day's end Brian closed the front doors and walked into the workshop.

'Only three lock-ups to go.' He pulled out a cold beer and the other boys joined him, except for Spike, who pulled on his Commandos vest.

'See you tomorrow, boys.' Spike pushed his bike out to the alleyway and kicked the engine over.

'He must be on a promise,' Ocker said, laughing, when Spike took off.

'Is everything organised for the run?' Winnie asked Brian.

'Everyone's paid their fees and we'll have one hundred per cent of our Chapter riding. We're booked into motels for the first night at Wodonga and for the rest of the week in St Kilda.'

Big Kev chimed in. 'I'll make sure there are no outstanding warrants so we don't have to bail any silly cunts out. We'll probably attract a lot of attention and we don't want to end up waiting around in some backwater and dealing with pigs.'

'Have you spoken to Swannie, Brian?'

'Yeah, they're going to meet us at the Five Ways at Liverpool, Wednesday.'

'Good,' Winnie said. 'Now Brian, what's this idea of yours for our new showroom? Are we bringing in a new partner?'

Brian looked startled. 'New partner, Prez?'

'Yeah, Kev told me that you wanted Gina in to run the clothes side.'

Brian smiled as he answered, 'Yeah, but she won't be a partner; it just gives her something to do. She'll be the buyer for us; she'll set it up and we'll sell the clothes. She won't be here all the time, Prez, no way.' He looked at Kev and Ocker. 'Whaddya reckon?'

Big Kev shrugged his shoulders. 'Doesn't worry me.'

'Someone's got to do it,' Ocker said, staring at the Prez.

'Okay, it's no bother to me,' Winnie said.

'I'm glad, Prez; it'll keep her away from the casino.'

Winnie hoped so.

'Oh and I wanted to tell you something that stays with us,' he said. 'My neighbour Marge has a garage she never uses; it's a safe place to stash the speed.' He looked at the boys. 'I'm going to rent it because it's over the road and I can keep an eye on it. Who'd suspect an old lady? I'll sign a lease under a bodgie name and won't tell her what's in there. She's offered me a roomful of old bike magazines and manuals so I'll tell her I want to set up a library in her garage. I'll put up some shelves and move the stuff out of the house and build a couple of hidey-holes for the goey and use it as a storehouse. How does that sound?'

Ocker looked at Winnie in admiration, 'You're the man, Prez!'

'While we're on the subject, Ocker, I think we should do maybe five or ten batches and store it so we have some in reserve. One day something might happen and we won't be able to make more.'

'I'm taking a break from the cooking, Prez. Steve's back. He failed one of his uni subjects, so he'll be here for another six months. He bought what's-her-name's ticket and gave her five grand's worth of traveller's cheques and then she fucked off overseas without him. He's really pissed off!'

Brian couldn't believe it. 'Fair dinkum?'

Everybody but Brian laughed at poor Steve's undoing at the hands of his sheila.

Ocker looked serious for a second. 'I'll tell Steve to teach Toothpick properly.'

'Anybody else?'

'Benny will be alright and he's keen. I had a word with him.'

Winnie looked at Brian. 'What do you think, mate?'

'They're two good blokes. I say yes.'

'Okay, Benny and Toothpick it is, then; we'll have a talk on the run to Melbourne.

'Next item of business is Gina's casino winnings. She has an appointment with Mimi this afternoon at the bank; she's funding the purchase of these buildings. I'll repay her out of the proceeds of the speed, so there's no problem with your money, Brian.'

Brian looked relieved.

'Okay, Ocker, when are you getting the hash?'

'I'm not, Prez — there's too much risk picking it up. I don't want to get hit.'

Winnie gave it some thought. 'You're right, mate. The Sergeant told me the waterfront is crawling with Customs agents. He'll let us know when it's safe.'

'The Hash King might have to stop bringing it in for a while, or find another way.'

'Well, you remember Rat told us about his mate with the fishing trawler up north?' Ocker nodded. 'What if we can get him to pick up the Hash King's gear at sea? It's almost foolproof and we'll get it much cheaper.'

'Have you spoken to him, Prez?'

'Not yet, but the Rat has, and we're meeting after Melbourne. I might have to go north for a couple of weeks.'

Brian looked dismayed. 'But we have to finish all the work on the new showroom.'

'You were born to do this, Brian, so surprise me. I'll bring the Indian in and you can show it a bit of love and a new set of tyres.'

Brian nodded; he was looking forward to checking out the Scout.

'My neighbour's also got her husband's FJ Holden panel van. If she wants to sell it, I reckon it'd make a terrific delivery van for the shop. Everyone'd notice it with "Western Choppers" lettered on the doors — it'd really stand out.'

'And when we open we can have a sausage sizzle and a band and balloons!' Kev said in his deepest voice. That got a big laugh.

Brian darkened. 'No, come on, fellas; we have to make Western Choppers the only place to come when punters think of custom choppers and parts.'

The Prez shot Brian a sincere appreciative glance. 'Customising with parts we import is where the real money is,' Brian continued.

Kev had his own ideas. 'We're going to build choppers too, Brian, and there's money in that.'

'I know, Kev, but most people will build their own, and that's our target market,' said Brian.

Target market? The boys looked at each other; Brian could have been speaking Latvian. The Prez looked at Brian. 'Who've you been talking to, Brian?'

'No one, Prez. On the way to the States in the plane I read an article in a marketing magazine about how to best approach your target market. It said the aim of start-up ventures like ours was choosing who we want as customers and then giving them what they want. It made sense to me and it suits what we're doing. So if we stock the shop well, build great custom bikes and give the customer what he wants, we get a good name and our business grows. Easy-peasy.'

There was stunned silence. Everybody in the room knew it made sense and it couldn't have been more simply stated.

Brian's sales lecture continued. 'I talked to the suppliers in the States, and they all agreed on one thing: the parts side is where the money is, especially if we sell quality at a good price.'

'The trip to the States was good for you, Brian.'

'Yeah, Prez, I'll go over again.'

'That's cool, Brian, as long as you keep coming back with brainwaves!'

'Okay, Kev, no balloons, but I'm going to put it in the newspapers and try for a radio interview.'

'You do that, mate. As long as you look after that side I don't mind talking to punters who want me to build their dream chopper.'

'Next on the agenda, before I go up north I want to make sure John Baker has settled on this place. I want the paperwork signed, sealed, delivered and legal before I go.'

'We're going to need some working capital to prime the pump, Prez.'

'When and how much, Brian?'

'The Yanks offered us three-month terms on the first invoice and a monthly account after that. I didn't ask, they just offered it to me, so I agreed right away. They sure know how to do business.'

'There's no favours in business, mate.'

'Don't worry, Prez, it's no favour. They know how hard it is to start a shop. They'd already checked us out. They know we're selling all-new products and what's good for us is good for them.'

'You've got a knack for this business,' Kevvie shook Brian's hand.

Then Brian threw a spanner into the works. 'Now I want to talk about wages.'

'What do you mean?'

'It's like this: I spend ten or twelve hours a day doing paperwork and ordering new stock and I'd like to be paid for it.'

Winnie was adamant. 'Not until we can afford it.'

Kev concurred. 'He's right — when the time is right we can work out a suitable deal for all of us.'

'Fair enough, Prez.'

'Now, what's the deal with Gina?'

'She's going to buy the clothing, take consignment jewellery and keep the shop looking shmick. We don't have to worry about that and we get our whack on every item. What do you blokes reckon?'

'How much commission?'

'Twenty per cent.'

'Is that a good deal, Brian?'

'It's fair, Prez. We have no outlay.'

'Okay, we'll go along with that.'

'When are you going to Bundaberg, Prez?' Brian asked.

'About a week after we get back.'

'Gina's cousin Bobby from the Brisbane Sharks wants a couple of pounds of speed. He's going to raise the cash, so if he's ready when you leave maybe you can drop it off? I'll give you his number before you leave and you can collect the cash.'

'That'll be no problem, mate. We're going up in Mimi's car, and it'll be safe.'

'Do you want me to service your bike before we leave for Melbourne, Prez?' Kev knew the bike backwards.

'No, you've got enough to do. I'll fix it myself.'

Brian looked up from his papers. 'Okay, no more business, let's have a drink.'

Kev and Ocker cheered.

On Wednesday morning, the Chapter gathered early at the clubhouse. The boys had their bikes looking good. 'We leave at nine sharp, Kev.'

'Okay, Prez.'

'Is everyone here, Brian?'

'Just about, Prez.'

A few members were working on their bikes. When the last member arrived, Big Kev's voice rang out. 'Ten minutes!'

The nominees chained the gate. One stashed two pump-action shotguns wrapped in a blanket in the back of the truck. Ocker checked his two-way radios with the back-up truck's driver. On the dot of nine, the forty-five bikes roared away in unison, with Kev and Winnie in the lead. Workers from neighbouring businesses gawked as they passed.

They rode in staggered formation towards the Hume Highway and their rendezvous with Swannie's Chapter at the Five Ways Hotel in Liverpool. Swannie met them in the parking lot. 'G'day, Prez. A good day for it!' The weather was perfect for riding — sunny, dry and cloudless.

'Your Chapter's thinned out a bit, Swannie?'

'You know what it's like, Prez, they come and some go. Anyhow, do you want a line before we go?'

'Never say no, mate.'

'Come with me.' They headed around to a motel room. Six members lined up around the table.

The Prez rolled a note and had his line then passed it to Swannie. 'I don't want to be here all day! Have a snort and let's go.' Winnie said it loudly enough that the other members scurried outside. By the time he and Swannie had the other half, many bikes had throbbed into life.

'First stop, Goulburn. I want to reach Wodonga tonight.'

Big Kev, Winnie and Swannie led the over fifty strong pack onto the broad highway heading south and wound up to cruising speed. Despite the intense concentration needed to keep the bike tracking, Winnie found himself reflecting on how quickly the Club had grown and what Swannie had said about members coming and some going. After an hour Ocker pulled up alongside and shouted over the exhaust, 'Benny's got a flat!'

Winnie put up his arm, signalling the pack to pull over and stop. Some of the early morning drinkers rushed over to the guardrails and pissed in the grass. Cars, trucks and buses sped past and beeped their horns; passengers stared out at them. A bus load of Japanese tourists craned their necks and aimed cameras.

'Ocker, tell the back-up truck to load Benny's bike and he can get it fixed in Goulburn while we're having lunch.'

'Okay, Prez.' The two-way radio crackled and Ocker passed on the message.

The Miners pulled up for lunch outside an old pub with a service station and tyre repair place on the Sydney side of Goulburn. Most of the boys fuelled up before going into the pub.

The locals looked wary and mostly ignored them. Some ate and left in a hurry. Winnie inspected the blackboard menu, which featured standard country pub fare, and some of the boys fell into line behind him.

A woman appeared at a square hole in the wall, pad and pencil in hand. 'Whaddyawantluv?' She didn't bother to look up.

'T-bone and chips, steak medium to well, please.' Only then did she look.

Winnie paid at the bar and headed outside to sit in the sun. A nominee offered to fuel his bike and Winnie slipped him a twenty-dollar note.

'Is the oil all right, Prez?'

'Yeah, just fuel; don't fuck with anything else.' He watched the nominee walk off and start his bike first kick.

Ocker sat down, radio in hand. 'The truck's about fifteen minutes behind, Prez.'

It occurred to Winnie that the radio was paying for itself in spades. He looked up and watched two local cops in a patrol car checking them out. He turned to Kev and gave him the drum. 'I don't want to give the pigs any reason to bother us. If anyone wants to smoke joints, get them to go around the back.'

The police car came back and turned into the car park. Two pigs emerged and stood with their hands on their hips.

'We'd better go and talk, Kev.'

'How you going, boys?'

'Not bad. Is there a problem?'

'No, just admiring the bikes. On a ride are you?'

Winnie just nodded.

'How far are you heading?'

'South,' Winnie replied.

'You're not staying in town?'

'No.'

'Just asking, that's all. There are a few idiots in town who might try and cause trouble.'

The pigs got back into their patrol car. 'Have a good ride!'

'Country cops, Kev; they don't want any bother.'

Button, the nominee, rode Winnie's bike back and carefully parked it. He gave Winnie his change.

'You can do that whenever I need fuel,' Winnie said. He checked his fuel anyway. He heard someone call his number from the kitchen — time for tucker.

He found the condiments among the knives and forks and spread hot mustard over his T-bone. Halfway through the fillet he heard the truck arrive. Benny unloaded his bike and wheeled it to the service centre, then came to sit with Winnie.

'It's not a bad meal here if you want one, but you'd better hurry: we're leaving as soon as your puncture's fixed.'

'No, it's all right, Prez.' Benny took out a cigarette and lit up. The smoke drifted over Winnie.

'Go over there and have that, or wait until I'm finished eating.'

'I'll wait, Prez.'

The eaters ate and the smokers smoked until the punctured tyre had been repaired.

'It's time to hit the road, Kev. Next stop, Wodonga.'

'Will we have enough fuel? The boys are saying we'll need fuel before then.'

'I didn't think it was that far.'

'It is, Prez. There's a town called Jugiong about halfway.'

'Jugiong it'll have to be, then.'

'The highway changes from here into just one lane either way. It's pretty rough.'

'We'll be right, Kev.'

'You haven't been to Melbourne before, Prez?'

'Haven't had to, Benny. You?'

'I lived down there when I was a kid. My father was in the Navy and we lived there when he got posted to the naval training station.'

'How come you never joined?'

'Are you kidding? I saw what the old man had to put up with.'

'Your bike's ready, mate.' The Prez watched a nominee push Benny's bike over to the pub.

'Didja fill it up?' Benny asked. They stared at each other and bit their lips.

'You'll stay a nominee that way!' Benny jumped on, started up, gunned it and sprayed the noms with dust and stones as he sashayed over to the pump.

Benny reckoned the highway was pretty shitty from there to the border but they'd soon get to the dual carriageway. He warned Winnie to look out for B-doubles because they ran the highway.

'They don't give bikies a hard time, Benny.'

Benny was right about the highway. They made Wodonga in good time but found themselves in traffic. The pack attracted huge attention when they stopped at the lights. Shoppers, schoolchildren and workers stared. Women came out of their shops and smiled and waved. The long ride and the heat of the engines had fostered an unnatural thirst so they headed for the first pub they saw. Big Kev removed his sunglasses and looked like a coal miner. It'd been a long ride; he rubbed his eyes and arched his back.

'Got to do something with the Hard Tail,' he uttered to nobody in particular.

'Yeah, but it looks good, Kev.'

A small group of locals gathered to admire the bikes as the Miners filed into the pub. A couple of nominees kept an eye on the bikes while the pub staff pulled beers non-stop.

Before they'd finished their first drink, a nominee whispered something to Big Kev. 'The pigs outside want to talk,' Kev said.

'Keep everyone in the pub, Brian. Come on, Kev, let's see what they want.' Winnie grabbed his beer and headed out.

'They most probably want to welcome us to Victoria!'

An inspector puffed up like a cocky and flanked by a sergeant and four extra bodies carrying clipboards stood before the bikes. Winnie and Kev headed towards them but didn't get a chance to say a word; the head Pig went straight on the attack. 'In Victoria you are, by law, required to wear approved safety helmets.'

The Prez turned to Big Kev. 'Where was the border, mate?'

'Don't get fucking smart with me,' the head Pig said. 'You know where the border is. You just rode over the river, didn't you?'

The Prez replied, 'Didn't see it, mate, but we'll wear helmets from now on.'

The Pig didn't expect that. He turned to his flunkies and nodded his head. They started writing down registration numbers.

'Why are they doing that?'

'If there's any trouble, we know who to look for.'

Big Kev towered over the copper and stuck his chin in his face. 'We've met your type before.' It was such an unexpected reversal that the Pig didn't know whether to shit or wind his watch. He turned white.

'Move your bikes off the footpath!'

Winnie nodded to the nominees, who wheeled the bikes elsewhere. The inspector began to lose it a bit because the boys grinned at him.

'And it's illegal to drink on the footpath!'

'Sorry, didn't know,' Winnie said. He drained his beer and wiped his mouth. It set the Pig off again.

'If any of your members do anything, and I mean *anything* wrong, they'll be locked up!'

Winnie's face set. 'If you lock up any of my boys we won't leave without them.'

He meant what he said and the Pig definitely wasn't used to being spoken to like that. He clenched his fists and motioned for his Sergeant to follow him. Behind his back, the sergeant shrugged his shoulders, smiled at Winnie and followed the top Pig back to the patrol car. He slid into the driver's seat, started the engine and took off. The top Pig looked straight ahead.

'Welcome to Victoria, Prez.'

'You'd better let everyone know about the helmets; we don't want any extra attention.'

Most of the members were too engrossed in bullshitting and drinking to know what had gone on. Brian and Kev walk back into the pub.

'On the rag, was he?' Swannie quipped. 'We were checking him out through the window.'

The Prez replied, 'I think somebody must've shit in his best hat; or his missus left him.' That brought the house down.

'So where is our motel, Brian?'

'Couple of blocks away. I've got a nominee up there now, confirming our bookings.'

'Good, I might have an early night tonight, I don't want to be burnt out before Melbourne. Anyway, after we have a feed tonight, Brian, I want the four of us in my room. Get Benny and Toothpick there for a talk.'

After a hot shower and a feed Benny and Toothpick turned up. 'Find a seat, boys.'

Big Kev locked the door behind them. 'We're about to put a lot of trust in you boys. If either of you has any doubts, you'd better leave now. What we're going to discuss has nothing to do with the Club; this is about our business. We want to bring you into it to make our speed. We can't do it with everything else we've got to do.'

Toothpick spoke up. 'We're ready for it, Prez. Whatever you want us to do, we're in.'

'You know the rules: if you get busted you're on your own, but we'll help with the legal shit and we'll look after your families. Is that understood?'

'Yes, Prez.'

'Okay, don't make any plans for when we get back to Sydney. You'll be going to our lab to take lessons on how to cook, and you'll both get ten per cent of our profits. Are you happy with that?'

Benny and Toothpick smiled at each other and looked around the room. 'Thanks, boys,' said Benny. 'We won't let you down.'

'You'd better not,' Big Kev said sternly. 'Okay, you can fuck off now and have a party, because when we get back, work starts.'

They shook hands and left the room.

Winnie and Kev talked it over.

'They'll be good for us,' said Winnie. 'Not only will they do the cooking, but after we get to know them better they can do some of our running around.'

'So that's why you offered them ten per cent!'

'That's it, mate. Then, if they like, they can get people to do the cooking and that way we'll be further away from the front line. We have other things to do. Are you and Ocker getting more brothels?'

Big Kev looked at Ocker. 'We're having a rethink. Soon it's going to be like a normal business.'

Ocker looked thoughtful for a moment. 'I've got other things to do and I've still got that tattoo shop to run. Maybe I'll start doing a bit more tattooing myself. The brothels are becoming a pain in the arse because most of the girls are on the hammer and they're unreliable.'

'What about you, Kev?'

'I really don't give a fuck anymore. Sandy and I will just have one up-market place with classy girls, who're going to work because they want to, not because they have to. Ocker's right, Prez — you have to be there all the time. We're doing alright anyway, Prez.'

'I know, Kev.'

'I'm going to build a new bike. That Hard Tail killed my back on the highway; it's all right for short trips but not on long runs.' He stopped to consider for a second. 'I might have two bikes; one for Sydney and one for runs.'

'Makes sense, Kev. What sort are you going to build?'

'I have a few ideas; we have a Jammer frame catalogue, so there are lots of options.'

'We could make it a shop project and put it on the showroom floor and you could use it for runs.' Kev was elated.

Brian stared at the floor. 'We can talk about that later — there's something else I want to talk about.'

'What's up, Brian?'

'It's like this, Prez. Have you noticed how small Swannie's Chapter's got?' He looked at the boys intently. 'Little Tony told me the reason is that he's making everyone in his Chapter sell an ounce of speed a week, and if they're late in paying, he fines them; but if they don't want to sell, he gives them the arse.'

'Are you sure about this, Brian? Did you say anything to Swannie?'

'No, Prez, I wanted to talk with you first. I just hope it's not true.'

'People change, mate, especially where there's money and power.'

'I don't know if it's true yet. I mean, we've known him a long time.'

'Did Little Tony tell anyone else?'

'No, he's shitting himself now; he thinks you won't believe him.'

'Where is he now?'

'In his room, Prez.'

'Get him, Brian.'

'Okay, Prez.'

Little Tony's dark eyes darted back and forth until they settled on the Prez.

'What's this I've been hearing about our mate Swannie making his members sell speed for him?'

In a strong voice Tony said, 'On my mother's grave, Prez, it's true. I don't mind doing the business, but we're losing a lot of members who don't want to be involved. Good members — that's not why they joined the Club.'

'Who else feels like this?'

'Most, Prez; we don't know what to do.'

'If you're bullshitting us, you know what'll happen. We've known him a lot longer than we've known you.' Kev wasn't happy; he had no reason to doubt Swannie's loyalty to the Club.

'I know, Kev, that's why nobody wants to say anything.'

'You don't just want to take over his business?' Winnie asked.

'That's not it, Prez.' Tony looked worried.

The Prez continued. 'This is what we'll do, Tony. You say nothing to anyone, let us find out for ourselves, and if it's true, your Chapter has to look after him.'

'Done.'

'We'll talk to you before the run is over. First we'll find out what's going on.'

'I—' Before Tony could say another word, Winnie raised his hand to silence him.

'That's enough! Get going now, we need to talk.'

Little Tony left and Brian patted Winnie on the shoulder. 'Don't worry, mate.'

'That'll put the cat among the pigeons,' Ocker said to no one in particular.

'We don't know if it's true yet,' said Brian.

'You're pretty close to him, Kev,' said Winnie. 'What's your feeling?'

'I hate to say it, Prez, but I believe Tony.'

'Let's find out for ourselves. If the other members are with him, they'll talk to us.'

'Swannie's doing a lot of business for us.'

'It doesn't matter, Ocker, if he's wrecking his Chapter. The Club comes first and there are plenty of members who'd take his place; he's a worry.'

'If it's true,' said Kev, 'we'll have to be there when the Chapter fronts him. It doesn't make any of us feel good, because Swannie's been with us for a long time.'

Chapter 20

The next morning, readying for the ride to Melbourne, members without helmets chased around looking for them. The pigs parked across the road and waited for them to leave, to escort them out of town. The Prez glanced at Swannie leading his pack down the highway and thought over what he'd learned the night before: one minute a bloke's your best mate and the next he's your enemy! He'd heard enough the night before, after speaking to some of Swannie's boys, to know that Swannie had to go. After almost a full day in the saddle they pulled up at a little town outside of Melbourne. Winnie rang Rastus for directions. While the members fuelled up and grabbed a feed, five or six pigs with long lens cameras took pictures.

Winnie was furious. 'What is this — a police state?' He couldn't believe it. 'Has anyone got a camera with them?'

Ocker went to his saddlebag and pulled out his camera.

'Take photos of those fuckers and see if they like it.'

The pigs freaked out and turned their backs when they saw Ocker's long lens. They jumped into unmarked cars and drove off. The boys laughed and tooted their horns.

'What's the plan, Prez?

'Rastus is going to get someone to meet us near Pentridge Prison and show us the way. Come on, let's go!'

Melbourne was a new experience for the boys, most of whom had never ridden alongside trams before. The Prez remembered them in Sydney, but it'd been long before he was old enough to ride.

The boys rode so close to the trams they could have spoken to the passengers clattering beside them. The found the bluestone walls of Pentridge Prison and pulled over to join the six Commandos awaiting them. Winnie wondered about the wisdom of having a jail in the middle of the city. The Commandos shouted out, 'Follow us!' and the mob took off through the canyon-like streets of Melbourne. They followed the Commandos into a side street and up to a huge set of gates emblazoned with 'Commandos MC' in solid letters. The gates opened and the fifty-odd bikes rode in and parked.

Rastus stood at the door. 'Welcome to our clubhouse.' He shook hands with each member of the Miners. 'Come in, boys, let's have a drink.'

Big Kev, Ocker and Brian joined Winnie and Rastus, introducing the boys to the Commandos members. The Commandos impressed the Miners with topless barmaids and a free bar for an hour. Their new clubhouse was the same size as the Miners' clubhouse but better set out, with a huge mural of the Commandos' colours covering a double brick wall. There wasn't a window in the place but it had been fully carpeted and in one corner was a commemorative shrine for members killed on their bikes. The place was warmed by a huge potbelly stove. Framed front pages of the Melbourne *Sun* displayed stories about the club.

Brian pointed out a public phone box in a corner. 'We need one of those, Prez.'

'Yeah, Brian, I don't think that's the only thing we're going to learn down here.'

The old Commandos looked scungy enough, but they displayed a lot of class and welcomed the Miners warmly.

'I'm impressed, Rastus.'

Rastus replied, 'We cleaned it up just for you. I'll give you a tour later.'

The prettiest topless barmaid Winnie had ever seen served their drinks.

'This is Amanda, boys,' Rastus said and gently rubbed her arse.

'Hi, boys. Rastus told me about you Sydney blokes.'

The boys couldn't take their eyes off her perfect titties as she pirouetted around like a ballet dancer and swung her arse and walked away.

She turned and said, 'I'll see you later, boys.'

'You like her, Ocker?'

'Fucking oath, mate. I'd drain a beer through her panties.'

Everybody laughed and Rastus remarked, 'You haven't changed a bit, you dirty little man!'

Swannie and Rastus embraced in a greeting.

The Prez gave Kev a look and said, 'I didn't know they were so close.' Kev shrugged but said nothing.

'The party isn't tonight, is it, Rastus?'

'No, Winnie, tomorrow night. I thought you might like a quiet night to get settled in your rooms. It's not too far from here. Later on tonight I'll pick you up and we can go for a feed. Orright?'

'That sounds all right, mate.'

'How was your ride down? Did that prick Pig give you a hard time in Wodonga?'

'He tried.'

'Don't worry, he does it to everyone.'

'What's wrong with the pigs down here? At our last fuel stop, they were taking photos!'

'That's a new one.'

'They didn't like it when we did it back to them,' Winnie said.

Rastus laughed and called over a few members and retold the story. They were suitably impressed.

'How come you've got no windows in here?' Brian queried.

Rastus didn't have to answer. The penny dropped for Brian.

'You're a dickhead!' Swannie laughed.

Big Kev just looked at Swannie; he'd said the wrong thing. 'Yeah, but he's our dickhead.'

Swannie put his arm around Brian's shoulders and apologised.

Brian just smiled. He knew more than Swannie thought he did. 'That's alright, mate.'

'Come on, Rastus, show us around.'

Rastus took them behind the clubhouse and out the back to some sheds. 'We can park about thirty bikes, nose to the wall, and there's a workshop down the back. Spike set it up.'

'Not bad!' Kevvie was impressed.

'He should be here soon,' said Winnie. 'He's flying down today from Sydney.'

'Here's our meeting room. Showers are down the back, and here's our gutting room.'

He unlocked the door, revealing a queen-sized bed, mirrored ceiling and walls, and a few chains scattered on either side of the bed. Two sets of handcuffs lay atop the bedhead, with a selection of whips and dildos sitting on a side table ready to go, and a large tub of Vaseline also at the ready.

'This is my type of room; you can smell the sex in here.' Rastus sniffed the air.

'Are you on heat, mate?' Ocker was curious.

'I'm always on heat!' Rastus grinned his toothless grin and dragged on his cigar.

'Come on,' said Winnie. 'Let's get out of here before Ocker starts jacking off!'

The boys followed Rastus out.

'If you want the key, Ocker, you gotta see me. I think Amanda has her eye on you.'

'Bullshit!'

'Let's wait and see. Now in here we have our special room.' He opened a heavy steel door and the boys entered a large room with a ten-seater table covered in green felt. Decks of cards lay in a wooden box.

'You play cards, eh, Rastus?' asked Swannie.

'Sometimes. You?'

'Love it!'

'You'll get a game here tomorrow, Swannie, and you'd better watch out — there are some good players here. Right now we have a small tournament on.'

'Put me down for it.'

'Anyone else?'

Silence reigned. Winnie, Kev and Brian inspected a row of Winchester pump-action shotguns chained to a wall and the small safe set in the floor.

'How do you get away with this, Rastus?' Winnie was amazed at the set-up.

'The pigs never get this far. Besides, they're all legal; we have licensed members and they just store them here.' His eyes darted to the floor safe. 'That can be hidden with a rug.'

'Not bad, mate.'

Rastus poured some speed out onto a mirror. 'Welcome to Melbourne — want some gas? We can go out for a drink later tonight and I'll show you around.'

'I've never heard it called gas before,' said Winnie. 'Good name, I like it; it makes sense.'

'We've got all sorts of names for it, mate; it all depends what suburb you're in at the time. We call it zip, goey and whiz. You Sydney blokes are way behind.'

'Not on all things, mate!'

'I know, Winnie.' Rastus passed Winnie a rolled note. 'Here, fill 'er up!'

Winnie snorted one of the huge lines, threw his head back and repeated the ritual then passed the note to Kev.

'There must've been half a gram in those two lines.' Winnie felt the effects in about three seconds flat. 'Mmm, that's good shit.'

'I know,' Rastus said in a wobbly voice. 'You'll be up for two days.'

'I never came down here to sleep, mate; I came down here to party with the Commandos!'

'Well, come on, let's party!' Rastus grabbed Ocker by the shoulder, 'Come on, you dirty little Miner, I've got a present for you!'

'I like presents, Rastus.' Ocker followed Rastus into the clubhouse.

Kev leaned in to Winnie. 'Ocker and Rastus've had girlies together before. Reckon they're going to do the same here?'

'Good chance, Kev. Did you see the gutting room, with all their little toys?'

'Some weren't so little, Prez.'

Winnie laughed at that. 'Has the back-up truck arrived yet, Kev?'

'Over there, Prez.'

The bald-headed driver stood at the crowded bar.

'Do you want him, Prez?'

'In a minute, Brian; let's find out what we're going to do first. I want to get to my room, have a shower and dress up for the tour of Melbourne with Rastus. Anyway, how far is St Kilda?'

'Find Benny,' said Kev. 'He knows his way around. We're going to need a couple of nominees to watch the bikes; there's too many bike thieves around here, so we'll put them on a roster, one day on and one day off.'

'There's enough of them, Prez,' said Brian. 'They can do eight-hour shifts.'

'You work it out then, Brian. I want all our bikes back there and we'll use taxis. The pigs'll be watching us, so I don't want to leave any of our members down here, Kev. Can you let the boys know?'

'Right now, Prez?'

'Get Benny and the bald one; get a look at him, will ya? I've never seen him without a beanie on before! He must shave his head, it's so shiny!'

'He oils it,' said Brian.

'Bullshit! It's shiny because it's bald.'

'He might shave the back?'

The bald driver came over. 'You want me, Prez?'

'Yeah, we all want to know if you shave your head.'

'Just the back, Prez.'

'Just joking, Baldy. We want you to take the truck to our motel.'

'I've got a map of Melbourne, Prez, just give me the address.'

'Here it is.' Brian handed it over.

'Get going now, Baldy. We won't be far behind you.'

Ocker and Rastus came back. 'Are we going, Prez?' asked Ocker. 'I haven't had my present yet.'

'She'll be here when we get back and I want all the bikes in the same spot.'

'What time do you want me to pick you up, Winnie?' asked Rastus.

'How about we meet you back here, mate?'

'That's fine, Winnie, I've got a few jobs to do. Anyhow, do you know where you've got to go?'

'We're organised.'

Big Kev returned with Benny. 'When are we going, Prez?'

'Tell them ten minutes, and Benny, you come up the front with me. Kev, I don't want any stragglers.'

'We ride straight through the heart of Melbourne, Prez,' said Benny. 'Have you heard of Flinders Street Railway Station?'

'Yeah, I've heard of it.'

'There's a famous pub across from it called the Young & Jackson; it's known all over the world for its nude painting. When I was about ten we caught the train into town with my mother and brothers. I remember her leaving us at the corner where the pub is — she'd forgotten to buy something. So I stuck my head in the door and looked at the nude painting. It was the first time in my life that I'd seen smut — well, my mother called it that when she caught me! She dragged me out by the ear. The pain was offset by the pleasure I got when I cracked my first fat. I went home and had my first wank that night!'

Everybody laughed loudly. Ocker reckoned they should call him Benny the Wanker!

'Where's Swannie?'

'He's getting one of the nominees to ride his bike for him; he's out with Rastus and a few of the Commandos, having a drink.'

'Shall I get him, Prez?'

'No mate, let's go.'

The boys had a clear run through to the motel, which was about ten minutes from outside the CBD. Winnie showered and dressed and chatted with Big Kev. 'What do you reckon Swannie's up to?'

'Don't know, Prez, but I'll bet my balls he's up to something. It'll come out. He's not showing you much respect by fucking off with Rastus and not hanging with us.'

'Does it show that much?' Winnie asked. Big Kev just nodded.

After they got ready Winnie knocked on Brian's door and Ocker opened up. 'Brian's on the phone to Gina.'

'Tell him we'll wait downstairs.'

In the foyer a few members sat around, ready for their first night in Melbourne. As excited as little kids, they headed for their taxi. 'Enjoy yourselves, boys, and stay out of trouble.'

Kev checked the bikes in the underground car park. They were guarded by two nominees, who were sitting comfortably in chairs and playing cards on the top of an Esky.

'Don't you blokes go getting too pissed and out of it.'

'We won't, Sarge; we're just making the time go by.'

'Make sure there's one of you here at all times. Do you have protection?'

They lifted up their baseball bats. 'Good, I'll see you later.'

The boys went out to their taxi. Winnie jumped in the front seat and directed the driver.

'You know the Commandos, eh?' the cabbie asked. 'They're good boys.' He pulled up in front of the Commandos' clubhouse.

'Say hello to Rastus for me.'

'How much is the fare, mate?'

'No, free for you boys.'

'What's your name?'

'Yusef,' he answered and drove off with a friendly wave.

Ocker was impatient to get inside. 'Come on, Prez; I'm going to get my present!'

'Someone else will have her by now.'

'Yeah, like fuck!' Ocker ran into the clubhouse.

'I like the way they're set up here, Kev. Our clubhouse is a tin shed compared to this.'

'We'll have to do something about it when we get back, get all the members involved.'

'Good idea, Brian.'

More taxis pulled up.

Spike met them, wearing his colours. 'How was the ride down, Prez?'

'No problems, Spike.'

'Rastus tells me that he's taking you out on the town tonight — you'll love it!'

'Why don't you come with us?'

'I can't, Winnie; I'll party with you tomorrow night. I've got people to see tonight, but I'll have a drink and a joint with you now.'

'I'll be in that,' Brian said. 'I'm revving off my head from the gas Rastus gave us!'

They followed Rastus to a table next to the memorial wall and Spike began rolling a joint from some brownish coloured grass from Tasmania. Spike looked at a nominee. 'These blokes are the officers of the Miners Motorcycle Club.'

'Yeah, we met earlier, Spike.'

'Well, you should know what they drink then, so bring them.' Spike smiled at the boys. 'Fucking nominees, they're too smart sometimes!'

Winnie took a close look at a photo of a Commando holding a huge fish; his colours hung nearby. 'What happened to him, Spike?'

Spike looked up from mulling the joint and his eyes clouded over instantly, his sorrow obvious. 'That's Scottie. We grew up together. He always got the girls! He'd just got out of jail and went fishing on Port Phillip Bay. They were swamped and the boat capsized. They stayed with the boat by holding onto a rope.' He paused to lick the papers on a massive joint. 'Whenever the boat went under, Scottie held onto the rope and he lasted eighteen hours. The other bloke wore a child's floatie and that saved his life — he was found after twenty-three hours, but Scottie was gone. They found eight state-of-the-art lifejackets in the bow, but they never found Scottie. We had to hire a helicopter to look for him, even though there were six RAAF helicopters at the base.'

'It would've been different if the Prime Minister went missing!'

'Yeah. Scottie, the silly cunt, never found the lifejackets. He was our Sergeant-at-Arms and that's why we have his colours. Sometimes I look at this photo expecting him to come walking into the clubhouse.' Spike's eyes brightened somewhat when he pointed to another photo of Scottie wearing a big grin doing a burnout and looking back over his shoulder at the gathered crowd enveloped in smoke from the rear tyre. He looked young and invincible.

The nominee returned with the drinks. 'I've got a message from Ocker; he said he got his present.'

Spike filled them in. 'You won't see him again tonight. It's Rastus' sister!'

'Fuck off! He's too ugly to have a gorgeous sister like that!' The boys all chortled — as ugly as Rastus was, his sister was beautiful. The joint did the rounds and the mood relaxed appreciably.

Winnie noticed that the Sergeant-at-Arms patch was missing from Spike's colours. 'You're not number two here any more, Spike?'

'No, Prez, Sydney's where I live now and I cannot be Sergeant-at-Arms from up there.' He lit up another huge joint and then handed it to Brian.

'Have you seen Swannie yet, Spike?'

'No, Kev, he's off with Rastus, but if Rastus says they'll be back, they'll be back. Worried?'

'No, just wondering.' Kev looked blank.

The Tasmanian weed wove its magic and the boys listened eagerly to Spike's Melbourne bikie stories. Turned out life there wasn't dissimilar to theirs in Sydney — same shit, different city.

Rastus turned up, looking nearly presentable under his Commandos beanie, pulled down nearly to his eyes. 'Are you ready, boys?'

Everybody knocked back their drinks and stood.

'See you at the party tomorrow, Spike.'

Outside a stretch limousine awaited. Rastus held the door open as the boys piled in. A nominee sat at the wheel.

Winnie's eyes widened. 'Where did this come from?'

'I own six of them and hire them out with chauffeurs.'

'With caps?' Kev asked, looking around at the plush interior and bar.

'With caps, mate, and they're always booked.'

Rastus passed around cold drinks and then made up four big lines on the mirrored table that folded down from the back of the front seat. He looked up with a dirty little smirk on his face. 'I wonder what type of mischief we'll get up to tonight. Do you have any preferences?'

'We're just bikies, mate,' said Winnie. 'We'll leave it in your hands.'

'Whatever we're going to do, at least we're doing it in style!'

'Cheers to you, Rastus!' said Brian.

'My pleasure, boys.'

'I haven't forgotten the first night we met you,' said Winnie. 'I thought we'd get into a blue that night and instead we ended up partying with you!'

'Yours was the first club to have anything to do with us,' Rastus said. He closed the sliding window. 'Now the nominee can't hear us.'

They snorted the lines through a McDonald's straw. Rastus leaned back in his seat, looked everyone directly in the eye then his face darkened. 'I thought you blokes were my mates?'

The boys did a double take. Brian and Big Kev didn't know what to say. Winnie stared point blank and then said quietly, 'Tell us what you're on about, Rastus, then I'll tell you if we're your mates or not.'

Rastus was obviously agitated but he kept it together. 'Yeah, well, a little bird tells me you're going to take over the Commandos and make Spike your President down here.'

Big Kev shouted instantly, 'Get fucked!'

Winnie just leaned back. 'You and Spike have been together for a long time; do you think he'd do that? No! Rastus, tell us what you heard.'

'There's someone causing trouble,' said Rastus, 'and I'll tell you who it is.'

Winnie spoke first. 'It's Swannie, isn't it?'

'Then you know what he's up to?'

'No idea, first I've heard of it, but you can tell us now, Rastus.'

Rastus lay back against the headrest and exhaled loudly.

'Alright. A few months ago he came to see me about getting chemicals and asked if I'd help set up a lab. I wondered why he didn't ask you but I never said anything and I helped him.' He stared at Winnie. 'Ever since, he's been very matey. About a month ago he told me about your plans and when I walked into the clubhouse tonight and saw you all at the table together I reckoned you were about to spring it on me.'

Winnie shrugged. 'When was all this supposed to happen?'

'He told me not to say anything to you until he was ready to get rid of you.'

'He'll never be ready, mate, believe me. I'll tell you something, Rastus: we're already onto him for other reasons and this is just one more, believe me. Don't say anything to him. We'll look after the problem when we get back to Sydney, but tonight' — he grabbed Rastus by the back of his head and knocked their foreheads together — 'tonight we're going to party!'

Winnie, Big Kev and Brian looked at each other. 'I'm glad you told us, mate.'

'Not as glad as I am, Winnie,' said Rastus.

'I never relished the thought of having trouble with you — you're our mate!'

Everybody laughed. The tension evaporated instantly. 'The hardest part's not to give it away before we get back.' Winnie stared out the window at the darkening streets. 'He's been keeping his distance from us, Rastus, and now we know why.'

'I never noticed.'

'You watch him!' Kev smacked his fist into his other hand. 'Cunt.'

'I will, Kev.'

The traffic slowed. People were walking about looking pretty relaxed, smiling and laughing. Brian watched the passing parade. 'There's a lot of people out tonight, Rastus. Is there a festival on?'

'This is a normal night in Melbourne. It's a people town; we don't have the pokies like Sydney and it doesn't cost a thing to walk the streets. It's more like Europe down here.'

'Have you been to Europe?'

'No, I've been told about it by my Italian mates. That's where we're going now, for a feed at Carlton — you like Italian, don't you? If not, we can go somewhere else.'

'Wog's fine, Rastus.' They stopped at Dominic's Restaurant and the nominee parked around the back. 'We'll be a couple of hours, wait for us.'

'Okay, boss.'

Winnie and his boys looked puzzled. They'd never heard Rastus called boss before. As they exited the stretch limo, patrons dining al fresco stared at them.

Winnie remarked to Kev quietly, 'We don't look too bad. It's Rastus they're staring at, because he doesn't look as if he'd have two bob to rub together, let alone be able to afford a limo!' They followed Rastus into the restaurant. Waiters waved and the owner greeted them.

'Rastus, follow me.' The owner led them to a quiet corner of the restaurant, to a table with a 'Reserved' sign.

Rastus introduced them to Dominic as 'his friends from Sydney'.

'Welcome to Melbourne, I'm Dominic.' He spoke with a faint Italian accent.

'You're pretty well known down here, Rastus,' said Winnie. 'How come you moved to Sydney?'

'It's a long story, but it's all changed now. I'll tell you about it one day. Order what you like, it's my shout.' He looked at the menu for a minute or so and then he looked up at Winnie. 'I can't believe that Swannie cunt. He used to be a good bloke. I don't know what's in his head; we had the same problem with one of our members.'

Winnie said it in one word: 'Money.'

Rastus nodded. 'Some people can't handle it; they're better people without it. Anyway, let's not spoil the night. He can wait.'

'So, what's the go with this place, are you in with the Mafia?'

'I don't know what you know, Kev.'

'I was in Vietnam with a bloke from Carlton. That's where we are, isn't it? Well, he told me about what goes on here.'

Dominic brought some glasses and a litre of red wine in a carafe. 'We're very busy tonight, Rastus. I'll come back soon.'

'Take your time,' Rastus assured him. Dominic hurried away.

Rastus filled the glasses from the carafe. 'This is Dominic's father's special wine. He grows his own grapes in his backyard, not far from here. Cheers, and welcome to Melbourne!' The boys raised their glasses and took a big sip. 'Now, I'll tell you about Carlton, Kev. Dominic owns this restaurant now. His old man worked on the wharves, while his mother cleaned houses.' He paused before continuing. 'Just to give their kids a chance in this country. I lived up the road from them and my old man gave me nothing. We rented, but they bought, and paid the fucking mortgage while my old man and mother gambled it or pissed all their money against the wall. I remember their house well; they fed us all and we ate and drank and laughed — it was my second family. Now Dominic owns this place because he works eighteen hours a day. His old man used to come in and do the washing up when he first started, and his mother washed and ironed their linen, so if that's the so-called Mafia, then so be it. His brother Vincent's a different story. He's just like us and he does a lot of business with his friends, just like we do. We're not Mafia, are we? We're just bikies! Do we hurt anyone who doesn't deserve it?'

Everybody just shook their heads.

'Dominic comes from a good family.'

'What's his brother do?' asked Kev.

'He runs a nightclub that morphs into a strip club late at night. We're going there later. Do you get the drift of Carlton now, Kev?'

'You can't believe everything you hear, can you, mate?'

Dominic returned with a loaf of garlic bread and a long serrated knife and placed it before Rastus. 'More wine, Rastus?'

'Yes, thanks, Dom.'

'Hey, I didn't mean anything.'

'I know, Kev, let's have a feed.'

'Come on, Dom, take our orders. We've got a big night ahead.' Dominic told them he'd bring a bit of everything and took off.

Rastus left for a leak and Winnie turned the conversation to Swannie. 'I don't feel much like a party tonight.'

Kev sat back in his chair and clenched his fists. 'I feel like getting stuck into him right fucking now.'

'No, mate, wait until we get back to Sydney. We have to find out what he's up to first. Rastus has no reason to bullshit us. If it's true, then we'll give it to him.' Winnie was as dark as he ever got, and when he darkened he got real quiet.

When Rastus returned the boys changed the topic. 'Do you want a moment, Winnie?'

'No, mate, we're just saying we might have an early night. The ride buggered us a bit and we want to be ready for the party tomorrow night.'

'I understand, Winnie. Well, let's have a great meal and some laughs.' Dominic started bringing plates of food and another carafe of vino rosso and they got stuck in.

Dominic brought salad, pasta and a plate piled with veal scaloppine, and a vanilla cake for afters. Rastus said it was the best food in Carlton, and no one could argue with that. When they finished, Rastus fired up a cigar and offered a box around. Brian and Winnie took one and Rastus held out his lighter to get them started. Brian exhaled a cloud of smoke. 'Nice, mate. Cuban?' Rastus smiled and showed him the box.

Winnie took a few puffs and leaned into the table. 'We have to keep this whole business to ourselves; we treat Swannie as before, you all agree?'

Nods all around, including from Rastus.

Dominic turned up with a bottle and a set of small glasses. 'A little something special from my father. Be careful, it could knock your head off.'

Rastus watched Dom pour. 'At Dom's house a friend of his father's came over before he went into hospital for a heart operation. They gave him some of this. He thought he could drink, had two glasses, said his goodbyes, put on his hat, walked out the front door, turned to wave at us, took a step and then collapsed backwards onto the lawn. First dead body I ever saw.'

Dom handed the glasses around. 'He tells that to everybody. Here, try it.' The boys' eyes widened.

Dom put his glass to his lips, winked and skolled it in one. Rastus didn't touch a drop. Winnie downed his and felt a burning sensation.

'You have to let it go down slowly,' said Dom.

The second glass went down a little better.

'Made from a blend of things, the old man's secret recipe.'

Winnie finished his drink and thought of his own father and how he changed after a few stiff drinks. He looked at Rastus watching him. 'You don't know what you're missing, Rastus.'

Rastus shook his head. He asked Dom for the bill and of course there was no bill. Dom spoke in Italian to Rastus, then Rastus stood and they hugged. 'Goodonya, Dom, see you tomorrow night.'

The boys staggered out to the limo. 'You speak Italian, Rastus?'

'No, mate, but over the years I've picked up a bit.'

'Is Amanda really your sister?'

'Yeah, mate, she looks the part, eh?'

'Ocker thought so.'

'Well, he won't get to fuck her. She'll line him up with some other girls. She's putting herself through university; she does that to make a quid. Takes balls, but she's good at it and she only works our clubhouse once a month or so.'

'Well, I wouldn't bet against Ocker getting what he wants.' Kev grinned broadly.

Rastus led them down a laneway to the waiting limo. He told the driver where to go and they piled in. 'Just a little stop first, boys.'

The car pulled up outside a disco lit with flashing neon lights. A queue a mile long waited outside while big bouncers let the pretty girls in and kept the uglies out. 'This is Dominic's brother's place. Strippers and late opening keeps the punters rolling in. I'll stay for a while and the nominee will drive you back to the motel. Goodnight, boys, seeyas later.'

When they got back to the motel Brian called home and Winnie went to his room and collapsed on the bed in his clothes. When Kev returned from checking the bikes Winnie was out like a light. Kev threw a blanket on him and thanked his lucky stars he'd only had one of Papa's specials.

Next morning at breakfast Ocker came in looking chipper. He poured a coffee and joined the boys at the table. Winnie moaned and promised he'd never drink anything ever again.

'What a night, boys.' Ocker was well pleased. 'He set me up with his bloody sister but it turns out she's not on the game. Anyway, she's an engineering student and we had a lot in common. She took me home to her place and we sat up and talked about portable phones and electronics. She reckons portables will be like arseholes — everyone'll have one.'

'Didja fuck her?'

'Plenty of time for that later, mate.'

Kev said nothing for a bit. He stared at Ocker. 'I think you're in love, you dirty little man. What will Rastus say?'

'I don't care, Kev. Rastus set me up, got me all hot to trot. Anyway, we're going out this arvo for a look at the town before the party.'

Kev had the last word. 'Goodonya, mate, hope it works out.'

Winnie waited until the banter died down. 'We've got a bit of bad news, Ocker.' Winnie told him all they knew.

Ocker was amazed. 'I'll talk to Little Tony later and get the drum. Find out who else might be in on this.'

Brian made some kind of excuse to get up and leave. He talked about locating Tony but Kev sussed it out. 'I reckon he's in the shit with Gina, Prez.'

Winnie waited for about ten minutes then followed Brian to his room. 'You alright, mate?'

'Oh, little Kitty joined the Brownies today and Gina's got the shits because I'm not there. I don't say a word when she goes off gambling.'

A knock at the door announced Little Tony. Winnie motioned for him to sit on the bed.

'What do you know about Swannie and the Commandos, Tony?'

'Nothing, Prez. He keeps to himself outside of club hours. I didn't even know he had anything to do with them, or that he came to Melbourne. He never told us. Turns out he's getting the chemicals from Rastus and cooking his own speed, as well as forcing his members to sell it under pain of expulsion from the Southside Chapter.'

Tony let out a long breath.

'There's more,' said Winnie. 'He's stirring up things between the Commandos and us, telling Rastus that we were trying to take over and install Spike as President.'

'Prez, I told you what I knew before, but I didn't know about all this. He's got a new nominee running around for him. A big cunt called Boris.'

'Well, we're going to look after Boris later, but first we have to sort out Swannie. Do you know where he is?'

'At the clubhouse with the Commandos, playing cards.'

Winnie leered. 'Hope he's winning, because I'm not waiting until we get back to Sydney.'

'Are you going to knock him, Prez?'

'No, it'll cause too much trouble with the Commandos if anything happens here. We'll pick him up, tell him we want him to meet someone and take him for a ride in the club truck. We won't kill him, just put him in hospital for a bit, and let him think it over while he's recovering. Let's get going. Kev and I'll take him, and you and Brian can go in the other truck.'

They walked out to the underground parking, where Boris guarded the trucks. 'You're Boris, eh?'

'Yes, Prez, g'day.'

'We're taking the trucks for a few hours and we'll be back around dark.'

They drove to the Commandos' clubhouse. Winnie didn't want to spook Swannie so he went in alone. Swannie was in good form and had the boys laughing around the card table while the nominees swept up and set up the clubhouse for the party. Swannie saw Winnie walk in, stood up, grabbed a drink and came over.

'You look like you're having a good time, Swannie.'

'Took all their money, mate.'

'There's someone I want you to meet, can you come now?'

'Sure, let me collect my winnings from the Commandos.'

Swannie slipped into the front seat between Kev and Winnie.

'Where are we off to, Prez?'

'We met a bloke manufacturing hydraulic clutches for bikes, needs investors; thought you might like a piece of the action.'

Kev was amazed at the bullshit Winnie dreamed up on the spur of the moment. Swannie bragged a bit more about taking all the Commandos' money. Kev kept looking for a likely spot. He saw a signpost pointing to a municipal tip, mulled it over for a heartbeat, slowed down and turned into the road. The sign on the fence said 'Closed' but Kev drove in past it. Swannie looked around nervously. 'Where are we? Looks like a tip.'

No one spoke. The trucks parked and the penny began to drop. Brian and Little Tony got out of their truck clutching baseball bats.

Ashen-faced, Swannie looked at Winnie. 'Why, Prez?' His voice changed, and he began to babble. 'Tony, tell the boys I'm a good bloke.'

'I already told them what a cunt you are, Swannie.'

A panic-stricken Swannie mumbled, 'I'm sorry, Prez, but it was Rastus, he wanted to take over and I told him I wouldn't be in it.'

Kev jumped out of the truck, grabbed Swannie's leg and pulled like buggery. Swannie held onto the steering wheel and wouldn't let go. Little

Tony leaned in and smashed Swannie's fingers, and then he let go. Kev heaved a sobbing Swannie to the ground. He screamed for mercy. Brian smacked him on the head and told the cunt to shut up. He fell silent.

Winnie leaned in real close and looked Swannie in the eye. 'You broke all our laws, Swannie. No loyalty, no mercy.' After some time, the blows ceased.

'Take all his clothes and toss his boots away.' They took his rings off his broken fingers and Kev grabbed his wallet and money belt, stuffed with thousands. He handed them to Brian.

'Look after these, will you, mate? Don't reckon he'll ride a bike again. Cunt.' He kicked Swannie's unconscious body again. Kev tossed Swannie's colours into the back of the truck and they drove wordlessly towards town.

Kev spoke first. 'Wonder when they'll find him.'

'Who cares?' said Winnie. 'I can't wait to tell Rastus.'

'What about the members, when do we tell them?'

'First night on the way back to Sydney we'll tell both Chapters at once. I doubt anyone'll stick up for him.'

'Not if they have any brains.'

'What about the members who left?'

'Fuck 'em. They didn't have the balls to stand up to Swannie. At least Little Tony had the front to tell us, instead of just leaving. He could be a good President.'

'Yeah, mate; he's a tough little bloke, a straight shooter. I like him. Hey, do you have a money belt, Prez?'

Winnie lifted up his shirt. 'No, mate.' They laughed, and it released the tension, wired as they were with adrenalin. No one liked hurting people, but it had to be done. The code was simple and clear: loyalty above all.

Winnie thought about the money belt — it had appeared chockers. He asked Kev, 'How much do you reckon was in that belt?'

'Must've been thousands, the sneaky prick. There was a pile in the wallet too.'

'I'll bet Brian is counting right now.' That started an involuntary laughing fit.

They parked the truck where they'd found it. Boris was waiting. 'I want you to have a chat with him tonight, Kev, and find out if he's in the Club for the drugs and money or for the Club itself. Get him talking; he'll tell you.'

'Done, Prez.' Kev pulled out Swannie's rings. 'What do we do with these?'

'Lose them.'

While Winnie got out, Boris appeared at the door and Kev flipped him the keys.

'Quiet night, Boris?'

'Yeah, Prez, I'm looking forward to the party tonight.'

Winnie gave Boris a big smile and assured him he was too.

Brian and Little Tony drove onto the lot. Brian jumped out before Tony reversed into his spot.

Winnie spotted a weird look on Brian's face. 'What's up, Brian?'

'Not here, I'll wait till we get up to the room.'

They walked into the room and Brian threw the belt on the bed. 'A shade under thirteen and a half grand. Why would he carry all that cash around?'

'He won at cards.'

'Not that much.'

'Maybe it was his safety belt.' Winnie's humour turned dark occasionally.

After three beats the joke found home. Kev let out a loud whoop, and they laughed like kids.

'Take a look at these, Prez.' Brian handed Winnie a handful of fifties from Swannie's wallet. Winnie peered closely; something was a bit off. They were pretty good, but they were forgeries. He tweaked them and rubbed them lightly with his fingertips. They looked okay, but they didn't feel quite right.

Brian inspected a note at arm's length. 'We could make a fortune if we could get onto these, Prez.' Winnie wasn't sure if he was joking. Kev rummaged in the fridge. 'Anyone for a beer? All kinds.'

A beer sounded just about right. 'Pass the chocolate out too, mate.'

Kev twisted the top off, drained the beer and belched loudly. 'That's better.'

'What do you reckon about these fifties, Kev?'

'Wouldn't touch 'em, Prez. Use 'em once and they're onto you.'

'I wonder if he got them here or in Sydney. We'll keep this quiet and maybe the supplier will get in touch with us when he works out Swannie's not around. Tony, when we get back to Sydney clear out his place of any Club gear and anything else of value. Take a truck and a nominee to help you.'

Tony knew what to do.

'I don't ever want to go through that again, Tony. We want you as the President of the Southside Chapter.'

'It's really up to the members, Prez.'

'You'll be right, Tony.'

'That's not why I gave him up.'

'We know that.'

'Thanks for your support, Brian.'

'She's right, Tony.'

Brian stared at the money on the bed. 'What do we do with the cash?'

'Half of all his assets go to each Chapter. Find out from Boris where he keeps his stash and we'll divvy that up too.'

'Leave that to us, Prez. He may not know anything.'

'Good,' said Winnie. 'I'm taking a long, hot shower and dressing up; I'm in the mood for a party.'

'Should we have a line first?' Brian was keen; he'd found Swannie's personal stash.

Tony did the honours with the knife and made four perfect lines that disappeared quickly.

'Tony, see if you can find his lab, too — it's ours now. Boris might help you.'

Kev and Winnie went to their room. 'Do you think Swannie'll talk, Prez?'

'I hope he won't be able to.' The Commandos' clubhouse seethed with partygoers, the stereo blared and people laughed and swayed with the music.

Winnie watched Rastus and a Commando having a quiet word. The frown said it all.

'I'll join you later, Winnie.' He disappeared into the back room with a few Commandos.

'What do you reckon's going on, Prez?' The door shut.

'Fucked if I know. Let's see.'

The band struck up and bodies started dancing. Brian pulled Ocker from behind the bar where he was fiddling with the stereo system and they joined Winnie and Kev outside in the quiet. 'Ocker, Swannie's gone. On the way back we'll have a meeting and let the members know. Until then, not a word to anyone. Kev, I want to leave by lunchtime tomorrow. We'll talk later, Ocker.'

Ocker said, 'You did what you had to do, Winnie.'

Brian pulled out a wallet. 'We found some counterfeit fifties on him. Do you know anything about them, mate?' He passed the note. Ocker held it up to the light and fingered it then passed it back to Brian. 'Pretty good, but not good enough.'

The doors of the clubhouse burst open suddenly and some punter went sprawling on his arse. Three Commandos soon followed and booted him scrambling on his knees across the yard until he got up and ran off into the night.

Rastus appeared a moment later. 'Caught the bastard passing dud money at the bar. He was a nominee for a time, but he gave up.'

Brian pulled out the note and gave it to Rastus. 'Did it look anything like this?'

Rastus stared at the note. 'Too right it did.'

'Was he playing cards with Swannie earlier?'

'He was.'

Brian produced a handful of notes. 'We found all these, too.'

Rastus grabbed the notes. 'I'm going to make an announcement about these notes; I'll be back later, Winnie.'

Rastus walked into the clubhouse, turned the music down and announced to one and all that bad fifties were floating around. He said if anyone valued their health they would not pass any, and then he turned up the music.

Winnie pulled Ocker aside. 'Little Tony is trying to find Swannie's lab; there's bound to be some equipment. When he finds it, grab it all.' Ocker knew the drill.

Brian pulled out the remaining bad fifty. 'What do we do with this, Prez?'

'Pin it up behind our bar so the nominees know what to look for.'

'Where's your girlie, Ocker?' asked Kev.

'Not here tonight, but she's coming to Sydney for the shop opening. Finds me irresistible.'

'What does Rastus say?' asked Winnie.

'Good luck.' They laughed.

Kev fired up a big joint and passed it around while the party raged inside. Rastus, a harmonica wrapped in his paws like a sandwich, belted out a blues tune. No one knew the whole Rastus, but he revealed himself a bit at a time. When he'd finished, everyone cheered and called for more but he'd had enough and joined the boys outside.

'I gave the members the drum about those bad notes. A few blokes had them and didn't even know it. I told them it's a matter of respect and that I didn't ever want to see that sack of shit we kicked out earlier. We're keeping his bike.'

'Did you tell Spike what Swannie was up to?'

'Yeah. He couldn't believe it, didn't know a thing. We've been brothers for years and I've never seen Spike speechless before.'

The band was playing loudly when Dominic turned up at the door with a bloke who had to be his brother Vincent, dressed to the nines. Rastus greeted them.

Vincent took a look around. 'Where are all the sluts tonight, Rastus?'

'Wives and girlfriends tonight, no sluts, Vincent.'

Winnie walked over and shook hands with Dominic and Vincent.

'Having fun in Melbourne, Winnie?'

'Yeah, Vincent, first time for me. I had a little too much of your father's grappa last night.'

'Gets them every time.' Vincent laughed. 'So what happened to you the other night? I was expecting you at the club.'

'Next time, Vincent. We wanted to be in good nick for tonight.'

'So Rastus tells me you run Sydney.'

Winnie laughed. 'We don't run Sydney; we just run a business in Sydney and do alright.'

'And you're opening a Harley chopper shop.'

'Yeah, in about two weeks. You should come up with Rastus for the opening and have a look for yourself.'

'I just might.'

'Rastus told me you and he are like brothers.'

'Yeah, we grew up together; he became a part of the family. He's the only one I'd say that about. When are you off, Winnie?'

'Tomorrow.'

'Well, I have to get going and keep an eye on the club. On Saturday night the yobbos come and get on the piss and go crazy; I don't want to lose my licence.'

'Good to meet you, Vincent. See if you can make it up to Sydney.'

Winnie watched the wives and girlfriends dancing and thought of Mimi. He wondered what he was doing there — he missed her.

Kev saw his face go blank. 'What's up, Prez?'

Winnie walked outside and lit a cigarette and stared up at the night sky. 'I think I've had enough of Melbourne, Kev. I just want to get on the road again. I'll find Rastus and say goodbye. See if Brian wants to come back now and I'll meet you here in ten minutes.'

Winnie found Rastus cutting lines in the back room for some of the girls. 'We're pushing off, Rastus, big ride tomorrow.' They walked outside.

'Thanks for coming down, Winnie. Glad you got to meet the boys and my Italian family. In future when you need chemicals or I need hash, we only go through Spike. I trust him with my life. If we have any other problems in future, I'll fly up and sort it out face to face, okay?

'Okay, mate, goodonya. I'll see you at the big opening of Western Choppers.'

Chapter 21

Next morning Winnie and Kev stood on their fifth-floor hotel room balcony and watched the Miners wheeling their bikes out into the sunshine and preparing for the ride north.

'They all know when we're leaving, Kev?'

Kev nodded, and then asked Winnie to take a look at a cop car parked on the street behind the motel. Winnie scanned the next door backyard and saw a figure hiding behind clothes on the clothesline. Another man with a camera peeked over a fence.

Kev yelled, 'What are you blokes doing down there?'

The head disappeared behind the fence and the bloke near the clothesline froze. 'You a snowdropper, mate?'

He stood behind the clothes but he was no less visible. The members below looked up and wondered what the fuck they were up to. Winnie and Kev almost fell over laughing. The cameraman poked his head up and Kev boomed out, 'Fuck off!'

The homeowner came out the back door screaming, 'What are you two doing in my backyard?'

Kev called out, 'He's a snowdropper.'

She grabbed a broom and made for the cop hiding behind the clothes. His badge got tangled in the washing and she took a swipe at him. He dodged the blow and took off, followed by the cameraman. Winnie watched them drive off in the patrol car. He looked over the balcony at the members staring up oblivious.

'I'll tell you what you missed later, boys.'

Kev waved at the lady with the broom who just shook her head and rehung her washing. 'That was pretty funny, Prez, but this is like a police state. I'll be glad to get home.'

'Then let's get this show on the road, mate.'

They filled Ocker and Brian in on the events witnessed that morning and the story passed around in a few minutes. Little Tony had the Southside Chapter members in a circle in the underground parking, telling them about Swannie.

'Do you want to join them, Prez?'

'No, leave them to it but make sure all the Miners are ready to leave, Kev.'

Toothpick had been partying since he arrived and was in no condition to ride, so they put his bike in the truck and he rode with the driver.

Brian had the shits with Toothpick. 'We can't rely on a bloke who gets pissed, Prez. I'm going to bring it up at a meeting.'

'Christ, Brian, we're fucking bikies. Try bringing up not getting pissed at the next meeting and see how you go.'

Brian shut up for a second then waded in. 'Well, I've never seen him this pissed before.'

'It's a one-off, Brian. Besides, I like the Toothpick.'

'You like his Ford Customline too,' Big Kev laughed.

Winnie smiled at Kev. 'You forget nothing, do you? Okay, Brian, when you bring it up remember to tell the members that while we're all brothers and we'd love to look after everyone who can't ride, there's only so many we can carry, so there's a good chance they'll get left behind. See if anyone gets pissed ever again.'

'Orright, Prez, I'll have a quiet word.'

'Better idea, just don't make him out to be a cunt because he had a few too many.'

Winnie looked at his watch and Kev checked his watch, boomed it out: 'Fifteen minutes to go!' His voice reverberated in the underground parking. Little Tony and his members looked out.

Ocker laughed. 'You're in stereo, Kev.'

Some of the boys mounted their bikes and fired them up. The Southside Chapter finished their meeting and walked out into the sunshine and Tony headed straight for Winnie. 'I told them Swannie's out and we'd talk tonight, Prez.'

'Good, any problems?'

'No, Prez. I spoke to Boris — he's okay, he just wanted to join the Miners. He didn't know what a nominee had to do so he did whatever Swannie asked. He liked the three hundred a week Swannie gave him to run around for him. I think his heart's in the right place.'

Winnie placed his arm around Tony's shoulders and walked a few paces. 'So's yours, mate.'

The noise of fifty-odd bikes firing up and riding off soon brought gawking motel guests and their offspring out onto the balconies. The Miners formed two long files, led by Winnie and Kev. They rode noisily at the speed limit though the streets of Melbourne. The boys took one last look at the city before hitting the highway, winding up to cruising speed and heading north. Ten minutes later a police car pulled even with Winnie and Kev and the nearside cop motioned for them to stop. Kev yelled over the roar, 'I'm getting a bit sick of this, Prez.'

They slowed the Miners down and pulled onto the side of the highway. Traffic rolled by and trucks tugged on their air horns as they passed.

A copper yelled out, 'Everyone stay with your bike!' Two plain-clothes cops and a few uniforms got out of the cars and approached Winnie and Kev.

One flipped open his notebook. 'Mr Kevin Hinchey and Peter Winifred, is that right?'

'That's right, and who might you be?'

'I'm Detective Sergeant Taylor.' He pointed at his offsider. 'This is Senior Constable Morris.'

'What can we do for you?'

'We're investigating the attempted murder of one of your Club members.' Winnie couldn't believe the cops were on to them so quickly, but he stayed calm.

'Who might that be?'

Just then the Club truck carrying Toothpick and his bike rode past and a cop immediately stepped out onto the road and pulled it over. A uniform opened the back door and revealed Toothpick's bike. The Sergeant with the notebook watched carefully.

'We want to talk to you about your mate John Swann. He was found not far from here.'

'I never even knew he wasn't with us.' Winnie looked around as if searching for Swannie's face amid the fifty-odd riders. Just then the second Club truck carrying Swannie's bike rode past and no one but the Miners noticed.

'Has anyone seen Swannie?' Winnie called out. The cops were taking down registration numbers and licence details. A few members within earshot shook their heads. 'He might have had an accident, Sergeant.'

'This was no accident. We're waiting for him to make a statement. If it turns out you blokes had anything to do with it we know where to find you.'

'Had a good time in Melbourne?' The offsider asked with a smirk.

Big Kev had had enough. He stepped forward and stuck his face in the cop's face. 'Look, I don't give a fuck that you're a copper, you're still a cunt ...'

The Sergeant suddenly saw the whole event about to spiral out of control. 'Go and take a look at that bike, Constable.' He nodded towards the Club truck and the Constable was gone in a flash.

Winnie stared at the Sergeant. He knew Swannie might be dumb enough to think about giving a statement, but he also knew he wouldn't — Swannie knew the rules.

The Constable returned from poking around Toothpick's bike. 'That bike belongs to the man riding in the truck, Sergeant.'

'Have you got all the registrations and names?'

'Yes, Sergeant.'

'Then let's get out of here, I've got a barbecue on this arvo.' The Constable walked a wide berth around Kev, who wore his most menacing face. 'Have a good ride back to Sydney. Maybe we'll see you later.' They walked back to their cars and screeched off.

'That was careless, Kev. We forgot about his club tattoo.'

Kev pulled out his pocketknife. He flicked open the blade and ran his finger along the sharp edge. 'I won't forget next time, Prez. Do you reckon Swannie'll talk?'

'I don't think he's that dumb. Come on, let's get out of here.' They mounted up, waited for a break in the traffic and took off again. After a fuel stop and a bite they crossed into New South Wales and Winnie breathed more easily.

'Let's get rooms in a hotel here, make an early night of it, and push on in the morning.'

When the Club truck pulled up everyone with a helmet exemption tossed their helmets in the back.

'I want to make sure we get that tattoo off Swannie. He can have it covered up or we take it off, it's up to him. First we have to find out where he is and how badly he's hurt, then get word to him and let him know his options. The papers should have the story tomorrow.'

Kev found Little Tony and they walked around the hotel to find a place to hold their meeting with both Chapters. Behind it was a wharf where they wouldn't be heard.

Kev gathered up the members and led them to the wharf. 'The Prez has something to say.'

'Doesn't he always?' said Ocker.

Winnie smiled at him then addressed the boys. 'Maybe you haven't heard about Swannie, so here's the drum. We heard from the Southside members that Swannie was forcing them into selling an ounce of speed a week. We only just found out about it and now we know why so many members left the Club. He was playing games with us and the Commandos. He told Rastus we were trying to take over the Commandos and install Spike as their president.'

Nestor reckoned Swannie had to be off his head. A few of the boys laughed.

Winnie asked Nestor point-blank, 'Did you know what he was up to, Nestor?'

'No, Prez, he was into the green until about six months ago but then he reckoned he was making too much on the powder. I reckon he was putting a little too much up his nose.'

'Well, the particulars aren't important. You can read all about it in tomorrow's paper. What's important is that he's gone. His bike goes to the Southside Chapter and they can sell it for whatever they want. The money we found on him and any proceeds from his gear we'll split between the Chapters.'

Little Tony held up his hand. 'Boris said the stash is at his dad's house.'

'After seeing the Commandos' clubhouse we'll use some of his cash to upgrade ours.'

'What about Rastus, Prez? Is he alright?'

'I think he was impressed with the way we handled it. Look, everything's fine, but I warn you to be careful with what you keep in your homes. If Swannie talks to the cops you can all expect a visit from the pigs. If he doesn't talk — and I think he won't — then it's business as usual. You Southside boys will have to elect a new President next week, so give that some thought. That's all, boys, meeting's over.'

The boys wandered back to the hotel and into the bar. Winnie and Brian walked together.

'What's up, mate?'

'I'm in deep shit, Prez.' Brian smiled for the first time in a day. 'Gina won't even come to the phone, so when I call home I talk to Kitty. It's nicer, but Gina can be harsh sometimes.'

276

Winnie shot Brian a look that said 'I wish I knew what to say', but nothing came out. Then he said, 'Why not call her when Kitty's gone to bed, mate?'

'Yeah, that's the go. I'll try later.'

Winnie left Kev in the foyer of the hotel. 'I'm going to call Sandy, Prez. She's up at her mum's place in Grafton recuperating.'

Later, Brian came into Winnie's room, looking very blue. 'Gina still won't talk to me.'

'We'll be back this time tomorrow. Just relax, come and have a beer and forget about it until you see her. No point in worrying about it until you do. I might even call Mimi, it's been four days.'

They walked into the crowded bar and had a few rounds. A smiling Kev announced, 'Sandy's fine but her mother still treats her like a kid and now she knows why she left home in the first place.' That brought a big laugh.

After a few rounds they headed for the dining room. Kev had been looking pretty sad, but he perked up. 'Since we won't be having any kids I just worked out she only has to look after me.'

'Put it there, Kev.' Winnie shook Kev's hand. 'That's two of us that aren't having any kids. My brother's got enough for the both of us.'

'You don't know what you're missing, boys.' Brian liked being a dad. Just thinking about Kitty made him happy.

'We don't have a choice, Brian,' said Kev.

'I'm going to talk to Mimi about kids when we go away later this week. Don't say a word to any of the girls, they all talk. Does Sandy's mother know you two run a brothel?'

'Christ, no! She thinks Sandy's still dancing.'

Brian looked at his watch and said he was off to try Gina again because Kitty'd be tucked up in bed.

Ocker couldn't believe it. 'If that's what married life is like, then it can get fucked. I'm going to bed. See you in the morning, boys.'

'Are you calling Mimi tonight, Prez?'

'No, mate, we'll be home tomorrow.'

The next morning the boys had their breakfast while reading all about Swannie. A picture showed him lying in a hospital bed connected to bedside monitoring machines. 'Have a look at this, Prez.'

Winnie read the story, which was headed 'Bikie Justice or a Settling of Scores?':

Members of the Miners, an interstate motorcycle gang, were questioned by state police yesterday over the vicious assault on one John Swann, aged 27, of Sydney, a long-time Miners Motorcycle Club member. Swann was found naked and unconscious on Sunday afternoon by council workers at a municipal tip near the township of Seymour. Police are treating the assault as attempted murder while Swann remains under police guard in a Melbourne hospital.

Kev looked over Winnie's shoulder ruefully. 'That fucking tattoo led them right to us, Prez.'

Winnie read on:

Detectives claim all attempts to get a statement from Swann have failed and he has repeatedly declined to be interviewed. 'The code of silence reigns. It's the bikie way,' said Detective Sergeant Taylor.

'It's not a very good picture of him, is it, Kev?'

Kev laughed. 'I've seen better, Prez.'

Brian joined them and wondered aloud if the same story was in the Sydney papers. 'It's bound to be, mate. Did you get to speak to Gina yet?'

'Funny that, I spoke to the good Gina last night. She's a real Gemini.'

'We'll be home soon, if Kev can get the boys on the road, and then you can settle her down, Brian.'

Kev overheard Winnie and boomed out in his loudest voice, 'Fifteen minutes!'

Winnie grabbed Little Tony and pulled him aside for a quiet word. 'When you get back, Tony, first thing I want you to do is go over to Swannie's place and pull every bit of our Club gear out. Check his washing and wardrobe and leave nothing behind, orright?' Tony nodded. 'Take a truck and a driver in case there's other stuff your Chapter wants. Call me when you finish and let me know what you found.'

The pack rode for the best part of the day. At their last fuel stop outside Liverpool the Southside boys split off and headed for Hurstville and Winnie and the Miners headed for the Parramatta clubhouse. Everyone made a beeline for the bar and a bottle or two of cleansing beer. Winnie hoisted a drink and toasted the members. 'Here's to the Miners!'

'To the Miners!'

Winnie took a long look around. Compared to the Commandos' clubhouse, theirs looked barren. 'We've been neglecting this place, Brian. When we build the new shop, if we have any material left over it could be put to good use around here.'

'Yeah, Prez, as soon as I can I'll have a draughtsman draw up some plans for this clubhouse and we can put it to the members and see what they think.'

'I like the idea of a separate members' bar at the back. We've got the space for it.'

Brian gave it thought for a moment. 'Maybe we should buy the place before we put too much money into it.'

'Rent money is dead money,' Ocker added.

'Good point, Ocker,' said Brian. 'We have more than enough money to put down a deposit.'

'Kev, let's organise a quick meeting before the boys go home and see what they think. It won't take too long, but if I'm going to be away for a while we might as well get on with it.'

'Meeting down the back, boys!'

Winnie addressed the boys. 'I'll be away for a week or two. There are a few little things we need to look after. First, the Southside Chapter is going to need a bit of support. It won't hurt for a few of our members to go over there for a drink with them.'

'Who'll be their new President, Prez?'

'That's up to them to decide, but I'm hoping they choose Little Tony. Now, after seeing what the Commandos did to their clubhouse and looking at what we've got, I reckon there's room for improvement here.' Winnie swept his arm around. The wall had holes in it where somebody had punched it. 'This looks like a shithole when we compare it to theirs, so I propose we start putting some money into it. Brian and Ocker reckon we should look at buying it first. We have roughly seventeen grand in the bank — that should be more than enough for a deposit. What do you reckon, boys?'

For a few minutes ideas flowed freely. 'One at a time!' Big Kev roared and the members shut up. 'Nestor, you first!

'Okay, Prez, so whose name is the property in?'

Winnie smiled. 'I never thought about that.'

'We could become an incorporated body, not for profit. We did it once with a footy club. There's a bit of paperwork like tax returns and annual reports we'd have to submit.' Everybody smiled. No fucking way were they going to do that.

'No, Prez, it's just a once a year thing. We could call ourselves the Miners Motorcycle Collectors Club. Being incorporated means no one person is responsible and we can apply for government grants.'

'What do you mean?'

'Every year, the government gives community grants to local clubs like footy clubs, lesbians and the cultural societies, so we'd qualify.'

'How much are they worth?'

'We got fifteen grand at the footy club, and you don't have to pay it back. That's not bad, Prez.'

'Imagine what the papers'd make of that,' said Ocker. '"Outlaw Motorcycle Club Obtains Government Grant."' That got a good laugh.

Winnie said, 'I don't think we need all that attention for a lousy twenty grand.'

'Well, it's an idea, Prez.'

'It isn't a bad idea, Nestor. You look after the incorporation paperwork with Brian, and Ocker can see if this place is for sale. If not, we'll move.'

'From here, Prez?'

'If we have to. So everybody here will have to vote: do we want to own our own clubhouse and do it up really good, or do we just keep renting? We can handle the repayments.'

Some of the boys looked at each other. They'd never thought of owning. They rented, their parents rented, but when a lot of the smarter members went for it, the doubters just shook their heads and went along with the majority.

'Okay, we'll look into buying it.'

They heard a loud knock at the door. Big Kev went out to the front where a nominee informed him that the pigs were there. Everybody looked to Winnie.

'Kev, Brian and Ocker, come with me. The rest of you just keep doing … not much. Remember, boys, we know nothing.' They made their way out to meet the two cops.

Winnie broke the silence. 'Are we glad to see you blokes! We went to Victoria for a ride and the coppers just wouldn't leave us alone down there!'

Kev and Ocker almost pissed themselves laughing.

One copper held up a copy of the local paper. 'What's this?' It showed the same photo as the Melbourne paper.

'We told the Victorian police, we know nothing about it. Do you think that they'd let us leave Victoria if there was any link? Have you spoken to them?'

'They're all off duty, but we want your side of the story.'

Brian adopted an indignant attitude. 'Do you always operate like this? Annoying us because you read some shit in the paper?'

The two local coppers looked at each other before replying, 'We'll be back.'

Winnie had heard enough. 'Okay, you go ahead. But for now, just fuck off.'

The coppers were walking away, but at this they turned. The younger of the two asked, 'What did you just say?' He looked like he wanted to take someone on.

'You heard him,' Big Kev growled back.

The older cop touched the other's arm. 'Come on, I'm getting too old for this job.'

Winnie and the boys walked back into the clubhouse and addressed the members.

'They've still got nothing on us and there's no complaint from Melbourne yet, but I'd be extra careful for a couple of days if I were you. Don't do any business with anyone and clean up your homes just in case.'

'Hey, Prez, you had a phone call while you were in that meeting.'

'Who was it?'

'She said you'd know.'

Winnie smiled. 'Okay, boys, the run's over. I'll see you all when I get back from up north.'

The members made their way towards Winnie for a final handshake and began to leave, eager to get home to lie down somewhere soft and think of nothing for a few hours.

'You're not leaving until Friday, are you, Prez?'

'No, Brian, I'll be around, but aren't you in a hurry to get home?'

'Monday's bingo day for Gina and she goes with her mother so she won't be back home until four. Feel like a drink, Prez?'

'Yeah, just a quick one.'

Brian told the remaining nominees to get going. They certainly didn't have to be told twice; they said their goodbyes and left with the other members, eager to hit the road.

'Is it just the four of us now, Brian?'

'It's just us, Prez.'

Winnie pulled out a bag of speed, cut up four lines on a mirror, snorted a line then passed Brian the rolled-up note. 'It's just us that matter, mate.'

'What are you up to, Prez?'

'I'm pushing off now, Kev. I'll be in tomorrow to give you boys a hand.'

'Yeah, sure, Prez,' Brian said with a smile. Brian was only openly sarcastic with Winnie when they were alone.

'I'll be here, but I might be a little late.' Winnie clutched his balls. 'They're getting heavy! I'd better call Mimi.' He went to call her.

Brian told Kev and Ocker he'd organised a lock-up for the tools and spare parts, and a couple of members to lend a hand. 'We're going to end up with a lot of room after the alterations.'

'I can't wait, Brian.' Ocker gave it some thought. 'Who'd have thought we were going to last this long when we started the Miners?'

Winnie came back and added, 'Just remember what brought us here in the first place — it's the business, and it comes first, before the shop.'

'Is everything okay with Mimi?'

'The story in the papers freaked her out but she'll be alright. She's just not used to it.'

'Not yet, Prez.' Ocker, as usual, had the last word.

The phone rang. Winnie answered and listened to someone on the other end for a minute, then hung up.

'Johnny Baker. Those bloody solicitors can smell a dollar a mile away. He wanted to know what kind of shit we're in.'

'Was he disappointed when you told him we're alright?'

'He seemed relieved.'

'Probably because we're worth more to him out than in.'

'No, I think he was genuine; he's always done the right thing by us.'

Winnie paused, then turned to Ocker. 'Ocker, get in touch with Steve to do some cooking for us. Now that Swannie's out of the way we're going to need extra product.'

'I've already spoken to him, Prez, and he's keen to make the money. We've only got him for another six months.'

'That'll give him time to train Toothpick.'

'We're running low on hash,' said Brian. 'Any news on the next lot?'

'That's why I'm going all the way up to Bundaberg. I hope the trip's worthwhile.'

Winnie waved to Marge watering flowers in her front yard. Mimi's Mercedes was in the garage when he rode in and he parked the Harley next to it. He decided to leave his saddlebags; he'd empty them tomorrow. He closed the garage door. I've got other bags to empty first, he thought.

Mimi opened the door and threw herself into his arms. 'Oh, Peter, I've been worried about you!'

'Don't worry about me, there's nothing to worry about; we had nothing to do with it. Come with me.' He led her to the bedroom. Afterwards he held Mimi and kissed the sweat gently from her forehead and neck. 'It feels like I've been away for three months, instead of three days.'

'Four,' she replied matter-of-factly, rubbing his back. 'I feel safe when you're here. Did Kevvie tell you his news?' she teased.

Winnie answered cautiously, 'What news?'

'He and Sandy are getting married! I don't know when.'

Winnie wondered what she was up to.

'They're made for each other, don't you think?' She looked at him mischievously as she continued, 'That's what people say about us.'

Fuck, I'm falling into a trap here! He smiled. 'What are you trying to say?'

'Don't worry, Peter; my parents won't let me marry you.'

'So they've worked it out and know I only want you for a fuck?'

'You're so coarse sometimes, Peter. Of course they love you and so do I. Anyway, did Kevvie tell you?'

'I remember something about getting married, but we haven't spoken about it; it's no big deal to us.'

'For a girl, it is.'

Smiling back at her he said, 'We're different; we don't have to get married, because you know I love you.'

'Come here.' She pulled him closer. 'When do you want to leave for Queensland? I finish work on Thursday. Our first holiday together!'

He smiled absently. In the back of his mind he was running through his itinerary, thinking about dropping off the speed in Brisbane and seeing the trawler captain in Bundaberg. He decided it was best for Mimi not to know too much.

'Have you got a feed for me?'

'I thought you just had one.'

'That was just a snack.'

'I bought the biggest porterhouse steak I could find, so have your shower and it'll be ready when you are.'

He watched her pull on shorts and a t-shirt, and thought, She's the best thing that's ever happened to me.

Chapter 22

When Winnie arrived at the shop the Snow's shop sign rested against the wall.

'What are you going to do with the sign, Brian?'

'I thought we could put it up on the workshop wall, a memento of where it all started. I'd like to have a little museum here and display the Indian, some Harleys, and all those magazines, posters and old signage you're getting from Marge. It'll keep the punters amused and might even draw people in.'

'That's a great idea, Brian. Who knows how many old magazines Marge has? I'll invite her to the opening and you can do a deal with her for the van. Once it's out of the shed we can start moving the rest of the paraphernalia out of the house and set up the library. I'll have to figure out where to put my hidey-hole — you'd better come and have a look with me.'

'Who are you getting to build it?'

'I'll do that myself. The only people to know where it is will be you, me, Ocker and Kev. I might get Kev to help; he's good at stuff like that. You should get a safe place too.'

'I don't keep anything at home, Prez. It's all in my mother's shed.' Brian added, 'It's perfect. Gina picks up for me when she takes Kitty over for babysitting.'

'You be careful, mate.'

'No one gets in there but me and Gina. When we first started in business, I sorted the green there. I give them a couple of hundred a week. I tell them how good the shop's going and they love it. I'm storing parts there now and it's pretty full at the moment with stock.'

'I hope you keep that secret. If people know about it you'll get knocked off. There's some bikie dickheads out there who wouldn't hesitate.'

Brian shot Winnie a worried look. 'You're right, Prez, it'd be easy to break into it. I might go and find another place. We don't want to tempt fate.'

'Bring in those pounds for Gina's cousin in Brisbane while you're at it.'

Brian grabbed one of the nominees to help load the parts back into the truck. 'I'll find another lock-up garage, Prez.'

'That's a good idea, mate.'

Big Kev and Ocker returned and saw Brian leaving.

'Where's he off to in such a hurry?'

Winnie smiled. 'He put a lot of the spares in his parents' shed as well as the speed and I'd hate to see us lose any gear, or powder for that matter. Ocker, the Rat has the phone number for the captain; did he give it to you?'

'He's coming around this afternoon.'

Big Kev passed Winnie a parcel. 'Here you are, Prez, put this in your luggage.'

'Do you think I'll need it?'

'Better to be caught with it than without it.'

Winnie inspected the shiny .38 pistol.

'She's ready to go, Prez.'

'When's Sandy coming home?'

'Tomorrow's train.'

'Mimi tells me that you're getting married?'

'It'll make Sandy happy, but it makes fuck-all difference to me. Not that she nagged me about it; as a matter of fact, she never mentioned it to me.' He paused for a moment and continued, 'It was me. When I saw her in that hospital bed I asked her; I knew it would make her happy and give her something else to think about.'

'It doesn't matter to me why you're getting married, mate. I'm just happy to see that she's better. How long do you think until we can open up the new shop, Ocker?'

'Brian reckons a couple of weeks but I think more like a month. He's pretty keen on it!'

'Yeah, I know, but looking at the empty shop, there's still a shitload to do.'

'Once they knock the wall out, it shouldn't take that long, Prez.'

'We'll see, Kev; I'll bet it's not finished by the time I get back.'

'You just go and have a decent holiday with Mimi.'

'I might do just that!'

'How're you getting up there, Prez?' Ocker asked.

'In her Mercedes.'

'That's pretty low-key, Prez.'

'I know what you're saying, mate. What Pig would suspect me of possession, especially when she tells them who she is, where she works and that it's her car!'

'How long are you going for?'

'A week, but I might take a few extra days and take Mimi to a resort; I'll have to see how much time she can spare.'

The shop phone rang and Ocker followed its shrill call to beneath a box.

'It's for you, Prez. I think it's the Pig.'

'Hello, Winnie, it's your old mate. I'd like to catch up for a beer today. When and where?'

'Three o'clock at the Frisco. I'll see you then.' Winnie replaced the receiver. 'Is Brian back yet?'

'He just pulled up. What does the Pig want?' Kev asked.

'Probably money, I'd say. I'll need to get some for him from our bank.'

'I hope there are no problems, Prez?'

'No, Kev, he sounded alright and I'll find out soon enough. I'm having a beer with him this arvo.'

'Do you want me to come, Prez?'

'Yes, Kev, we'll go in the car, no bikes.'

'Here's Brian now, Prez.'

'All sorted out, mate?'

'All done. That was a much better idea. I'd have hated it if somebody'd broken into the parents' garage.'

'Me too, Brian. I've got to see the Pig today and he's going to want money. How much do we owe him, Brian?'

'Ten grand, Prez. I'll get it for you.'

'Ocker, have you spoken to Little Tony about Swannie's place?'

'Yeah, he found eighty-two grand in a safe in the wall of a shed, exactly where Boris said it was. The rest is tied up with his father in real estate according to Boris — Swannie'd been bragging he was playing monopoly with all his profits.'

'I don't like our chances of getting any of that.'

'I'm going to see Boris this afternoon to dismantle his laboratory before the pigs find it.'

'Just be careful,' Winnie said. 'Brian, I'll leave my bike at your place while I'm away. I don't feel safe leaving it at my joint.'

'Sure, Prez.'

'Can you take it from here? I'll get Kev to drop me at home after we see the Pig.'

'Sure,' Brian said. 'Here's the money for the Pig, the speed and a phone number for the Sharks in Brisbane.'

'He knows it's cash up-front, right?'

'Sure does, Prez. If they like it, there'll be a new market for us.'

'The only way they won't like it is if they jump on it, and if they do, then that's their problem. We're giving them good product.'

'I explained it all to him, Prez; let's see how greedy they are.'

'I'll get you to stop at my place on the way, Kev.'

Winnie glanced down at his haul. Speed, money and a gun. 'Fucking hell, I wouldn't want to get done with this.'

The Rat arrived in his yellow Zephyr, a surfboard still on top. 'He's still getting around in that old shitheap and it still looks odd parked outside a bikies' joint.'

'Don't worry, Prez, I've spoken to him about how obvious it is. He never uses it for business,' Brian replied reassuringly.

'It's the connection, Brian — those pigs aren't that stupid.'

'I'll tell him again.'

'Ah, the Rat.'

'How're you going, Winnie? Boys?'

Winnie decided it was time to get up the Rat about his car and motioned him aside. 'Listen, mate, Brian spoke to you about your car, but we're fair dinkum now. It just stands out like dogs' balls around here.'

'I don't use it for business, Prez.'

'It's the connection to us, can't you see that? Just use it over your side of town — it won't stand out so much at the beach. Can't you afford another car?'

'I can't help it, Prez, I'm a hoarder. But you're right, I'm going to have to put it away. I can afford another car; I'm doing pretty good at the moment.'

'Surfboards, is there any money in that?'

'I invested some money with a couple of blokes manufacturing and selling board shorts and t-shirts as well as boards to all the surf shops. They piece out the work to all these housewives working at home and then we collect the goods and distribute them to the shops. We've only just started and we're already behind in filling the orders. It'll be a goldmine and it's all legal. We're making a good earn so I have some spare cash. I saw what you blokes did with the spare parts and bikes and decided I could do the same with surf gear.'

'Good on you, Rat, smart thinking. But be careful, there are lots of crooks out there.'

Winnie and the Rat shared a good laugh.

'I've known these blokes for a while, Prez. They're legit, and they couldn't have got started up without my seed money.'

'That's terrific, Rat, I wish you the best of luck. Now did you speak to your Bundaberg mate?'

'Call him Skipper to his face, Prez. If he likes you he'll refer to himself as "the Smuggler" in the third person — he's a funny cunt! Here's his phone number. He drinks at the Royal Hotel. I'm sure his boat is going up to the slipway soon, so he'll be around.'

'He knows what I want to talk about?'

'Prez, remember this: he's not dumb.'

'Come on, Rat, you know me.'

'On the way up north I had a relapse and he's the one that got me off the hammer. When he took me out to sea he locked me below for three days straight when I was going full-tilt cold turkey. He gave me two blankets and some water and it worked. I owe him a lot, Prez.'

'There'll be something in it for you, Rat.'

'Prez, you owe me nothing. You and the boys have done a lot for me already.'

Winnie hugged the Rat. 'I'll see you when I get back.'

'You know I love you, mate.' The Rat glanced up at Winnie. 'You and the boys helped me a lot. That means a lot.' Tears welled up.

'Go on; fuck off before you get me going!'

The Rat scurried away and the last thing he heard was 'Don't forget about the fucking car!'

Winnie took a closer look at the construction. Intrusively loud banging had started on the other side of the wall.

Brian looked as proud as a new father. 'They're knocking the wall out and when it's gone we'll know how big the shop's going to be. I can't wait! Come and have a look at this, Prez!'

Brian held a set of drawings for the new shop. 'Three shop fronts joined into one. Whaddya reckon, Prez?'

Winnie was amazed at how much room there was. 'Fuck, it's going to be huge!'

'When we're finished, the counter's going to be here.' Brian paced it out. 'The custom and spare parts will be behind it and over there we'll display our choppers.' Winnie looked on, astonished.

'You've got it all worked out, mate.'

Big Kev came back with a box laden with burgers and called out to the boys doing the renovations to put down tools and come for a feed. He looked at Winnie. 'What do you think?'

'It's going to be like a supermarket!'

'That's just what it is, Prez — a bikies' supermarket!'

'And your workshop will be down the back.'

'I'm always down the back.'

'That's the way you like it, isn't it?' Winnie said, laughing. 'I'm only pulling your leg, mate. Here's the keys to my bike, Brian. Are you ready, Kev? Let's go see the Pig.'

Brian hugged Winnie. 'Have a good holiday, mate. I hope to have this finished when you get back.'

Winnie wrapped his contraband in his jacket and followed Kev out to his car.

They rode to Winnie's place and stashed the gun and the speed then headed for the meeting with the Pig at the Frisco in Woolloomooloo. The public bar was chockers; sailors spilled out onto the street clutching beers, happy to be ashore.

Kev parked the car and Winnie did his best to shove the bundle of ten thousand dollars down the front of his jacket, but it bulged ostentatiously.

'Here, Prez, use this.' Kev passed him a shoebox. 'There's some tape in the glove box.'

'You're a real boy scout, Kev!' Winnie stashed the money in the box under the front seat. 'I'll give it to him when we leave; I just hope nobody rips the car off.'

Big Kev pulled out a steering lock and fastened it in place. 'Just make sure you lock the door, Prez.'

The pub looked like the United Nations — sailors from five different countries stood shoulder to shoulder drinking and having a laugh. Big Kev bought beers while Winnie looked around for a suitable place to await the arrival of the Pig.

'Over there.' Winnie spotted the Pig standing near the doorway leading to the hotel's upstairs rooms.

The Sergeant indicated for them to follow him, and led them out the back to an empty table near the kitchen area. 'How're you going, boys? I forgot the Navy's in town.' He looked at Big Kev and nodded. It was the first time he'd ever met Kev.

'It's alright, Sarge; Kev's my right-hand man. Now, what's up?'

'The hash is ready. Pick it up just like you did last time. The keys are in the van. I spoke to our friend, and he wants to know if you've made your connection in Bundaberg yet. He's keen to use you but you have to organise everything. He'll get it there and the rest is up to you and your mate.'

'That's no problem at my end if the captain wants to get involved. I can't get it from where it's made and your man can't get it into the country, but together we can make it happen.'

'Well, your man is going to have to trust us.'

'I haven't spoken to him yet, but if I were him I'd want a fair bit of cash up-front and I wouldn't be cheap.'

'Just see what he wants, Winnie. If he wants to be in it, good. He won't have to work with the Buddha sticks anymore.'

'Oh, what do you mean by that?'

'The syndicate in Thailand was busted. A word to the wise: don't even think of doing business there, because they'll shoot you.'

Big Kev sipped his beer and took in the conversation silently, marvelling at how the Prez could sit there drinking beer with a corrupt Pig and planning on importing a massive amount of Afghani hash. He couldn't help but admire Winnie's foresight. A couple of drunken sailors wandered past and were about to light a joint when they saw the boys. They quickly headed back to the bar.

'Have you got the money?'

'It's in the car; we didn't want to bring it in.'

'There's a back way.' The Pig indicated the exit.

Big Kev stood up. 'I'll get it, Prez.' When Kev had left, the Sergeant asked Winnie, 'Are you sure you can trust your mate Kev?'

The Prez said nothing for a while, then answered very slowly, 'I look at you betraying your brothers in the police force for a few dollars and you ask me if I can trust my mate? You can get fucked.'

The Sarge leaned back in his chair and laughed. 'It's all bullshit, Winnie. There's no brotherhood except me and my mates; we don't care about the rest and it's a simple case of us and them.' He took a swig. 'Besides, we work good together; don't go spoiling it.'

Big Kev returned, shoebox in hand, and handed it to Winnie. 'I'll get some beers.'

Winnie slid the box across and the Pig placed it on his lap, under the table. Putting both elbows on the table, he rested his face in his hands and leaned towards Winnie. 'That was a naughty bit of work you did to your mate Swannie.'

Winnie didn't answer. The Pig went on, 'You're lucky I've got a copper mate in Victoria.'

'What are you trying to say — you want more money for us not getting arrested?'

'No, not at all, Winnie. Besides, they've got no evidence linking the Miners unless he makes a statement.'

'He hasn't so far and he won't in future. Positive.'

Big Kev arrived with the beers.

The Sarge picked one up, drained it, wiped his mouth and then stood. 'Let me know the score when you get back, Winnie.' He picked up the shoebox and disappeared out the back.

'What's up with him, Prez?'

'Nothing, mate, he's just trying to play games. Come on, let's get out of here before we end up in the fucking Navy.'

Chapter 23

The small coastal town of Brunswick Heads was a welcome stop-off point after the long drive north along the Pacific Highway from Sydney. Winnie and Mimi pulled up in the Mercedes outside the Brunswick Heads Hotel as the setting sun lit the sky in a blaze of orange light. Mimi breathed in the healthy sea breeze wafting over the breakwall. Waves pounded on the bar and a small river snaked past opposite the hotel.

They walked through the beer garden and passed tables full of holidaying families, surfers and fishermen. They stepped inside the crowded bar and made their way to the office, which was lit by a single light bulb suspended from the ceiling. Winnie knocked on the door and waited. An older man dressed in old trousers that were much too big welcomed them with a warm smile. Winnie reminded himself that they were in redneck territory, where they despised blacks and bikers alike.

The old hotelier asked 'Owyergoin?' Before Winnie could reply he asked, 'Travelling on, or are you staying?'

This time Mimi was first off the rank to answer him, in her best 'posh' voice. 'Just the night, thanks.'

He pushed the travellers' book under Winnie's nose. 'Fill this out while I work out where to put you.' They both signed the book then Mimi suddenly smiled and looked at Winnie. He just shrugged. He'd written a fake name and address. He then tried to inspect what Mimi had written, but she closed the book before he could get a look.

The old man checked the reservation list and then looked up triumphantly. 'There you go, the only room left, the best room in the pub! It was booked but the people never turned up, so it's all yours. Good luck.'

While he was settling the bill, he lowered his voice and said quietly, 'I don't know if you're a bikie or not, mate, but if you are, a word: there's a few blokes in the bar tonight that don't like bikies. The Sharks from Brisbane touched up a few of the locals. It got pretty nasty.' The old bloke shook his head disapprovingly. 'Some of the locals went back to get guns and we had coppers from everywhere here. I don't like that.'

'Okay, thanks, mate.'

Mimi whispered in Winnie's ear, 'I wonder why he doesn't like the police here.'

'I noticed a heap of betting slips he'd forgotten to put away on his desk. I'd say he's the local SP bookie. He probably pays off the local cop and Saturday would be his biggest payday. That wouldn't be too good for business.'

'You're very observant.'

'It pays to be.'

Winnie parked behind the pub, unlocked the boot and asked Mimi, 'What bags do you need?'

'Just those two.' She pointed to two of her three bags.

He opened his bag, took out the .38 and the speed and hid them in the spare tyre well. Winnie carried the bags to the room.

'I'm going to have a shower,' Mimi said, looking forward to freshening up after their lengthy journey.

While Mimi showered, Winnie snorted a quick line. He laid out the map on the bed and studied it carefully.

'What're you doing, babe?'

'Just trying to work out how far it is to Bundaberg from here.'

'How far is it?'

'About eight hours, I'd say. We'll be there about this time tomorrow.'

'Is there any hurry?'

'No, but I'd like to get the business out of the way first; then maybe we could have a few days out on one of those island resorts.'

'Why did you write down a false name when we signed in?'

'Just a habit, babe; I always do it. What name did you put in?'

'Not telling,' said Mimi.

'I'll go and have a gander.'

'You would too!'

'Don't worry, I won't. You can have your little secret.'

'I'll tell you one day.'

'Come on, get dressed and we'll go and get something to eat.'

They left the noisy pub and crossed the little footbridge over the river and walked down to the beach.

Mimi thought she could live there except that it was too far from Sydney and a bit quiet.

'Maybe one day we could buy a few acres away from Sydney?' Winnie suggested.

'That's what I'd like, Peter.'

'I've always wanted to build my own home. Maybe we could design it ourselves so it suits us exactly.'

'Are you proposing?'

He looked at her with a cheeky smile. 'One day maybe, but not tonight.'

They were off early next morning, headed north again.

When they neared Brisbane, Winnie asked Mimi to check the map and find out the direct route to Redcliffe. 'We have to cross a bridge soon.'

She asked, 'What bridge?'

'Can't you see it up ahead?'

'Oh, that little thing? I was expecting something like the Harbour Bridge.'

'Look for a sign to the Bruce Highway.'

'After you cross the bridge, keep right.'

'How far do you reckon it is to Redcliffe?'

'Miles yet, but why do you have to stop there? You might have told me, but I can't remember.'

'Keep an eye out for a phone box,' said Winnie.

'There's one up ahead outside the newsagents.'

Winnie parked in a no-stopping zone and stood in the phone booth rummaging through his pockets for change. 'Fuck, no change, but at least it's working.' He hung up the receiver and went back to the car where Mimi handed him some coins. After a brief conversation he returned. 'That was Gina's cousin; we met him at Brian's housewarming.'

'The blond?'

'What do you mean "the blond"?'

'Well, he has blond hair, doesn't he?'

'Yeah, but it's— no, don't bother, you're right, he has blond hair.'

Mimi giggled at Winnie's reaction. 'You're jealous, Peter!'

Winnie pulled a face. He focused on the road and avoided looking at her.

'Where do you have to meet him?'

'At the pub in Redcliffe. He said I couldn't miss it, it's at the end of the bridge he called the bumpety-bump. It can't be that hard to find.'

'Here comes the bridge.'

'Look at that!' A long wooden bridge extended across the water and almost disappeared into the distance. As they crossed the bridge the tyres made a bumpety-bump sound and on the other side they saw the pub. The blond cousin had it right: you couldn't miss it. Winnie parked, pulled out the speed from his stash in the boot and stuffed it inside his jacket.

'You can come with me if you like, but I'm going to discuss business with him for a bit.'

'No, give me the keys. I'll use the ladies room and freshen up. Take your time.'

He headed towards the public bar, crowded with working men on their lunch break. He made his way around to the pool table area, found a view from a window that overlooked the bay and positioned himself in the best vantage point to spot Gina's cousin.

Small yachts darted around Moreton Bay like white flies. Ever since he first rode the Sydney ferries, he'd loved the sea, but never the surf. His reminiscence was interrupted by a shrill bell. Every elbow lifted from the bar, and patrons downed their drinks and hurriedly left the pub. Gina's cousin walked into the room, and as he entered everyone in the place greeted him with a 'G'day'. He made his way over. 'Winnie, how are you?' They shook. 'How's your trip going? I saw the Merc outside. Not many of them get around up here.'

'It's been a good drive and the Merc handles the highway alright. Are you the mayor or are you just popular?'

'Most of us grew up around here. See that chick behind the bar?' She waved at them while she stacked the empty glasses, a wide smile lighting up her pretty face. 'I used to finger fuck her in high school.' He lifted up his glass and toasted her. 'That's how local I am. So when I meet people for business I use this as my office.'

'I see.'

'That little cutie behind the bar will make sure you're not being followed by pigs and that way you won't walk into a trap. She can smell a Pig a mile away — her father's one.'

Winnie smiled. 'I wish I went to a co-ed school.'

'Brian was saying that you're building a new shop; you should do alright there.'

'Yeah, he reckons they'll have it ready in a few weeks.'

'How far are you going, Winnie?'

'Not too sure yet. I just wanted to get away with my girl for a week or so while the boys are renovating.' He paused in thought and added, 'You're right about the shop. Harleys are really becoming popular in Sydney.'

'Same up here, mate.'

'I stopped in a place called Brunswick Heads yesterday; it seems the Sharks aren't too popular down there.'

'Fuck, don't mention that place, mate. We went there on a run and got in all sorts of shit.'

'What happened?'

'A couple of our blokes gave it to a local girl and her fisho boyfriend found out and she started screaming rape. Pigs came from everywhere and went right through us, taking every penny we had then charging two of our members for rape, with no bail.'

'Fuck.'

'Yeah, you're right, they don't like us down there.'

'Did they rape her?'

'Who knows? Did you bring the gear, Winnie?' Winnie patted his pocket reassuringly.

'Now, this is pure; cut it up to five times and you'll do alright with it.'

'There's only shit around here.'

'Well, if you don't get greedy you'll get the market. Put it this way: it's like pot with seed or without.' Winnie paused for effect. 'Even if it's cheaper you still want quality, so if you sell quality you charge a good price and you watch; in a couple of months you'll be doing a fucking pound a month. Be nice, and you can do it every month of the year.'

'Never thought of it like that — you're right.'

'So where do you want to do this?'

Gina's cousin slid a single key across the table. 'In the toilet there's a cleaning locker. You'll find the money on the top shelf.'

Winnie located the locker and turned the key in the door. The smell of ammonia hit him as he made the switch. He stuffed the money in his back pocket and made his way back.

'When you want more, ask Brian,' he said. 'You'll either have to drive down to collect or we can ship it through …'

'Don't worry, mate, we've got a couple of truckers in our club; they do two trips to Sydney every week, so the money goes down and the goods come back the same way. Easy and clean.'

'Good, as long as it's organised. I've got my girl with me so I'm heading off.'

They shook hands on a deal well done, and as Winnie left the bar he waved to the barmaid and conjured up the image of Gina's cousin finger fucking her.

Mimi waited outside in the Merc.

The sign said it all: 'Bundaberg Home of Bundy Rum 5 miles'.

Closer to town, motels sprouted on both sides of the highway.

'Where would you like to stay?'

'There's an information centre. Why don't we ask there?'

He swung the car into an empty parking lot outside the information centre.

Inside Mimi talked to the girl at the counter while Winnie looked over a map of the harbour. It was huge; he'd never guessed it was so big. He thought that unloading cargo there wouldn't look that out of place. Mimi passed him pamphlets offering local accommodation.

'Which one do you like?'

'The one with the hot tub!'

'The hot tub it is, then.'

Mimi thanked the girl and they walked out, hand in hand.

Winnie parked outside the Bonanza Motel. He registered using another fake moniker. Mimi read the bullshit he'd written. She just shook her head and smiled. Inside the room she switched on the spa and Winnie said he was going out to make a phone call and would be back in a few minutes.

'Take the key with you; I'll be in the tub by the time you get back.'

He found a public phone offering some privacy and called the Skipper. 'Hello, I'd like to talk to the Skipper?'

'Speaking.'

'This is Winnie from Sydney, Rat's mate.'

'Oh yeah, he told me you were coming up for a holiday.'

'I'd like to catch up for a beer.'

'Okay, tomorrow at the Royal Hotel, around two o'clock. Do you know where it is?'

'No, but I'll find it.'

'Good.' The Skipper hung up abruptly.

Winnie felt a strong sense of excitement in his stomach at the thought of meeting the man. He knew there'd be a good earn in it for them, if it worked out alright. He wondered who it was who reckoned the drugs business was easy. The cattle sales report blared on a radio nearby. The only thing Winnie knew about cattle was that you could eat them.

Steam emanated from the bathroom and Mimi lay in the hot tub enveloped in bubbles, her eyes closed. Winnie joined her and began to relax as the weariness of their journey caught up with him. He fell asleep and when Mimi woke him the water had turned cold. She held out a hot towel for him.

'What time is it?'

'Nine-thirty. Come on, I'm ready for bed.'

The next morning Winnie felt like a tourist, walking beside Mimi, who was taking pictures. He'd never toured for the sake of it and wondered what he was doing there until he spotted the Royal Hotel near the railway station. He remembered the business meeting and a slightly queasy feeling gripped his stomach.

'I have a meeting over there at two. Maybe we can have lunch there after.'

'That's a bit late.'

'You don't mind, do you?

'I thought we were on holiday.'

'We are.'

'Well, how come everywhere we go, you have meetings?' She wasn't thrilled. 'It's okay, Peter, I want to ring work anyway. Will you be long?'

'An hour tops, babe.'

At two on the dot Winnie entered the pub and spotted a bloke wearing an old sea dog's cap. He made his way over. The bloke stood up as Winnie approached. 'You look exactly how the Rat described you. Pleased to meet you, Prez.'

'They call you the Smuggler, don't they?'

The Skipper lowered his eyes and said firmly, 'Not in public.'

'The same with me, mate. I'm Winnie up here. The Rat tells me we might be able to help each other out.'

'In what way?'

'You're not going to play silly buggers with me, are you, Skipper?'

'No, the Rat tells me you're okay. What do you have in mind?'

'First, I'm going to do you a big favour.'

'What would that be?'

'You were going to bring in a shipment of Buddha sticks from Thailand.' Winnie immediately had the Skipper's full attention. 'They're onto it.'

'Are you sure?'

'One hundred per cent, Skipper. If you pick up you'll be no use to us because you'll be in deep shit. You'd better cancel.'

'The people I know won't do that, Winnie.'

'What will they do if you don't pick it up?'

'Drop it somewhere else. Are you sure the cops know it was destined for Bundaberg?'

'Well, my contact said the Federal Police know Buddha sticks are on their way.'

'Winnie, that one job is worth a couple of hundred grand to me.'

'Is it worth going to jail for, Skipper? I have a contact in the Sydney cops. Customs Australia-wide know when it left Thailand. The leak was from the Thai end. Whoever was behind it will get busted. If I were you I wouldn't touch it. The reason I came to see you is to see if you want to work with us.'

'Who are you?'

'Me and my friends. It doesn't matter who they are.'

The Skipper gave the proposition some thought. 'If I do, I'll only do business with you and the Rat. Is that clear?'

'I'll talk with my friends. Our deal will be one hundred up-front and another hundred after. Interested?'

'I'll let you know. But not heroin, I don't touch that shit.'

'I'll tell you what, Skipper, the Rat wasn't doing heroin when we knew him — that was his own trip. We're just as pleased as you are to see him off it.' Winnie looked at him seriously and continued, 'If I might add, the Rat told me how you got him off it cold turkey.'

'He told you? I locked him below for three days!'

'He reckoned it was pretty rough, but you saved his life.'

'Rough on him?' the Skipper exclaimed. 'He nearly kicked the side of my boat in. Is he still clean?'

'Yeah, he's clean, Skipper.'

'When do you want to employ me?'

'I'll let you know. I might even get the Rat to drive up and pick up the first load when it's on.'

'What do you want to bring in?'

'Hash. A few tons, maybe as much as five.'

'There's something I'd like to tell you now, Winnie.' The Skipper looked serious. 'When you ship south by truck there are lots of variables. Anything can happen. Accidents, police, or worse, the main roads inspectors. It's just not worth taking any risk. You should look into bringing a twenty-foot refrigerated container to the wharf and we'll offload straight into it. It's easy to load it and truck it to the Bundy rail yard then ship it by train and pick it up in Sydney. Getting caught in possession isn't a good thing and the chances are pretty good you won't have the same scrutiny on the rail.'

'But what about Customs up here? Don't they check you when you come in?'

'We go out light; I'll stay outside for seven to ten days with the booms out and trawl. Customs patrol out there. They won't bother me if they see me working; they know me and they're too busy looking for foreign registrations. They wave as they pass while we're sitting on a couple of tons of Buddha!' The Skipper chuckled like a naughty boy.

Winnie knew he could trust the Skipper. He raised his glass. 'A pleasure to know you, Skipper.'

'Likewise, son, and you see, when I go back into port, the five tons makes me low in the water so everything looks normal. No one bothers me.' He smiled, 'Besides, my cousin works for Customs and he always lets me know if anything is up. That's the beauty of being a local.'

Winnie looked around the now almost empty bar. 'You can have it, Skipper.'

'It all depends on what you want. I like it.' The Skipper picked up his rum, leaned back in his chair and surveyed the bar. Two old blokes sat at the far end drinking beer and sherry chasers and watching a soap opera. 'All my responsibilities end at the wharf, so you need to organise the refrigerated container ready for loading at dockside. We freeze and pack our prawns onboard, load them into the same container as the hash and the whole thing goes straight onto a train. There are no more Customs from here to Sydney or wherever.'

'That sounds fair enough.' Winnie held out his hand. 'You're on board.' He leaned over and whispered, 'You old smuggler.'

The Skipper said with a wry smile and quite proudly, 'Three generations.'

Winnie looked at his watch. 'I have to go.'

The Skipper leaned over to Winnie and whispered, 'Prez, are you expecting someone?'

'My girl is with me.'

'Is that her?'

Winnie turned to look and there indeed was Mimi, standing on the footpath peering in. The Skipper laughed.

'No women allowed in here, mate; they've got to go to the ladies' lounge. I'll come out with you.'

'No, mate, I don't want to mix business with pleasure. You'll hear from the Rat or me within a few days, a week tops.'

The Skipper casually waved a salute and Winnie walked out to meet Mimi on the footpath. He thought he should explain the rules of the pubs in Queensland.

'Don't worry, Peter; I've already been informed up the road. I walked into a pub and everybody stared at me. I wondered what was wrong then the barmaid pointed to the Ladies' Parlour.'

'What did you do?'

'Turned around, walked out and came here looking for you. Who was that old man you were talking to in the pub?'

Winnie thought there was no use telling her everything. What if they broke up? 'He was the bloke that got the Rat off heroin. The Rat asked me to drop in and say hello and I wanted to thank him too.'

'That was your business? I could've come with you.'

'Secret men's business, babe. Let's have lunch in here.' They walked into an old-fashioned milk bar with booths. Winnie ordered a tomato sandwich and a chocolate milkshake.

Mimi smiled and lowered her menu. 'Do you feel like a peasant?'

He shot back angrily, 'Don't say that!'

'I'm sorry, Peter. I didn't mean to upset you.'

'It's alright, babe. You know the only time I ever ate out as a kid we went to a milk bar just like this. And that's what I had. I think my uncle paid.'

'I'm sorry, I had no idea.'

'You have no idea how poor our family was. But my mother managed to give the church a donation every Sunday.' He shook his head sadly. 'Fucking incredible.'

Mimi reached over and held his hand. 'What can I say? I'll have a tomato sandwich too.'

He looked around. A waitress slowly cleaned a nearby booth while talking to her friends.

'They sure don't rush things up here. I couldn't do it; you'd have to be born here.'

The waitress came and gave their table a quick wipe over with a clean cloth. 'On holidays are you, or on a honeymoon, maybe?' Mimi blushed. The waitress didn't stop for an answer. 'It's lovely, isn't it? Now, what can I get you?'

'Two tomato sandwiches and a chocolate milkshake with two straws. Oh, and make the sandwich on white bread, please,' Mimi added.

'That's all we have, love. You know we grow the best tomatoes in Australia here; we're famous for them.'

'I thought you were famous for your rum?'

'More people eat tomatoes than drink rum.' She smiled and went off to place the order.

'I have to go back to Sydney soon, Peter. I spoke to Dad and a couple of my clients need urgent attention. In three days.'

'Plenty of time.' He started to think about how much he was missing the boys and how keen he was to see the progress in the new shop. His business was finished up north.

'We can go down the New England Highway. It'll be an easier drive, too.'

The waitress placed their order before them. 'Enjoy your stay.'

Chapter 24

They got back to Sydney with just one overnight stay. Winnie let the Mercedes have its head on the long straights and although the distance was long, they arrived the night before the first of Mimi's scheduled meetings. At the bike shop the next morning Winnie admired the work out the front, then shouted into the shop.

Brian and Ocker stuck their heads out. 'What are you doing, checking up on us?'

'Someone's gotta do it!' Winnie gave the boys a hug.

'How was the holiday, Prez? Everything alright with Mimi?'

'Yeah, no worries, Brian, she had to come back for work. I'd had enough, anyway. What's been happening?'

The boys took him on a tour of the shop. Inside was even more impressive than out. It only needed a coat of paint.

'When do you think we'll be opening, Brian?'

'In a couple of weeks, Prez. We have most of the stock from the States in storage.'

'Come and have a look at this, Prez.' Big Kev led them down some stairs to his workshop.

'Well, look at this!' The Prez was pleased with what he saw. Row upon row of spanners and other tools lined the wall and Winnie's bike sat on a hydraulic platform, detailed and sparkling after a polish. 'How'd you know I'd be back early?'

'Well, Mimi rang Gina and I thought you might just want it here.'

'Too right, Brian.' He admired its shining splendour. 'Somebody's done a good job!'

'It was me, Prez.' Ocker beamed.

'Yeah, like fuck you did!' said Kev. 'The nominees polished it.'

'Yeah, but I got them to do it,' Ocker replied, and they all chortled.

'So, what's been happening while I've been away, Ocker?'

'The labs are up and running, Prez. That Toothpick's a natural and he's busy doing his first solo cook as we speak. Also, the Mario brothers called in to see you. They said there were no problems, but wanted you to give them a call when you got back.'

'How'd things go with the Smuggler, Prez?' Kev asked.

'He's in.'

'What'd he say when you told him that the pigs were onto the next shipment?'

'I don't know if he believed me, Kev, but if he's smart he'll stay away from it. If not, he's not going to be much use to us. We'll just have to wait and see.' Winnie paused for a moment. 'He's not a bad old bloke, and if he's smart enough to get Rat off the hammer, he's smart enough to smell it's off. Did you see the real estate boys about buying the Club property, Ocker?'

'Yes, Prez, it's in the works. They're going to contact the owners and let us know.'

'I hope they don't tell the owners we want to buy it — they might not want to sell to bikies.'

'I don't think so, Prez; the real estate wouldn't want to lose out on the commission.'

'Yeah, that's a good point, Ocker — did they say how much it'd be?'

'About a hundred and twenty-five thousand. I reckon it's a fair price, Prez, and we'll be able to build a clubhouse we can be proud of.'

'Too right, boys. Have you heard back from the Sharks, Brian?'

'Yeah, we have Prez; they're very impressed with the quality.'

'Well, can you take care of that with Gina's cousin?'

'No worries, there.'

'He's on the ball up there.' Winnie told them how the exchange had gone, and they were all suitably impressed.

'We'll need more distributors, now we've got the new labs open.'

'The Tigers can't get enough, Prez; a few of our members are supplying them now.'

'Tell the boys to keep their ears open. Knowing Twister, he'd be charging too much and cutting it. Fuck, I wouldn't mind gaining a few of his members if they're any good.' He squinted as he paused in thought. 'Just to stick it up him.'

'Fucken oath!' Big Kev replied.

'Anyway, how's Sandy, mate?'

'She's good, and after being at home with her mother she realises how good she has it with me.'

'But she was pretty sick, Kev?'

'Yeah, I know, I was just mucking around. She's fine, Prez.'

'Go on, tell him the news!'

'What news, Ocker?'

'Kevvie's getting married!'

'I knew that.'

Ocker feigned hurt. 'I thought I was the first to know.'

'You know women,' Big Kev said as he wrapped his big arm around Ocker's shoulder.

'What about the hash, Ocker? How's that going?'

'Everything's fine, Prez. Rastus is taking a lot for Melbourne.'

'Don't let us get short.'

'He's paying a good price.'

'That's alright, then. I just hope we can keep it going.'

'There are other importers, Prez. I don't think it'll be as easy getting it through the wharves anymore, with all the extra Customs checks.'

'No, we're onto a good one with the Smuggler. If the Hash King wants to keep bringing it in and we have the Pig's information, there'll be no problems for us. We'll make more if the Hash King doesn't have to bring it in; there's a lot less risk for everyone.'

'How much cheaper do you reckon, Prez?' Kev asked.

'Half.'

'Fuck, do you think he'll be in that?'

'I wouldn't ask if I didn't think he would. There's only one thing: once it hits the wharf in Bundaberg, it's all ours, and we look after it from there to Sydney. The Hash King will have to cooperate with *us* in future, not the other way around, and that's what I'm going to tell him — but that's only for us to know.'

'How do we get it here?'

'The Smuggler reckons the go is to ship it in a refrigerated container via rail. It'll be in a load of frozen prawns. It may take a little longer, but it's a lot safer that way. If the Pig ever wanted to give us up, we'd be able to get a long way away from it and the Hash King will wear the cost.'

'Sounds a sure thing, Prez.'

'I still don't trust the Pig; he's just in this for himself. Actually, it just might be a good idea to get a few photos of him with us, preferably when we hand him some cash. Think you can do that, Ocker?'

'You know me, Prez; my new camera has a telephoto lens.'

'I know a good place, Prez!' Big Kev piped up. 'Down at the Frisco, the day we went there and I went to the car, I could see straight through the window, right to where you two were sitting.'

'That'd be perfect for next time. Good thinking, Kev! Ocker, you can go early and set up.'

'Why do you want photos, Prez?' Ocker asked.

'I'll show them to him and let him know that if we go down, the cunt will go down with us.'

'That's not a bad idea, Prez. Our little insurance policy.'

'That's it, Brian, and he'll know we don't trust him.'

'Yeah, maybe he'll give us more respect. He fucking acts like the schoolteacher with us.'

'That's what I reckon. We'll have him by the balls.'

'Come on, Prez, I'll show you my new toy.' Ocker beamed excitedly.

'Not another mobile phone, Ocker?'

'No, Prez, but the phones are getting smaller.'

'Yeah, but they don't work; you need phone lines, I keep tellin' ya.'

'Come and have a look at this!' Ocker opened the door to his room and revealed what looked like a sound studio.

'This is my new spray booth!'

'Very nice, Ocker!'

'Have you heard about airbrushing? It's new from the States. You can paint whatever you like. It's just like tattooing!'

'I might get you to do the Club colours on my bike.'

'No problem, Prez, just wait until I get used to it. I'll tattoo the Miners logo on your back one day, Prez.'

'We'll see.'

'Prez, you know I'm going to paint masterpieces in here.'

'If you're that good,' said Winnie, 'why don't you paint on canvas?'

'I already am.'

'I didn't know that. Are there pictures of sluts in the raw?'

'Some.' Ocker replied with a devilish grin.

'Yeah, you're a dirty little cunt.'

'So?'

'Have you got your bike here?'

'Yeah.'

'Let's go see if any of the other blokes want to go for a ride.'

'I'll be in that. Don't worry about this paying its way, Prez. I can sublet it from the shop. That'll be easier for all of us tax-wise.'

'Yeah, tax, Prez; we're going to have to start paying tax. Maybe you should speak to Mimi about it. We've got to do something with all our cash.'

'Yeah, I know, Ocker, but you don't know what I'm up to with the Mario brothers,' the Prez said. 'It's just some private business, but when it happens, I'll have a good legitimate investment, even if I have to subsidise it until it gets off the ground. At least it's bricks and mortar, not like your mobile phone pie-in-the-sky.'

'We'll see, Prez.'

'Let's ask Brian and Kev if they want to come for a ride with us.'

Big Kev lowered Winnie's gloriously polished bike from the hoist. 'Where do you want to go, Prez?'

'I'm sick of the country. Let's go into Sydney from the north and ride over the Harbour Bridge — see what I've missed and grab a drink. What do you guys reckon?'

'Sounds good.'

'Before we go, Kev, can we have a quiet word?'

'Sure, Prez.'

'How's Brian been?'

'Something's not right; one day he's up and the next he's down. You never know what mood he'll be in.'

'He's not doing too much of the speed, is he?'

'Don't think so, mate.'

'Maybe it's the shop?'

'Could be, but I'd say it's her. She thinks she's a bloke sometimes.'

'I'll have a talk with him later; you never know what it could be.'

Brian walked in. 'What what could be?'

'Nothing, mate. Do we have to lock up?'

'No, Prez, a couple of nominees still have work to do.'

Winnie kicked his bike into life then slowly dropped the choke and let the engine settle into a nice rhythmic 'thump, thump' that echoed loudly down the lane.

Winnie smiled at the feeling: his pulse raced. 'It's the best feeling,' he told Mimi that night.

The pack looked pretty official; their colours flapped in the breeze and Winnie's mind flooded with childhood memories of the ferries creeping across Sydney Harbour. The Prez paid the bridge toll and the female tollbooth attendant tried to grab his hand when he handed her the note; there was no way he was waiting for his change.

They headed down the Woolloomooloo ramp and straight to the doors of the Frisco Hotel. A mix of sailors and girls came out to admire their bikes. Ocker wasted no time and started trying his luck with two women while Big Kev went to the bar.

Winnie and Brian found an empty table on the footpath.

'Fuck, I loved that ride,' Brian said.

'I'll drink to that, mate!' Kev said, arriving with the drinks.

'Kev, when Ocker stops being a dirty little cunt, show him where he can take photos of the Pig, will you?'

'I'll go and check it out again, Prez.'

Ocker walked back out and sat down. 'I used to work a couple of those girls up the Cross. They're married to sailors now!'

'What are they doing here?'

'Fleet's at sea, mate.'

'Go out the back with Big Kev. He wants to show you a good spot for taking photos.'

'Okay, Prez.' Ocker took off.

'Is everything alright with you and Gina, Brian? The boys are worried about you.'

'Why haven't they said anything to me?'

'I don't know, you'd better ask them. All I know is they're concerned — we're brothers, remember?'

'I know, Winnie. Wait until they come back, I'll tell you all together.'

'You don't want to leave the Club, do you, Brian?'

'No, Prez, nothing like that.'

'Good, you had me a bit worried then. Anyway, how's Kitty going, mate?'

Brian's face lit up at the mention of Kitty. 'She's really into Brownies and she loves her dancing. You'll have to bring Mimi to her next show. There's one in about a month and Gina always makes sure I know well in advance, ever since I missed Kitty's Brownie induction.'

'Did she make you pay for it?'

'Fucking oath she did, I'll never hear the end of it. But Kitty said she understood it was because I was on a Club run. It brought me to tears, mate.'

'You can't teach that, mate.'

Kev and Ocker come back from their reconnaissance mission. 'There's one clear shot from the toilet window, but if Ocker goes upstairs he'll get three different angles.'

'Is he safe?'

'Yeah, no chance of getting caught.'

'Make sure you get the Pig taking the money.'

Brian leant forward in the chair and they all paid attention. 'So, if you blokes were worried about me, why didn't you talk to me?'

'Because we wanted to wait until the Prez got back — is that alright?'

'No need to get uppity, Kev. I was just surprised when Winnie told me; I never knew you were worried.'

'It stood out like dogs' bollocks, Brian, that's all.'

'I'll tell you what the problem is. Gina's been onto me about the new shop. You already know how she's doing the shirts and jewellery. Well, now she wants to turn it into a fashion house.'

'It's a bike shop, for Christ's sake!'

'Yeah, I know. You should see some of her ideas, Winnie.' He leant back and smiled. 'I have it all worked out. I'm going to set her up in her own shop. It won't cost me much and she can do her own thing and she won't be in *our* shop.'

'That's the way, Brian,' Ocker said. 'I hate it when our women are around; I can't be myself.'

'What's that? You dirty little cunt. Wait until you get your own woman.'

'I've got lots of them!'

'You'll lose your balls one day, mate!'

'Not too soon, I hope. I look at you blokes and see what you go through, and I'm glad I haven't.'

'It's called love, mate.'

'It's not for me, Brian.'

'I thought you were onto Rastus's sister from Melbourne?'

'Me too, but it turns out she's off to university in the States. She reckons it's an opportunity too good to miss. She got offered a scholarship to experiment with fibre optics.'

'What's that?'

'Don't worry, boys, you'll hear all about it in the future, I'm sure.'

'So what are we going to do with the space Gina was going to use?' Winnie asked.

'The same thing: t-shirts, belt buckles, jeans — we'll see what there is.'

'Who's going to run it?'

'Maybe we should hire a girl?'

'That's the go.'

'Shut up, Ocker.'

'It'd be good for us to have an attractive woman on the floor,' Winnie said. 'It'll just go to show how classy we are. Gone are the days of sitting around in overalls with bikes lying everywhere. We're going to give the punters carpet, chrome and tits — we'll set the pace!'

Ocker gave the idea some thought. 'Yeah, but if we have a sheila there everyone will want to fuck her.'

'No, Ocker, that won't happen; part of her deal with us is that she doesn't fuck any of us.' He paused for a few seconds. 'I know what to do.'

'What's that, Prez?'

'We'll get a good-looking dyke. Most blokes wouldn't know and then there'll be no competition for our girls.'

'She might try and fuck one of our girls.' Everybody looked at Ocker in wonderment. 'Just kidding, boys.' He smiled crookedly.

'Where'll we find one?' asked Brian.

'Oh, I'll get you one!' Ocker said, laughing.

'We want somebody full-time,' Winnie said, 'and no bikie sluts connected to other clubs.'

'I know a fag and he knows others,' Ocker said. 'They have their own scene; they're like us.'

'Like fuck they are!'

'Well, they're not accepted and neither are we.'

Brian hoed in. 'We're getting all philosophical, aren't we, Ocker?'

'The way I live, I get to meet all types and I don't care who's a queer because that just leaves more girls for us, as long as they don't hit on me.'

'I think you're safe, mate,' said Brian. 'Anyway, I want our shop to be the best in Sydney and we all have to play a part.'

Winnie wondered aloud, 'What part do I play?'

'The same part as you played in the old shop, Prez — help out everywhere and nowhere. You're too important for our other business.'

'Yeah, you're right, Brian; nothing changes, does it?'

'We'll look real legitimate.'

'Well done, Brian, it's your baby.'

'Cheers!' Brian said, and they drained their glasses. Brian hurried off to the bar for more drinks.

'I haven't seen him that excited in a while.'

'Whatever it takes, Prez. God only knows what he puts up with.'

'So where and when are you getting married, Kev?'

'We're in no hurry, Prez. I might just wait until we fix the new clubhouse and have it there.'

'That's not a bad idea, Kev.'

'What's that?' Brian asked, returning from the bar.

'Kevvie's getting married at the clubhouse!'

'Get married and have the reception at the same place — good idea!'

Over the next few weeks, everybody worked at getting Westside Choppers operational. Parts arrived and Brian utilised his newly acquired business skills and set up an inventory system on a computer. He organised letters of credit for the suppliers, a Customs broker for imports and everything else he could think of, so when the time came they'd be ready. Winnie was amazed at his skills.

'Brian, I'm off to see the Pig today; I'm taking Kev with me. We don't owe the Pig any money but the cunning bastard wants to meet me in Balmain. I'm going to tell him that the Skipper is in, and I'll pass on a word to the Hash King about the way it's going to be from here on in.'

Winnie walked over to Big Kev, who was working on a custom bike for the showroom floor.

'The swing arm shaft was bigger than it was supposed to be.' Kev was frustrated but stayed cool. 'I need a break from this, Prez. I can't do more today. I have to get new bearings, too.'

'Well, we're going to meet the Pig in Balmain; you should be able to get some there.'

'How come we're not going to the Frisco?'

'He changes all the time, but don't worry, Ocker's turn to get a photo will come. The Pig always gives me plenty of advance warning of a meeting, and I'll make sure Ocker doesn't bring a huge camera and stays out of sight. The Pig's a creature of habit, he never stays long. I've worked out he always collects at the Frisco, but I don't know why.'

'It's close to the city. Maybe he has to pay his mates in head office?'

'Maybe, Kev.' Winnie thought Kev might be onto something.

* * *

Winnie and Kev entered the pub via the beer garden, where they saw the Pig waiting in the shadows.

'Grab some drinks, Kev. I'd like a few private words first.' Winnie sat down.

'What did he say?' The Pig's voice had a nasty edge. Winnie knew when Burrows was serious and he knew when not to fuck around.

'The Skipper's with us. He's smart enough to keep away from the Buddha sticks.'

'I know; they brought it down to Gladstone and the blokes who picked it up got done today by the Feds. They're running around Sydney now, arresting the whole syndicate.'

Winnie asked, 'Didn't your mate up there tell them it was off?'

'It seems he did, seeing as he went all the way to Gladstone, but they couldn't have believed him.'

'Is there any way there was a Federal officer onboard?'

'No, the ship dropped it off at sea, but their syndicate had been infiltrated and my mate went with them to pick it up. We wanted them to fuck up,' the Pig said. 'It only makes the Feds look good; it gives them a little victory and makes them feel like they earn their pay, but if it weren't for the crooked cops, they'd get nothing.'

'It sounds like a turf war between the Feds and the state police?

'Sort of.'

'What if the Skipper's been compromised?'

'He hasn't — well, not yet anyway. I'll know when he is.'

'You don't know who he is.'

'I would have if he'd touched the Buddha. Someone would have given him up.'

'I need a meeting with our friend the Hash King.'

The Pig's eyebrows raised perceptibly. He drained his beer. 'I'll let you know.' He got up and left at the moment Big Kev walked back with beers.

'Has he gone?'

'Yeah.'

'Good. I don't like that cunt.'

'They got the load of Buddha sticks up in Gladstone,' Winnie said. 'It makes getting our hash look good.'

'Too right, Winnie. Did you tell him you want it cheaper?'

'No, I'll tell the Hash King to his face.'

'When's that?'

'The Pig's going to set it up. He's usually prompt.'

'I heard that Twister's opening a new Chapter in Newtown.'

'That doesn't bother us, Kev.'

'No, but a few of them are getting a bit cheeky, now Swannie's gone.'

'Have you spoken to Little Tony?'

'He told me. He wanted to know if he could belt them. Now that Kero Ken's in jail Twister has no one to control his boys.'

'Tell Tony to give it to them. If Twister's got any problem with that he can see me.'

'Alright, Prez.' Kev changed the subject. 'Are you ready for the big shop opening?'

'Yeah, it's going to be a success, with Brian running it.'

'We've done alright, Prez.'

'No, he's done it almost single-handedly; even Snow's was Brian's good management. He always paid the rent without using any of the pot money.'

'What about the hot bikes?'

'He sold them.'

'Yeah, I never looked at it like that, Prez.'

'Come on, let's go. You can pick up those bearings down the road and I'll help you put them in when we get back to the shop.'

Friday night, and all the members rolled in on their bikes. It had been a few weeks since Ocker had seen the real estate people. He stood behind the bar fidgeting with a new toy. Winnie ordered a drink.

Ocker leaned over the bar and told Winnie, 'I got a price today for the clubhouse — a hundred and twenty-two thousand. It's a good price, Prez. In a couple of years, this place could be worth a lot more.'

'Most of our blokes will think a hundred thousand is a lot.'

'We'll have to convince them,' Ocker said.

'Some of them are pretty dumb.'

'Too bad it's a majority vote.'

'There are enough smart ones to give us the majority,' Winnie said. 'I don't want to force it on them unless I have to.' He surveyed the clubhouse, taking in the peeling paint and the old posters of girls straddling bikes. 'Yeah, we can do a lot with this joint, after seeing the Commandos' clubhouse.'

'We can score building materials cheap; I know a bloke, Prez.'

'Let's just wait until we get the plans drawn; there's a few builders in the Club.'

'Have a look at this, Prez — it's my new toy.' Ocker produced an item no larger than a matchbox. 'It's my new camera.' He took a photo of Winnie and handed the camera over.

Winnie looked through the rangefinder. 'That's the go, mate. Where'd you get that?'

'Out of one of my geek magazines.'

'Here, give me a look.' Big Kev held out his hand and put the camera against his eye, 'Fuckin' too small for me, mate. You and your fucking gadgets, Ocker.'

'I reckon it's because when I was young, my stepfather used to pull my toys apart and then put them all back together to see how they worked.' Everybody laughed.

Nestor appeared. 'How're you going, Prez?'

'Good, mate.'

'Can I have a quiet word, Prez?'

'You've got no problems out at the farm, have you?'

'No, Prez, it's good, and I've got another farm too.'

'Yeah, I knew that. What's up?'

'You know my young nephew Amber? He wants to nom-up for the Club.'

'He's a bit young, don't you think, Nestor?'

'That's what I told him, Prez. He's here tonight.'

'I'll have a talk with him after the meeting.'

'Thanks, Prez. Would you like a drink?'

Winnie held out his empty glass. 'You turned out alright, mate.'

'Meeting in ten minutes!' Big Kev yelled. Everyone made their way to the meeting room. Brian took them through the minutes of the last meeting.

'Right, the Prez has something to say.'

Winnie took the floor. 'We wanted to see if we could buy the clubhouse, and we can. It's going to cost a hundred and twenty-two thousand.'

The news was met with whistles and shocked faces. An anonymous voice called out, 'How can we afford that?'

'You've seen the Commandos' clubhouse. We could do ours like theirs and be proud of it.'

'What's wrong with ours, Prez?'

'It's a shithole compared to theirs.' He looked around at their meeting room, filled with old torn lounges and five-gallon drums used for chairs. 'The beauty of owning this place is that we won't have to pay rent. What we make from the bar, we put towards the mortgage. If we're short, we'll make it up with fees. We've talked about this before and you were all keen when we came back from Melbourne.'

'Let's have a show of hands,' Big Kev called out. All except for a couple held up their hands.

Winnie looked pointedly at Ed, the loudest voice against the idea. 'In a couple of years you'll realise what a good idea it is.'

'Maybe, Prez. It looks like we're going to buy it. The only reason I was against it was the cost, but I've got an idea how we can raise some cash towards a good deposit.'

Winnie looked surprised. 'How, Ed?'

'We could raffle a new Harley, sell a couple of thousand tickets at ten dollars each and there's twenty grand.'

'We have to buy the bike out of that, Ed. It doesn't leave a lot for us.'

'Not if we get somebody we know to win it!' Members' murmuring swept the room.

'Now you're talking, Ed. We rig it so we get all the profit?'

'That's right, Prez.'

Heads nodded — simple, clean and indisputable ideas always got the nod.

'We can sell tickets in the shop!'

Someone called out, 'My brother's a printer, he'll print the tickets.'

Winnie gave it thought. That way everyone was involved, and it paid the twenty per cent deposit for very little work.

'Each member'll have to sell two books of tickets,' Winnie said.

'How many tickets in a book?' someone asked.

'Twenty.'

'It's going to be hard selling tickets to our friends.'

Brian said, 'Tell them to think of it as a building fund donation. I'll bet everyone here that I can sell the most tickets.'

Winnie spoke again. 'If we all agree, then that's the plan. All in?' All the heads nodded.

Ed beamed.

'Okay. Don't forget, boys, the opening's in two weeks. Everyone here, alright?'

Kev called out in a small voice, 'Are we going to have balloons?' It brought the house down.

Then Kev got serious. 'Has anyone had trouble with the Tigers lately?' No one said a word. 'Well, a few Tigers were sniffing around the Southside Chapter and Little Tony's boys gave it to a few of them, so just keep an eye out; there might be some payback.'

'We don't have to worry about it for now, Kev. I heard the Tigers are having problems with the Cabramatta slope-heads.'

'Are they?' Kev grinned.

'We'll have to watch out for them, Kev. Those slopehead cunts are mad!'

'So am I,' said Kev. Some newer members had no idea how mad Kev was, only knowing him as the biggest bloke in the Club; they just stared at him and wondered.

Winnie stood up again. 'Don't forget to bring all your friends to the shop opening. We'll make the raffle announcement on the day; it won't be hard to sell the tickets, especially if we borrow a Harley from Fraser's for the day, and tell them a non-rider won it so we can return it. We tell the punters that someone not connected to the Club won it, and then we'll keep the cash. Organise someone, Ocker.'

Chapter 25

A few of the Friday night girls played pool. The nominees behind the bar serving drinks stared at a beautiful girl waiting for a drink. Ocker tapped Winnie on the arm.

'That's Bernice, Prez.' Ocker motioned Brian and Kev to come over. 'Bernice, I want you to meet Winnie, the Miners' President, Brian, our Vice-President, and Big Kev, Sergeant-at-Arms. You'll be working for all of us.'

'I thought we wanted a dyke to work in the shop, but she's not a dyke, is she?' Kev couldn't get over her.

'What a waste!' Winnie said to no one.

Bernice couldn't have given a stuff what the boys thought.

Brian didn't know where to start. 'Can you use a computer?'

'Yes.'

'What do you know about Harleys?' Big Kev asked.

'My three brothers ride them and I rode a Sporty in Adelaide.'

'Do your brothers ride with any Club?'

'No, they do their own thing.'

'How come you left Adelaide?'

'It's only a small town. Do I get the job or not?' Bernice must've had more balls than a billiard table; she looked anyone who spoke to her squarely in the eye. The boys were dumbfounded.

Winnie took over. 'Well, you're exactly what we want — there's not too many good-looking, queer, Harley-riding women in this town — so I guess you've got the job.' He stopped to look at everybody else and said, 'Unless anybody has a problem with it?'

'Not me!' said Ocker.

'Or me,' said Brian.

'I'm with you, Prez.' Big Kev said.

'Looks like you've got the job then.'

'Thanks, Brian. When do I start?'

'Monday. You know where the shop is?'

'Yes, Ocker showed me.'

'Well, good. There's a lot to do before we open.'

'How do you know Ocker, Bernice?' asked Kev. 'Do we call you that?'

'No, Bernie'll do. I met Ocker through a mutual friend. He's a cutie, don't you think?'

'Yeah, real cute.' Big Kev patted Ocker on the head.

'Would you like a drink, Bernie?'

She glanced at her watch. 'No, thanks, I have a date tonight. See you all on Monday.'

'I think she's going to be perfect for us.'

'In more ways than one, Brian.'

'How's that, Prez?'

'Well, we've wanted someone in Adelaide for our business and she has brothers that are bikies. I'll have a chat with Bernie about it. She seems pretty switched-on, but I want to do some checking on her before I say too much.'

'How'll you do that, Prez?'

'I'll get the Pig to see if she's who she says she is; we can't be too careful.'

'Don't you trust me, Prez?'

'That's not it, Ocker, you know that; we have access to the information, so we might as well use it.' Winnie walked over to Nestor and Amber.

'You remember Amber, don't you, Prez?' Amber shook Winnie's hand.

'Yeah, g'day Amber. You've grown a bit since I saw you last. Grab your drink and come for a walk with me.' Amber followed him outside. 'You're still working with Nestor, eh?'

'Only job I've ever had, Prez, and it pays good money. I bought a Harley last week.'

'So Nestor says. He said you want to nominate for the Club?'

'That's right, Prez.'

Winnie looked him in the eyes. 'Don't you think you're a bit young?'

'It's the only thing I've ever wanted, Prez.'

Winnie smiled at him. 'What can I say? I'll talk to Nestor.' They walked back inside the clubhouse where the Rat stood talking to Ocker. 'Where did you come from?'

'Just got here, Prez. Can we talk?'

'Yeah, a little later, Rat. How've you been, anyway?'

'Real good.'

'Grab a drink and join the boys. I have to do something first.'

He signalled Nestor to join him. 'Amber will be alright. You nominate him at the next meeting.'

Nestor broke out in a wide smile. 'Goodonya, Prez! He won't let us down; he's a good kid and he's up for it.'

Winnie grabbed the Rat and they joined Brian, Kev and Ocker. 'Let's go have a line. Let the boys know that we're not to be disturbed, Kev.' They filed into the back room; Brian cut five lines and they took turns in 'powdering their noses'.

The Rat let out a big breath. 'The Skipper called me today, Prez. He said to say he owes you one.' Rat knew nothing of Winnie's meeting with the Skipper. 'What's that about, Prez?'

'I saved him from going to jail, Rat.'

'How's that, Prez?'

'He was going to pick up the Buddha sticks that the Feds busted. We had a tip-off they were onto it, and I left the rest up to him. He made the decision not to be in it — lucky for him. Now this is the go, Rat: we want you to be involved in bringing in the hash.'

The Rat looked amazed.

'All you have to do is go up to Bundaberg and pick up the hash in a container, load it onto the train and pay the Skipper what we give you.'

'Just like the prawns, Prez. When?'

'We'll let you know; we'll give you plenty of notice. You'll have to go outside with him, too.'

'I'm a sailor now, Prez, that's no problem for me. The Skipper said we just might be working together again.'

'That's it then, Rat. I'm going back to the bar. Come on, and I'll buy you a drink.'

'I have to give money to Brian first; I'll join you in a minute.'

There was a loud banging on the door. Big Kev hurried over to open it. 'What is it?' Kev demanded.

'Trouble.' Nestor looked worried. 'You'd better come here, Prez.'

Brian had his head down, counting money. Winnie told him to finish with the cash first and then to come out. The rest followed Nestor out into the bar area. Billy, one of the Miners, sat on the floor with a blood-soaked towel over his head.

Winnie made his way over to Billy, who attempted to stand. Winnie placed his hand on his shoulder: 'No, sit, mate. Just tell me what exactly happened.'

Billy coughed and cleared his throat. 'I stopped at the lights and about five or six blokes with baseball bats and iron bars got out of a car and attacked me for no reason.'

'Do you know who it was?'

'That's the queer part, Prez — they were slope-heads!'

Winnie and Kev exchanged looks. 'Kev, get everybody who's not meant to be in the clubhouse out of here; this is Miners business.'

All the Friday night girls and hangers-on were quickly ushered out of the clubhouse. A senior member, Doc, who'd served as a medic in the Army, examined Billy.

'How is he, Doc?'

'He'll live, Prez, but he needs a few stitches and maybe a tetanus shot. He should go to the hospital.'

'Okay, get a few of the boys to take him.'

'Where's Billy's bike?'

'He's a staunch cunt, he rode it back!'

Winnie turned around. 'Right, first we have to find out who the fuck they were.'

'Do you want the nominees out of here?'

'No, Kev, if we're going to war, they're going to be in it too. Who said the Tigers were having trouble with the slopes?'

'Me, Prez!' Johnny piped up. 'A few of them were down near Chinatown last week doing business when they were attacked.'

'Go on.'

'The Chinese blokes they were doing business with ran off pretty quickly. The Tigers said they shit themselves when the slopes arrived.'

'So what happened to the Tigers?'

'Nothing, Prez. One of them had a gun and took a shot at the slopes and the rest took off.'

'They've mixed us up with them,' said Kev.

'It doesn't matter — nobody touches a Miner and gets away with it.'

'Listen to this, Prez!' Ocker had his scanner tuned in to the police channel. 'It's not a one-off, Prez. Here, listen to this.'

Crackling voices emanated from the scanner, calling for back-up and ambulances in Kings Cross. 'There's trouble between the Tigers and the slope-heads up the Cross.'

'Ring up the Tigers clubhouse and see if they know what's going on, Kev. No one's to leave until we find out what's going on.'

Kev let the call to the Tigers ring out, then hung up.

'Keep on the scanner, Ocker.'

'It sounds like an ambush, Prez.'

'Do we know anybody down in Chinatown?'

'I do, Prez!'

'Well, get on to them, will you!'

Brian walked into the clubhouse and Winnie filled him in.

'Sounds like a case of mistaken identity, Prez.'

'Our colours are nothing like theirs.'

'You know that the slopes all look the same to us. It might be the same for them.'

'It doesn't matter, mate. We have to find out who they are first, and we have to talk to Twister.'

Paul had friends in Chinatown and called his mates down there. 'They're not Chinese, Prez: they're Vietnamese.'

'What's the difference?'

'They hate each other. That's all my mate could tell me.'

'Keep ringing the Tigers, Kev, until you get somebody.'

'The scanner's gone silent; it might have blown over, Prez.'

'No, it hasn't; it's only just started for us. I'll talk to the Pig. He'll know what's going on.'

'I've got Twister on the phone, Prez!' Kev shouted.

Winnie took the phone. 'You've had a bit of trouble tonight, Twister?'

'Word gets out pretty quick, Winnie.'

'Well, I want to talk about it.'

'Why?'

'Because they got one of my boys tonight and I'd say it's a case of mistaken identity, that's why.'

'What about tomorrow, Winnie, around lunchtime, then I'll tell you the story.'

'Where'll we meet?'

Twister went silent for a few seconds.

'Come to our clubhouse,' said Winnie. 'Yours'll be too hot.'

The Miners spoke among themselves. For most it would be their first war, and none was sure what would happen or what would be asked of them.

'Kev, I'll tell them the score and then I want you to select a war party of ten men. Then we'll go over to Cabramatta and give some of them a belting.'

'Who, Prez?'

'Any cunt!' Winnie replied. 'Go by car.'

Big Kev bellowed. 'Listen up!'

A silence fell immediately.

'We don't know completely what's going on yet,' Winnie said. 'We'll find out the story off Twister tomorrow, but we know it's the slopes in Cabramatta.' A haze darkened his eyes; he meant business. 'Kev is taking ten members over to Cabramatta to give a few of the fuckers a serve.'

'I know just the place, Prez; I just came from there and there's a pool hall where their members hang out.'

'Good one, Reg. You talk to Kevvie.'

Brian announced that he was coming too. 'I like Billy.'

Kev selected his men. 'No knives, just baseball bats.' His men armed themselves.

'Okay, boys, let's go!' Kev led the war party outside. 'Now, before we get too excited, this is how we're going to do it. Reg here knows the area.'

They stood in silence awaiting Kev's next word. 'When we get to this pool hall we'll just walk straight in and start smashing whoever's there.'

'Women too, Kev?'

'No, not the women, unless they attack you.' He smiled. 'We'll only be there one minute.'

Someone asked, 'One minute?'

'You'll be surprised how slow it goes. If anyone goes down, they leave with us. Got that?'

'Yes, Sergeant!' The reply came in unison.

'Good, let's go!'

Reg drove the first car. 'Not too fast, mate!' Kev ordered. The other members in the car swapped jokes nervously until they reached Cabramatta.

'It's up here, Kev, on your right. I'll turn around at the railway station and come back down the road.'

'It looks like there are a few in there, Sarge.' Gregg the Egg said from the back seat. He'd been around for a while but his voice bore a tinge of nervousness.

'Everybody right?' Big Kev asked, and then he patted Brian on the knee and gave him a wink.

'I'll keep the engine running, Sarge.' Reg glided past the poolroom then pulled the car up a few car lengths away.

The other car parked behind them. It was late and hardly anyone was on the streets.

Kev calmly led the war party up to the front doors. He stopped outside for a second, looked at the boys, then mouthed, 'Okay?' The boys all nodded.

Kev pushed the poolroom doors wide open and stepped inside. 'Let the mayhem begin.'

The bloke behind the counter looked up as Kev ran over to him. He didn't comprehend for half a second, but when he saw the danger he reached for the phone. Kev smashed it with one mighty hit. The slopes looked up from their games of pool but they were so caught by surprise they barely had time to use their cues as weapons before the Miners were on top of them with baseball bats. Blood spattered everywhere. Some women screamed and ran into the toilets. The blokes tried to stand and fight but they didn't have a chance in hell. In less than a minute there wasn't a man standing except for the Miners.

'That'll do!' Big Kev called out. 'Everybody out!'

Adrenalin pumping hard through his veins, Kev led them out. One slope leapt to his feet unsteadily, a torrent of blood flowing from a gash in his head, and stabbed Brian, embedding his knife up to the hilt in Brian's arm. Kev saw it happen in slow motion; he took a few giant steps and swung his bat and sent the slope sprawling across the floor. Brian stumbled forward, dropped his bat and sprayed blood over the pool table. Kev grabbed Brian's bat, wrapped his arm around Brian and helped him back to their car. Reg screeched away.

Kev screamed, 'Give me a bandana!'

They'd been driving for less than a minute when he noticed that Gregg the Egg was missing. He assumed Gregg was in the other car and went back to taking care of Brian's injury, telling him, 'You're going to be alright, mate.' Brian's face had turned grey; his eyes rolled back in his head, and the blood flowed copiously.

Kev applied pressure around the area where the knife had entered. 'It's alright, mate, it hasn't hit the bone.' Kev pulled out the knife in one swift motion. He tied the bandana tightly above the bleeding wound and Brian began to shake uncontrollably, incapable of saying anything. Kev tried to reassure him, but he was himself close to panic. 'Not far to go now, mate.' By the time Reg pulled into the clubhouse Brian had turned white.

Reg sprinted from the car to find the Doc while Kev carefully lifted Brian from the back seat. The Doc emerged with Winnie and some other members. The boys in the other car still had no idea that Brian was injured and they spoke excitedly about the fight until they saw the boys gathering around Brian.

The Doc inspected the bleeding arm. 'We've got to get him to hospital. I think he's cut a vein, Prez.'

'I'll go,' said Ocker. 'Come on, Reg, this is an emergency.'

The Prez asked Kev, 'How'd that happen?'

'As we were leaving, one of them was playing possum. I looked after him.' Kev held up the blood-soaked knife for inspection.

'Keep it, Kev; we'll see if we can give it back.'

The boys back at the clubhouse made their way to the bar and told and retold the story to the other members. Pommie, a Miner who'd been riding in the other car, spoke to Kev. 'Whaddya reckon about Gregg the Egg?'

'What do you mean?'

'He done a runner before we went into the pool hall.'

'Did he just?' Kevvie snarled. 'I thought he was in your car. Is his bike here?'

'No.'

'We'll go and visit him tomorrow and get his colours,' said Winnie. 'Our colours don't run — hear that?'

'Yes, Prez!'

'Who nominated him?'

'I did, Prez.'

'Well, Pommie, it's your job.'

'I know, Prez.'

'Do you know what to do?'

'Yeah, we kick his fucking guts in!'

'Don't wait until tomorrow, Pommie. Go now. Kev, you stay here with me. Pommie can take a couple of blokes with him.'

Kev looked at Pommie. 'Well, you heard the Prez!'

'I'm on my way.'

'Don't forget to get him to sign the registration papers for his bike before you give it to him, and bring the bike back here.'

Winnie checked his watch. It was almost daybreak. 'Do you reckon I should ring Gina and tell her about Brian?'

Big Kev just stared. 'It's a bit early, don't you think, Prez? She'll give you an earful of shit and blame you, you know.'

'Yeah, I know, Kev; he might be back soon anyway.'

'Geez, mate, you seem more worried about telling Gina than bashing those fucking slopes.'

Winnie didn't bother replying. 'Make sure these boys don't get up the piss too much, Kev, and organise some food, will you?'

The boys arrived back from the hospital with Billy. He didn't look too bad as he walked uncertainly toward them.

'You'd better go home and relax, Billy.'

'No, Prez, I want to stay here.'

Winnie put his arm around his shoulder. 'Alright, mate, you just sit down and take it easy.'

'How's Brian?'

'I dunno, mate. When he gets back we'll all know. Just take it easy.'

When the Doc came back from the hospital he filled the members in. 'Brian's in shock and needs microsurgery on his arm.'

'Okay, thanks, Doc. You boys go and grab a drink. Good job.'

'Are you going to ring Gina, Prez?'

'No, mate. I'm getting Mimi to go to the hospital with her, and maybe Sandy too.'

'I'll call Sandy.'

'Thanks, Kev.'

Twister arrived with two car loads of Tigers armed to the teeth. Winnie told Kev to make certain they left their guns in their cars.

Winnie grabbed Twister by the arm and led him out to the back room. 'Come on, let's talk. Now, Twister, what the fuck's going on?'

'Last week, a couple of my boys sold some really piss-weak speed to these Cabramatta slopes. When they tried to return it my boys got stuck into the little cunts and we thought that'd be the end of it until last night. Then they ambushed us up the Cross. There must've been fifty of them!'

'You don't look too bad.'

'We've got six Tigers in St Vincent's Hospital. Thank Christ the pigs were there in numbers real quick, but the slopes were well organised. One group bashed the shit out of us and while that was going on another crew gave our bikes a belting as well. By the time we figured out what was going on they'd fucked off.'

'When they bashed our Billy tonight, they must've been on their way into town to have another go at you.'

'Is Billy alright?'

'He'll be right. We went to Cabramatta earlier and bounced some of them in a pool hall. We don't know who they were but they'll get the message.'

'So, Winnie, we're in this together.'

'Like fuck we are, Twister. No, you're in this by yourselves. We'll sort out our own problems and you and your Tigers will have to sort your own shit out.' He added pointedly, 'We're not guilty for your sins.'

'They're hard to find; no one will talk to you, Winnie. They're Vietnamese — tough cunts.'

'We'll find them, Twister.'

'If that's all you want, Winnie, we're off. We're going after them.'

'Good luck, Twister.'

Big Kev had overheard it all. 'Geez, Prez, I'm glad you didn't join forces with the Tigers.'

'We don't need a war for no reason, Kev. Business is good at the moment and a war would only bring heat we don't need. Let Twister have it.'

'What are we going to do, Prez?'

'First thing is we have to find out who they are.'

Doc called out from the clubhouse, 'Prez, you're wanted on the phone. It's your missus, I think.'

'Thanks, Doc.' Winnie went back inside to answer it.

'Hello, Peter, are you alright?'

'Yes, Mimi, I'm fine. How's Gina?'

'She's not too happy about Brian. Sandy's at the hospital with us.'

'Have they said how long he's going to be in?'

'Not yet, but how'd he get hurt?'

'I'll tell you later. Is Ocker still there?'

'No, he's gone back to the clubhouse.'

'Okay, I'll see you soon.'

'Look after yourself, Peter.'

Pommie and the boys arrived back from visiting Gregg the Egg. They had his bike on a trailer.

'How'd it go, Pom?'

'He lay down and screamed like a mongrel dog, Prez. Here are the papers for his bike.'

'Good. When we sell his bike the money goes towards the deposit on our clubhouse.'

'What'll I do with these, Prez?' Pom held out Gregg the Egg's colours.

'Burn them.'

Ocker walked in, smiling. 'I'd rather face the slopes than Gina, Prez. She's not too happy.'

'Yeah, I know.'

'How is he?'

'The knife cut his vein and he lost a lot of blood but they're stitching it up now, so they reckon he'll be home tomorrow or Monday.'

'Can we visit him today?'

'No, Prez, he'll still be out of it until tomorrow. The pigs turned up at the hospital.'

'What did they have to say?'

'I haven't seen Brian since they spoke to him,' said Ocker. 'That's all I know.'

'I wonder how they knew.'

'The hospital would've informed them; they have to. But they didn't stay long.'

'We'll find out tomorrow.'

'Did Twister turn up, Prez?'

'Yeah, mate; it was his blokes who ripped off the slopes in the first place. The slopes were on their way into the Cross when they came across Billy. I bet they mistook him for a Tiger and bashed him.'

'I bet they don't know the difference.'

'How do you think we can contact them, Ocker?'

'Reg should be able to find out for us, Prez. He's from Cabramatta.'

'Well, get him over here quick smart.'

Big Kev located Reg and brought him back to the clubhouse.

'Do you know any of the slope gangs?'

'No, Prez, I moved out of there before they arrived.'

'You know any people out there?'

'I was only young, Prez, but it can't be too hard to find something out.' He stopped to think then said, 'I'll go and see an old mate.'

'Can't you ring him?'

'He hasn't got a phone.'

'Well, go and see him, then, and go by car.'

'Alright, Prez.'

'Tell the boys to go home, Kev, but tell them to stay near their phones just in case.'

'I don't think there'll be any trouble,' Kev replied. 'I'm sure the pigs will be onto them by now.'

'Prez, someone from the Redbacks is on the phone.'

A voice on the end asked, 'Are you blokes okay down there, Winnie?'

'Yeah. Why are you asking, Sorrow?'

'It's been on the radio. I heard two Miners are in hospital after getting bashed up the Cross by slopes.'

'They always get it wrong. You know the press, they fuck everything up. It's a long and complicated story, mate, but the short story is the Tigers caused the trouble. Somehow or another we got caught up in it. I'll tell you the story next time I see you.'

'If you need any assistance, we're here, mate.'

'Thanks, Sorrow.' Winnie hung up.

Kev called out, 'It's all over the radio, Prez. Fuck-all we can do about it. I'm going out the back to check our weapons.'

'No, leave them for the moment. You never know, we might get a visit.'

The unmistakable roar of a pack of Harleys filled the air. The Southside Chapter had arrived.

'I forgot to tell you, Prez — I called Little Tony earlier on and let them know the drill.'

'Thanks, Kev, I forgot all about them.'

'You can't think of everything, Prez.'

'Don't let on, Kev.' Winnie winked at Kev and walked out to meet a very worried-looking Little Tony.

'Prez, what's going on?'

Winnie brought him up to date.

'So what do we do, Prez?'

A ringing phone interrupted them. 'Someone wanting to talk to Peter Winifred?'

Winnie took the call and after a brief conversation hung up. 'I've got to go out for a while. Stay here until I get back.'

After Winnie left the compound, Little Tony asked Kev, 'Where's he going, mate?'

'That'd be a Pig for sure. No one calls him Peter, except his own mother and his missus.'

Tony didn't ask any more questions.

Winnie came back about half an hour later. 'The pigs know what's going on, but the funny thing is, they don't give a shit. They just said not to be so public about it.'

'Did he say who they were?'

'They're not sure themselves, except that there are a few different gangs and apparently the blokes we hit in the pool hall aren't the ones warring with the Tigers.'

'Good chance they'll think it was the Tigers.'

'Who knows how they think, Kev. The Pig reckons they're bad cunts.'

Reg made his way over. 'I saw a mate, Prez. His sister goes out with a slope in a gang. My mate doesn't talk to him because he doesn't understand him, but his sister does.'

'Well done, Reg; go to the top of the class!'

'Thanks, Prez.'

'How do you think we should go about talking to them?' Little Tony asked.

'I really don't know, mate. What do you think, Kev? You've been in Vietnam.'

'We never really got close to them, Prez, except for the bar girls and laundry ladies. One thing's for sure, they're cunning cunts. What they say is not what they think. They don't like losing face.'

'Who does, Kev, as long as we both win?'

'In what way, Prez?'

'I don't know yet; we'll have to wait and see.' Winnie walked outside with Little Tony.

'This is just what we don't need at the moment, Prez.'

'How's that, mate?'

'We've just got back into business after Swannie's exit. We've just built up the business now and if we have a long war it'll suffer and the pigs'll be right onto us.'

'I know, but there's not much we can do about it. How's your Chapter going, Tony? I see Boris has his colours.'

'He's a good one, Prez. He's my Big Kev.'

Winnie looked at Tony. 'He's got a long way to go to be half of Big Kev.'

'You've got to start somewhere, Prez.'

'So business is good?'

'It's a good product, plus we're the only ones with hash.'

'Don't get greedy, mate; let everyone make an earn.'

'Oh, I know, Prez; I don't put too much on it.'

'That's good business, Tony. I don't think you and the boys have to wait around here. Thanks for coming over.'

'One together, Prez.' He put his arm around Winnie's shoulder.

'Goodonya, Tony.'

The nominees kept up a steady flow of coffee and tea until the phone rang. 'Reg, it's for you!'

Reg had a conversation then replaced the receiver. 'We won't be able to find out anything until tomorrow, Prez. The sister's boyfriend is locked up with a bunch of mates and they won't be out until Sunday.'

Winnie announced that it was time to get stuck into the good gear. The tension eased immediately, the music got louder, the bourbon and beer flowed, joints were lit and white lines of speed appeared and disappeared.

'Whaddya think the women are up to, Prez?' asked Kev.

'Still with Gina, mate; you know how they stick together.' Winnie laughed. It had been a long night. He grabbed his drink and raised it in a toast. 'Who cares?' They both laughed.

Sunday at the hospital was busy during visiting hours, but when Winnie walked into Brian's room the only smiling face belonged to Brian. Gina, Brian's mother, Sandy and Mimi showed absolutely no emotion. Big Kev whispered to Winnie, 'It looks like we shit in someone's best hat.'

When Kev and Winnie filled the doorway Brian's mother and Gina muttered something about getting a cup of tea and quickly left the room. Kitty ran towards them.

'Uncle Peter!' she yelled excitedly.

Winnie scooped her up and walked over to Brian's bedside. 'How are you, mate?'

'Good, Prez. I'll be out of here tomorrow.'

Mimi walked over and stood beside Winnie. 'Don't I get a kiss, or a hello?'

'Sorry, babe.' He gently placed Kitty down on the bed and warmly embraced Mimi.

'I've been worried; I haven't heard a word from you.'

'Didn't Ocker tell you?'

'That's not you. Anyway, I have to go.'

'Where?' Winnie was exhausted; he couldn't think straight.

Mimi looked over at Kev and Sandy cuddling one another. 'I'm going to my parents' place for dinner. You were invited — you forgot, didn't you?'

Winnie just smiled. 'We've been a bit busy.'

'You're a bastard,' she whispered then walked over to Brian, gave him a peck on the cheek and kissed Kitty. 'Get well, Brian,' she said, and left the room.

'Are you in trouble, Uncle Peter?' an observant Kitty enquired innocently.

'Maybe, Kitty.'

Sandy said, 'She'll be alright, Prez. She's not used to this; just give her some time. I've got to go now.'

Big Kev smacked her on the arse. 'I'll see you tonight.'

Brian watched silently. 'How's everything going, Prez?'

'Fine, mate. We might be able to talk with them and find out what's been going on. Has Ocker kept you informed?'

'Not all of it, Prez. I've been out of it for a while.'

'How's Gina taking all this?'

'It'd be alright if my mother wasn't here, but when they're together ...' he looked at the ground. 'You know?'

'I know, mate. I might get going before they get back.'

'I'll see you at the shop tomorrow, Prez.'

'No, mate, take some time off.'

'It's not as bad as it looks, Prez. Besides, I have to show Bernie what to do.'

'Can't we do that?' Big Kev asked.

'No.'

'Well, take it easy, mate.'

Back out in the sunshine Big Kev walked toward his car. 'Looks like you're the bad guy again, Prez.'

'Nothing changes, mate. Let's go back and see if Reg has anything for us.'

Back at the clubhouse Ocker had the scanner doing its business. Before Winnie uttered a word he turned it off. 'They want to talk with us, Prez.'

'When?'

'It's up to us. They suggested St Felix's church on the highway at Bankstown.'

'What do you think, Kev?'

'Well, it's neutral ground and pretty open.'

'Well, we won't take any chances, so arm up two cars and come with us. How do we contact them?'

'Reg is waiting to hear from us,' said Ocker. 'I'll ring him and get him to organise it for today.'

'Better get Reg here. I want to find out more about them before our meeting. There's no use mucking around.'

'I'm on to it, Prez.'

'What time is it now?'

'Three o'clock.'

'Make it seven.'

Big Kev selected Doc, Pom and Slippery to carry the guns. 'Come with me.' He pried a couple of floorboards up and handed out arms. 'Doc, take the rifle; you too, Slippery; Pom, you take the shotgun.' Kev stared at the Pom. 'You have to be careful with it. If — and I mean if — you use it, just make sure the Prez and I aren't anywhere near it.'

'No worries, Sarge.'

'We don't want any accidents. Now check your guns; they should all be empty.'

The smell of the gun oil and the sound of sliding bolts and the pumping shotgun brought back memories to Kev of rabbit hunting when he was a kid. He divvied up the ammo among the three of them.

'No loading until we're in the car. Put them in the boot for now.' Kev slid the floorboards back.

'What have you got?' the Doc asked Kev.

'Nothing too big.' Kev slid a blue Police Special .38 from the back of his pants.

'Looks good, mate.'

'Have you ever shot anyone, Pom?'

'No, but if I have to, I will.'

'You don't have to prove anything, mate. This is just back-up.'

Ocker listened intently to the scanner and then looked up at Winnie. 'I'll be glad when they get portable phones going. They'll change everything.'

The boys relaxed with a game of pool until Reg arrived. 'They won't have the meeting tonight, Prez.'

'Why not?'

'There's a mass on and too many people will be there.'

'Aren't they Buddhists?'

'No, Prez, a lot of them are Catholic.'

'When do they want it, then?'

'Tomorrow morning at ten o'clock.'

'Are you sure they'll turn up?'

'I'm not too sure, Prez, but they know it was a mistake with Billy, if that's anything to go by.'

'It's a funny time to have a meeting. What else have you found out about them, Reg?'

'The gangs are mainly orphans sent here from Vietnam. They only have their uncles or aunts here and they have enough trouble just looking after themselves.'

'Right. Go on.'

'These blokes formed gangs that were into extortion but now they're into drugs. That's why they had trouble with the Tigers. They're close because they only have each other. Their leader's name is Tran.'

'You heard what Reg said, boys; we'll meet here at eight in the morning,' Kev said. 'Get the guns back out of the car and go home.'

'What're you going to do, Kev?'

'Stay with you.'

'How do you know what I'm going to do?'

Kev just smiled back at him. 'I'll give Sandy a call.'

'I want you to open the shop tomorrow, Ocker.'

'Why, Prez? I want to go to the meeting with Kev and you.'

'Brian's going to need you, and believe me he'll be there. Besides, Bernie will be turning up, so you'll need to be there by nine at the latest.'

'What if there's trouble?'

'It feels good, mate. Don't worry. Why don't you organise a few girls for us tonight?'

Ocker pulled out his little black book and with barely a glance stated, 'I've got just the girls.'

'Who?' Big Kev asked.

'The nurses!'

'Beauty, mate!'

'But with just the three of us, I think we might need a bit more of this!' Ocker retrieved his bag of speed and made three huge lines on the bar. They had a big night with the nurses and not much sleep had been had by the time the boys began turning up in the morning. Ocker put the girls in a cab and Big Kev brought out the guns again and gave the orders.

'Right, Pom, Slippery and the Prez will come with you. Keep those guns out of sight. We don't want any mistakes.'

'Yes, Sarge.'

'Only fire if I call out to you. When we get there we'll ride around the block, just to make sure it's not an ambush. Okay?'

The boys were tense as they rode through the early morning traffic. At St Felix's they saw two Asian blokes standing inside the church doors.

'What've they been up to, I wonder?'

'Getting their last rites in!' Reg said. It made everybody laugh.

'Come on, Kev.'

Winnie and Kev walked towards the church and the two Asians walked out to meet them.

It must've looked like the shoot-out at the OK Corral. They stopped about three metres from each other and at that moment Winnie whispered to Kev, 'We'll just play it as it comes.'

Their leader spoke in broken English. 'There has been mistake.'

'Fucken oath there has been!' Kevvie roared.

'Hold on, Kev, let him have his say.'

The leader put his hands together as if to pray, bowed his head and looked up. 'My name is Tran and this is Phuong, and we apologise for what happened to your friend on Friday night.'

Winnie just stared at him. 'Are you taking responsibility?' It wasn't what either of them had expected.

Tran stared back at Winnie. 'What more do you want?'

'No more fucking mistakes, or you'll all go back to Vietnam in body bags!' Kev pulled his gun out to show them he meant business.

'That'll do, Kev.' Winnie noticed that they didn't react at all. 'Okay, there's been a mistake. You'd better punish those involved, then we might be able to do business.'

'Get fucked, Skippy!' Phuong said before Tran could stop him. 'You skippies are robbers!'

Winnie held up his hand. 'This is getting us nowhere. We accept your apology. Now, are we going to have any trouble with the blokes we hit in the pool hall last night?'

Tran smiled. 'No, no problems.'

'Good, that's it, then. Just remember: if you want to do business, you get a message to me. Come on, Kev.'

They turned and walked back to the car. Kev kept glancing over his shoulder. 'I don't trust those cunts, Prez.'

'I think you might be wrong this time, mate.'

Kev got the boys to put their guns away.

Reg was keen to know what had gone down, 'How'd it go, Prez?'

'Good, Reg, we're not going to have any worries. Let's go back to the clubhouse. Also Reg, don't be surprised if those slopes want to do some business with us. After being burnt by the Tigers they were pretty pissed off, but if we show them respect this could work out well for us both.'

'What do you think the outcome will be between them and the Tigers, Prez?'

'Twister doesn't have much stomach for a war. I reckon he'll just let it die down and get on with business.'

'What about our Billy? He might want to carry it on.'

'I'll talk to him. He'll understand.'

Chapter 26

At the shop Brian supervised the work with one arm in a sling while Ocker took the piss out of Bernie, who looked hot in her body-hugging clothes.

Brian beamed. 'You'd never know she was queer, Prez. So, what was the result with the Vietnamese blokes?'

'Let's go out the back,' Winnie said. 'How's the arm, Brian?'

'It's alright, mate. It wasn't as bad as it looked, but it just missed the main artery.' He grinned cheekily. 'I'm getting plenty of sympathy, too.'

'Okay, this is the go. They're not that much different to us; they're just after an earn. It seems Twister and his Tigers robbed and bashed a few of them.'

'Fuck, eh, Prez?'

'Yeah and they weren't happy about it, so on their way to the Cross they ran into Billy. An unfortunate case of mistaken identity — it won't happen again.'

'So that's it, Prez?'

'Well, mate, what else would you like to do?' Winnie asked. Brian's silence was his answer. 'One thing that came out of it is that they might go into business with us. I don't think they'll be going back to Twister, anyway. What did the pigs say when they came to visit you in hospital, Brian?'

'Fuck-all, Prez. I just told them it was an accident and they said that us bikies never talk. I just played with them, so they got the shits and left.'

'Okay, if everything's alright I'm going home early. I don't think Mimi's too happy with me.'

'Good luck, Prez.'

* * *

Music was playing as Winnie walked in and saw Mimi sitting on the lounge looking miserable, her eyes red. Her hands twisted a handkerchief. He stood there for a moment, watching. 'A man's got to do what he's got to do, babe.'

In between sobs she blurted out comments on the Club, his late hours and everything else on her mind. It didn't make sense to Winnie, but he got the drift. He took her in his arms and she let go another flood of tears. 'What are we going to do, Peter?'

'Just try to understand, Mimi.'

She wrapped her arms around him. 'I'll try, but I worry about you.'

Winnie had the sense to say little except 'She'll be right, babe' and other soothing things meant to deflect deep discussion on any topic. After a while Mimi calmed down and snuggled up to him on the couch. They sat quietly for an hour and nothing more was ever said about the matter.

The work at the new shop went smoothly. It took six weeks from go to whoa, and eventually the big day of the grand opening arrived. The Commandos came up from Melbourne and the Redbacks rode down from Newcastle. Everyone brought their wives and girlfriends and a crowd of more than two hundred turned up. Bernie played chief greeter and made sure everyone had a drink the moment they walked in the front door.

Winnie introduced her to Mimi. Bernie didn't stick around — there was too much for her to do — and the moment she left Mimi turned on Winnie. 'Does she work here?'

Winnie just nodded. 'Beautiful, isn't she?' He waited for a few seconds as Mimi digested that nub of information. 'Don't worry about Bernie, Mimi. She only likes girls. She's a dyke.'

Mimi looked intently at Winnie. 'Is she?'

'That's why we hired her — no problems there.' Mimi was temporarily satisfied, though a little curious.

When Rastus and Spike arrived, Winnie shook their hands warmly. 'Help yourselves and take a look around, boys. I'll catch up with you later.'

They were amazed at the shop. Their faces told the story. Brian had ridden the builders hard and the place looked tiptop. 'Go for it, Prez.'

Even Big Kev was awestruck. 'Fuck, Prez, we've got some people here!'

'Where's Ocker?'

'Selling raffle tickets for the Harley.'

'We're going to have to get some of the boys to do security for us out the front,' Winnie said, 'We don't need any bikes going astray — you know who'll be getting the blame, and it's not good publicity. Things are different now.'

'What about the raffle for the Harley?' Kev asked with a smile.

Winnie grinned back at him. 'That's different too. Have you worked out who's going to win it?'

Kev smiled again before answering, 'Ocker's queer mate from the university.'

'Have you seen him? What does he look like?'

Big Kev just said, 'You'll see.'

Brian's arm was nearly back to full use and he busied himself behind the counter. The display had an array of quality custom parts ordered from the US. It was what most bikies wanted, and they always had money for their bikes. Bernie explained the qualities of different products, while showing off her luscious body in tight jeans to a gobsmacked audience, who were amazed at her technical knowledge and her nice arse. Bernie ignored the oglers and outsold everyone. Big Kev helped cook sausages. When food was free, people ate more.

Winnie wandered over to Mimi. 'What are you doing behind there?'

'Helping Gina. She never expected so many people.'

'Thanks a lot, Mimi.'

Amber helped set up the beer tent around the back while his mates admired Kevvie's workshop and the latest equipment and tools laid out neatly before a custom bike on a hydraulic stand. Ocker wandered around doing a brisk trade selling raffle tickets for the bogus Harley raffle.

Kev reassured Winnie about security. 'Little Tony organised it.'

'That's initiative! He's a good one.'

Spike took a long walk around and joined Kev. 'Whaddya reckon, Spike?'

'I'm impressed, Kev. I like what you did with the panhead.'

'I want to build an Aussie Chopper; something to suit our roads until they get better.'

'What's Ocker up to, Kev?'

'Hasn't he got you yet? We're running a raffle for a new Harley and it's being drawn today.'

Rastus smiled. 'Yeah, right, and who's going to win it?'

'Just think of it as a donation.'

A bloke with a camera and a huge bag slung over his shoulder walked into sight.

'Who's that, Kev?'

'I don't know, but I'm about to find out.' He caught the man's attention and gestured to him. Struggling through the crowd, the man made his way over. 'Where are you from?'

'The *Advocate*. I'm doing a story on the shop opening. I saw Brian out the front. He told me not to take any pictures unless I asked first, and I haven't.'

'It's too crowded here for photos.'

'No, I'm not here for photos, I'm after a beer.'

Kevvie laughed. 'Come on, mate, I'll buy you one!'

Ocker arrived with the raffle tickets. 'Come on, Rastus, a chance to win a new Harley!'

'Yeah, fuck-all chance!' Rastus laughed. 'We tried it and nobody bought — they smelled the fix.'

'They're not as generous as us Sydney boys,' Ocker said. 'Come on, how many, Rastus?'

'Give me five.'

'Me too.' Spike held out his money.

Rastus motioned to Winnie and they slipped out the back for a smoke. Bad news: the pseudoephedrine had gone up another five grand and it was harder to get. Rastus reckoned Winnie should look around for another supplier in Sydney. They both knew sending away clients wasn't good for business. If Winnie found a supplier and kept the price down he had a ready market through Rastus and his huge network. Someone in pharmacy supplies would be hard to find, but if he put the word out about the price he'd pay, someone would turn up; everybody had a weakness for cold, anonymous cash. The more people wanted it, the more he could jack up the price — he knew what it was worth.

Winnie and Rastus talked about what else they were up to. Rastus had some of his crew employed in his private security business. Of course it was unlicensed, but he owned it outright and they did 'other things' as well. Everything was good in his world. Winnie filled Rastus in on buying into a couple of pubs with some Italian mates. 'Top blokes. Old schoolmates. We understand each other.'

Ocker stuffed the raffle ticket stubs into a drum. He'd organised little Kitty to draw the winning ticket; she looked innocent enough. Her job was simple: she'd draw a ticket from the drum and hand it to Ocker. Ocker would make a switch with a ticket secreted in his hand and announce the winner. Winnie hoped Ocker was very good at it.

Big Kev and Sorrow from the Redbacks had a little chat about the trouble the Miners had had with the slopes. 'Nothing to do with us, Sorrow. They jumped the Tigers at Kings Cross but when they thumped Billy we went to a pool hall and settled the score. Then the Prez set up a powwow and sorted it out.' The noise of the band drowned them out.

Ocker got on the PA and made the announcement everyone had anticipated all afternoon. 'We're drawing the raffle in five minutes.'

A bloke Winnie had never seen before kissed Bernie. He had bleached hair and wore skin-tight leather pants. Ocker carried the drum over to where Brian stood with the microphone, little Kitty following behind him. The music stopped. 'Welcome to Westside Choppers, Sydney's newest shop for custom motorcycle parts,' said Brian. The crowd roared. 'Thank you for coming and making our opening grand!' The crowd roared again. 'You've all been waiting for the raffle drawing, so get your tickets out. My daughter Kitty will draw the winning ticket. Are you ready?'

The crowd roared back 'Yes!'

Brian rolled the barrel out and opened the lid.

'Here you go, Kitty, it's all yours.' Kitty stuck in her hand and pulled out four tickets at once.

'Just one, darling.' She threw them back and pulled out one.

She started to read aloud. 'The winning number is ...'

'No, darling!' Brian called. 'Give it to Ocker!'

Ocker took the ticket, made the switch and read out the number. 'Number one, seven, three.'

Ocker's gay mate squealed in feigned delight. 'I won! I won!' He stood out with his bleached hair and tight trousers when he made his way up to the stage. Everyone looked stunned.

Someone yelled out 'Redraw!' while Brian inspected his ticket, then made a big show of handing him the key for the bike while the crowd booed.

'Now, what's your name?' Brian asked the winner.

'Jim Roberts.'

'Well, Jimmy, thanks for supporting the Miners Motorcycle Club, and happy riding!'

A queer had won the bike. Some — most — were not too happy.

Gina rushed Kitty off the stage, fearful there could be trouble, and the band burst into life. Winnie looked at Big Kev and winked as the crowd drifted away. He spotted the Mario brothers talking to Rastus and Spike.

Winnie wandered over. 'So you've met my mates from Melbourne?'

'Yeah, Winnie. Rastus knows our cousins Dominic and Tony. Small world, hey?'

Winnie just shook his head.

'You did a good job here, Winnie. A great way to open, with the raffle and everything.'

'Thanks, Mario. Maybe when our pub's ready we can do the same. How much longer until you open?'

'The paperwork's done. Now we renovate.'

Ocker joined them with Bernie and Jim. 'Prez, I'd like you to meet my friend from the university, Jim Roberts.'

It was their first meeting; Winnie gave him a firm handshake. 'Congratulations on winning the raffle, Jimmy.' His mind raced, thinking of all the people Ocker had found through Jimmy over the years; he'd even found their first cook.

'It's Jim, not Jimmy,' Ocker whispered to Winnie.

'Alright, Jim, goodonya.'

Rastus checked out Bernie flitting around. 'Where have you been hiding?'

'Bernie, meet Rastus, up from Melbourne.'

'Are you a friend of Ocker's?'

'Yes, we're good mates. I work with him.' Rastus thought she was a street girl. 'I work with all the boys in the shop, don't I, Prez?'

Winnie didn't want to let Rastus know she was a dyke — that was up to her. He hoped she'd keep it going for a while longer and she did just that by being friendly to Rastus and offering him a drink, which he quickly accepted. A wide grin spread across Rastus's face. 'I think she likes me.' He even pulled his beanie up from his eyes a little.

'You should get your teeth fixed, mate. She'd like you more.'

'You reckon she likes me?'

'Fucking oath, mate. I've never seen her act like that with anybody else. She doesn't like cigars, but.'

'Doesn't she?' He put his cigar out on the floor and ground it in with his heel. 'Me neither.'

Bernie handed over a drink and gave him a beautiful smile. He must have thought he was in with a chance, so he pushed ahead. 'Would you like to come out the back with me? I've got some good Melbourne speed.'

'Okay, I know a good place to go.' She led him away and he followed; as they walked off, Rastus smiled and gave Winnie the thumbs up. When they were out of earshot everybody erupted in laughter and Spike and the Mario brothers looked on, wondering what the hell was up. Ocker couldn't stop laughing.

'She's queer!'

The Marios looked incredulous.

'You didn't deserve to win that bike,' some drunken egg said to Jim.

Winnie looked at Ocker and mouthed, 'Leave it.'

The drunken egg, bolstered by the lack of response, went on. 'You're not even a bikie!'

Ocker saw where it was going and intervened. 'That'll do, mate. You've had a good time.'

'Got protection, have we, you little faggot?'

The egg put his arm on Jim's shoulder to spin him around. Jim handed his drink to Winnie and quick as lightning seized the egg's arm in a wrestling grip, spun him around and brought him down on the ground hard. Still holding his arm Jim smashed the palm of his free hand down on the egg's nose and broke it, all in less than a few seconds. Blood flowed freely then the egg's eyeballs rolled back in his head and he lay still, quite unconscious.

Winnie looked at a couple of the egg's mates. 'Get him out of here!'

They grabbed an arm each to cart him away. Jim leant over him. 'Tell your mummy that a poofter bashed you!'

Winnie handed Jim's drink back and looked at him with new-found respect. 'That didn't take too much, Jim.'

'I broke a nail,' Jim said, looking at it casually. 'I think I cost you some customers, Prez.'

'Don't worry, Jim. We don't need eggs.'

A beaming Rastus came back with Bernie. The boys watched him light a cigar and blow out the smoke. 'Bernie does like cigars, you smart cunts. My turn will come! I'll get you bastards. You're a good sport, Bernie. Let's get you a drink!'

The Mario brothers seized the opportunity to collar Winnie. The pubs they had bought were all heritage listed. They were having all sorts of problems with Stan Ogilvy in the Planning and Heritage Department, mainly to do with changing the façade. Someone kept knocking their plans back. The cost could run into thousands and they didn't have it, so they thought Winnie might know someone who knew him.

'What about your cousin?'

'He's too scared to approach him. He can't help us and this cunt hates wogs.'

'Okay, don't get too excited about it. I'll see what I can do.'

'We're sorry to have fucked you around like this.'

'I can't promise you anything. What's the worst-case scenario?'

'We can sell them as they are and we'll make a profit, but that's not the reason we're in it. The city's coming back to life. They'll take off once we get them going.'

'Alright, I'll ring next week, and see what I can do.'

The band packed up, most of the crowd left, and the nominees cleaned up the aftermath. Spike and Rastus flew back to Melbourne. The women went to Brian and Gina's. Kitty was tired and Mimi planned on staying there the night.

Winnie talked to Ocker about his little queer mate. 'Now, about the raffle — what's the go with it? What are we giving him for the scam?'

'I thought we could pay him out of the shop money, but he wanted to do it just for a laugh so I gave him an ounce of speed, a donation from the Club.'

'I don't think the punters will fall for the raffle too often. We'll have to find another way to make a quid,' Brian said thoughtfully. 'Maybe we could have a casino night.'

'Maybe, Brian. What do you feel like doing tonight?'

'I'd better get home. Gina will be expecting me. Why don't you come with me? There's plenty of room.'

'I'll see, mate. I wouldn't mind going out for a bit of a party. It was hard work today.'

Suddenly Bernie stuck her head in the doorway to ask, 'Do you want me any more today, boss?'

Winnie looked at Brian. 'No, Bernie, you might as well piss off. Thanks for today — you're a champion.'

'Stop it or you'll make me blush.'

'I don't believe that. Where are you off to?'

'Jim has a party to go to. You want to come?'

'I've never been to a queers' party. Do you want to come, Brian?'

'No, I'm going home.'

Winnie looked at Ocker and Kev and raised his eyebrows.

Kev nodded and Ocker said, 'Yeah, we'll come.'

'What'll I tell your missus, Prez?' asked Brian.

'Nothing; not a word. It might be fun and we need some. I've been neglecting myself lately.'

'Me too!' Big Kev agreed.

Jim and Bernie went ahead to the warehouse in Balmain to tell their friends that the bikies were coming to have fun, and not to shit themselves, but the queers still shit themselves anyway. While Kev and Winnie looked for parking spots, two police cars with lights flashing pulled up out the front.

Big Kev yelled over the roar of the motors, 'Well, that's fucked that.'

Ocker rode past, beeped his horn and pointed up the road at Bernie. 'I'll get her.'

Bernie jumped on Ocker's bike.

'What the fuck is going on, Bernie?'

'Some politician sent the pigs; he reckoned there were under-age children in there!'

'Where's Jim?'

'He's still in there!'

'Do you want to come with us?'

'No, I'll find Jim.'

'When you find him, come back to the clubhouse.' Ocker turned to Winnie. 'Looks like the party's fucked here, Prez. They can come to the clubhouse. I'll open up.'

'We'll all come back with you, mate.' Winnie gunned his motor and passed the pigs so closely that they jumped for the safety of the footpath.

Back at the clubhouse Ocker answered a ringing phone. It was Jim, wanting to know how many of his mates he could bring.

'As many as you like.'

When the gay boys started arriving, some were a little scared; they'd never been to a bikies' clubhouse. They brought their own band, who got busy setting up. Bernie's girlfriend hadn't liked the idea of coming one bit.

Bernie said she'd had a hard time with bikies some time back. 'Give her time, Winnie; she'll be okay. Do you want any drugs?'

'What've you got?'

'Some nice trips. Here, share these with the boys.'

Bernie passed over ten hits of LSD. Winnie walked around popping them into the mouths of those who wanted them.

When Amber asked for one, Big Kev laughed at his cheekiness. 'Fuck off! Someone's gotta work.'

Sorrow took one. 'This could turn into a good party, Winnie.'

'We'll see. The only thing I can't stand is when they kiss. I can't stand seeing blokes kissing.'

'I'll tell Bernie to tell the boys no kissing in the clubhouse.'

Some were dressed as boys, some as girls. Jim pranced over. 'You're a darling, Prez.' He pranced away.

Winnie blushed. He grabbed Sorrow and pointed at Jim. 'Did you see the little cunt in action today?'

'No, but I heard about it. You never can tell.'

Everyone was soon off their tits. Kev admitted as much to Winnie.

'So am I, Kev. I hope we don't have any bother here tonight.' They laughed.

'These trips are alright, Prez. There might be a decent earn in it for all of us if we can get hold of enough of them cheap enough. Let's talk to Ocker.'

They looked at each other and laughed again. In the throes of the first rush of the acid everything seemed a bit whacko. 'I think it's going to be a long night,' said Winnie. 'I'm going outside. It's too hot in here.'

The queers hit the floor dancing to disco songs. Winnie noticed Bernie dancing with her partner and rubbing her crotch. 'Just like a bloke,' he thought and made his way out into the cool night air. He felt mellow and shared a joint with a couple of hardcore dykes dressed as bikies.

Inside the clubhouse Ocker danced like a madman while Big Kev looked on and shook his head from side to side as if to say, 'When is this going to end?'

Suddenly six uniformed coppers walked in. The sergeant stood at the door. 'Get the Prez,' he said to no one in particular.

'This is a private party!' Big Kev shouted. 'Find your own!'

Winnie walked in. 'Now, Sergeant, what's this all about?'

The sergeant began by shouting, 'I am the —'

Winnie held up his hand to stop him. 'No need to shout, mate.'

The Sergeant started again. 'Look, I'm the new Licensing Sergeant, and I believe you're running an unlicensed bar.'

'Have you got a search warrant?' Winnie was as cool as ice.

'I don't need one.' Some of the members gathered around them. The Sergeant looked around.

Winnie began again. 'You don't need a search warrant if it's licensed, but seeing as we're unlicensed, you need one. Now why don't I come down to the police station on Monday and we can talk about it? This is a private party.'

'I don't see why you'd want to party with faggots,' the Sergeant hissed.

'I understand how you feel.' Winnie nodded towards Big Kev. 'See, Big Kev's brother is a fag. We're doing it for him,' he said with the straightest of faces.

'I'm on afternoon duty this week,' the Sergeant said before turning to his boys and leading them away.

'Fuck, Prez, where did you get that from?'

'Which part, Kev?'

'About me having a queer brother?'

'It was better than saying you're a queer.'

'What about the other shit about the search warrant?'

'I think that's right. Besides, it is a private party, after all. We're not charging admission.'

'But if we don't do something about it, we'll end up in the shit one day. You'd better go and talk with him next week, Prez.'

'I'll talk to the Pig about it first; he'll know what to do. How come they got in unnoticed, Kev?'

Nestor answered. 'It's my fault, Prez. I saw them and thought they were queers dressed up.' That got a big laugh. The acid continued to weave its magic.

Everyone was so off their heads no one else noticed the pigs arrive or leave. Those were good trips.

In the morning, after the party crowd left, the clubhouse looked as if a cyclone had blown through. Winnie stood among the debris and wondered aloud to Ocker if it was all worth it.

'Well, Prez, the queers passed the hat around for the club and we raised over two thousand, plus what we took at the bar.'

'That's worth it,' Big Kev said. 'We never expected an earn, but we did alright.'

'Ocker, who gave us those trips, do you remember? They were different.'

'Bernie.'

Sorrow wandered in from outside. 'It was a good party, Winnie. I never know what to expect when we come down. I thought we were only here for the shop opening.'

'So did we, mate. That's Sydney for you.'

'Don't forget about coming up for a run to our clubhouse. I'll give you a call.'

'Okay, Sorrow.' The boys shook. 'Ride safely, mate.' Sorrow and the boys took off for Newcastle.

Chapter 27

In the morning the shop looked spotless. Even the floors had been polished.

Brian had had the cleaners in. 'I did a little myself. All we need now is customers.'

Winnie couldn't believe how professional the shop looked. 'Don't expect too much too soon, Brian.'

Brian's faith was rewarded by lunchtime. The phones never stopped ringing; people enquired about what services they offered and what chopper parts were available. Bernie took names and addresses for the mailing lists while Big Kev enthusiastically led a customer through the process of ordering his custom bike and Ocker showed a bloke how his bike could look in different colours. Winnie wandered around the shop and familiarised himself with the custom parts catalogues.

Gina came in, full of piss and importance. She approached Winnie. 'Is the boss in, Prez?'

Winnie yelled out, 'Hey, Brian! Your missus is here.'

The people in the shop turned. Gina turned to Winnie, smiled and whispered, 'You're still a cunt, Prez.'

They didn't close the shop doors until six o'clock, giving the workers with big money time to come and browse after work. It was another one of Brian's cheap but profitable ideas. A few of the punters looked as if they had never ridden a motorcycle before. One spoke to a smiling Ocker.

'I wonder what he's up to,' Brian said to Winnie. 'He doesn't look like a Pig, but you never know.'

Big Kev walked out of the workshop rubbing his hands on an oily rag. 'I've got enough work for three months, Prez. I'll need an offsider.'

Winnie spoke up. 'I can help you, Kev.'

'Yeah, I know, Prez, but I need someone I can train.'

'Anyone in mind?'

'Not yet.'

'Well, if you need one, start looking, but no one from the Club. We need someone here when we go on runs.'

Ocker walked the punter out the door and saw him off, then made his way over to the boys.

'What are you so happy about, Ocker?'

'That bloke is a stockbroker. I told him about my Nokia shares and portable phones and he reckons I'll make a million one day.'

'Yeah, mate, one day. Now, how's the painting booth — get any work?'

'Enough for a couple of weeks. And a few blokes are making up their mind about what colours they want. That'll give me about another month. This is just the start.'

Brian smiled proudly. 'I knew there was a real market for these custom bikes.'

'We have these, too.' Bernie held up her list of customers' names and addresses.

'Fuck, we'd better keep that list secure. Bike thieves would love to have that,' Big Kev said, and he and Ocker had a good laugh. 'Even though we're retired, some other blokes we know would love to get their dirty little hands on that.'

Brian reached for the list. 'Here, better give me that list, Bernie.'

'Don't you trust me, Brian?'

'I don't know who your brothers are.'

Winnie came to Bernie's defence. 'I checked her with the Pig; she is who she says she is.'

Bernie was a bit shocked. 'Have you been spying on me?'

'You can't be too sure in our business, Bernie.'

She looked suddenly very unhappy. 'Ocker? What's the go here?'

'It's just business, Bernie. That's the way it is. Just think of it like this: you know we can trust you now.'

'I suppose so.' Bernie looked at the floor. 'You can be too trusting; my girlfriend fucked somebody else the other night.'

'What did you do?'

'Took her back, of course. She's going to make it up to me tonight.'

Brian looked over the list Bernie had compiled. 'Christ, there must be forty names here. This shop will be a fucking goldmine, boys.'

'Hey, Bernie, where did those trips come from last night? Can you get more?'

'I don't know. A dyke I know only makes small batches for parties. I'll see. Look, I'm exhausted — is it alright for me to leave now?'

'Yeah, go and have your orgy.'

The phone rang. 'Don't they know we're closed?'

'I'll get it,' Brian said. 'Westside Choppers.' He held his hand over the phone. 'It's the Pig, Prez.'

'Hello,' said the Pig. 'Congratulations on opening your new shop. It's time we had another talk.'

'Where?'

'Down the Frisco.'

'Okay, make it seven … Right, boys, it's on for tomorrow; he wants his pay.' He looked at Ocker. 'Got your camera working?'

'No worries, Prez.'

'Right, we'll knock off early tomorrow, boys. Brian, you'll be right with Bernie here, and we won't leave till five-thirty to meet him at seven o'clock.'

'I don't know if there'll be enough light to take the photo then, Prez.'

'Fuck, I never thought of that. It'll be too dark for sure. Oh well, never mind. We'll do it another day. Okay, you stay back here with Brian. Kev and I'll do it. Brian, bring his money in, will you?'

'Sure, Prez. I hope the hash is back on; we're running low. Rastus told me the speed chemicals are going up again. He reckons we should look for other sources up here; it must be harder for him to get.'

'I know, but if his source dries up we'll be fucked. Does anyone know anybody?'

Everyone shook their heads.

'Don't worry, there'll be somebody out there. We just have to find them.'

'Hey, Prez, what about picking up the Indian from Marge? I'll give it a respray and a polish; it'll look good in the shop.'

'Yeah, I forgot about it.'

'We can pick it up tomorrow, Prez.'

Kev parked the truck around the corner from the Frisco.

'I'll see if the Pig's here, Kev. You can never tell with him, he's a cunning cunt.' Winnie walked out past the kitchen. 'He's here, early again.'

'Hey, do you mind if I don't come? I just saw an old Navy mate.'

'No, it's alright, Kev.' Winnie sat down with the Pig. The conditions would have been perfect for the picture. Winnie handed over the bulging envelope.

'Ah, good, Winnie, this is better than a shoebox. Large bills. I hope they're not dodgy. There's a few floating around. You don't know anything, or anyone involved, do you?'

Winnie couldn't believe the Pig, onto every little trick. He just shook his head.

The Pig leaned in. 'There's a shipment of hash on the way. It's from the man in Afghanistan. Karmal can't see you right now; I know he's hard up for cash, so here's the deal. There's ten tonnes. You can have it for five million, but he needs two and a half within a week.'

'That's a lot of cash.'

'It's half price.'

'How come it's so cheap?'

'You don't read the papers, do you?'

'Not much.'

'The Russians invaded Afghanistan. The hash comes from a place called Mazar-e-Sharif. This'll be the last shipment until they kick the Russians out. The money raised goes for guns to protect his village.'

'That's not our problem.'

'It will be if you can't find the cash — there are other people who will. It's a good deal for you, Winnie.'

'I'll talk to the boys and let you know.'

'Here's a phone number you can always reach me on. Don't mention money or hash when you call. If it's on I'll call around to your new shop on Friday for it.' With that he got up and left, just as Big Kev arrived. They nodded to each other.

Kev sat. 'What's his hurry?'

'Sit down and I'll tell you. The hash is on its way. That's the good news. The bad news is we need two and half million up front and this is the last shipment for a while. It'll be half price but he needs the cash in less than a week.'

'The Russians have invaded, haven't they?'

'How do you know?'

'I read the papers. They won't be there long, Prez; this'll be their Vietnam.'

'I don't care about the politics, Kev. We just need the cash.'

* * *

Winnie explained the hash deal to Brian at the shop. 'Can we do that much cash, Brian?'

'Well, I have roughly four million.'

'He wants two and a half up front and the other two and a half a week after it's loaded. It's nearly half price for ten tonnes.'

'That's alright, Prez, but what if something goes wrong? We'll be out of pocket.'

'That's why it's so cheap. Do you blokes want to take a punt on that much?'

'What can go wrong, Prez?'

'Anything. The shit can be intercepted, apart from that. The rest is up to the Smuggler. How long will it take to get the rest of the money, Brian?'

'Well, we have some outstanding but that's normal. I can find out by the week's end.'

'This'll be the last for a while. There are others who'll take it.'

'We don't have a choice, Prez.'

'Yes we do: we either take a gamble or we have no hash.'

'Take it,' Big Kev said.

'Ocker?'

'Take it, Prez.'

'Brian?'

'I say we take it, but it's a bit of a worry. All our cash will be tied up in it.'

'Well, you worry for us. I'll need the two and a half on Monday.'

'It'll be here, Prez.'

Friday morning, Brian arrived lugging a fat suitcase stuffed with twenties and fifties.

'Is it all there, mate?'

'Gina and I were up half the night counting. It's all there, Prez, but we're going to be half a mill short for the other half.'

'We'll be right, I might know someone.'

A car pulled up outside the shop. Ocker took a quick peek. 'Here's the Pig, Prez.'

Winnie grabbed the suitcase and lugged it outside and threw it into the Pig's open boot then slammed the lid down. 'It's all there.'

'It always is, Winnie. Now here are the radio frequencies and call signs.' He handed Winnie an envelope. 'Your Smuggler'll understand. I'll see you in two weeks for the rest of the cash.'

'That's if there's no fuck-up.'

'Have faith, Winnie.'

With that, the Pig left. The boys looked worried. It was a few years of hard work up in smoke if there were any fuck-ups. 'I hope we did the right thing here, Prez,' said Brian.

'Too late to worry about it now,' said Ocker. 'Easy come, easy go.'

'Yeah, like fuck, Ocker. This is a chance for us to go one step further; we're going to make some serious money or we'll be broke. We all made the decision and we're all in this together, right?'

Kev said aloud what everyone else was thinking. 'Yeah, but we never handed two and a half million to anyone before, let alone a bent cop. I feel a little sick in the guts.'

'Look at it this way, Kev — we'll know within a few weeks. We have to make some plans, Ocker. We need a new place to store this load. Keep using the shed you have now, but find another one.'

'Why's that, Prez? The place we have now is safe.'

'Just fucking change it!'

'Okay, no need to get up me.'

'Come on, Bernie'll be here soon. I have to go into town. Something I thought of, Brian. I don't suppose you had your name and address on that suitcase, did you?'

'Are you trying to be a smart cunt, Prez?'

Winnie turned very serious. 'It's always the small things that bring you undone.'

'It was new, Prez. Are you worried?'

'Of course I am, but we'll be right, I hope.'

Brian put his arm around Winnie's shoulders. 'We're all in this together, mate.'

Before leaving, Winnie stuck his head into Ocker's spray booth. Ocker put down the spray gun and pulled off his mask and shook Winnie's outstretched hand. Winnie didn't say a word.

'It's alright, Prez. It's a fuck of a lot of hash. I'll hide it well.'

'Look at this, Prez.' Big Kev stood at the workbench staring at a set of chopper plans. 'It looks good, but it won't corner very well. I got these in the mail from some bloke who won a pisspot full of money in the lottery. I don't want to put my name to it if it can't fucking corner.'

'Don't worry, Kev; it most probably won't leave his shed.'

'You think I should build it?'

'Why not? As you say, it looks good. I've got to go, Kev.' They winked at each other. 'She'll be right, mate.'

With the envelope in his back pocket Winnie jumped into his car and drove to John Baker's office. A big new sign proclaimed it to be the offices of John Baker & Partners. A new girl, Annie, sat at the front desk.

'Is John Baker in?'

'Do you have an appointment?'

'Tell him it's the Prez. He'll see me if he's in.'

'There's somebody called the Prez here to see you, Mr Baker.'

His door opened. 'It's been a while, Prez.' They shook. 'What can I do for you?'

'I need Squizzy Taylor's phone number.'

'You could have rung me up for that.'

'No, mate. I have a delicate matter to put to you. I need to borrow five hundred thousand for one month. You'll get seven-fifty back.'

'You sure?'

'One hundred per cent, John, but we need cash.'

'I know a bookie who might help.'

'I don't want to meet him.'

'You won't have to. I'll do that.'

'When can you find out?'

'Ring me tomorrow. I'll have an answer and I don't need to know what it's for.'

Winnie smiled.

The intercom buzzed. John took the call. He hung up and looked at Winnie. 'They busted your mate Nestor on a marijuana plantation near Windsor.'

It wasn't Winnie's worst nightmare, but it rated up there. 'Did he make a statement?'

'No.'

'Good. Will he get bail?'

'I'm on my way there now. Do you want to come?'

'No, that won't look good. As far as we're concerned, this is his own affair, not the Club's. Better give me Squizzy's number and I'll call you later today. I'll let the boys know.'

'Here, use this.'

John slid his phone over.

'Hello, Brian, it's me. Nestor just got done.'

'Yeah, we already know, Prez. Amber is here now. He got away.'

'Well, tell him not to go home until we know what's going on. John Baker is on his way to see Nestor and find out about bail. I'll be back late this afternoon.'

Winnie waved to Annie as he left the office. He knew there was little or no real connection between Nestor and the Club and he knew Nestor would keep mum. He found a phone box.

'Rat, hello. We need to meet today, one o'clock at the Frisco.'

The Rat waited among dockyard workers rushing back to work. Winnie headed to the back door and the Rat followed. 'It's time for work. You have to go north and see the Skipper. A shipment is on its way.' He passed the envelope over. 'Guard this with your life, it's the call signs and frequencies. The Skipper will understand. Get him to show you how to order a refrigerated container, maybe two. There's ten tons; load them and get them delivered to Sydney by rail. That's the good news. The bad is that Nestor got done today. It looks like our pot supply will dry up.'

'I've still got my north coast connections, Prez. Besides, I'm doing alright with the speed. How did he get done?'

'Don't know yet, but it was at the farm near Windsor. They probably got the lot. He'd be spewing. When will you head north?'

'As soon as you can organise my money, Prez.'

'I'll meet you at the clubhouse at ten tomorrow. I've got to go now.'

Winnie headed back to Brian's office.

'Nestor got out on twenty grand bail,' Brian said. 'I used Club money; he can pay us when he gets out. Amber took the money to John Baker's office. Kev wants to see you and Mimi rang to say she'll be back tomorrow night.'

'Thanks, mate.'

Ocker and Big Kev looked up as he walked in.

'Looks like we're out of the pot business.'

'Not yet we're not, Prez,' said Kev. 'Nestor still has a couple of farms that haven't been looked at yet.'

'Bernie was telling me about her brothers in Adelaide growing hydroponic pot indoors,' said Ocker. 'They'll be here next week. Maybe we can swap: speed for pot.'

'I've never heard of growing it indoors.'

'They grow it under lights and the roots grow in water with chemicals to feed them. It won't hurt to talk to them.'

Winnie sat down. 'Fuck, what a day.' He pulled a bag of goey out of his pocket and poured a small mound onto a motorcycle magazine.

Big Kev pulled out his knife and Ocker rolled up a note. Big Kev started making three lines.

'Make that four.' Nestor appeared at the door in his farmer's outfit.

'Come on, what happened?' asked Winnie.

'I was lying down in the caravan having a beer when pigs with guns out stuck their heads in the door. I thought it was some cunts trying to rip us off. When I saw it was the pigs, I yelled. Amber was checking the crop and I wanted to let him know so he could fuck off. The local noxious weeds inspector was looking for Crofton weed, and he found the pot. It was just bad luck. He only had a couple of local coppers with him.'

'What have they charged you with?'

'Cultivation and trafficking. They found the scales.'

'I'll see if the Pig can do anything. Did they mention the Club?'

'No, Prez, I never have Club gear on out there.'

'Have you seen Brian yet?'

'I haven't got time to hang around, Prez. I want to get home and clean my house just in case the pigs decide to come for a look-see.'

'Do you need a hand?'

'No, Prez, Amber'll help me. I'll see you Friday night.'

'Well, boys, we've just got two new distributors for our products, one in Perth and one in Adelaide. Perth's the go, this bloke from out west told me; there's lots of money about with all the mines opening up. We need to talk money now,' said Winnie. 'I've got the chance of borrowing five hundred from a bookie and we pay back seven-fifty, no questions asked.'

'Well, only if we need it, Prez,' said Brian. 'The speed's going good.'

'Okay, I'll hold off, but I need two hundred and twenty in the morning for the Rat to take north.'

'We're going to be a bit short.'

'Any money owing?'

'The Marios owe us two hundred grand. They pay on Friday.'

'Okay, what do we do about Nestor?'

'I rang Little Tony, Prez. He's pretty cool and maybe if we're short we can see him.'

'No, no one in the Club must know what we're doing. Let's just keep the four of us in on it.'

The phone rang and Brian answered. 'Prez, it's Squizzy Taylor.'

'Squizzy, long time no see, mate. I want to catch up. When would that be possible?'

'Tonight if you like, Winnie. I'm going away for a week from tomorrow with the Minister.'

'Okay, tonight. Say the clubhouse, seven-thirty.'

Winnie looked at the boys. 'Squizzy must be getting pretty high up in the public service; he's going away with a Minister for a week.'

'Yeah, but they all go,' said Brian. 'It's the perks. He might just be an arse-wiper.'

'Maybe, but he'd be good enough.'

'What do you need to talk about, Prez? Is it alright if I'm there?'

'Of course, Kev, I was going to ask you. Do you blokes want to come for a drink with Squizzy? I haven't seen him for a while.'

'No, not me,' Brian said, 'I have to organise the money for the Rat.'

'Yeah, good, Brian. Bring it around to the clubhouse in the morning. I might just stay here the night, seeing as Mimi's still away.'

Ocker gave the idea some thought. 'I might join you, Prez. We'll get some sluts, eh?'

'We're not all like you, Ocker.'

'Speak for yourself, Brian.'

'I'll see you boys in the morning,' Winnie said.

Chapter 28

Squizzy was waiting for them as they pulled up at the clubhouse. 'You look good in a suit, Squizzy.'

Squizzy blushed. 'It's my work clothes. The clubhouse looks great.'

'It'd better — we're buying it. And then we renovate it any way we want. What are you up to, Squizzy?'

'I'm going to Canada tomorrow on a trade mission for the state. It's no fun and I work like a black ant.'

Winnie poured out a line of speed then handed the bag to Squizzy. 'Take this with you. Gets you up when you're feeling down. Stick it in the Minister's bag, he won't get looked at.'

Squizzy tucked the bag into his wallet. 'John Baker told me you needed to talk, Winnie. How can I help?' He pulled out a notepad.

'I'm in partnership with the Mario twins from school. We're developing a couple of pubs in Sydney and they're having trouble with some cunt on the council. They can fill you in. Can you help us?'

'I should be able to, Winnie. It all depends on what it is. I'll talk to them when I get back.'

'Good, I'll let them know. Here's their phone number.'

Big Kev lit a joint and Squizzy undid his tie and leaned back on the bar. 'Fuck, I reckon I could enjoy this life.'

'You get the best of both worlds, Squizzy.'

'No, you have the freedom.'

'Don't tell Brian that.'

'What's the go with him? Has he changed?'

'He's got a family, mate. So what's your Minister like?'

'Don't know him that well. They say he's a bit of a punter. I've only been working for him for a month. It's my job to check anything he might sign — they're not all lawyers.'

Big Kev passed the joint around and marijuana smoke filled the air. Ocker wanted to know if he could phone around and get a few girls to come over. They all agreed it was a bloody good idea.

Squizzy smiled. 'I'll be in it, Ocker.'

'Do you like blonds, Squizzy?'

'I like 'em all, mate.'

Ocker held up his portable phone, and Squizzy took a look at the latest gadget. 'They don't work.'

'Squizzy, they're getting better.'

'Yeah.'

'You watch this. Who do you want to ring?'

Kev yelled out, 'Ring my missus; you've got the number.'

'Sandy wants to talk to you, Kev.' Ocker held out the phone.

'Don't fuck me around, Ocker. Can't you see I'm playing pool?'

'No, here, talk to her.'

Kev grabbed the phone. 'Hello?' He listened intently. 'I'll see you tomorrow. I'm staying at the clubhouse tonight.' He passed the phone back to Ocker. 'You're right, they are getting better.'

A taxi pulled up and Ocker paid the cabbie. 'This way, girls.' Two tall blondes followed him into the clubhouse.

'Fuck, he wasn't kidding.' Squizzy stared in disbelief.

Ocker stopped at the bar. 'Who else wants to play?'

Winnie and Kev were playing pool. 'No, mate, you and Squizzy go.'

Ocker and Squizzy disappeared out the back.

'You're a dirty cunt, Ocker,' Kev called as they went.

Ocker came back out to the bar and got a few drinks and yelled out to the girls what he was going to do with them. Winnie heard the girls giggling.

Kev leaned into the table and sank the last ball. 'It's not your night, Prez. Oh, I've got some more bad news for you.'

'What's that, Kev?'

'Do you remember Robyn?'

Winnie looked up. 'Robyn the dancer, Sandy's friend? Fuck, that's been a while.'

'Well, she lives down the coast and she's in town and she wants to catch up with you.'

'Do you know what that's about?'

'She had your kid.'

Winnie stared at Kev, speechless.

'Didn't you know?'

Winnie shook his head.

'A boy. He'd be about seven now.'

'How do you know?'

'Sandy wrote to me in Vietnam. When you never mentioned it to me after I got home I just thought you weren't worried about it.'

'This is the first I've ever heard of it. Does Mimi know?'

'You'll have to talk to Sandy. Robyn and Sandy exchange Christmas cards, but that's all I know.'

'When does she want to meet?'

'Tomorrow night.'

'It was a boy, yeah? What's his name?'

'I really don't know, Prez. You know as much as I do now.'

'Does anyone else know?'

'I haven't mentioned it to anyone.'

'Good, Kev. Let's leave it that way. Could you find out if Sandy told Mimi?'

'I'll do that now, Prez.'

After a brief conversation Kev hung up. 'Mimi doesn't know. Robyn is coming to my place after lunch. That should give you plenty of time before you see Mimi.'

Winnie's mind raced — he was allegedly a father. The news gave him a feeling like no other feeling in his life.

Girls' squealing filled the clubhouse. 'They seem to be having plenty of fun out there.'

'Do you want to join them, Prez?'

'Not now, mate. I feel gutted. I'll see you in the morning; you're staying the night still, aren't you?'

'Yeah, mate. I might just go and join Ocker and Squizzy.'

'Tell Squizzy not to forget to ring the Mario brothers in the morning.'

Next morning, early, Winnie found Ocker and Big Kev still at the bar. 'Are Squizzy and the girls gone?'

'Yeah, Prez. Are you alright, mate? You don't look too good.'

'No, I'm alright, mate, but the Rat will be here soon.'

Brian arrived all cheery. 'It looks like you guys were up all night.'

'Bring the money?' Winnie asked gruffly.

Brian threw an airline bag on the pool table. 'It's all there. Two hundred and twenty large. What's up, Prez?'

'Sorry, mate, I got some unexpected news.'

'Anything I can do?' Brian looked at Big Kev, who just shook his head. 'Alright, I'm going to the shop.'

Ocker brought Winnie a coffee. 'Do you want to tell me, mate?'

Winnie took a sip and stared at the floor. 'Yeah, Ocker. It looks like I'm a father. I don't want Brian to know yet. He'll tell Gina and then the world will know before I tell Mimi.'

'Who's the mother?'

'Robyn, the dancer.'

'I remember her, she disappeared real quick.'

While waiting for the Rat to arrive, Winnie played out a variety of scenarios. A child was the last thing he needed; he had too much on his mind to attend to anything other than business at hand.

The Rat arrived on time. 'G'day, Rat. Are you ready to go?'

'Yeah, Prez, I want to stash the money first. Have a look at this.'

Winnie followed the Rat out to the Zephyr, where he unlocked the boot and pulled out the spare tyre, exposing a cavity underneath stretching under the back seat. Winnie loaded the cash in. 'Just don't have any accidents. Now, you know what you have to do?'

'No problems, Prez.'

'Good, give me a ring when the job's done and you're on the way back. Say hello to the Skipper for me.' They shook hands and the Rat jumped behind the wheel.

Winnie's emotions almost got the better of him when he rang the bell at Kev's apartment. He felt as if it were happening to someone else, as if this was part of a story he'd been told that had nothing to do with him. He wanted to turn and walk away and forget about it, and in that instant he knew he should have, but a few scant seconds later the door opened and there stood Sandy, wearing a face that told him more than he wanted to know. He followed Sandy inside to the living room where a skinny, ashen-faced Robyn sat.

'You remember Robyn, Prez?'

Nothing could have prepared him for Robyn's appearance. Without thinking, he blurted out, 'She's a junkie slut.'

Robyn started crying. Sandy grabbed him by the arm and pulled him out of the room.

'You're a stupid bastard, Winnie. Robyn's no junkie, she's dying of cancer. Take it easy on her. I'm going out now. You go back inside and talk to her. You're not the reason she's here; it's for your son. I'll be back in an hour. Be gentle.'

Tears welled up in his eyes as he entered the room. Robyn just stared at him.

'I apologise, Robyn.'

'You weren't to know, Winnie.'

'You never told me you were pregnant.'

'What would you have done? Married me?'

He smiled at that. 'No, but I could've helped you.' A silence fell between them; neither wanted to fill it and for a full minute no one spoke. 'What's his name?'

'Harry. He's seven now. Here are some photos.' She passed them over.

He studied them. 'What's he like?'

'You. Confident, rebellious and selfish.'

'Selfish?'

'It's all about you, Peter. You and your stupid motorcycle club. That's why I never told you. You were too young in the head. Now I only have months to live, and I want what's best for Harry; that's why I'm here. My parents are dead and I only have an aunt in South Australia.'

He cradled her in his arms while she sobbed uncontrollably.

'I have money,' he said. 'We can get another opinion. I'll do whatever you want.'

'There's nothing that can be done. I've accepted it.'

'Does he know?'

'Yes, but I don't know if he fully understands.'

'What does he know about me?'

'I told him you were dead.'

'How are you going to tell him I'm not?'

'You'll figure something out.'

'How can you be so sure he's mine?'

'Look at him. Who does he look like?'

Winnie stared at the photo and saw himself aged seven: same distant look, same intense dark eyes. The likeness was uncanny.

'When can I see him?'

'It's up to you.'

'You know I have a girl now, Robyn. Her name's —'

'Mimi. Yes, I know. Sandy told me. I know she's a good woman. I don't want to get in your way, but I'm only here for a couple of days for chemotherapy. I get pretty sick from it, so I won't keep you long.'

'I need to talk with Mimi first. This affects us both. What if I bring her around tomorrow?'

'That'll be fine.'

'Robyn, I'm sorry, I truly am, and I just don't know what to say.'

'Don't say anything. I chose my own path and now I'm dealing with it. I should never have listened to the bloody priest who advised me in the first place. I should've just had an abortion.'

'Think of Harry's future. I promise I'll look after him.'

'All I ask is you don't let him become a bikie.'

That was too much, he thought. 'Robyn, I can't promise you that. It'll be up to him. One thing I will do is make sure he gets a proper education, and then his life will be up to him.'

'You're right, Peter. Go on and pick Mimi up. I know you'll be a good father.' Robyn started crying softly again. The door opened and Sandy walked in carrying groceries. Robyn excused herself and left the room. Sandy put down the groceries and put things away, every so often glancing at Winnie.

'Well, Prez, what are you going to do if you can't look after him? What if Mimi says no? If she does, Kev and I'd do it.'

'I don't know what you think of me, Sandy, but he's my responsibility now.'

'Okay, Prez. You'd better pick up Mimi and tell her the story.'

'She doesn't know anything, does she?'

'Not a word.'

'Good. You know, I thought telling Mimi was going to be hard, but it'll be a piece of cake compared with seeing Robyn like this.'

'Off you go, Prez.'

While he waited at the airport for Mimi, Winnie tried to think of what to say before he decided that, in this case, only the truth would do. He spotted Mimi rushing over towards the car. He grabbed her bag, threw it in the boot then grabbed her. Mimi threw her arms around his neck.

'I've missed you so much, Peter.' She kissed him but felt his squirmy resistance, as if he were only partly glad to see her. 'Didn't you miss me?'

'Too right I missed you, babe.'

'You don't sound like you did.'

Winnie opened the door for her and then slid in behind the wheel. He stared straight ahead for a few seconds, turned and said quietly, 'I have something I have to tell you now.'

Mimi looked straight ahead, expecting something awful because his tone was so deadly serious, so uncharacteristically sombre. She felt dread overtake her, fill her; she dug her fingernails into her palms and waited for him to start.

'I just found out that I have a son.'

The relief she felt gagged her. 'A son? Who with?'

Winnie told her Robyn the dancer's story.

Mimi remained silent throughout and tears rolled down her cheeks. 'The poor woman. What are you going to do?'

'I don't know. I had to talk to you first.'

'You don't have any opinion?'

'I wanted you to meet her first. I need you to help me make my decision: what you want, I want.'

'That's not fair, Peter ... Well, there's no way I can argue with you about this. He's your son; I know you'll want to have him, care for him, and I love you, Peter, so what you decide will be good enough for me. What do you want?'

'To keep him.'

'I already knew that. What's he like?'

He showed her the photo. She studied it for two minutes. 'There's no doubt he's your son, and Harry's such a strong name.'

'Yeah, I like it.' Winnie smiled. 'We'll have to get a bigger house.'

'Why don't we build one?'

'Come on, babe; let's not get too carried away just yet. I don't want to be there tomorrow when you meet her. I'll let Sandy and you handle it.'

'That's a good idea, Peter.'

At the shop the next morning Brian greeted Winnie with a smile. 'Hello, Dad. Word gets around fast; you know women.'

'No, I don't, mate.'

'What are you going to do?'

'Learn how to be a father, I suppose.'

'You'll be a good at it, mate.'

Winnie knew the topic wouldn't be covered in a few sentences so he turned his thoughts to the things he could control. 'Have you worked out how much money we're going to be short?'

'I think we'll be pretty close. I got onto a few members who owe and Ocker reckons he can cover what we don't have. We'll be right.'

'That's good, mate. Make sure you have it ready to go. It'll happen real quick and when we get the shipment on our boat, the Pig will be straight around here.'

'You don't think it's a trap, do you, Prez?'

'No, we know too much. I'm not going to worry about it until we have it stashed away down here.'

Bernie entered Brian's office. 'Congratulations, Prez.' There were no secrets in the shop.

'Not you too?'

Bernie just nodded.

'Well, I'm going out to work with Kev.' Winnie walked to the workshop. 'How you feeling, Prez?'

'Not as excited as everyone else.'

'I won't say anything, then. Come on, give us a hand with this chopper.'

That afternoon Kev and Winnie went to see how the girls' meeting had gone. They found them in good spirits — two empty wine bottles' worth. The alcohol had helped relieve them of some of the pent-up stress.

'We made a decision, Peter,' Mimi said. 'I'm going to legally adopt Harry and we'll be his parents.' She reached for his hand. 'Kev and Sandy are going to be his godparents, because he hasn't been christened yet.'

'I'll explain what it means to him.' Robyn appeared a little drunk but a lot happier.

Winnie was filled with anxiety about meeting his son; he had no idea how to prepare for it. 'When can I see him?'

'At Easter, a few weeks away. He hasn't been to the city before. I promised he could go to the Royal Easter Show. Mimi and I thought you could both take him; it'll be too much for me.'

He hugged Mimi. 'That sounds alright, Robyn. I haven't been to the Easter Show since I was a kid. I can show him some of the things we did.'

'No, you won't,' Mimi said and they all laughed. 'I can imagine what you two got up to.'

In the car on the way home Winnie looked at Mimi. 'Do you know how long Robyn has?'

'Yes, a matter of months; maybe weeks.'

'She can't stay down the coast and she's got no one to look after Harry. What can we do?'

'She's going to move in with Kev and Sandy. Harry can come and stay with us when she gets sick.'

'How often is that?'

'We don't know yet. It'll give us a chance to bond with him. It's going to be a bit of a rough time, Peter, on all of us.'

'Thank god you're patient, Mimi. I haven't been a father before and I haven't a clue what to do or say. The only thing I'd like to do is get him into a good school.'

Mimi laughed loudly. 'Look who's being uppity.'

Winnie almost reddened. 'No, I don't mean it like that. I just want him to go to a school and be there when he's supposed to be. I don't want a school like mine where they don't give a fuck if you're there or not so long as your parents pay the fees.'

'I understand, Peter. Your mother will be thrilled.' Mimi stifled another laugh.

'She's already got three grandchildren.'

'But this is yours; you know you're her favourite. She'll love Harry when she meets him and it'll be good for Robyn. She'll see how we're a family and that'll make it easier on her.'

Winnie knew in that instant that it would somehow all be alright. 'What about your parents, Mimi?'

'It's something they'd expect from me.'

'Will you keep working?'

'I haven't even thought about it. Do you want me to?'

'You don't have to. It's not as if we need the money and you do go away a fair bit.'

She put her hand on his leg. 'And you don't?'

'Someone has to earn a crust.'

'Okay, that's what I'll do; I'll be a stay-at-home mother.'

'At least you won't be single.'

She looked at him expectantly. 'Are you proposing?'

'When it's time. This is all so quick. Let's build a new house first. Besides, it's going to be quite hectic in the next six months; we won't be able to make any plans.'

'Oh, you're so practical, aren't you?'

He swerved the car into a loading zone and parked. 'Come with me.' He raced around to her door, pulled it open and helped her out.

She looked up at the sign above the door: Prouds' Jewellers.

They walked hand-in-hand up to the counter and stood before the showcase. 'Which one do you want?'

'Is this a marriage proposal?'

He nodded. Mimi wrapped her body around his. She kissed him and some shoppers clapped.

He opened his eyes and said, 'Let's get out of here.' They got back into the car.

'That was the most romantic thing, Peter.' She kissed him again. 'When can we get the ring? When can we get married?'

'Give me twelve months.'

'To buy the ring?'

'No, we can do that next week. The married bit, I mean.'

'I'm making plans already.'

On the Friday afternoon the Rat called with a four-word message: 'Big haul of prawns,' he said, and hung up. It was time for Winnie to get the money together for delivery to the Pig.

'All ready, Brian? Do you have any idea what we'll make out of this?'

Brian shrugged. 'If it all comes off, after expenses, around twenty million dollars. But don't get too carried away just yet — there's a lot to be done before we start counting it out.'

Winnie and the Pig arranged to meet at Garden Island near Harry's Café de Wheels. It might be the last big earn from the Hash King and Winnie expected to have his arm twisted for one last big sling. He and Brian loaded the money into two beer cartons and taped it all up neatly. Winnie parked where he'd be able to keep an eye on the car. Garden Island was unusually busy: two Navy ships readying to leave port, wives and girlfriends kissing their boys goodbye. Winnie leaned against the rail overlooking the harbour and watched the goings on.

'They wouldn't want to be late, would they?' The Pig's voice spoke quietly into Winnie's ear.

'Do you want a pie?'

'Yes, with peas.'

Winnie ordered, paid and handed the Pig his pie. They ate as they strolled slowly towards Woolloomooloo and the Garden Island gates.

'Everything go off okay, Winnie?'

'Yes, so far.'

'It's such a nice day. Why don't we sit down and have a talk?'

'Okay,' Winnie replied, knowing what the Pig was after.

'You and your boys are going to do alright out of this. Seeing as it'll be the last earn from my mate, I think I deserve a bonus from you and your boys. A big bonus, — say half a million.'

'You've done alright out of us.'

'No, don't get me wrong, Winnie. I'll still work with you. It's just that you got a bargain. I could have upped the price and you'd never have known.'

'Okay, Sarge, I'll talk to the boys, but you'll have to wait to see if they agree.'

'I know that, Winnie. Now, do you have something for me?'

Winnie pointed to his car.

As he lifted out the cartons, the Pig asked how he intended bringing the shipment from up north.

Winnie smiled. 'You don't need to know. You can't help being a copper, can you?'

'Just curious, that's all.'

'I hope you're not playing games,' Winnie said.

'You'll be right, Winnie.'

Back at the shop, the boys were bristling with questions.

'How'd it go, Prez?'

'He's a greedy cunt. We haven't even got the shipment yet and he wants a bonus — half a mill. He reckoned he could have jacked the price up and we'd never have known, so I reckon he's on the level. Anyway, if you're right with the figures, Brian, it'll be well worth it. What do you blokes think?'

'I just don't like the way he does things, Prez.'

'What other way can he do it? He's a bent copper.'

'Why don't we wait until we get our investment back? Then we can decide what he gets.'

'Good idea, Brian. Is that alright with you, Kev? Ocker?'

They nodded.

'I reckon we should give the Rat a bonus, seeing as he did all the work. We have him down for two hundred now. Why not give him what we give the Pig? He's a loyal cunt.'

They all agreed, and that's how both the Pig and the Rat ended up with a lot of folding money.

Chapter 29

A couple of cheeky cunts came into the shop and talked loudly about another patch club, the Hunters, that had just started up out near Penrith. Bernie heard them say that they drank at the Log Cabin in Penrith. Winnie and Kev had a chat about it and agreed that they needed to pay them a visit the following Friday night. If the Hunters were alright they might consider doing business with them, and if they weren't, he and Kev would give them the business.

The Marios called Winnie to say a council bloke came to see them and gave them the all-clear. Squizzy had got things moving fast. 'That's good, Mario. I didn't think he'd do anything until he got back. So when are we having the big opening?'

'About three months. I'll keep in touch. We're up to our ears in renovations. Seeya.'

Winnie hung up, feeling light-headed. The hash was in, the Marios were on top of things, he was going to be a father and Mimi loved him, but despite all the euphoria his mind kept returning to Robyn and her disease.

Bernie's brothers, Wayne and Paul, turned up and Bernie introduced them to Kev, Ocker and Brian. They'd drove up with a stash of the home-grown, hydroponic pot. Paul pulled out an airline bag, unpacked some tightly wrapped parcels and spread the pot out. Ocker stuck his hand into it and grabbed a handful and sniffed. It was nothing like the stuff Nestor grew. Besides the overpowering stench of tomcat's piss, it had huge sticky resin heads.

Wayne pulled out a magazine from his pocket and handed it to Ocker. 'This shows you how to grow it indoors. You can grow a crop in four months if you stay on top of it. The plants can get attacked by mites, so you need to keep it clean. If you do it right, it's all female so you get the best quality.'

'You should talk with Nestor; he'd like to grow indoors.' Ocker busily scanned the magazine. 'You could grow this shit anywhere.'

'That's it, Ocker. We like the idea of swapping it for speed; we can't get it in Adelaide.'

'How much do you want a pound?'

'Three grand, delivered, and fifty pounds minimum, cash up-front. Have a smoke first. Sample it with your mates, see what they think.'

'We pay three grand now?'

'This stuff has no seed; it's a better smoke and the punters will pay more for it, you'll see.'

Ocker grabbed a big handful and filled a tin.

'Take as much as you want. Now, what about the speed? That's what we're after.'

'How much do you want?'

'We'll take a pound for starters.'

Winnie turned to Wayne. 'I'll give you a price before you leave tomorrow.'

'Good. We know enough blokes with Harleys in Adelaide who love it and we do good business with them.'

Ocker motioned Winnie and Kev to follow him into the spray booth. 'What do we know about these blokes, Prez? They've just blown in from South Australia, and they want to buy a pound of speed right off. We have to be very sure about this.'

'The Pig checked out Bernie and she is who she said she was. No history. If the brothers are who they say they are this could be a good connection in Adelaide. They're not affiliated with any one club. It's perfect for us — they can do business with everyone, irrespective of who's at war.'

'Well, Prez, if you think it's alright, I'll agree.'

'Brian, what do we charge them for a pound of pure?'

'Sixty-four grand, Prez, no matter how many pounds they buy. Our problem will be having enough supply if it takes off there like it has here.'

'Okay. Are you happy with that, Kev?' Kev nodded.

Brian gave Bernie's brothers the news. They said they'd be back with the cash and left.

* * *

On Friday night Winnie addressed the meeting and let the members know what he intended for the Hunters. A throaty cheer arose. A couple of nominees went by car and called to confirm that the Hunters were there. The plan was simple enough. If there was trouble they'd whack them and take their patches. No guns, just bats.

On the way out to the bikes, Big Kev whispered to Winnie, 'I hope you don't mind, but I'm carrying.'

It was warm, a perfect night for a ride up the Great Western Highway towards Penrith. At the Log Cabin, a mob of Hunters were drinking outside, chatting up girls and passing joints around. When they saw the Miners ride in, one ran inside. A few seconds later a bunch of about eight walked out together and tried to look like as if didn't give a fuck.

'At least a few are staying. Are you ready, Kev?'

Kev looked both ways and checked out the area. The Miners hid bats behind their backs. A big, tough-looking bloke with Tiny written on his patch stood barring the doorway, his arms folded and legs spread apart. Kev thought he left himself wide open. It looked good, though.

Tiny spoke up. 'This is our pub; you blokes'll have to find somewhere else to drink.'

Most of the Hunters were too young to know that they should have talked with the Miners before starting a club, and most wore the one per cent badge without a clue as to its significance. Big Kev smiled, took two steps towards him, raised his bat and brought it down hard on Tiny's shoulder. He crumpled to the ground. A few ran off and three others tried to put up a fight but were no match as the boys got into them. In less than a few minutes Ocker had torn off four patches and hung them over his arm like trophies. He chucked them into a nominee's car, mounted his bike and the Miners took off together in a thunderous roar.

'It's the fucking Miners,' someone yelled from a crowd pouring out of the pub.

Police cars with lights flashing and sirens wailing drove into the pub twenty minutes after they left and met a wall of stony silence. Back in the clubhouse the Miners exulted at how easy it had been. A fire built outside blazed as it burned the Hunters' colours. Ocker saved one set for the trophy wall and handed out the rest to senior members to toss into the fire. The boys roared their delight as each set burst into flames. To ensure they burnt completely, the nominees poured petrol on the fire and nearly blew themselves up, which pleased everyone more. Someone played a garden hose on the glowing embers and the boys all went inside to celebrate.

Ocker said he'd found a couple of girls in the women's toilet at the Log Cabin hiding one of their boys. 'He gave me his colours straight away seeing as he had his pants around his ankles. He'd shit himself.' All the boys laughed at this story.

'Ocker, did you tell Nestor about the hydroponic pot yet?'

Nestor looked surprised.

Ocker pulled out the bag of skunk weed and handed it to Nestor. 'Here, try this, mate; it'll blow your head off.'

'Yeah, I've heard that before.'

'No bullshit, you try it, mate. Everyone loves it.'

Winnie looked at Ocker. 'I bet you say that to all the boys.'

'No shit, Prez. You want to try some?'

'No thanks, Ocker, I'll stick to the speed.'

Someone called out, 'Prez, there's a phone call for you, long distance.'

'That might be the Rat.' It had been a week since anyone had heard from him.

He came back shaking his head. 'That was Rastus; he's coming up from Melbourne next week with Spike.'

'It'll be good to see them, Prez. I bet I know what he wants.'

'He never mentioned anything, but I know what you mean, Kev. If only the Rat would turn up.'

'Just a fucking phone call to let us know if he's alright.'

'No, Brian, I told him not to ring, just in case the pigs get lucky.'

'Or the Pig sold us out.'

'Don't think like that, Kev.'

'Speak of the devil, Prez,' said Ocker.

The Rat stood smiling at the clubhouse door. 'Come on, boys, let's talk outside.'

Winnie lifted the Rat into the air and swung him around.

'Ocker, organise some drinks. Come on, Rat, this is a double celebration.' Winnie stopped and looked at the Rat seriously. 'You didn't have any problems, did you?'

'No, Prez. It was a long drive and I'm knackered.'

'Come with me, I have something for you.'

Winnie pulled out the mirror and emptied out a pile of speed. Big Kev knifed some lines up. A nominee arrived with the drinks, and when he'd left Ocker closed the door behind him.

'Now, Rat, how'd it go?'

'Exactly as planned, Prez. The Skipper done all the work, I just handled the paperwork, but I shit myself the whole time because I knew you could lose a lot of money if it went bad.'

'Well, it's not over yet — we haven't got the stuff yet. When does it arrive?'

'Monday, Prez.'

'So how's the Skipper?'

'He told me to tell you that you owe him a case of rum.'

'If it wasn't for you, Rat, we would never have found him so we've decided to give you a bonus.'

'Here take this.' Big Kev handed him a rolled-up note.

The Rat snorted his line. 'That's not a bad bonus.' He wiped his watering eyes.

'That's not your bonus. Have a talk to Brian.'

Brian put an arm around the Rat's shoulders. 'I've got something for you.'

The Rat looked puzzled. 'I'm not in trouble, am I?'

'Fuck off, Rat, you're our mate! We're giving you a bonus of five hundred grand.'

His eyes widened. 'Fuck, I'll be able to buy a home over near the beaches when the stuff arrives.' That got a good laugh. 'What was the other celebration?'

Making it sound like nothing, Big Kev related the story about the hit on the Hunters. 'Here, Rat, have a smoke of this. Some new weed called hydroponic or something. It's from Adelaide.'

The Rat took a long pull on the joint, held it in for a moment or two, then coughed and spluttered like a sick lawnmower until tears streamed down his face. He tried to say how good it was but whenever he opened his mouth he coughed some more, and the more he gagged the louder the boys laughed.

Monday morning at the shop, the Rat arrived early to go with Ocker in the hired truck to pick up the hash. The boys waited all afternoon for a call. Late in the afternoon the phone rang. Winnie picked up and listened. Every so often he'd say something like 'Fuck!' or 'Jesus!' and finally, 'Fuck off!' It didn't sound good. Winnie's face had turned pale.

Brian's face went white too. 'I couldn't handle it if we've lost it.'

Kev grabbed Brian's shoulder. 'Just hold on, Brian, until we find out what's going on.'

Winnie finally hung up. 'What's up, Prez?'

'The container's not here.'

Brian screamed, 'What does he mean, it's not there?'

'Come on, calm down everyone. Don't get too excited. There's a railway strike; they're chasing it up now. Ocker told them it's perishable and saw a mate in the railway union who might be able to help.'

Ocker returned after dark, with a weak smile creasing his face. 'It's stuck somewhere between Brisbane and Sydney. My mate in the union reckons it'll take up to two weeks for us to get it after the strike's over.'

'Didn't you tell them it was perishable?'

'The refrigeration lasts for up to three months, Prez; there's no real problem. I didn't want to cause a scene in case they got suspicious.'

'Does anyone know when the strike could be over?' asked Brian.

'They have a meeting tomorrow. You see, Rat, this wasn't that easy after all. You did wait in Bundaberg to see the train leave, didn't you?'

'Exactly as you told me to, Prez.'

'Don't you trust the Smuggler?'

'It's not that, Kev. There's a lot of hash in that container, and we had to trust him. Once we get possession, not even the Rat will know. Ocker, you might as well take the truck back and keep on to your mate in the union.'

'I thought everything was going too smoothly.'

'What's up, Brian? Has anything we've ever done gone smoothly? We have no control over this. We just have to sit it out.'

'No, we don't, Prez — why don't we just go and steal it?'

'Not if we don't know where it is.'

'Let me do some sniffing around. I have a mate in the signal box at Enfield. He might be able to help.'

'Brian, we don't want to stir up too much interest.'

'This bloke is alright.'

'Just be careful.'

Next morning Brian was all smiles. 'Right, this is the go, Prez: it's stuck in the Chullora goods yard but the union cunts are allowing perishables to be picked up.'

'Ocker, you've got the paperwork, let's get the truck. I'm coming.'

Winnie waited in line at the goods yard while Ocker handled the paperwork with the foreman. Within an hour the container was on the truck.

'I didn't know if this was a trap, Prez.'

Winnie looked over his shoulder at the container. 'All I see is money. We better stop at a phone box so I can ring the boys.'

'Here use this, Prez.' Ocker tapped his portable phone. 'Go on, try it.'

Winnie dialled the shop number. 'It's ringing.'

'Of course it is.'

Brian answered.

Winnie said, 'We meet at the warehouse in an hour.'

Ocker backed the truck in and Kev broke open the seals and the locks and swung open the doors. All they could see was undisturbed blocks of hash as big as number plates, wrapped in red cellophane. Everyone just stared at the piles of hash.

'Okay, boys, let's unload this.' Winnie opened one package. The hash looked just like black putty and smelled strongly. It took almost all night to unload and weigh it all.

'Right, we're back in the hash business. Let your dealers know.'

'What about the price, Prez?'

'It stays the same; they're not to know how much we've paid. Sydney has been dry for so long, they'll pay anything.'

Rastus and Spike drove up from Melbourne the next day.

'You're just in time, boys! We just got our hash. How much do you want?'

'We can talk about that later. First, Winnie, have you done anything about the pseudoephedrine? We only have about three months' supply.'

'Fuck, Rastus!'

'Well, I told you.'

'I know, mate, it's just we've been busy. I'll get onto it.'

Spike and Rastus smiled. 'We're only taking the piss out of you. We're onto another supplier. We have a warehouse full, fell off a ship. We have a few members working on the wharves and they misdirected a couple of containers.'

'You beauty, Rastus! Why don't we make a swap?'

'Our price went up on the chemicals — they're getting harder to get.'

'So is the hash, mate. This is our last load.'

'Until when?'

'Fuck knows. It all depends on the war in Afghanistan.'

'Talking about wars, we brought some things up from Melbourne for you to have a look at. Go and get them, Spike. You'll love these, Kev.'

Spike brought in a small suitcase and placed it on the workbench. He unlocked the case to reveal an array of handguns sitting in rows, each in its own resting hole. 'These are samples.'

Kev grabbed a long-barrelled blue Smith & Wesson. 'What a beautiful gun!'

'How many have you got?' Winnie fondled a 9 mm Browning windmill automatic.

'There's enough. These are brand-new and all for sale.'

'How much?'

'They average about a grand each.'

'Where do you get hold of them?'

Rastus smiled. 'Off the wharves, where else?'

'It must be like a supermarket.'

'The thing is, Winnie, they don't know where they lose them. As far as they know they could've been stolen in any port, or even lost at sea. At least when you buy these, they haven't been used; they're all clean.'

'How long are you up for?'

'Just to do business. Do you want any?'

'Who else are you selling them to?'

'Don't worry, Winnie; we only sell to friends.'

Everyone put in an order.

'When can you deliver?'

'With the next load of chemicals.'

'Send them up next week and you can take the hash back with you.'

'That'll work out good, Winnie.' Spike closed the case.

'Are you going now?'

'We have other people to see,' said Rastus.

'That was short and sweet.'

'Business first, Winnie.' Spike and Rastus tidied up and left.

Kev went into a reverie. 'I wonder who else they're selling to.'

'The Italians, I imagine; you know how close he is to them.'

'They're no competition; they have their own customers,' said Winnie. 'I'm taking a week off, boys. Robyn is bringing the boy up. It's time I met him. If there are any problems you'll know where to find me.'

Chapter 30

They waited at Central railway station for half an hour before the train pulled in and disgorged people clutching bicycles and baggage. Winnie saw Robyn struggling with her suitcase and guiding her boy.

They made their way over and Winnie took the suitcase. Robyn smiled weakly. 'Thank you.' Mimi leaned over the boy. 'Here, let me take that bag.'

'I can do it.' He was only small but he was big enough to manage and he warned Mimi off with a look. Mimi looked into his eyes and in them she saw Winnie and the way he held himself.

'My name's Mimi. What's yours?'

He looked at Robyn, unsure. Robyn nodded and smiled encouragingly. 'Harry.'

'Well, Harry, why don't you let me help you?'

'Okay.'

Robyn introduced Winnie. 'And this is Peter.'

Harry held out his little hand. 'Pleased to meet you.'

Winnie shook his hand. 'How are you, Harry?'

'Good.'

Winnie would've bet a few dollars that Robyn hadn't told him anything. 'Did you have a good trip?' he asked her.

'It wasn't too bad.'

'He's a real little man.'

'Harry's had to learn early.'

Winnie picked up the suitcase and took Robyn's arm. Mimi and Harry carried Harry's bag together. 'Did your mum tell you we're going to the Royal Easter Show?' asked Winnie.

A wide grin flashed over Harry's face. 'Yes, are you coming too?'

'I wouldn't miss it for quids. We can get show bags, see sideshow alley — everything! You can even watch the boxing with me, mate.'

'No, he can't.' Both women said it together.

'Just joking.' Winnie winked at Harry. He knew something was going on over his head so he said nothing.

'Thanks, mate,' he said to the ticket collector as they left the railway platform.

'You haven't told him yet, have you?' he whispered to Robyn.

'I couldn't. We have to talk about it.'

'Mum, can I get something to eat? I'm starving.'

'Yeah, why don't you and Mimi go, mate, while I have a talk with your mother?'

'Have you got money, Mum?'

'Mimi will look after it, Harry,' Winnie said, then when they'd gone, 'He's an independent little bugger, isn't he? Looks like you did a good job raising him, but why didn't you tell him about me?'

'Because I'm a coward.'

'No, you're not; you have a lot on your plate at the moment. Mimi will think of a way.'

Mimi and Harry returned, Harry clutching a pie and licking tomato sauce off his fingers. 'They're nice pies, Mum.'

As they sat around the kitchen table, Robyn sipped a cup of tea and watched Harry fall asleep on the sofa after his big day.

Mimi and Robyn spoke intermittently. 'When's your first hospital visit, Robyn?'

'Next week.'

'Good, I'll take you shopping and we can have a look around for a decent school for Harry.'

Winnie gritted his teeth. 'Enough girlie talk. Harry has to know what the score is; he's old enough. I reckon tomorrow we can go for a walk and I'll tell him. It's the best way.'

Harry propped himself up on one elbow on the sofa. 'Are you talking about me?'

Everyone's head turned towards Harry and the girls' faces reddened.

Winnie smiled. 'Yes, mate, come over here.' Winnie put his arm around Harry and looked him in the eye. 'You see, mate, I'm your father.'

Harry's eyes darted to his mother. Robyn nodded, then looked at Winnie.

'Your mother thought I was dead.'

'How long have you known about me?'

'Just a few weeks, ever since your mother was last in Sydney.' Winnie was rattled by the question. His love for this young boy he'd just met almost overwhelmed him. He wrapped him in his arms. 'We have a lot of catching up to do.'

Harry squirmed a bit but soon relaxed in the embrace. 'Do you ride a motorcycle?'

Winnie could only nod. Mimi watched, and tears filled her eyes.

Harry looked up. 'Why is everyone crying, Mum?'

'We're happy, not sad. Now off you go to bed.'

He looked at Winnie. 'Will you take me?'

'Sure, son.' Winnie was surprised at how easily the word came out.

The phone rang and Mimi answered.

'Mimi, it's Kev. Is the Prez there?'

'He's just gone to put his son to bed. Can you ring him back in a few minutes? It can't be that important.'

'Yes it is.' Mimi heard a deadly serious note in his voice.

'I'll get him.'

'What is it, Kev?'

'The clubhouse has been firebombed.'

He looked at the girls. 'I have to go out.'

Mimi smiled, but said, with obvious contempt, 'You're a bastard, Peter. The first night with your boy, and you go out?'

Winnie surmounted his panic and his temper and told her about the firebombing. Robyn came out of the bedroom. She saw something was up but didn't say a word. Winnie grabbed his colours and told them he'd ring to let them know what was going on.

Many of the members were already at the clubhouse, watching the firemen and the police picking over the smouldering ruin. Winnie approached Big Kev. 'What's the story, mate?'

'They won't let us in, Prez. The fire chief and police reckon it's a crime scene. The fire chief says they couldn't get in and fight it because there were too many secondary explosions. I don't know what he meant.' Big Kev grinned.

'Good job we had plans to rebuild,' said Winnie.

'Who do you think might have done it? We haven't had trouble with the Tigers for a while.'

'Twister wouldn't have done it, Kev; he's not that stupid. Do any of the boys know anything?'

'I haven't had a chance to ask yet, Prez. I bet it was those young cunts we gave it to last Friday; I'll bet my balls on it.'

The head cop made his way over. 'Who's in charge here?'

'I am,' Winnie replied.

'Now, I want you and your boys to keep out of this investigation, leave it up to us. Do you think you might know who might have been involved?'

Winnie's silence infuriated him. The Pig got more and more agitated as he tried to think of something to say that wouldn't make him sound like a dickhead. 'If you blokes think you're above the law, I want to tell you that you're not, and if there's any payback,' he poked his finger into Winnie's chest, 'I will hold you responsible.'

Winnie grabbed the jabbing finger and pushed it back at the cop. The Pig knew he had gone too far. Winnie just stared at him, watching him retreat and join the other pigs and get in their cars and leave. The firemen cleaned up their gear and the fire chief approached Winnie.

'Sorry we couldn't save your clubhouse, boys. Whoever started this used a lot of accelerant. You can go in now and salvage what you can.'

The boys made their way in and surveyed the heartbreaking damage. They walked around in a daze, picking up singed picture frames and other mementoes of the Club's history. Memories flooded back of their opening night, when Big Kev met Sandy having an onion on the pool table and the girls stripped and danced for them. The bar was nothing but a pile of ashes and the wall behind the stage where Kevin Borich had played was completely burnt out. They could see straight through to their meeting room.

Winnie was angry. 'Come on, you cunts, stop dreaming.'

'Have a look at this, Prez,' Ocker held up two bottles of bourbon, the labels singed but both still full.

'That's a start, mate. What else have we saved?'

'Brian's checking the safe.'

Big Kev came back smiling — his guns were alright.

'Were those explosions yours?'

'No, Prez,' he smiled broadly. 'They must have been the shells in the shotgun. Take a look at what's left.' What was left was little more than twisted metal; the shells had exploded inside the barrels.

'The pigs didn't look too thoroughly,' said Ocker.

'They don't want to get involved,' said Winnie.

An unmistakable smell of petrol hung in the air. 'Well, they didn't have to test for what started it.'

'Good chance the pigs'll be back here soon to warn us not to touch anything and to leave it up to them to sort out who did it.'

'Yeah, like fuck, Prez. We'll find out who done this' — Big Kev's eyes glazed over — 'and they're going to be taught a lesson.'

Ocker watched from the doorway as two cops got out of an unmarked car and waited outside, hands on hips. 'Why do they always stand like that?'

Winnie went outside to meet them. Ocker saw him nodding every so often. After ten minutes the cops put their notebooks away and left.

'What did they want, Prez?'

'The usual, Brian. How did the safe take the fire?'

'It got a bit hot, but the Club books and money are okay.'

'Bring those bottles over, Ocker.' All the boys gathered around. 'Right, we've got to find the cunts responsible for this. Anybody have any ideas?'

'What about the slope-heads, Prez?'

'There's no reason for them to do this. We do business with them. This is not their go.'

'I reckon it's the Hunters from last week,' said Kev. 'They've still got the shits with us, and they're young and stupid.'

'Yeah, well, they're not that fucking stupid,' said Ocker. 'They managed to burn our clubhouse down.'

'They'll be shitting themselves by now,' said Winnie, 'so we'll have to be careful. Good chance they'll be armed up. We don't want any dead heroes. If anybody hears anything, let me know. I want everybody out today. Visit pubs, check your dealers — someone'll know, 'cos these cunts'll brag about this. Open those bottles, Ocker; let's have a drink to the old clubhouse. Looks like we'll have to scrap the plans for the extensions. Now we can build exactly what we want. Let's not take our time with the plans. Get them done today, Ocker, just a rough plan, something with a members' room upstairs.'

'I'll get onto it, Prez.'

'Okay, boys, let's get this place cleaned up.'

* * *

By lunchtime next day it was hard to tell a building had ever been there. Nothing remained except for the naked concrete slab. Everyone was covered in soot and ash and they were standing surveying the desolation when a car pulled up.

'It's that big cunt Tiny we hit from the Hunters, Prez,' said Ocker.

'Don't tell me he's after more.'

'Hold on, Kev, he's not after trouble — not with a broken arm, anyway.' Tiny had a driver with him. They walked over slowly. 'He's got balls, Kev, that's all I can say.'

Tiny stood with his arm hanging uselessly in a sling. 'I'm here to tell you Miners that I had fuck-all to do with your clubhouse burning down.'

Kev pressed his advantage. 'Who the fuck are you, cunt?'

'Tiny,' he answered. He was trying not to sound nervous but he only half succeeded. 'You know me — you broke my collarbone the other night.'

'We tried for both. We must be getting slack, Prez.'

Tiny turned to Winnie. 'I never got a chance to come over here. I'm sorry for you blokes.'

'Do you have any idea who might've done it?'

'We had a meeting and disbanded the Hunters. Then we talked about what we could do about your Club. A couple of blokes we didn't know talked about torching you. We told them not to even think about it. We're not give-ups but we just thought it polite to offer you them.'

'Where will we find them?'

Kev was onto it immediately. 'Wait on, do they have guns?'

'We're not sure. They have a panel-beating shop out near Blacktown, two of them. We'll drive in as if we're visiting them. You park outside, and if everything is alright I'll walk out — that can be your signal to come in. You're not going to kill them, are you?'

Winnie walked away, then stopped and told Tiny to wait.

'Right, this is the go, Kev: when we get the go-ahead, I want to tie them up and gag them, then we'll have a little fun.'

'Who have you picked?'

'Brian and Ocker, Slippery, Toothpick and Doc — he's always good to have around.'

Tiny parked his car in a nearly deserted factory unit. They walked to the end unit, with a sign that read P & B Smash Repairs above the door. Some of the boys carried baseball bats. Tiny walked out of the shop — that was the signal.

'These cunts are going to pay.' Winnie led them in.

Before they got in a fearful voice screamed out, 'No!'

Winnie quickly had one bloke up against the wall, with the barrel of his gun jammed in the cunt's nostril. His eyes were each as big as a meat pie. Big Kev headed for the other one, who'd picked up a big shifting spanner for protection.

'Good,' Kev said. He put his gun away then turned to Brian. 'Give me that bat.'

He didn't stand a chance as Kev started whacking him.

The bloke wailed 'I'm sorry, I'm sorry', but Kev was past caring.

'Not yet, you're not.'

Kev tied them up and gagged them. Winnie went out to Tiny and told him it would be for the best if he fucked off right about then. Tiny left. They pulled down the shutters. 'What'll we do, Prez?'

'They burnt us — let's see how *they* burn.'

Winnie picked up the oxyacetylene torch, opened the gas outlet and lit it up. Then Winnie told Kev to take their boots off. That got their attention quick smart.

Kev cut their laces. Winnie said, 'Don't worry about the socks.' He started playing with the length of the flame, up and down, then waved it under their feet, then he turned up the flame and held it in one place until the smell of burning woollen socks was overtaken by the smell of burning flesh. Their screams, muffled by the gags, couldn't have been heard two metres away. Winnie wondered how long the bloke could hold on before he passed out and he intended to find out.

'Next,' Winnie said and pulled the flame away, leaving a trail of black smoke wafting out of the black hole in the bloke's foot. He started on the other foot and repeated the dose. The man fainted.

The other cunt fainted before Winnie started on him.

Ocker looked around at their spray-painting guns. 'Look at these, Kev. Brand-new.' Kev grabbed a box and loaded them in.

Winnie extinguished the torch and threw it onto the floor. 'They won't be walking anywhere for a while.'

They sure looked funny lying there, soles up, smoke drifting out of their socks. A couple of his boys dry retched.

'Is that all we're doing, Prez?'

Winnie looked at Big Kev. 'Isn't that enough?'

Brian looked pale. 'What now, Prez?'

'Let's go. Someone'll find them.'

'What if they talk?'

'They won't.'

On the ride back to the clubhouse no one said a word. That day would become legendary in Miners Club history. A fair fight was one thing, but burning down their clubhouse was altogether different. A line had been crossed from which there was no going back. Lessons had to be taught, and people would learn: don't fuck with the Miners.

Chapter 31

By the time the boys got back to the clubhouse a couple of demountable rooms had been delivered for use as a temporary clubhouse. The remaining bourbon disappeared quickly, the mood remained sombre, and the smell of the burnt clubhouse was a reminder of what had just happened, and why. Winnie collapsed on a sofa.

'Prez, Mimi dropped by while you were away. I don't think she was too happy. She wanted to know when you'd be back.'

'It's okay, Nestor. I'll go home soon and sort it out.'

'Before you go, Prez, take a look at this.'

Ocker spread out his plans for a new clubhouse on the floor. Winnie's mind was so focused on Mimi and his boy that he hardly took any notice, even though some other members showed excitement at the drawings. Winnie stood looking without properly seeing, and finally he turned to Ocker. 'Get them costed and we'll see how much it is. We won't have a meeting this week, Kev. Tell the boys to lie low till this blows over. I'm going home.'

Kev followed him to his bike. 'What's the boy like, Prez?'

That brought a smile to Winnie's face. 'He's a bright kid, looks a bit like his old man. I think it'll be alright, Kev. Why don't you come to the Easter Show with us?'

'No, you do it with him; there'll be plenty of time for me to get to know him.'

At home Winnie parked his bike in the empty garage. Mimi's car wasn't there.

He made his way inside and found a note from Mimi. 'Robyn in St Vincent's Hospital, please come, Mimi.' On the way Winnie realised he didn't even know Robyn's surname.

He walked over to the Enquiries desk. 'I'm looking for a patient, first name Robyn, I don't know her last name. She has cancer.'

'I'll look for you. What's your relationship to her? She's only allowed close family.'

'I'm the father of her son.'

'Her name's Robyn Prior, sixth floor, room 622.'

'Thank you.' He made his way to her room, hoping he wasn't too late. He stood before the closed door and gathered himself to face whatever he'd find behind it. He pushed the door open a crack and peeked in. Harry stood between Mimi and Sandy, who had their arms draped over his shoulders. The room was eerily silent, the monitors were off and Robyn's eyes were closed. Winnie knew instantly that Robyn was dead. When he stepped into the room, Harry turned his head. He'd been crying, his eyes red and raw. In that instant Winnie knew his life was forever changed. His role was clear. He'd make sure Harry had a loving and stable life; there was no other option and that knowledge gave him a clear moment of peace. Both Mimi and Sandy had been crying, and when they saw him they started up again. Winnie hugged them and to his surprise Harry put his arms around him and hugged him back. They stood in a sad little circle.

'I'm sorry, Harry.'

Harry started to cry again. Winnie looked up and saw hospital staff staring into the room. Nothing more could be done for Robyn; it was time to care for the living. He had no idea what to do but leaving seemed the best option.

'Come on, girls.' When he spoke it was as if they all awakened from a bitter dream. Mimi reached for his hand and they turned as one and walked out. Outside, Winnie stopped. 'Give me a minute,' he pleaded. He went back in, closed the door, walked to the bed and took one long, last look at Robyn, the dancer. 'I know you don't want him to grow up to become a bikie. I can't promise that, but I promise I won't give him any encouragement.'

Two nurses entered, pushing a stainless steel trolley. It's a job, I suppose, Winnie thought as he joined his little group at the lift. 'Where do you want to go?' he asked. He had no idea what to do or say next, but he knew they couldn't stay there.

'Home,' said Mimi, with little joy.

They rode down to the ground floor wordlessly and walked out into the mercifully fresh air.

'We have two cars,' Winnie said. 'Could you drop Sandy home? I'll take Harry with me and I'll see you at home.'

Mimi hugged Harry and released his hand. 'I'll be home soon, Harry. You go with your father.' She hugged Winnie and turned and walked away with Sandy.

On the ride home Winnie tried to think what best to say to Harry. 'You know Mimi can't replace your mother, Harry, but I promise you this: as long as you're with us she'll be the next best thing, and you'll always be safe with us. Do you understand that?'

'Yes.'

'You know I'm your father, don't you?'

In a strong voice Harry said, 'You're the dad I never had.'

In a stronger voice, Winnie added, 'I am your dad now.' He reached over and touched Harry's head. 'I bet you're hungry. Want to get something?'

'Can we have McDonald's? We don't have them down home.'

'This is your home now, mate; you can have whatever you want. Within reason.'

At that, Harry smiled widely, 'A Big Mac and chips then.' They laughed together, and for the first time in his life Winnie thought if he were to die right then and there he'd go a happy man.

By the time Mimi arrived home Harry was nodding off on the couch in front of the television set. Winnie carried him up to his room. Mimi tucked him in and as she did, Harry reached up and kissed her.

Winnie pulled the covers up to Harry's chin and tousled his hair. 'Sleep tight, son.'

Mimi switched the light off and closed the door and collapsed into Winnie's arms and sobbed.

'Don't worry, baby, everything'll be alright. It's good this happened so quickly. That way we'll do everything on instinct and it'll work out fine.'

Mimi pulled back. 'That's alright for you to say — you're never here.'

'What? You just wanted me to let the clubhouse burn?'

'It didn't burn for two days.'

'We had to do other things as well.'

'Like torture people.'

Winnie pulled back and looked into her face. He wondered what she knew, but he had no intention of speaking of those two days to her or anyone else.

'It was all over the news — two people were tortured in a panel-beating shop.'

'Come over here, Mimi.' She resisted until he pulled her down beside him on the couch.

Winnie turned on the television for the late news. It was the lead story: two people had been found bound and gagged with holes burnt into the soles of their feet. The police spokesman said there might be a link to the Miners Motorcycle Club and that the assault might have been a payback for burning down the Miners' clubhouse. They showed the Miners patch on screen and the smouldering ruins of the clubhouse. Big Kev and Ocker appeared briefly before the cameras. The spokesman said police were continuing their enquiries and, in a twist, that the two men involved were to be arraigned and charged with car theft and rebirthing.

Mimi was fired up. 'That's what I mean. How could you do that?'

'Don't believe everything you hear.'

'Are you telling me you had nothing to do with this?'

'I am.'

She stared into his eyes, searching for a crack in his armour. He stared right back. She threw herself into his arms. 'I knew you could never do anything like that.'

He knew Big Kev or Ocker wouldn't say anything, and he believed that his best weapon was to never apologise and never explain. To change the topic, he asked about Robyn's sudden death.

'She had a heart attack. There was just too much happening in her body — the emotion, the chemotherapy … and it was just her time. Before she died she spoke to Harry about you.'

'What did she say?'

'I really don't know, but becoming parents is going to be one hell of an education for us both.'

'I know, Mimi, but you don't need a licence to be a good parent. We'll start by just loving the kid and see how we go from there.'

The funeral was well-attended. Winnie was proud that many members turned up and was gladdened by the mass of floral tributes. The minister provided a good sermon, made better by its brevity. He wisely concentrated mainly on Harry. After the service, Mimi and Sandy introduced Harry to Gina and Brian.

Big Kev whispered in Winnie's ear, 'Those two cunts were pretty staunch, Prez. They mustn't have said a word to the pigs.'

'Have the pigs talked to any of our boys?'

'We'd probably have heard by now. We'll be right.'

Mimi brought over a couple who had come up from Robyn's hometown for the funeral. They made a point of saying what a good boy Harry had been with Robyn. It brought tears to Winnie's eyes.

After the hearse left, the funeral director handed Winnie the cards from the wreaths and Winnie thanked him.

Chapter 32

John Baker fast-tracked their plans through council. As construction neared its end, Ocker sat down with Winnie. 'Prez, how big a party do we want for our opening? Who do you want to invite?'

'As many as we can fit in.'

'I'll talk to Little Tony. He's coming over today. We'll get an idea of numbers.'

'Well, before the opening I'd like to sketch an idea for a mural in the clubhouse,' said Ocker.

'Will it be ready for the party?'

'A month at worst.'

'The clubhouse has to be one hundred per cent. Let's aim for a month.'

'Okay, you're the Prez.'

'Show me where you want it.'

Ocker pointed. 'Over here along the back wall. I'll do some portraits of some members on their bikes.'

'That'll work alright, mate.'

Little Tony pulled up in the yard. He hugged Winnie and Ocker and shook hands with Brian. 'It's coming along well, Prez. When's the grand opening?'

'We'll let you know. I was thinking of a day–night party — what do you think, Ocker?'

'That's not a bad idea. I could organise a tattoo show during the day and then we can have the party at night.'

'That way the women and children can come in the day.'

'Yeah, and when they go home, we can play.'

A few members overheard and cheered lustily.

'Would you like a drink, Tony?' asked Winnie.

'Is the bar open already?'

'Not yet, but Ocker runs a temporary one out of the caravan. Grab a drink and let's go for a walk. How are things going with the Southside Chapter?'

'Real good, Prez. It's amazing how many blokes Swannie scared away by making them flog his drugs. What was that shit on the news about the Miners supposedly burning two blokes?'

Winnie smiled grimly. 'That'll teach them, but you never heard that from me.'

'For sure, Prez. Now I have something for you. How would you like to help a bloke out with a bit of larceny?'

'What do you have in mind?'

Little Tony whispered. 'A truckload of pseudo.'

'How big a truck?'

'Big enough, Prez. I have a mate who works at ICI in Botany.'

'He's not the driver, is he?'

'No, the dispatcher. There's no special security on it.'

'Who knows about this?'

'Not a soul, Prez.'

'How come he offered it to you?'

'I sell him ounces.'

'What does he want?'

'Fifty grand,' said Little Tony. 'He knows how valuable it is.'

'How well do you know him?'

'We grew up together.'

'Okay, what's the go?'

'After they pick up their load they go to the weighbridge, then they're on their way. Normally they go to Brisbane. We'll follow the truck until the driver stops for some tucker, then knock the truck off, get it back to Sydney, unload and dump the truck.'

Winnie smiled. A devilishly simple plan. 'What's in it for you, Tony?'

'Ten pounds of pure, plus the fifty grand.'

'Who's involved with you?'

'Only Boris. You just have to let us know where you want it delivered.'

'Let me have a talk to the boys about it first. How do you like the hash?'

'It's a winner, Prez. Seeing as we're the only ones with it, my boys are raking it in.'

'That's the way, Tony; keep them happy.'

'They tell me you're a father now. How's that going?'

'I don't know yet, mate. Slowly, I suppose. He's a good kid and Mimi took to him straight off, but I need to spend more time with him. Look, Tony, if we decide to take the pseudo shipment your mate can't know about us.'

'He won't, Prez.'

After Little Tony and his boys left, Kev rang and asked Winnie and Ocker to meet him at the shop. They found him in the workshop, putting the finishing touches to one of his new creations. 'So what's up, Kev?' asked Winnie.

'I'm worried about Brian. Gina was in here earlier going off her head.'

'What's so unusual about that?'

'It was louder than usual. She's off the rails, mate.'

'I might just go and see what's happening. Did he say anything?'

'No, I just kept my head down. Not my business, but something's wrong there.'

Winnie joined Brian in his office. He was sifting through a pile of invoices.

'How's the clubhouse coming along, Prez?'

'Good, mate. I reckon we can have the bar open in a couple of weeks.'

Brian said nothing; he just stared at Winnie, who stared right back. 'Kev's told you — I can see it in your eyes.'

'Told me what?'

'Come on, Winnie, don't play fucking games with me. I can tell you know something. Gina won't set foot in this shop again. I've barred her. Good enough for you?'

'Brian, I'm your mate, remember? Is there something I can do for you?'

Brian sat back in his chair and rubbed his eyes for a moment. 'She won't stop gambling. It's a disease. I closed her shop down — she was employing a woman to run it and then she was off to the fucking casino. She kept shop hours.' He grinned at his little joke.

'You better not leave so much money lying around.'

'It's not only the money, it's the habit. She's at it as soon as she can get away. I can't stay home all day and watch her, can I?'

'Yeah, but she'll end up pissing away all your money. What do you own besides the house?'

'Fuck-all, except my share of the shop and cash from our business.'

'Well, you'd better convert your cash into assets and transfer them to your parents or Kitty. Put it out of reach. John Baker knows how to do it. In our game you never know when things can go belly up.'

'You're right. I have to admit, though, when Gina wins, she wins big. Remember Las Vegas?'

'I remember, Brian, but no one ever got rich gambling. I'd say barring her from the shop won't work too well, mate. Just don't argue with her in the shop. It's bad for morale. I think you should say something to Kevvie, mate; you embarrassed him.'

'I will, Prez.'

'Come out to the workshop. I have something to tell you all.'

In the workshop Kev fired up his newest creation. He twitched the accelerator intermittently, making conversation impossible. Winnie waved, pointing towards Ocker's spray booth.

Big Kev shut the door behind them. 'What's up, Prez?'

'You all know how expensive pseudo is and getting hold of it is almost impossible. Well, Little Tony has a hijack for us if we want it.' He told them Tony's plan. 'Not much risk if it works to plan. What do you think? Good one or not?'

The boys stared at the floor and gave the matter thought. One by one they agreed it sounded like a simple and profitable heist.

Winnie outlined what he planned to do with it. 'Ocker, you organise a new lock-up for us and we stash it away for a year or so. It'll be insurance against a time when we can't get any from Rastus.'

Brian did the maths in his head. 'There'd have to be a fair amount if we have to carve off ten pounds of pure for Tony and fifty grand for his mate at ICI.'

'We're paying nearly fifty grand a drum now, Brian.'

'I suppose you're right, Prez, if you look at it that way.'

'Don't worry, if it's not a bargain we can cut Tony down from what he wants. Do you blokes want to be in it?'

They all nodded. 'Okay, Ocker, you organise a lock-up. Brian, can you get fifty grand for Tony?'

'When's it on, Prez?'

'I told Tony I'd let him know next week. He's bringing his Chapter over, and we can discuss the opening with them.'

'How's the hash going, Ocker? Have we got our investment back yet?'

'Nearly, Prez.'

Kev stood at the doorway, ready to leave. 'Is that all, Prez? I want to get this bike finished.'

Winnie nodded and they returned to their stations. He followed them out to the showroom, where Bernie was fitting a leather jacket on a young, keen bikie. She looked good; Winnie always thought it was a terrible pity she was queer.

Mimi arrived with Harry, who was dressed in his new school sports uniform. He looked around the shop, wide-eyed.

Winnie kissed Mimi and hugged Harry. 'This is a nice surprise, babe. So what do you think of the shop, Harry?'

'I love it.' He stood before a showroom Harley. 'Is this yours?'

'No, mate, mine's out the back. Come on, I'll show you around.' He looked at Mimi and raised his eyebrows, hoping she'd agree.

'That's a good idea, Peter. I'll chat with Bernie.'

They walked around the shop until Harry stopped before a case displaying chromed handlebars, mirrors and bits and pieces. 'What are these, Dad?'

'Blokes put these on their bikes to make them look better. They order the parts and we send them in the mail.'

Harry was fascinated; he carefully examined every part. He wanted to know the name of each and what it was for. Years later he would amaze Winnie by remembering everything.

'Come and meet your Uncle Brian. We've known each other since we were about your age.' Harry trailed Winnie into Brian's office. 'Brian, say hello to Harry.'

Harry shook Brian's hand expertly. 'You're about the same age as my daughter Kitty, Harry. When's your birthday, mate?'

'April the fifth.'

Winnie had read Harry's birth certificate in the last week and had been surprised that Robyn got his own name right. 'This shop was mainly Brian's idea, Harry.'

'No, not all of it — it was your father's idea to have a shop in the first place. It was about a quarter the size of this, but it gave us a start.'

'Where does Uncle Kev work?'

'Out the back.' A bike started up with a roar in the workshop at the back. Harry jumped. It sounded much louder in the confines of the shop. He gripped Winnie's hand tightly as they entered Kev's area. Kev slowed the engine to a lazy idle, wiped his hands and shook Harry's hand.

'Uncle Kev built this bike. What do you think?'

Harry just grinned.

'Would you like to sit on it, Harry?' Kev asked.

'Yeah.'

'Just be careful of those exhaust pipes, Kev.'

Kev lifted Harry into the saddle. 'Now lean forward.' Harry reached forward and gripped the handlebars. 'Okay, Harry, now twist this handle back.' Harry gave the accelerator a little twist and the engine roared loudly. He smiled every time he gunned the engine, amazed at the noise and the power. Winnie saw Harry's joy and worried for a moment that he might not be able to keep his promise to Robyn. But he knew it was up to Harry — as long as he didn't encourage him.

Winnie plucked Harry from the Harley saddle and swung him to the floor. 'Come on, Harry; let's see what Uncle Ocker's up to.' They looked through the spray-booth window where Ocker swept layers of glistening forest green paint onto a set of petrol tanks. Ocker, all masked up, looked up and waved but continued his work. 'Do you like the colour, son?'

Harry blushed. 'Yes, Dad.'

In that simple moment something clicked between them. Winnie took Harry in his arms and they hugged. Standing at the far side of the workshop, Mimi, Bernie and Big Kev watched. It was Winnie's turn to blush. Winnie hitched up his jeans, Harry copied him by pulling up his tracksuit pants, and they ignored their audience.

The members arriving early for their first meeting in the new clubhouse admired Ocker's newly finished mural at the back of the stage. It still smelled fresh. John Baker and Squizzy Taylor stood out like dogs' balls in their suits and ties.

'This clubhouse is a bit more flash than the old one, Winnie.'

'Yeah, Squizz, everything worked as planned. I'll show you around.' Winnie led them into the newly carpeted back room with the long wooden table with a mirror set in the middle. He pulled out a bag of speed. 'Might as well christen it, hey?' He poured out a mound, made up some lines and handed Squizz a rolled up note. They each had a snort.

'You always have the best stuff, Prez.'

'Thanks, Squizz, but what did you expect?'

'Nothing else.'

'Thanks for getting this through council so quickly.'

'All part of the job, Peter. Just keep sending your members to me.'

Winnie laughed at that. 'I hope we don't have too much work for you, mate.' They all laughed at that.

John Baker raised his glass. 'I'd like to propose a toast to you and your clubhouse and a bright future, Peter.'

They clinked glasses. Winnie felt as good as he had for months.

'How are your pubs coming along, Peter?'

'I'll find out tonight, John. The work should be finished soon, thanks to Squizzy. Both of you sure have good contacts. Thanks, boys.' He raised his glass and toasted them both, looking them squarely in the eye. The night was suddenly disturbed by the sound of a mob of bikes arriving. 'That'll be Little Tony and the Southside Chapter. Come out and meet them.'

'We'll have to leave you to it, Peter; we have a Law Society function tonight.'

'It'll be more fun here.'

Squizzy drained his glass. 'I'll be back, Prez.'

'Only because you like blondes, Squizzy.'

Winnie greeted Little Tony and Boris. 'I'll organise drinks, boys, and then we can go out the back and have a talk.'

Once they were in the back room, Tony asked, 'What's the go, Prez? Do you want in on the pseudo caper?'

'It depends, Tony. You want ten pounds of pure but what if there are only a couple of drums? It may not be worth it.'

'Don't worry, Prez. My mate tells me the truck's loaded; there's a lot of it.'

'Okay, then we're in for sure. When do you want the fifty grand?'

'We'll know next week.'

'See Brian. He'll have it at the shop. You're sure your mate doesn't know about us?'

'Don't worry; mum's the word, Prez.' They shook on it.

Out in the clubhouse Ocker had turned up the music. Winnie knew there'd be no point in trying to have a meeting, especially after two topless barmaids sidled up to him and kissed him and pressed another rum into his hand. They'd worked hard for their first night; no point fucking it up with business. 'We'll meet in the morning. Let everyone know, Kev.' Winnie gave Ocker the thumbs up. He mouthed 'Nice tits' and they both laughed.

Ocker yelled over the music, 'Wait till you see what I laid on, Prez.'

A dwarf came from behind the bar wearing a hat with a mirror mounted on the top bearing about twenty lines of speed. He handed Winnie a straw.

'Only Ocker could think up something like this.'

'It's good pay,' the dwarf's voice said from under the hat.

Winnie had his snort. 'Yeah, you're worth it, mate.'

'Finished?'

'Yeah, finished, mate.'

A hand popped up and took the straw and the dwarf moved on. Tony strolled around the clubhouse, stopping to look at the new photos that had replaced the burnt ones. 'It looks good, Prez.'

'Yeah, I like it; it has a good feel and we made it out of bricks and mortar — harder to burn.' That got a good laugh, though a slightly bitter one.

'I invited Tiny tonight. He comes into the shop a bit. I think he'd like to nom up.'

'Have you spoken to him, Tony?'

'I asked him if he was interested, after we'd bashed him. No hard feelings. He said at least he'd been bashed by the best.'

Winnie gave it a moment's thought. He liked staunch blokes who took it and gave it in equal amounts. 'Yeah, Tony, I'll have a drink with him later.'

Ocker walked around with his topless waitresses carrying drinks. Winnie shook his hand. 'You've done a great job, Ocker, as usual. Goodonya.'

'Watch this.' Ocker turned to one girl. 'Do your trick, miss.' She stuck out her tits and moved each nipple independently.

Winnie laughed. 'What other tricks do they do?'

'They come later,' the waitress said with a warm smile. The boys were loosening up, the bar was crowded and the music so loud everyone was shouting to be heard.

The Mario brothers walked in and surveyed the dwarf doing the rounds. Winnie greeted them with a big handshake.

'We heard about the fire. Hope everything's all right now.'

'We don't want a repeat, that's for sure. So whaddya think, boys?'

'Nice job on the new clubhouse, Winnie. We like your new mascot too.'

'I don't think they'd let him into our pubs. Private parties only!'

'Can we go somewhere private, Prez?'

'I'd like Kevvie to come.'

'Sure, Prez. We have something for you both.'

They whistled as they entered the back room. 'Very plush.'

'Okay, boys, tell me about the pubs.'

'They're getting there; that's what we want to talk about. We need more money.'

'Go on.'

'You know we haven't sold a lot of drugs in our pubs. We found out that the security firm we're using is doing it for us, but we want to control it.'

'Isn't it your security company?'

'No — when we bought the pubs, we sold it.'

'So what's the problem?'

'We went and saw the people who bought it and they told us to get fucked; if we don't like it, we could sell the pubs. Even if we sack the security they'll still sell drugs, 'cos it's their turf. So we thought we'd come and talk with you. After all, you're a partner.'

'What you're saying is, if we can fuck them off, you can sell our drugs?'

'Just until we can cash ourselves up, Prez; then we want to buy more pubs in the eastern suburbs.'

'A lot of pubs are closing. Why stay in pubs?'

'Prez, we heard they're legalising poker machines in a few years. We reckon it'll be a licence to print money. The more pubs we own, the more poker machines we can have.'

'If you start dealing in the pubs you can't just stop, or you're back to where you started.'

'Maybe you know someone who'd like the security business?'

'I'm sure we'll find somebody. Now who are the cunts you sold the business to?'

'The Gibbses from Balmain; the whole family is into it. We don't know how to handle them.'

'The Gibbses? I see what you mean. Leave it with me, Mario.'

'Congratulations on the new clubhouse. We're off — this is our biggest night. Gotta keep an eye on things.'

'Okay, boys. Kev and I might come for a ride down there when the Gibbses are around. Oh, Mario, by the way,' they turned, 'you should hire some topless waitresses in our pubs.'

'No, our patrons don't have control like you blokes; it's good the way it is.'

'Wait until you see us with them in the morning — then you'll see our control.' They all roared with laughter. Winnie saw the Marios off and wandered back inside.

Kev said, 'The Pig reckoned they were into selling hammer. He said they were bad cunts.'

'Well, let's see if they want trouble with us. Anyway, I don't want anybody selling hammer in our pubs.'

'How do you want to handle it?'

'We should go for a ride with a few of the boys. I'll find out when the runners are around. We'll hit them and wait for the Gibbses to come and take it from there. Before we do that, I'll have to talk to the Pig. It won't hurt to have some information on them.'

'We'll have to hit them pretty hard, then.'

'I know, Kev. Come on, let's see what's going on inside.'

The strippers were putting on their show.

Ocker was beside himself. 'Watch this, Prez.' One girl pulled out a huge cucumber, rubbed it with oil and stuck it up the other. 'Don't you love it?'

Winnie didn't know what to make of it but he knew Ocker was a dirty cunt and since he'd organised the entertainment and the crew was enjoying it, he just rolled his eyes. 'Sure, Ocker.'

The girl took her hand off the cucumber and the other one moaned, sucked in her arse and shot the cucumber out like a rocket flying into the crowd.

'She's got good compression, Kev.'

'You're a dirty cunt, Ocker.' Kev laughed loudly. 'Here's Squizzy back.'

'You just missed the show, mate,' said Ocker. 'I'll see if I can organise a private one.'

'I love coming here.'

'Come on, Squizzy,' said Winnie. 'Let's get you a drink.'

'Have you got a line I can have?'

'Sure, Squizz.'

'I don't want to have it in here.'

'I understand, mate. Grab your drink and come with me.'

Winnie closed the door and set up a few lines. Squizzy rolled up a note and snorted it greedily.

'What do you know about poker machines becoming legal in pubs?'

'Who told you that?' Squizzy looked amazed.

'Why, is it true?'

'Yes, but keep it to yourself. It's definitely on the cards in a few years. Who told you?'

'I can't tell you who tells me anything, Squizz, and it's the same when people want to know what you tell me. I never know, if you follow me?'

'Sure, Prez. Look, my Minister is on the cards to take over as Sport and Recreation Minister; it'll come under his ministry if they win the election. From what I see and hear, the pubs are funding their campaign very heavily, so it's only a matter of time.'

'Your Minister's a bit of a punter, isn't he?'

'He's mad about it, Prez.'

'Well, let's see if we can get him some winners.'

'How can we do that?'

'There's a way, mate.' Winnie touched his nose with his forefinger. 'If we can help him pick a few big winners it might come in handy one day, hey?'

Squizz nodded and snorkelled up the other half of his line.

'Come on, let's join the party.'

The dwarf sat at the bar having a drink and dangling his legs in the air; he had a pretty funny look on his face, as if he'd been sampling the product. Ocker arranged a private show for Squizzy and the dwarf as well in the new gutting room, where the two strippers waited. The dwarf had his clothes off and he gripped his dick and pointed it like a missile at the girls. Squizz wanted to know what they could do with them.

'Anything you like, you dirty bastards.'

Ocker closed the door behind them and walked over to the one-way mirror. 'Hey, Prez, come and see this.'

'No, mate, I don't want to watch; I want to talk.'

The dwarf was getting ready to mount one of the girls. 'He's a horny cunt.'

'Ocker, do you know anyone working out at the track?'

'I sell hash to a trainer at Randwick. He knows what's up.'

'What's he like?'

'A black rogue.'

Winnie laughed; he had little interest in the ponies because he suspected everyone at the track was a rogue. 'Talk to him and see if you can find some horses about to win — you know, when they give them some goey.'

'Why's that, Prez? You taking up punting?'

'No, but Squizzy's Minister likes a big punt. It'd be good for Squizz to feed him some winners.'

'Yeah, good for us too.' The party was going off and they were doing big business at the bar so Ocker went back to his job.

'Hey, Prez, do you want to talk to Tiny?'

'Yeah, Brian, bring him over. Where's Little Tony?'

'Gone to the pub to watch a band and get some more sluts.'

Brian introduced Tiny to Winnie.

'The Vice-Prez tells me you want to hang around with us. You did the right thing by us, Tiny, goodonya. I reckon you'll become a good Miner. Brian will nominate you at the next meeting and I'll second it; you won't have any problems. Just keep it to yourself till the next meeting. Go and have a drink but don't get too pissed — we're having a meeting in the morning.'

When the sun rose, a stream of taxis arrived to take the girls home. Kev pulled on his last drink of the night. 'Ocker, Squizzy and the dwarf are still in the gutting room with the girls.'

'Fuck, I forgot all about them.'

'When do you want this meeting?'

'Soon, Kev. I want to spend some time with Mimi and Harry today.'

'Okay, Prez, I'll get everyone together.'

Squizzy walked out smiling, his coat slung over his shoulder. He looked rooted. 'Prez, you always look after me. Here's my new phone number.'

'I'll call you if I get a tip.'

'That'll make me look good, Prez.'

Ocker put the girls and the dwarf in a cab and handed the driver a fifty. Winnie thought that was a bit generous.

'You have to look after the cabbies too, Prez.'

Kev stood by watching. 'Where did you get that dwarf, Ocker? I bet you have a house full of freaks.'

'You're jealous you're not in it.'

'Are you calling me a freak?' Big Kev looked nonplussed. 'Why, thank you,' he said, then he grabbed Ocker in a headlock.

'No, not the nose!' Ocker screamed as Big Kev squeezed his nose. Ocker moaned until Kev let him go. 'You big cunt. I'll get you one day.'

Everyone there laughed.

Kev yelled out, 'Come on! Let's have our meeting.'

Little Tony stood up before them. 'Prez, the Southside Chapter congratulates you on the new clubhouse.' The boys clapped and cheered.

'First thing we want is a grand opening, involving both Chapters,' Winnie said. 'We want it to earn a few bucks for the Club, prime the pump, and your Chapter'll share it, Tony. We were thinking about a tattoo show during the day and a party at night after the wives and kids leave.'

'I can organise that, Prez.'

'Good one, Ocker.'

'We'll need to advertise.'

Everyone endorsed that plan.

'The next thing this morning is: Brian wants to nominate Tiny. Now, Tony, your boys don't know this bloke, but he's helped us a lot.'

'It's your Chapter, Prez.'

'Get Tiny and bring him in, Brian ... Tell the boys why you want to join.'

'Because I think you boys have a great Club.'

'Even though we bashed you?'

'The best bashing I ever had.' The boys cheered as Brian handed Tiny his Miners top and nominees' patch.

'Brian will tell you about the fees later. Now go out to the bar and wait for us to join you for a drink. Next thing, I have an interest in a couple of pubs in Sydney we just reopened. Has anybody here ever heard of the Gibbs family?' A few of the boys nodded.

'They're supposed to be real bad cunts, Prez.'

'That's what I heard. Well, we'll see about that. They sell hammer in the pubs and told our managers to get fucked. They reckon they'll do what they like.'

The boys listened quietly. 'This week a few of us are going for a ride down to the pubs. If anybody wants to come, they can, but we don't need the whole Club.'

'Me and Boris'll come, Prez.'

'Thanks, Tony. Now the next thing is just for my Chapter. Tony, do you mind waiting in the clubhouse?'

'Sure, Prez.'

The meeting got real quiet when Brian stood up. 'Thanks. Prez, is there anything else?'

'Yes, Brian. A few of you are behind in your dues. I want you to catch up. You know who you are. Meeting closed.'

In the bar Ocker lined up shot glasses filled with Sambucca.

Big Kev shouted for everyone to grab a glass. 'Here's to our new nominee, Tiny!'

'To Tiny!'

'We're going to get going now,' said Tony. 'I'll call you soon.'

The sound of many bikes starting up still excited Winnie and he stood and watched them roar off, Miners vests flapping in the wind.

Chapter 33

Winnie read the note from Mimi, saying she'd taken Harry to soccer, and she'd be home by lunchtime. He was exhausted and threw himself on the bed. He awakened with Mimi sitting on the bed next to him; she leaned over and kissed him. He pulled her down on top of him and kissed her but she pulled away.

'Stop, Peter. Harry's in the kitchen making us coffee; he'll be in here in a second.'

'Well, having to look after his mother would've exposed him to a lot.'

'Robyn did say he organised her medicines for her before he went to school, and after she taught him to cook he looked after that too. Independent little bugger.'

'I'm glad for that.'

'You're a bastard.'

'Come here.'

Before he could grab her again, Harry walked in slowly, unsteadily carrying two coffees and trying not to spill them.

'Put them here, mate.' Winnie put his arm round Harry's shoulders and looked into his face and smiled. 'How'd you go at soccer?' Just looking at Harry filled him with the love only a father can have for his son; it was a wholly new experience and one he enjoyed more than he'd ever thought he would.

'We drew one-all, Dad. Can you come and watch next week?' Harry's eyes fell to the floor.

'Of course I can. I'll come.'

'He's too modest to tell you he won the best and fairest award — he's a little champion.'

'We can all go together,' Winnie said, bright-eyed, then, 'What do you think, Mimi?' He reached for his wallet. 'How much pocket money should Harry have each week?'

'He helps me a lot … let's say ten dollars.'

Harry's eyes lit up. 'Ten dollars. Yeah!'

'Yes, but you have to bank half every week.' Winnie pulled out a note and handed it over.

'Okay, Harry, don't forget we're going to visit your Grandma this arvo.'

While she dressed, Mimi watched Winnie changing into his street clothes. 'Have you spoken to Warren lately, Peter?'

'No, we don't see each other too often.'

'I think you should before we go up.'

'Why's that?'

'Warren told me your mum has dementia.'

Winnie leapt up and went to the phone. 'Hello, Warren, it's Peter. Mimi was just telling me about Mum.'

'You'd know if you went and saw her more often. It's too late now.'

'Listen, cunt, I never rang you up for a lecture. Just tell me what's up.'

'You should go and see for yourself. She can't keep living on her own.'

'Why not?'

'She forgets things.'

'Like what?

'Having a shower, things she puts on the stove — do you want me to go on? It's going to be a job looking after her; she'll have to go into a nursing home. I can't do it. Go and see for yourself.'

Winnie immediately felt guilty about getting up him. 'I'm sorry, Warren, you're right. I'm going to see her today and I'll ring you when I get back. What does her doctor say?'

'What I told you.'

'Okay, see you, mate. I'll just go up by myself.'

'What's up, Peter?'

'Like you said, Mum has dementia. It sounds quite advanced.'

'I'll come with you, Peter.'

'I want to see what she's like before I take Harry to see her.'

'Don't you think he can handle it? There isn't much he hasn't seen. Tell him before we get there.'

'Tell him what? I don't know myself.'

'Just tell him the truth.'

Harry overheard. 'What truth?'

'Come here, mate. It's my mum — she's pretty sick. I have to go and visit her. Do you want to come?'

'Does she have cancer too?'

'No, she's just not too good. Get changed and we'll go and see her.'

Driving out of the city in the slow Saturday traffic as the shoppers went about their business, Winnie said quietly, 'This city is getting harder and harder to drive around. How would you like to live out in the country?'

Mimi looked at Winnie. 'What brought this on?'

'Look at this!' he exclaimed as crowds of people flooded across the pedestrian crossing. 'I'd like something different for Harry to grow up in.' He glanced in the back seat, where Harry dozed. 'Somewhere he can roam around; after all, he used to live in the country. Where we live in the inner city, there's hardly anything for him to do. He's got soccer, but there's more to life than that. When I was a kid we got up to all kinds of things.'

'Like what? No, don't tell me what you got up to; I can just imagine. I hear enough from Gina.'

Winnie smiled. Brian must have told her.

'Come on, Peter, tell me what you have in mind.'

'How about we build a house?'

'Where?'

He shook his head. He wasn't sure exactly where, but he gave the matter some thought on the freeway. He looked at the estates on both sides. 'They're starting to develop everywhere, but I don't want to live around here; I'd rather live down near Camden. Brian and I ran away from home once. We caught a steam train and that's where we ended up. The Hume Highway goes past there; it's only forty minutes to the clubhouse. Every time I go past Camden I get this feeling I'm at home.'

'I have an aunt down there. I know the area. This is all pretty new and exciting, isn't it?'

Winnie loved her girliness. 'And let's get married soon.'

Mimi turned to face him. He couldn't read her. 'I'm still waiting for the engagement ring.'

'I thought we could have a double wedding in the clubhouse with Kev and Sandy.'

Mimi smiled. 'You just don't get it, do you? No girl wants to share the most precious day of her life with another girl.' She reached over and pinched his cheek.

'Ouch! What was that for?'

'Especially in the clubhouse. My mother will kill me if I don't get married at St Mark's at Darling Point.'

'That's a bit posh.'

'You can hire a suit. So, of all your mates who'll be your best man?'

'That's easy.' He looked at Harry.

Her eyes filled with tears. 'That'll be special; I can't wait to tell my mother.'

'What do you think she'll say?'

'She'll be happy. She loves you.'

'Wake Harry up, please, Mimi. Mum's place isn't far.' Winnie looked in the rear-view mirror and caught Harry's eye. 'We're nearly there, mate.'

Winnie parked outside his mother's cottage. He knocked on the door and they waited for a few minutes. He knocked again. The door slowly opened and a grey-haired woman he hardly recognised appeared at the door. 'Who is it?'

Tears came to Winnie's eyes. She'd shrunk, her skin appeared waxy and grey and her eyes looked rheumy and unfocused. She tottered on unsteady feet.

'It's Peter, Mum.'

Her eyes were blank but they brightened for a second as she struggled to recognise him. 'It's Peter!' She opened her arms and hugged him.

'Go on, Harry, give your grandma a hug.'

Mimi, Harry and Winnie's mother sat on the lounge saying very little. His mother appeared not to know what was happening. She didn't properly recognise him, kept calling Harry 'Peter' and had no idea who Mimi was. Winnie looked around at the uncharacteristically untidy house. His mother was never like that; she had always been houseproud. This is not fair, he thought. His mother's life had been tough enough.

Mimi followed him into the kitchen and wrapped her arms around him. 'I don't know what to say, Peter.' She surveyed the kitchen sink, filled with burnt pots and dirty dishes. Mimi plugged in the kettle and got on with cleaning up.

'This isn't good enough. I'll talk to Warren. She needs full-time care for her own safety. There's a new retirement village opening nearby, we can look into that. But until then I'll hire someone to look after her. There's no other way; she can't stay with us, not in our unit, and I know Warren doesn't have room. I can afford it and that's what I'll do. They know how to look after people like Mum; I'm sure there'll be some type of therapy. Do you mind staying here with Mum while I go and get some fresh food and supplies?'

'Don't be long, Peter.'

He headed to the nearest shopping centre, in Woy Woy, and started buying everything he thought his mother needed. Then he stopped off at the florists and bought a large bunch of lilies. He lost all sense of time, and when he pulled into the street and saw the ambulance parked outside, its lights flashing, his heart skipped. He watched in horror as two attendants wheeled out a stretcher bearing a body bag. Mimi and Harry stood crying at the door. He ran to the ambulance, stopped at the stretcher. 'It's my mother.'

The attendants stood back respectfully as Winnie pulled the zipper down and exposed his mother's face. Death had released all the tension; she looked twenty years younger. Her lips were still warm when he kissed her. 'What happened, Mimi?'

The attendants said nothing as Mimi took Winnie by the hand.

'Harry was talking to her and she closed her eyes, let out a breath, fell back onto the sofa and just died. We had no way of contacting you so I called the neighbour over and she called the ambulance. I'm so sorry, Peter. Harry's in a bit of a state; you'd better talk to him.'

Winnie said his goodbyes there and then and reached for Harry, who looked stunned. The attendants zipped up the bag and put his mother into the ambulance while Mimi watched, sobbing. Neighbours gathered at the front door and offered their condolences. Winnie took Harry gently by the shoulders and ushered him inside.

'I'm sorry, Dad.' Harry looked up at him.

Winnie wanted to cry, but tears would come later, when he was alone with Mimi.

For someone who'd only lived in Woy Woy for a short time, Winnie was surprised there were so many people at his mother's funeral. 'They're from the housie,' Mimi whispered.

His Club mates who'd known his mother came; he expected nothing less. He and Mimi sat next to Warren and his wife Carol. After the service the brothers embraced.

'She was a great mother, Pete.'

'Yeah, I know, mate. I'm glad I got to see her alive again. It was as if she'd been waiting for me to come.' Winnie felt an enormous love for his brother at that moment and he hugged him unashamedly for the first time in twenty years, maybe more.

Big Kev, Sandy, Brian and Gina came over. They said nothing, but each hugged Winnie.

Kev looked around. 'Where's Harry?'

'He's had enough funerals in his short life. Marge from across the road is looking after him.'

After the funeral they drove home to Sydney in a sad silence. Mimi stared out the window.

Overcome with the emotion of recent events, Winnie stared straight ahead and concentrated on the road. 'How would you like to have a child with me?' As soon as he spoke those words he couldn't believe he'd said them. He and Mimi had never spoken about children until Harry came along.

'I've been dreading this moment.'

'Why's that, babe?'

'I don't think I can have children. Don't say anything, Peter; I've been to countless doctors about it.' She cried silently. 'It's alright, Peter. I accepted it years ago.'

'Why didn't you tell me?'

'It never came up. Besides, I didn't know you wanted children, and now we have Harry. I want to be a good mother to him.'

'You are already.'

Chapter 34

Winnie returned to the shop the next day and Bernie came out to see him as he pulled up on his bike. 'I'm sorry about your mother, Prez.' She hugged him warmly for a moment or two, then said, 'Don't get any ideas, now.' Winnie laughed at her cheekiness. 'The Mario brothers want you to call.'

Winnie called them straight away.

'Hello, Winnie. Remember we told you about the hammer boys? Well, they'll be here tomorrow.'

'When?'

'Normally about three or four.'

'I'll see you then.' Winnie joined Brian in his office. 'Kev and I are going to see the Gibbses tomorrow. And I'm going to see the Pig this arvo — have you got his money?'

'Fuck, I almost forgot.'

Brian reached into a drawer and pulled out a fat envelope. 'How do you reckon it'll go with the Gibbses?'

'Don't know, mate, but if someone had a go at our dealers, we'd do something.'

'This is different, Prez — it's your pub.'

'Yeah, that doesn't seem to bother the Gibbses. Anyway, do we have any cash? I reckon it's time I looked for a house.'

Brian's eyes darted around as he ensured that no one was listening and then he lowered his voice to a whisper. 'I nearly piss myself just thinking about it, Prez, but we have almost sixteen million from the sale of the hash.'

Winnie let out a long whistle. He silently mouthed the words 'sixteen million' and burst out laughing. 'Yeah, we've been lucky, mate. Time to build a mansion.'

'Where?'

'We're going to look down near Camden. Mimi and I are getting married.'

'Congratulations, mate. About time. When?'

'There's no date yet. I'll leave all that to Mimi. She wants to get married in a church so I have to get dressed up in a penguin suit. Harry's going to be my best man and I'd like you, Kev and Ocker standing next to me.'

'It'll be my pleasure, Prez. Now, when do you want the money? It'll take me a day to get it.'

'Why, where do you keep it?'

'That, I don't tell anyone.'

'What if something happens to you?'

'There's a sealed letter in John Baker's safe. Not even Gina knows. There's just so much cash and I'm not sure she can be trusted with it, but she helped me count it — she's good at that.'

'What about on the weekend? Will you be able to bring it in on Sunday?'

'No problem.'

'I'll let Kev and Ocker know about the Gibbses.' Winnie left the office with sixteen million things on his mind.

'Hey, Kevvie, can you let Little Tony know we'll be seeing the Gibbses tomorrow afternoon? At the Horse and Cart.'

'I know where it is. We'd better be prepared for trouble.'

'I'll see you here tomorrow. I have to see the Pig today.'

'Do you want me to come with you, Prez?'

'No, it'll be alright.'

'Where are you meeting him?'

'At the Hollywood on Broadway.'

The Pig motioned Winnie to go out to the beer garden. Winnie ordered a drink and followed him to a table in the corner.

'Have you come prepared?'

Winnie pushed over the envelope. The Pig looked around and opened it under the table, scanning the contents before putting it in his breast pocket.

'I need some information on the Balmain Gibbses.'

'I already told you to be careful with them; they're well connected. What's up?'

'They're selling hammer in a pub I co-own.'

'How do you know it's them?'

'I was told.'

'That'll be Neil, the youngest one. A real dickhead, thinks he knows it all. His old man won't be happy when he finds out.'

'Can you do anything?'

'It's a hard one, Winnie. They have protection, and I'm not the only cop who does favours.'

'Could you say something to someone?'

'I don't advertise what I do. The Gibbses are with another crew. If I say anything they'll be onto me. I don't need that.'

'Looks like it's my way, then. I'm not going to let the Gibbses or anyone else stand over us.'

'Just be careful. He's known to carry.'

'We're ready for anything.'

'Alright, be careful then, and don't bite off more than you can chew. Here's some news. I have to do a management course down at the Academy so I won't be around for six months. I'm in line for a promotion but I still want this every month.' The Pig patted his pocket.

'How do I get it to you?'

He slid a piece of paper over to Winnie. 'These are my banking details. I'll see you in six months.'

'What if I need to speak to you?'

'Don't worry, Winnie, if you end up in the shit, I'll know.' The Pig drained his drink and stood to leave. 'Remember, don't fuck with the Gibbses unless you know you can win.' He winked as he walked away.

Winnie finished his beer and waited a few minutes until the Pig was well and truly gone. He decided to give Mimi a thrill by going to the jewellery store and buying the ring she'd picked out.

Back at home, Mimi gently unwrapped the box and opened it carefully. Once she saw the diamond glinting inside she squealed loudly. She slipped it onto her finger, held her arm out and admired the stone glinting under the lights. Harry came running into the kitchen, his eyes wide — he didn't know what to expect but he knew something good was up.

'Look at this, Harry! What do you think of this diamond? Isn't it a beauty?'

'It's a beauty alright, Mum.'

It *was* a beauty. A flawless, four-carat, crown-cut diamond mounted in platinum and surrounded by baguettes doesn't come cheap, and Mimi knew it. She kissed Winnie and danced him around the kitchen. 'Thank you, Peter. It's the one I loved the very first time I saw it. Thank you, thank you, thank you!' Winnie blushed while Harry looked on, only half-comprehending what was happening.

The next day at the shop Winnie told the boys what the Pig had said about his six-month absence.

Brian was a bit unsure. 'I don't know why we should still pay him if he's off the scene, Prez.'

'He's still working for us; let's just think of it as insurance. That make sense to you?'

Brian gave it a moment's thought, then remembered the millions sitting in the secret hiding place. 'Yeah, Prez, cheap at twice the price.'

'Is our new nominee Tiny here, Kevvie?'

'Out the back with Toothpick and Slippery.'

Winnie and Kev joined the boys. 'Listen, boys, we don't know how this'll go down. Kev and I will do the talking. I just want you as back-up.'

They parked their bikes outside the Horse and Cart and met up with Little Tony and Boris in the bar.

One of the Mario brothers greeted them. 'That's them playing pool, Prez.'

Winnie looked over at them. 'Which one is Neil Gibbs?'

'The one shooting now.'

'Right, this is what we'll do: Kev, you and I will take him into the shitter. Tony, you and the boys make sure the others don't follow — you got that?' They nodded. 'Tiny, you stand out on the footpath with the bikes. If the pigs turn up, you let us know.'

Tiny grinned.

The Gibbs mob turned and stared at the Miners crowding the bar. Winnie and Big Kev approached the pool table. 'Having a good day, boys?'

'Just put your money up if you want a game, or fuck off.'

Winnie smiled and shot Big Kev a look. He watched Kev grab the Gibbs boy by the throat, lift him off the ground with one hand and say, 'We want a game, cunt, but it's not pool!'

Gibbs tried to pull Kev's hand away from his throat while his mate swung his cue at Kev. Kev sidestepped the clumsy blow and tightened his grip on Neil Gibbs's throat. The bloke swung his cue again but only managed to collect Gibbs's face. Boris lunged at the bloke with the cue, smacked him with a balled-up fist and dropped him to the floor.

Gibbs's other mates backed into the corner, not wanting any of the same treatment. Kev half-dragged and half-lifted Neil Gibbs into the toilets — he was still stinging from the good hit to the head. Kev threw him up against the wall. Some bloke who'd just finished a piss quickly left. Winnie stuck his own face as close as he could get to Neil Gibbs's face without touching him. His voice stayed calm and he spoke in a hoarse whisper. 'Now listen to me, cunt. I own part of this pub and a few others around here, so if you and your boys are told not to sell your drugs here, you don't fucking sell your drugs here! You hear me? You can get fucked!'

'You cunts think you're tough. Don't you know who I am?'

'Yes, we do, Neil. But we don't care. We're businessmen and you and your hammer are bad for our business.'

Neil Gibbs's eyes opened wide. He spit back, 'Wait until my old man hears about this!'

Winnie saw Gibbs's hand go to his jacket and caught a glimpse of something metallic. He shouted loudly, 'Look out, Kev!'

Kev reached for the gun and pushed its nose towards the floor at the same moment as a shot rang out. Neil suddenly squealed like a pig. The .38 bullet had torn a hole through the top of his boot and bitten off a toe or two, and his precious blood spurted up like a geyser. Kev wrestled the gun away and served Neil Gibbs a nice backhander with it. Neil collapsed in a bloody pool on the tiles. He might have said something but his blubbering made it hard to understand a word.

'Come on, Kev, let's get outta here.'

When they walked out Neil's mates definitely wanted no part of it. They huddled in a corner of the pub and avoided any eye contact. Kev slipped Neil's gun into his belt as Winnie motioned the boys to mount their rides and leave.

Back at the shop Winnie got the boys together and gave them an account of the events at the Horse and Cart.

'Is he dead, Prez?'

'No, the silly cunt shot himself in the foot.' He stared at Kev. 'Did you toss his gun in the river, Kev? If he goes to the pigs they probably won't believe us.'

'It's already in Canada Bay, Prez.'

'And you other boys, get going and keep your heads down for a couple of days. They'll only be looking for Kev and me.'

'Yes, Prez.'

'Tiny, good job for a nominee.'

'Thanks, Prez.'

After everyone but Ocker and Brian left the clubhouse, Brian asked what Winnie thought the Gibbses would do to retaliate.

'I doubt they'll go running to the pigs. They're old school, so one of two things will happen: we'll either end up in a war or they'll work something out with us. In any event, I don't want to take any chances with them. You'd better let all the members know the score.'

'If I can get onto them all, Prez.'

'You could if everyone had one of these!' Ocker held up his newest portable phone. 'They're much smaller now.'

'Can we afford to buy them?' Winnie enquired.

'These aren't on the market yet, but these are.' Ocker pulled another gadget from his pocket. 'It's a pager. You send me a number to ring you back on. They work really well. I think everyone in the Chapter should have one, and they're cheap.'

'Okay, mate, bring it up at the next meeting. Are you selling them?'

'No, you buy them at the Telecom shop. Watch this!' He asked Brian to take it out to the front of the shop. 'When you get a message, Brian, just press this button.' The rest of them followed Ocker to the phone. He dialled a number, and then hung up. A few minutes later Brian walked back into the shop smiling and looking at the pager. He showed Winnie and Kev the shop number on its screen.

'That's the go, mate.'

'It'll do until the portable phones are available.' Ocker said. 'They're going to make me rich!'

'We're going to be rich on Sunday, mate; we're divvying up the hash money.'

Bernie burst into the workshop, looking worried.

'Winnie, the pigs are here.'

'Right, we've all been here today working.' Winnie headed out to confront the pigs who'd walked into the shop.

'Can we help you?' Winnie asked.

The pigs looked around before answering. 'I'm Detective Sergeant Green and this is Senior Constable Mason. We want to know your whereabouts today.'

'Been working in the shop all day.'

'You sure?' Detective Green prompted. 'You sure you haven't been at the Horse and Cart Hotel?'

'No, what's the problem?'

'You're a smart cunt, aren't you?' the detective said.

'What's your problem? Maybe I can help.'

'You're the President of the Miners Motorcycle Club and some of your members were involved in a shooting there, earlier today.'

'I told you we've been working here all day. These bikes don't build themselves.'

'We've been told you and your Sergeant-at-Arms were involved. So where is he?'

'He's working out the back.'

'Get him; you're both coming down the station for an interview.'

'You can interview us here, or charge us and then we'll go. Do you have witnesses?'

The detective began to lose it and spat back, 'We ask the questions, you fucking answer them. Got that?'

Winnie stood eyeball to eyeball. 'I told you where I was. Are you calling these people liars?'

The detective stared at Brian and Bernie and mulled over his options. 'I'll be back,' he said, then stormed out of the shop with his sidekick in tow.

'Whaddya reckon, Prez?'

'They know fuck-all. They thought by coming here we'd shit ourselves and put our hands up. At least we know that cunt Neil Gibbs hasn't dogged it.'

That night he lay on the sofa with Mimi and watched her write down names of invitees to the wedding. She flipped the page over and announced, 'These are just my friends and family!'

Later, on the television news, the lead story went something like this:

Police fear a drug war is about to erupt over turf between the Gibbs family and the Miners Motorcycle Club, after Neil Gibbs, the youngest son, was shot in the foot. The incident follows an altercation at the Horse and Cart Hotel. Police are continuing their enquiries.

* * *

417

Mimi questioned Winnie. 'Are you involved, Peter?'

'Don't worry, Mimi; it'll be alright.'

'It's not me — what about Harry? He's still only young. What do we tell him when he gets older?'

'He'll understand.'

'I don't know if he will. I just know that he'll be growing up with us.'

'That's another reason why I'd like to move out of town. We should start looking.'

'What was that all about? You own shares in that pub.'

'Mimi, I've told you not to ask questions about my business, except for the banking.'

She held up her hands. 'Okay! I don't need to know.'

'Come on, babe, cheer up and let's get this list finished. Have you picked a date yet?'

She smiled happily. 'The twenty-second of August.'

'Christ, that's only two months away!'

'The church is booked out until next year. We were lucky to get a cancellation.'

'So, where's the reception?'

'At Dad's golf club.'

'The boys'll love that.'

'Will they behave?'

'At least until we leave.' She looked at him sternly and he rephrased what he'd just said. 'They will behave.'

'How many do you want to invite?'

'I'll write up a list. What's the go on the costs?'

'You and Dad can work that out.'

'I want to see him next week, anyway. I have money I want him to look after.'

'How much?'

'Four million.' He stated it coolly. Mimi stared back at him, wide-eyed. 'No questions, remember? It should buy you a wedding dress.'

'I don't need one; I'm wearing my mother's dress. It's something I've always wanted.'

'It's your choice. You'll look good in anything.'

Mimi wrapped her arms around his neck. 'I love you, Peter.'

Chapter 35

The next morning some members called in to find out about the fallout with the Gibbses. Of all people, Twister came in, incognito and alone. 'Winnie, I need to talk to you.' He looked uncharacteristically nervous but he smiled.

'Follow me.' Winnie motioned him out to the back alley. 'What's up?'

'Old man Gibbs came to see me. He wants to have a meeting with you, by yourself.'

'He can get fucked!'

'You don't know him; he's a real bad cunt.'

'Listen, Twister, I don't give a fuck. What happened was that young cunt's fault.'

'He knows that. He just wants to talk to you.'

'Are you in business with him?'

'No, but I used to be. He's the reason Kero Kev's in jail. I found out that he gave us up on our hash deal.' Twister looked meaningfully at Winnie. 'You remember, down on the docks?'

Winnie remembered alright; he knew it wasn't the Gibbses, that the pigs were already onto it, but he wasn't about to enlighten Twister. 'How do you know that?'

'I don't know it for a fact; it's just a feeling I have, since he was the only one who knew we were onto a big hash deal. I don't do business with him any more.'

'So how come you're here?'

'Like I told you, Winnie. He knows that I know you, and that's all. He said you can name the place.'

'Wait here, Twister. I want to talk to the boys.' Winnie went into the shop where the boys waited with bated breath.

'What's Twister want, Prez?'

'Old man Gibbs wants a meeting with me. I can choose where.'

'Anything's better than a war, Prez,' said Ocker. 'It's bad for business. But it could be a trap.'

'Try this, Prez,' said Kev. 'You go to the meeting and we keep Twister here with us.'

'I don't think Twister's close to him any more.'

Kev gave it a moment's thought. 'Who told you that, Prez?'

'Twister.'

Kev just smiled.

'Alright, Kev, some people never change. I'll see if he'll be in it.' Winnie went back to Twister. The boys watched Winnie doing the talking. When he finished, Winnie and Twister stared at each other for about five seconds. Twister nodded in agreement. It reminded Kev of the shoot-out at the OK Corral.

Winnie walked back smiling. 'He must still be working with them; why else would he do it?'

Big Kev said, 'That's Twister, Prez. I'll tell you something I heard: that hash they got busted with was never destroyed, it was on-sold to the Gibbses.'

'So the only one to miss out was Twister.'

'I'll bet that old Gibbs is just using Twister.'

'That's a change, Kev.'

'You can always scam a scammer; it's in their blood,' said Ocker.

'So how are you going to set the meeting up?' asked Kev.

'We can go for a drive in his car and just talk. We don't need to go far and Twister said he'd stay here — we agreed on three o'clock.'

'Prez, I have an ankle holster; come with me, they take a bit of fitting.'

'I don't need it, Kev.'

'You're not going unless you do.'

'Okay, mate, maybe you're right.'

'I've got a nice little automatic to go with it.'

At three o'clock, a black Mercedes with tinted windows pulled up outside the shop. Twister got out and Big Kev and Winnie met him.

'He doesn't want any trouble, Winnie.'

'We're just talking, Twister. Now you wait here.'

Kev held Winnie back. 'Hold on, Prez. Tell Twister to open the boot first.'

Twister popped the boot. Big Kev inspected it then closed it, satisfied. Winnie got into the back seat next to old man Gibbs. He stared at Winnie with cold blue eyes. 'I don't like what happened to my boy,' Gibbs said calmly.

His delivery put a shiver up Winnie's spine but he felt reassured that he had Kev's nice little automatic in the holster strapped to his ankle. 'It wouldn't have happened if he hadn't pulled a piece out.'

'Where is it now?'

'We threw it in the river to see if it floated — it didn't. You never know with those things. He was told not to deal in our pub by the owners and he told them to get fucked. That's bad manners and bad business. I don't take it lying down when people ignore what I say.'

Gibbs's face lit up. He chuckled. 'Yes, he's a cheeky little bugger, isn't he?' The smile quickly gave way to his previous icy demeanour and his thin voice grew cold once again.

'If there are any more problems you come and talk with me. It might just smarten him up a bit.' There was a silence and then the raspy voice went on. 'You run a pretty good operation, Winnie. Why don't you and your boys come and work with me?'

'You and Twister have something going on already from what I hear.'

'Now and then. He's pretty dumb, you know. I have plans to sell product and you and your Miners would be ideal for it.'

'Yeah, well, what's good for you may not be good for us.'

'Can't you see what I'm offering you?'

'Just make sure that your boy doesn't sell drugs in our pubs.'

'You might just live to regret your decision. I've got plenty of contacts.' He paused and a puzzled look creased his leathered face. 'I don't understand — you do business with the wogs but you won't deal with me. Why not?' Clearly the old man wasn't used to anyone knocking him back.

Winnie just stared back. 'I trust the wogs.'

The old man gave Winnie a last steely stare as they pulled up at the back of the shop.

Twister eagerly awaited their arrival. He jumped into the car as soon as Winnie left it, and the driver squealed his tyres as he raced off.

The boys walked out. 'How'd it go, Prez?'

'I don't think he gave a fuck about his boy getting shot. He just wanted us to sell his drugs for him.'

'What did you say?' asked Kev.

'More or less told him to get fucked. From what I can see he uses Twister and anyone else who's scared of him. He's an evil cunt and you can tell he's not used to anyone saying no.'

'Do you expect trouble?'

'I think he might be setting something up and he doesn't need any problems. He seemed kind of glad that his son got shot. I reckon he thinks it's a badge of honour.'

'No one likes their son being shot, Prez,' said Brian. 'You'd better be careful.'

Winnie went into the members' room and sat down with Kev. 'The Pig told me the Gibbses have a few friends on the force who look after them. So old man Gibbs is dangerous, but if I've got it right he doesn't want this to get out of hand. We'll keep an eye on the Horse and Cart and see what happens, but my instinct tells me we'll be right. You might want to keep your head down though, Kev.'

'Yeah, Prez. By the way, Little Tony called. They're putting the truck job off for a few weeks.'

'That's most probably a good idea.' Winnie changed the subject. 'I'm getting married on the twenty-second of August, so make sure you have no plans.'

'What's the hurry, Prez?' Ocker looked concerned. 'I was organising the Tattoo Show for then.'

'Is it much of a problem changing the date? It's the only time we can get the church.'

'I'll make it the week before.'

'How're you going with the organising, mate?'

'I ordered trophies. Tooheys will send a caravan and a beer tent to sell piss. We've ordered port-a-loos, seating and bands, and the Lions Club is set to cater, so I'll have to change all that. Plus the advertising.'

Kevvie just leant back in his chair with arms folded. 'Geez, he does a good job, Prez.'

Winnie tried not to smile. 'I'm sorry, Ocker. You are doing a great job.'

'She'll be right, Prez.'

'Kev, why don't you give Ocker a hand?'

'We have been helping him.'

'Yeah, the boys have helped a little, but I'd better change the advertising.'

'When you go on your honeymoon, will you take Harry?' asked Kev.

'That's all part of the wedding plans. I'll have to ask Mimi. Why do you want to know?'

'I know Sandy would like to see more of him.'

'I'll let you know, Kev.'

They arrived at the shop on Sunday morning to split the cash. Everything was quiet. As Brian opened the door, he beamed from ear to ear.

'It's payday, boys. Come and have a gander at this!' He ushered them inside the lunch room, where four huge piles of banknotes stacked up like bricks lay on the table. 'They're all the same, boys. Take any pile you want.'

The boys stared in awe at their individual piles of four million dollars. The cash represented almost five years of solid work.

'What are you going to do with yours, Ocker?'

'Buy more tattoo shops.'

'Kev?'

'Gold bars, Prez,; we're cruising now.'

'Brian, what about you?'

'I took your advice. John Baker's onto it for me. What about you, Prez?'

'I reckon this'll buy me a pretty decent house.'

'I want to take a photo of this!'

'Ocker, are you mad?'

'They do it in the movies!'

'Yeah, they also get caught in the movies. Put the fucking camera away! No one is ever to know about this. Let me say this again: what happened here today is for no one else to know about. No one. Not a fucking soul.' On reflection, they all agreed.

'Kev, did Mimi call Sandy and set up for Harry to stay with you?'

'Yeah, Prez, it's all good. We'll look after Harry while you and Mimi are on your honeymoon. I thought I might take Harry for a ride on the chopper.'

'Not until his feet reach the foot pegs, and then I'll be the one taking him.'

'Well, he's staying with us for a few days and I wanted to do something with him.'

'Take him to the movies. Oh, by the way, your old mates Rastus and Spike are coming up for the wedding.'

'It'll be good to party with them. It always seems to be business every time they visit.'

'Has there been any more trouble in your pubs from the Gibbses?'

'Quiet as a mouse, Kev. Their security is gone and we've got some new blokes.'

'Why didn't you give our members the job?'

'I don't want any connection to us. The blokes we hired are legitimate and I don't want to give the licensing police any excuse to stick their snoots into our pubs. Come on, boys, let's get rid of this!'

Ocker pulled out a folded mailbag and Winnie and Big Kev headed straight for their cars and returned with large suitcases. Ocker filled his mailbag, slung it over his shoulder and walked around the shop saying, 'I feel like Santa Claus!'

The meeting's business settled, they all rode off at, or under, the speed limit to their own hidey-holes and disposed of the cash.

The Tattoo Show signalled the official opening of the new clubhouse. Ocker and a couple of the boys helped entrants complete entry forms and explained the contest's procedures while the band carried out their sound checks. The Tooheys boys set up the outdoor caravan bar and began doing early trade with the workers. Winnie and Big Kev walked around the site, checking the jumping castle for the kids and giving heaps to the members, who weren't supposed to be drinking. 'We need everyone in control today.'

The Lions Club set up their food tent, full of enthusiastic helpers wearing aprons. At first, people drove past slowly to see what was happening. Winnie joined Big Kev at the gate. 'Once they see the castle and the beer tent and smell the sizzling sausages, they'll walk straight in.'

Kev was apprehensive. 'You reckon, Prez?'

Winnie gave him a look that said 'She'll be right, mate.' Slippery and Doc, seated at a small table, took ten-dollar donations from the adults, and it added up quickly. A pack of bikes — the Redbacks from Newcastle — come roaring up the road. They were the only other club Winnie had invited. Kev opened the main gate, waved them in and directed them to the parking. Big Kev and Winnie greeted the Redbacks with back-slapping and warm hugs.

'Hey, Doc, if there's any problems at the gate, get me or Big Kev.'

'Do you reckon Twister and the Tigers will turn up?'

'They weren't invited,' Winnie replied and his eyes narrowed for a second.

They joined Sorrow. 'Sorrow, how are you, mate? It's been a while. How was the ride down?'

'Beautiful, mate. Come and show me the new joint.'

Sorrow walked around and took in the details. 'What a flash clubhouse!'

The Redbacks wandered around, checking the place out. Winnie shouted drinks for Sorrow and his members and left them to it. 'Sorrow, I'll catch up with you later.'

Winnie walked back outside to see the place filling up with people from every walk of life. Many weren't bikies and Winnie soon saw that the advertising had paid for itself.

Mimi, Harry and Kitty, Sandy and Gina turned up together. Winnie led them to a tent they'd set up earlier.

'One week to go,' Mimi said quietly as she kissed him.

He smiled like a little boy. 'I know, babe, I know.'

'Is it alright for the kids to walk around?'

'Yes, just not into the clubhouse.'

'Hello, Uncle Peter.'

'Hello, Kitty. You look beautiful all dressed up!' Kitty blushed and gave Winnie a big hug.

'Harry, you look after Kitty, okay?'

'I will, Dad.'

'Can I get you girls a drink?'

'Yes please, Prez,' said Sandy.

Winnie spotted Tiny and told him to look after them — anything they wanted, they could have.

Gina thanked Winnie for the drink and raised her glass to him. 'Mimi tells me you're planning to build a new home. Where?'

'We don't know exactly, but I like the area to the southwest of Sydney, down Camden way.'

Mimi pitched in. 'Whenever we get ready to look, something comes up. We're going to spend a few days looking after our honeymoon.'

'Where are you going, Prez?'

'That's a surprise. I can't tell you or it won't be a surprise.' Winnie winked at Mimi. 'I'll be back later, babe. Tiny will look after you and the kids.'

As he walked away he realised he'd forgotten all about planning for the honeymoon. It was one more thing to think about, but right there and then he had other things on his mind.

Brian was busy directing nominees who were erecting another tent. 'Hey, Prez, it looks like we're going to have a full house today. Have you seen some of the tattoos? They're amazing. Ocker had some naked bloke who was completely covered, except for his jocks.'

'He can't have a life, mate.' Winnie laughed. 'Brian, where did you go for your honeymoon?'

'Katoomba.'

'What was it like?'

He glanced over his shoulder, then said, 'Honestly, it was shit, mate. Gina was up spewing every morning and there was no sex.' He checked again to see if they could be overheard before continuing. 'After we got married, sex became a chore.'

'You should buy her a dildo.'

'That's what Kev said. I'm telling you, mate, don't get married.'

'Women are not all the same, Brian.'

'Yeah, mate, they're not all the same. What about Lord Howe Island? I read about it. They cater to honeymooners — lots of bed and breakfast places and quiet hotels. It's not too far and it's away from everything, if that's what you want.'

'That's exactly what I want.'

''I'll tell you what, I'll see my travel agent on Monday. She books my trips to the States. Seven days will be more than enough, hey?'

'Perfect.'

'I'll organise it, Peter. It's my wedding present to you and Mimi. I didn't know what to get you, so it'll be a nice surprise for Mimi and you can pretend you didn't know.'

Winnie hugged him, thinking that he couldn't really remember the last time Brian'd called him Peter. They'd always been generous to one another but this was a real surprise. Winnie whispered, 'Thanks, mate.'

Slippery pulled Winnie aside. 'Hey, Prez, the cops are here!' Winnie walked to the main gate to meet the cops.

Winnie strode straight up to the Sergeant and his Constable. 'Any problems?'

'Just the parking on the street. I saw a bloke on the gate and they said they'd sort it out.' The Sergeant looked around. 'You have a fair crowd but I can see it's under control, so we're not here to bother you, but we'll be around to keep an eye on things.'

'Okay, then.' Winnie watched them get back in their patrol car.

'That was simple, Prez.'

'It's the best way, Brian.'

When the band took a break, Ocker, the master of ceremonies, stood onstage with microphone in hand and announced the categories and the entrants for the tattoo competition. The inked-up contestants displayed their work to the enthusiastic crowd.

Girls giggled as the bloke wearing only his jocks climbed onstage. Winnie noticed Harry and Kitty laughing together; it made him happy to see them getting on.

Brian was checking it out and commented to Winnie, 'I'm glad Gina's in the tent.'

The thunder of bike engines arriving got Winnie's attention. It was Twister and the Tigers.

The crowd was so occupied with the Tattoo Show they hardly noticed. Winnie and Big Kev walked out to meet them.

'Are we welcome, Winnie?' Twister asked.

'Not today.'

'Why not? I only have a few members with me.' Twister thought pleading his case might prove favourable. 'Come on, Winnie, it looks like a great party.'

'That's the way we'd like to keep it.'

In a surly tone Twister said, 'Old man Gibbs says hello.'

Big Kev stepped forward. 'Fuck off, Twister, you're holding up traffic!'

'Are you a traffic cop now?' Twister spat back sarcastically.

Kevvie advanced a step. 'Yes, but I don't give tickets, so fuck off!'

Twister shot him a sneaky grin. 'Okay, but you might just get this back with interest one day.' He looked over his shoulder and gave the signal to his members. 'Let's go!' They left as noisily as they could.

'I wonder what that cunt's up to, Prez.'

'You never know, Kev. He must've known we wouldn't let him in.'

'He's pretty dumb. Remember how pissed his boys got at the last show?'

'No, Kev, he's playing with us. He wants us to think he's working with the Gibbses, but I'll bet he isn't.'

Kev thought about it for a second or two. 'What about that bit about paying us back with interest? What's he playing at?'

'He just can't keep his mouth shut, Kev.'

'Guess we'll find out soon enough, Prez.'

'Fuck him, Kev. Let's go inside.'

Slippery and Doc at the gate announced that they'd had four hundred and eighty-seven visitors so far.

'That's pretty good, Doc.'

'Have a look at that, Prez!' Doc exclaimed in awe. 'It's Bernie from the shop!' And there she was, striding down the street in full get-up, dressed like a high-class whore.

Winnie kissed her on the cheek and remarked, 'You look as beautiful as always.'

'Why, thank you, Prez!' She planted a kiss on his cheek. 'Hello, Kevvie.' Bernie stretched up to give him a peck.

'We'd all love to fuck you,' Kevvie whispered and she just giggled.

'I know. Pity I'm queer!'

'Yeah, it is! Come on, Bernie, I'll take you to meet some of the girls.'

Winnie stuck his head into the food tent where the Lions were well organised and doing a roaring trade. The bloke in charge handed Winnie a sausage smothered with burnt, crispy onions and a squirt of tomato sauce. 'Free for the boss.'

Winnie hadn't eaten since the night before, he realised — he was starving, and got stuck into it, then watched the tattoo contestants lining up, displaying their numbers like entrants in a beauty pageant. Harry and Kitty stood transfixed, mouths agape as they pointed at the punters' tattoos.

'Which one do you like the most, Harry?'

'Kitty likes that girl's best.' Harry pointed at a girl with her back fully covered in jungle artwork and wild animals.

'That's pretty good, Harry, but what do you like?'

'That one!' He pointed at the mammoth, taut physique of Boris, whose back was inked with the Miners patch. He'd been the first Miner to do it.

'Yeah, that's good too! You can both help with the judging. Just remember the number they're holding and tell Ocker.'

'Oh, can we, Uncle Peter?'

'Yes, Kitty, and you can vote in the People's Choice award. You write their number on a ticket and put it in that box over there.' They both cheered, pleased to take part in the affairs of the day.

Winnie sighted the Rat with a blonde surfie chick on his arm. He held up Harry and Kitty's hands when the Rat pointed to the clubhouse, and mouthed 'Later'. He led the kids to the voting box. 'There you are.' He lifted them up in turn and let them deposit their tickets. 'I might have a go at this too.' He wrote down Boris's number.

'Who'd you write down, Uncle Peter?'

'It's a secret, my dear Kitty.'

'I thought you said no more secrets, Dad?'

Winnie smiled. 'I did, Harry, but this one's different.'

Ocker's voice boomed out announcing the end of the judging and the trophy presentation after the next bracket. The band resumed playing. Winnie took the kids into the food tent and ordered sausage sandwiches and lemonade for them.

The Lions boss was thrilled. 'This is going to be a great day for us, Peter. We must have sold two hundred kilos of snags.'

'I'm very happy for you; hope the proceeds are going somewhere useful?'

'Children's Hospital in Camperdown, for a new MRI unit. This'll help, thanks.'

'It's our pleasure. Come on, kids, I'll carry the drinks. Let's go see if we can find the girls.'

Tiny sat at the back of the tent keeping an eye on the girls, who looked as if they'd been hitting the grog pretty hard. They were laughing their guts out when Winnie turned up with the kids. They made a big fuss over Kitty and Harry, who only wanted to eat their snags and sip their lemonade. Winnie sat down with Tiny. 'The sheilas keeping you busy, Tiny?'

'It's worth the ticket price. They're bloody funny, especially since Bernie arrived.'

'You know she's queer, don't you?'

'Yeah, Prez, what a waste!'

'Where's Big Kev?'

'In the back room. The girls were in there with him for a while powdering their noses. They just got out, that's why they're talking so much. Must be the goey.'

'They don't need drugs for that, mate. I'm going there now, if anyone's looking for me.' He looked at the kids. 'Harry, Kitty, I'll be back later.'

'Before the judging, Uncle Peter?'

'Yes, Kitty.'

Harry was busy eating and just waved.

Winnie opened the door to the back room, full of smoke and some Miners and Redbacks. He headed for the speed and snorted the entire line. 'Just what I needed.'

'It's turned out pretty good, eh, Prez?' said Ocker.

'Beauty, mate. We'll do alright, and so will the Lions and the Tooheys boys.'

'Kev told me Twister turned up.'

'Yeah, that queer cunt's up to something. We'll worry about that tomorrow but today I want to make sure Boris wins the People's Choice award. Can you organise that, Ocker? I'd like to see our colours up there at the end of judging.'

'He has already, Prez. I got all the boys to vote for him. My best tattoo artist did him, and it'll be good advertising for my shop.'

'That's our Ocker!' Winnie smiled. 'Kitty and Harry seem to be getting on alright.'

Brian looked really happy. He was always at his best when it came to Kitty, the love of his life.

'All right, all you blokes, I don't want you puffing in here all day. Let's go out and show the colours.' Most of his members rose and filed outside, exhaling clouds of dope smoke.

'You Redbacks are alright. You're welcome to stay as long as you like.'

'That's good, they left their pot,' Sorrow replied with a grin.

'Then they must want you to smoke it!' Winnie glanced at Kev. 'Kev, the Rat's here with some hot surfie chick.'

'Yeah, that's his wife, Prez.'

'I didn't know he got married!'

'Neither did I, Prez, until today.'

'What's she like?'

'Who knows, Prez; they always seem alright at first, don't they?'

'You know what blokes are like, Kev. Have you had a talk with him about keeping everything under his hat? The Rat knows a lot about our business.'

'I haven't had a chance, Prez, but he knows to keep quiet.'

'Where are they?'

'He won't be hard to find — just look for her blonde hair.'

Ocker, the self-appointed MC, picked up the microphone as the band wound up their set and announced that the judging was complete and he'd make the presentations in ten minutes.

'I promised the kids I'd watch the presentations with them, Kev.'

They made their way back to the tent and met two Miners escorting a pissed punter off the premises, where he wouldn't be a hindrance to the other patrons.

'Don't bash him,' Winnie instructed. 'It's not a good look.'

Winnie and Kev found Kitty and Harry craning their necks looking for him.

'I told you he'd come!' Harry said to Kitty, and they both raced towards him.

The women were a bit worse for wear and didn't even notice him; they were heavily engrossed in each other's tales. He was about to walk out of the tent when he saw Mimi and Bernie sitting close together. A pang of jealousy coursed through him for a millisecond, then he realised Mimi had to talk to someone, so he turned away to get to the judging.

Ocker introduced the winners, who stepped onstage and collected their trophies. Kitty's favourite, the lady with the jungle scene on her back, won her category.

'See, I told you she'd win!' Kitty said happily.

The People's Choice category was yet to come and Winnie said quietly to Harry, 'Who do you reckon will win that trophy?'

Harry whispered back, 'Can't tell you, Dad. It's a secret.' Their eyes met as they both laughed at his joke.

'Now, last but not least,' Ocker announced, 'the People's Choice award goes to …' he paused to milk the moment, 'Boris from the Miners' Southside Chapter!'

Big Kev and Harry both threw their arms in the air and yelled, 'Yeah!'

Boris climbed onstage to retrieve his mammoth trophy and the crowd cheered wildly. He posed a few times then turned his back to the crowd and displayed the Miners patch tattooed all over his back, and everybody cheered.

'Boys,' Kitty said in her exaggerated way, 'will be boys!' She smiled at Harry, who blushed scarlet.

'I'm just going to have a talk with the Rat,' said Winnie. 'Tell Sandy to keep an eye on Mimi, if you don't mind. She's right into the piss.'

'I understand, Prez. We'll look after her.' Kev took the kids back to sit with the girls.

Winnie got the Rat's attention away from yet another blonde surfie chick standing beside him. The Rat's wife turned to Winnie, while the other blonde just stared back at him with a 'Come fuck me' look.

Winnie thought about it for a second but knew it would end up being trouble, since he was getting married next week and his bride-to-be was ten metres away. He didn't look back. He and the Rat walked off a short distance.

'How're you going, Rat?'

'Real good, mate.'

'Kev tells me you got married. Congratulations!'

'The same to you, Prez. Next week, eh? Come and meet my wife. We only had a little ceremony and didn't invite many people, just her folks and mine.'

'Don't worry about it, Rat. Besides, I forgot to put you on my list.' Winnie paused for a second. 'Anyway, we don't want to be public with our connection. Come on, I'll get you a drink and we'll have a chat.'

Winnie signalled a nominee, who brought them drinks, then they went out the back to some relative quiet.

'I heard you had a bit of trouble with the Gibbses?'

'It's over now, mate,' Winnie said between clenched teeth.

'They're real cunts, Prez. When I was on the hammer my dealer was right up there and dealing direct with old man Gibbs himself,' Rat recalled. 'Some shit went down between my mate and the "young" Gibbs; I think he might have been taxing the ounces. Anyway, my mate got the blame and we haven't seen him since.'

'He never showed?'

'No, Prez, so just be careful, even though I know I don't have to remind you.'

'There's something I need to tell you,' Winnie said, and the Rat followed him to the members-only gutting room.

'We don't let the wives or girlfriends know about this room; it's locked when they're here.' He retrieved the keys from his pocket and they entered. 'We tell them it's a storeroom.'

Winnie closed the door behind them and flicked on the light.

'Fuck me, Prez!' An astounded Rat took in the double bed in the centre of the room, adjacent to a dressing table with a full mirror and boxes of condoms and lubricants displayed on it. A mirror covered the entire ceiling.

'This is like a brothel, Prez.'

'Whaddya think? Ocker set it up.' Winnie raised his eyebrows as he looked at the Rat. 'Don't suppose you'd care for a line, would you?

'Too right, I would.'

Winnie cut up two lines as the Rat rolled a note. They stuck their noses in it and let out deep breaths.

'Look, mate, it's very important that you tell your missus nothing about our dealings.'

'She knows nothing, Prez; she's pretty dumb.'

'It doesn't matter. Sometimes they're the worst.'

'We're building a house together.'

'Where'd you tell her you got all your money from?'

'Catching prawns in Queensland. Don't worry, Prez, she's a good girl.'

'Well, the less said the better then, hey?'

'I suppose I shouldn't tell you, but her cousin Teri's got the hots for you.'

'You just tell her to be careful because the wives will zero in on her if they spy her trying to hit on me. Tell her this is a bike club, not a surf club; at least tell her to wait until the girls leave.' Winnie winked at the Rat and the Rat laughed.

'What time will you go till tonight?'

'All night, mate,' Winnie replied. 'Come on, let's get outta here. I'll catch up with you later on and then you can introduce me to your wife.'

In the tent, Winnie found Mimi pissed as a newt. He looked at Sandy, who just nodded as he walked over.

'She'll be right, Prez. It's her hen's party. I'll drive her home and take Harry as well. We're all staying at your place tonight.'

'It'll be a bit crowded.'

'You blokes won't be there, so we're just going to have some fun.'

Thinking of Teri, the surfie chick, he agreed that was a good plan and asked Sandy to tell him when they were leaving. He was suddenly glad to see Mimi surrounded by the other wives and girlfriends; it pleased him that she had made friends and got on with them all.

'Where are the kids?'

'With Kev.'

When the crowd had thinned noticeably, Winnie stepped up to the bar, where Ocker was holding court with Brian and the Redbacks.

'Hey, Prez, you know why Aussie men like girls with big tits and tight pussies?'

'No.'

'Because they've got big mouths and small dicks! One of my girls told me that.'

Winnie laughed but he was beginning to feel the effects of the many drinks and the lines and the day spent on his feet. He sat with Squizzy. 'So how are you, Squizzy?'

'Good, mate. I've been putting some bets on for the Minister.'

'How'd he go?'

'Done his arse. He won't be too happy on Monday.'

'Why doesn't he go himself, or just bet with the bookies?'

'He owes them too much. It might be time to see if we can get him some winners, Prez.'

'I spoke to Ocker. It's in the works, mate.'

'If you could, Prez. Might be good for us all. Brian told me you were getting married. Congratulations.'

'Haven't you got an invite? You're on the list. Give me your address and I'll see you there. Hopefully we'll have something for your Minister too.'

'I hate asking for it, Prez.'

'Don't worry, Squizzy. It'll be good for both of us, and it won't cost a thing.'

'Onya, mate. I have to go, Prez. I'll see you next week at the wedding.'

When most of the non-bikie crowd had left, the first band packed up. Ocker had another one setting up inside for the Miners' private party. Winnie found Tiny looking after the kids and girls in the tent.

'You can go inside, Tiny. I'll look after them now. You've done a good job. Time to party — have fun!'

Mimi came back from the ladies' and shook water from her hands then wiped them on his face. He caught her hands in his. 'Did you have a good day, babe?'

'The best, Peter. God, that Bernie's a funny girl! We had a few laughs, I can tell you — but I'm feeling the effects of all that booze. The girls are coming to our place for the night.'

'Will you be alright?'

'I'll be fine, Peter. We're getting takeaway and a couple of videos for the kids.'

'I'll walk you out to the car.'

Sandy joined them; she had stayed off the grog and was the only one fit to drive. 'We're off now, Prez. The kids are already in the car.'

'Take it easy on the way home, Sandy.'

He held Mimi's hand tightly as she wobbled on unsteady feet. Winnie guided her over to Gina, who was also a little worse for wear. 'Come on, Gina, time to leave.'

'Trying to get rid of us already, Prez? I suppose you just want to party with your sluts.'

'Gina!' Sandy spoke in a menacing voice that said, 'Don't be a dickhead. Shut the fuck up.'

Winnie got the girls to the car. He kissed Mimi, pulled her seatbelt on and clipped her in.

'I'll see you in the morning.' Winnie had the shits with Gina. He knew there was no use saying anything to Brian, but he sure felt like it. When the girls had driven off he joined the boys at the bar.

'It's been a good day, Prez,' said Brian. 'We had over nine hundred pay at the gate.'

Winnie saw the Rat and his two surfie chicks dancing and when the Rat saw Winnie he tried to entice him to dance. Winnie shook his head but he watched the two girls jiggling and giggling. They seemed to be off their heads.

'Want to come outside for a hash joint, Prez?' The Rat's little stoned eyes twinkled merrily.

'Why not? You better bring your missus and her friend. I wouldn't want to leave them in here with these blokes.'

'Oh, they're coming too, don't you worry about that.'

Everyone was so wasted at that point that no one took any notice of anyone else, so Winnie walked outside into the dark and joined the Rat, who introduced his wife Carol and her cousin Teri.

He shook each of their hands and gave Teri a look that said, 'If you want it, you've got it.' 'You and the Rat are married, eh, Carol? Did he tell you we went to school together?'

The Rat lit up the hash joint and passed it to Winnie.

Teri asked, 'Which is your bike, Prez?'

Winnie pointed to a cluster of ten bikes. 'It's one of those.' He passed her the joint.

'Come and show me.'

The Rat pulled another joint out of his pocket. 'Go for it, Prez.'

Winnie walked to his bike and Teri followed. 'Can I sit on it?'

Winnie had never ridden a surfie chick or a surfboard; suddenly both appealed. 'Okay, come around this side.' She passed him the joint and brushed her tits against him as he guided her hands to the handle bars.

'Now, just swing your leg over.' He thought he wouldn't mind throwing a leg over Teri as she settled in the saddle.

'Put your legs here.' She placed her feet on the foot pegs. 'Now, how does that feel?'

'It'd be good if we could have the motor going. I'd like to have something hot and throbbing between my legs.'

'That won't be happening.'

'Won't it?' She slid her hand up and down his leg then stopped at his groin.

He helped her off the bike and slipped a hand over her bum. His other hand moved down her shoulder and stopped at a nipple. 'You're a sexy bitch.' His eyes darted around now — the last thing he wanted was the Rat and his missus watching. He pulled Teri towards him and she shoved her crotch into his groin.

'I'd like to fuck you,' she whispered. 'Where can we go?'

'Come with me. Hey, Rat, I'm going to show Teri the clubhouse.' The Rat was so stoned he just waved. Winnie fumbled for the key to the gutting room while Teri massaged her tits.

'I hope you're a tit man.'

'I'm an everything man.' He flung open the door and she followed him inside.

'Would you like a line?'

She nodded. She picked out a small cat o' nine tails from Ocker's bucket of toys as Winnie cut up the line. 'What's this for? Would you like me to use this on you?'

'No,' he smiled, 'I'm not into that.' He wondered how he could explain the marks the whip would inflict on his back to Mimi. 'But if you like, I'll use it on you.'

'No, I'd rather have this.' She pulled out a foot-long dildo and waved it around like a sword. Then she took the note off Winnie, bent over in front of him, and snorted the line. Winnie shoved his hand between her legs. He took off his colours and folded them before putting them on a chair. It didn't take long for her to get naked and stretch out on the bed while Winnie pulled off his boots. He looked at her perfect tits and her hairless cunt.

'How come your cunt's bald? You haven't had crabs have you?'

'No, why is that?'

'I thought you only shaved if you did.'

'I shave myself. The sex is much better — come and try it.' She began playing with herself and using the dildo while Winnie tore off his clothes. He switched off the light and she was right: her cunt was the most amazing thing. Two hours of fucking passed quickly.

'I have to go, Teri.'

'You haven't got any friends who'd like to visit me, have you?'

'How often do you do this?'

'First time, Prez. I always dreamed about it.'

He smiled. 'Well, your dreams are about to come true if that's what you really want.'

'Oh, I do.'

In the clubhouse Winnie saw Ocker standing at the bar, drink in hand.

'Is her dream going to come true?'

'You know, don't you?'

Ocker nodded. 'The Rat told me.'

'Off you go, then; she's in the gutting room. It's unreal, mate.'

'Thanks, Prez.' Ocker grabbed some drinks. 'She might be thirsty, Prez.'

'Ocker, just remember her dream and don't sheriff her.'

'Would I do that, Prez?'

Winnie joined Big Kev, who was watching the band.

'Been having some fun, Prez?'

'Who else knows?'

'Who doesn't? You know no one here'll talk. Did Tony tell you about the change in plans for the heist? He reckons it'll be a lot easier to just rob the depot.'

'I don't care how they get it, Kev, but I better have a talk with him first.'

'In the morning, Prez. They're off their faces at the moment. Sorrow gave them trips.'

In the morning the Rat wandered around looking for Teri. 'We have to go, Prez. Do you have any idea where she is?'

'I'll bet she's still in there with Ocker. I'll ask Kev to get her.'

'All the best for your wedding, Prez.'

'Thanks, Rat.'

Sorrow and his members readied to leave for Newcastle. 'We're off, Winnie. Thanks for a great party.'

'Take it easy, Sorrow.'

As the drugs wore off a few members sat outside in the early morning sunlight and shared a laugh or two. Brian organised the dismantling of the tent and cleaning up of the clubhouse. Winnie pitched in, prompting other members to join them, and they soon had most of the heavy lifting finished. The phone rang and Ocker answered. His face suddenly darkened. He looked at Winnie, cupped his hand over the receiver and whispered, 'One of the Redbacks was hit by a car on the freeway on the way home. Rocky. He's dead. He was pretty out of it when he left.'

Winnie turned down the music and asked the members for a moment of quiet. He told them what he knew. Everyone took it pretty badly; it had been a great day and evening until this bad news. 'I never want that to happen to any of us. If any Miner sees one of his brothers pissed or out of it and trying to ride, you have to stop him. We don't want to go to any more of our brothers' funerals. Give them a lift home, or they stay at the clubhouse till they're okay — have you got that? It's a Club rule.'

The death quickly sobered everyone up. Those who knew Rocky talked about what a good bloke he was, and the memory of the great party soon faded, to be replaced with a sombre silence.

'Brian, get Little Tony and Kev and Ocker and come outside for a chat. If Rocky's funeral is this week we'll all go, but if it's next week, after the wedding, I want Brian and Tony to take the Club up to Newcastle to show our respect.'

'Alright, Prez.'

'Now, Tony, what's this Kev's telling me about the pseudo?'

'It'll be a lot easier this way, Prez. We'll be better off, less risk, and we'll have about half an hour start before anyone can raise the alarm.'

'Why didn't you think of this earlier?'

'Better late than never, Prez.'

'When do you look like doing it?'

'They're waiting for a shipment now, Prez, so it won't be long.'

'Ocker, how are you going with the horseracing tips?'

'I'm on it, Prez. My mate at the stables gave me a list of what he needs for the horses to go fast. My university friends are making it up for him.'

'As soon as you know will you give Squizzy a ring? Don't go giving the tips to anyone else.'

'I know the score.'

'That's it, Ocker. Did the surfie chick's dream come true?'

Big Kev spoke up. 'No, the dirty little cunt sheriffed her and locked the door from the inside.'

'I never heard anyone knock.'

'Bullshit, Ocker, we nearly broke the door.'

'We must have been asleep.'

'Yeah, like fuck you were.'

'You should've been quicker,' said Ocker. Everybody laughed. 'What about a buck's party, Prez? Do you want one?'

Winnie thought about it. 'I think I had it last night. That surfie chick was something else, eh, Ocker?'

'Yes, Prez, she sure was.'

'I remember the nickname we had for him before he became Ocker,' said Kev. 'It was Lizard. If there was anything to be had he'd pounce on it and keep it for himself.' The boys laughed.

'You know I don't like that name, Kev.' That made the boys laugh more. Big Kev tousled Ocker's hair. 'I'm sorry, Lizard.'

'You cunts are just jealous, aren't they, Prez?'

'Don't bring me into it. Anyway, I'm off. What are you blokes doing?'

Brian answered. 'There's a lot of cash in the safe. Maybe Ocker and Tony can help me count it.'

Winnie gave that a moment's thought. 'Okay. Tony, your Chapter gets half the gate money, after expenses.'

'We can count it now,' said Brian. 'Come on, Ocker, Tony, let's get on with it.'

When Big Kev and Winnie got back to Winnie's, Harry came out at the sound of their bikes.

'G'day, Harry, where are the girls?'

'They're sick, Dad.' He lowered his voice. 'I think they drank too much.'

'Who's up there?'

'Just Mum and Auntie Sandy.'

'Come on, let's go up and see them.'

The place was spotlessly clean and the girls sat at the kitchen table holding their heads and sipping tea. Mimi looked up and said hello weakly.

Winnie put an arm over her shoulder. 'Feeling a little unwell, are we?' Mimi just nodded.

Sandy stood up. 'Let's go now, Kev, before I collapse.'

Winnie walked out with Kev and Sandy and saw them off. Mimi held her head and sat immobile. 'Mimi, you should have a nap and an aspirin. This'll be a big week. Take it easy.'

He helped her into the bedroom and pulled the bedclothes back for her and she climbed in. She opened her arms for him to join her but the memory of the night before with the surfie chick made him stop. 'Let me have a shower first, babe. I must stink of sweat and booze.' He showered, and by the time he returned Mimi was sound asleep.

Chapter 36

Mimi had arranged for Winnie and Harry to have suits tailored for the big day. Winnie decided there was no point in fighting it so he and Harry went to get the job done: new suits, new shoes, and even a cummerbund embroidered with the Miners Club colours. Mimi had thought of absolutely everything.

As had Brian, Winnie discovered. He'd left an envelope inside Winnie's jacket pocket when the Miners had come in to have their suits fitted. Inside was a map of Lord Howe Island, plane tickets and a letter confirming the hotel booking. The accompanying note said simply, 'Cheers, Brian, Gina and Kitty'. 'Top man,' thought Winnie, with real appreciation.

The hard work done, the boys decided to stop at Binky's for a hamburger, opposite the railway on Elizabeth Street. They pulled up outside, before Winnie abruptly took off again.

'What's up, Dad?' asked Harry.

'Nothing, mate. I just remembered a better place up the road. Look up there, Harry, on top of the Golf House — the neon man swinging a golf club. I used to look for it when we caught the train into the city.' They drove slowly through the traffic. 'Here's the place.'

They stopped outside a shop with a big sign saying they had the best hamburgers in Sydney. They parked and went in and ordered. They found a booth and played the juke box for Harry while he ate his burger. Winnie used the payphone to call Kev. 'Listen mate, I just saw Twister in a burger joint with old man Gibbs and two blokes in suits who looked like pigs.' Winnie wished his Sergeant was around to tell him what was going on.

They got home to find Mimi loading her car in the garage. Winnie wouldn't see her again until the wedding. She stopped and watched as Harry carried his boxed suit inside.

Winnie whispered, 'Do I really have to wait until Saturday to play with you?'

'Yes.'

'I suppose a head job's out of the question?'

'You're so crass; I don't know why I'm marrying you.'

He smacked her on the arse. 'Because you love me?'

'Now, where are we going for our honeymoon?'

'Can't tell you.'

Mimi drew close and rubbed his crotch.

'That won't work,' he said.

'Come on, Peter. I have to know what clothes to take.'

'Just take holiday stuff and some good clothes.'

'Thanks, that tells me everything. Are you starting to feel excited?'

'About what?'

Mimi walked away, shaking her head. 'See you Saturday.'

On the Saturday, Toothpick arrived to pick up the boys twenty minutes early. He put Winnie's bag in the boot and Harry walked out dressed up in his suit and new shoes.

'You look terrific, son,' said Winnie, 'but I feel like a goose dressed like this.'

'You do look a bit like a penguin, Dad.' They exchanged glances and shared a laugh.

Toothpick slid behind the wheel, gunned the motor and drove off slowly. 'We're a bit early for the church, Prez.'

'First we're going to the Centennial for a beer with Brian and the boys. It's where I met Mimi, but it's a queers' pub now. Nothing stays the same, does it?'

Toothpick parked in front of the purple pub. They found Brian, Big Kev and Ocker at a table.

'Don't laugh! Look at yourselves.'

'We're not laughing, Prez. What would you like to drink?'

'Just a beer, mate, and a squash.' Looking around the bar, memories flashed through Winnie's mind. He recalled the hundreds of bikes, and the drinking and spewing and fighting. Now it was a genteel place with bottles of wine on the shelves, and hardly smelled like a pub any more. 'This pub sure has changed, eh, boys?'

Kev looked around at the other patrons. He leaned in and said quietly, 'Yeah, these blokes all have little moustaches now. I can't stand the cunts.'

'They're not bad blokes,' said Ocker. 'I sell a little to a couple of them. I said to one of them once, how did you know you were queer? He said, when he had his first wank over a bloke at school.'

Kev said, with a look of disgust on his dial, 'It's not natural.'

'Don't worry, Kev, it's not compulsory.'

Big Kev shook his head and Ocker laughed at him.

'I remember the night you met Mimi here,' said Brian. 'Who'd believe nine years later you'd be back here to marry her?'

'Yeah, who would? A toast to the old Centennial!' They hoisted their glasses and took long swigs. Harry watched carefully, then he did it too.

Winnie looked at his watch. 'Time to go, boys.'

Toothpick opened the back door of the car. 'In you go, Prez, Harry.'

Winnie wound down the window and watched Brian and the boys climb into a new Mercedes. 'Is that yours?'

Brian turned and dangled a set of keys. 'Yep.'

'Very classy.'

'Thanks, Prez; it's the result of a lot of hard work.' He winked at Winnie, who winked back.

On the drive down to the church Winnie took the wedding ring out of his pocket and handed it to Harry. 'Now, you know what to do, mate.'

'Yes, Dad, I know what to do.'

The bridal party waited at the side of the church with the priest while the rest of the guests filed into the church. Sandy, Gina and Mimi's cousin in their long yellow dresses looked terrific. Sandy pinned a carnation to Winnie's and Harry's lapels. Winnie felt the first wave of excitement sweep over him — whatever was about to happen was wholly beyond his ken. He knew it was serious, but his thoughts flew to spending a week alone with Mimi on an island in the Pacific.

'Are we ready?' the priest asked.

'You know it,' said Winnie. He straightened his bow tie, pulled his jacket down, clenched and unclenched his fists a few times, took a deep breath, and he and Harry marched off. The organ played as they followed the priest down the aisle. Winnie nodded to the Miners and smiled his biggest shit-eating grin. As he passed his brother and sister-in-law Winnie thought he ought to give Warren some money for a new suit. He gave a small wave to Mimi's mother and brother and wondered how they really felt about seeing their little girl marrying him. At least he looked the part on the day. He and Harry stood at the altar with the priest and chatted briefly until the organ played the Wedding March. All heads swung around to watch Mimi walking down the aisle, arm-in-arm with her father. Of course she was absolutely beautiful in her mother's wedding dress, trailed by Kitty, who was holding her train. Mimi's eyes locked on Winnie's, then on Harry. She beamed.

'What a lady,' he whispered, and she looked down to hide her blush.

Winnie felt something he had never felt before — immense humility. This vision before him was about to accept him as her husband. Her father left her at the altar and sat with his wife, glancing at the suited Miners, who were grinning like schoolboys. Harry was the only one concentrating on the priest and he listened intently as Mimi and Winnie exchanged vows. Winnie heard the priest say the words he and Mimi had concocted and then Harry gave him the ring. The ring found Mimi's hand, the priest said more words and then Winnie lifted Mimi's veil and kissed her. Tears flowed freely as she looked up at Winnie and kissed him back. 'I love you.'

They followed the priest and signed the registry and legal papers, and the first five minutes of their married life came to an end. Then, at last, they walked down the aisle as man and wife. Mimi's mother turned on the waterworks and dabbed at her eyes with a handkerchief, clutching her husband's arm. Cameras flashed, Mimi waved and Winnie smiled and nodded. Inside, his stomach churned, his heart thumped; he wanted to scream with sheer happiness. There was a long line of well-wishers, faces known and unknown, kisses, sweet-smelling cheeks and hearty hugs. It was all a blur as they stopped for introductions to prick relations and more photos, and the whole time Winnie's thoughts were on boarding the plane for Lord Howe. A half hour later, the long line ended at last, and Winnie turned to Mimi. 'I will always love you, Mimi.'

Mimi answered slowly. 'I love you, Peter, and always will, no matter what.'

They were the first words they had spoken to each other since the ceremony. The photographer arranged and rearranged groupings and fired off his flash and waved his arms about gaily. The wedding party beamed and Winnie's faced ached from his unforced grin. Mimi, radiant, her brilliant blue eyes shining, said all the right things and cried some more. A long, white limousine arrived and a chauffeur drove them through the streets to the leafy, posh golf club. They walked inside to a table armed with a battalion of champagne-filled glasses. Toasts were offered, glasses clinked and the party began.

Winnie looked around and acknowledged the good wishes of the guests. He saw Squizzy talking to Mimi's brother and John Baker outside on the lawn. Squizzy suddenly looked at his watch, peeled away and pulled out a transistor radio, put it to his ear and paced up and down. Finally he put it away, gave Winnie a thumbs-up and a big smile. Winnie sidled over.

'Congratulations, Prez.'

'What was that about with the radio, Squizzy?'

'Ocker gave me two winners. The Minister will be very happy. Hope you have a wonderful honeymoon, Prez.'

Mimi's brother stuck his head out the door. 'You're wanted inside, Peter.'

'Not more photos.'

'No, speeches.' Mimi's brother, the master of ceremonies, said all the appropriate things, avoided any ribald stories and made his sister blush.

Finally it was Winnie's turn. His heart raced but he too said the right things, and he made a point of thanking the people who deserved it. Then he turned to Harry. 'Last but not least, allow me to introduce my son, Harry Peter Winifred. I want to thank him for performing his manly task so well today.'

There followed warm applause and then Mimi's brother announced the bridal waltz. Winnie swung Mimi onto the dance floor and they danced as one. The Miners looked astonished.

By the third day on Lord Howe they had just about seen everything. Mimi had been delighted by the destination, as Winnie knew she would be, and they'd decided to learn scuba diving. Winnie could hardly believe the colours of the teeming fish. That night, sitting on the veranda of their bungalow, Mimi doubled over in pain. Winnie rushed to her side.

'What's up, baby?' Sweat poured down her face. 'Come and lie down.' He helped her into their bed, where she curled up in the foetal position. 'Is it your appendix?'

'No.'

'I'm going to get a doctor.' He rushed away to the office. The doctor appeared in ten minutes, and gave Mimi painkillers and a sedative.

'We have to evacuate her.'

The air ambulance got them back to Sydney and St Vincent's Hospital within twelve hours. Winnie remembered the last time they were there, to visit Sandy. Mimi's mother and father met Winnie in the ward. A doctor, a friend of the family, approached Mr Gregson, who did the introductions.

'We're not sure what her problem is just yet. I saw the X-rays and we're going to operate. There's a spot we need to check.'

'Did you know, Peter, that Mimi's had problems with her plumbing before?'

Mrs Gregson turned to the old man. 'Don't talk about it like that.'

Sandy and Big Kev arrived with Harry. When Harry saw his father he threw himself into his arms. 'Not again, Dad!'

'Everything's fine, son.'

Mrs Gregson and Sandy cried.

'Come on, Prez, let's find a coffee.'

'I'm going nowhere, Kev, until I find out what's going on.'

'We went up to the funeral, Prez.'

'Do you have to mention that word, Kev?'

'Sorry, Prez. You know what I mean — up in Newcastle.'

'How was it?'

'The Redbacks were impressed. I gave Sorrow your condolences.'

The doctor walked out from the operating room. He smiled warmly. 'She's fine, son. The problem was a gallstone stuck in her fallopian tube. This is good news: it may now be possible for her to conceive.'

'Thanks, Doc. Does she know?'

'Not yet.'

'Can I tell her?'

'Of course.'

When the family returned to the waiting room they saw Kev and Winnie smiling. Winnie relayed the doctor's message. Harry held onto Winnie's leg and Mrs Gregson hugged her husband. Winnie peered into Mimi's room through the observation window. The doctor told him, 'You can go in now.'

Mimi opened her eyes. 'I'm sorry for ruining the honeymoon.'

He kissed her. 'It's okay, they discovered the problem and it's all fixed now. You might even be able to have a baby.' Her eyes widened and she smiled and squeezed his hand. 'That's what the doctor said. I suppose it's up to me now.'

She was asleep before he left the room.

Chapter 37

With the success of the new Harley-Davidson model, the brand was on the up and sales in the shop reflected its resurgence. In twelve months the shop tripled sales and people from all walks of life started buying. A few even enquired about the Miners Club and Bernie helped source new nominees. They were not all stereotypically working-class boys either. A new kind of member — the private school type — started joining.

The next week little Tony and Boris pulled off the pseudoephedrine robbery. Kev and Winnie met in the back room and discussed what to do with it. 'We have at least two years of stock for our laboratories. We can continue to buy from the Commandos and keep this for when their supply runs out.'

Ocker walked in holding a letter. 'Check this out, fellas — my Nokia shares went through the roof in Europe. The mobile phone is here. Not only in Europe, but in Australia as well. They'll take our business to another level. What have I been telling you?'

'Seeing is believing, Ocker.'

'No, hearing is believing.'

'What are you going to do, retire?'

'No, mate, I love this life.'

After a few trips down to the Southern Highlands, Winnie and Mimi found the land on which to build their dream home: close to the highway but not too close; a running stream; level, with lots of old trees.

'We haven't talked about what sort of house we want to build,' said Mimi. 'Do you have anything in mind?'

'I like your parents' home.'

'It'd be expensive building a timber place.'

'So?'

Winnie thought of how his business was going. The hash was almost gone, the labs were working overtime and the pubs had become trendy — the Mario brothers knew what they were doing.

'I'm going to see the doctor this week.'

'Is there anything wrong?'

She smiled. 'I missed my period.' Winnie felt a wave of excitement. 'Don't get too excited,' she said. 'I don't want you to be disappointed.'

'How much have you missed it by?'

'Don't you know?'

'Blokes don't run by the calendar.'

'Two weeks.'

'Don't think I don't care, babe.'

'I know you do, Peter.' She touched his cheek with her fingertips.

Winnie showed an architect some pictures of Mimi's parents' house and asked for preliminary drawings along similar lines. While they were underway, Mimi had a few more appointments with her doctor, who confirmed her pregnancy. Winnie was beside himself with excitement. He loved the idea of having children with Mimi, and beamed while he ate breakfast. As he watched Mimi help Harry get ready for school he reflected on the first pure happiness of his life. A sudden, loud knock on the door shattered his reverie. Mimi opened the door to confront two detectives and a pair of uniformed cops. One detective flashed a badge, pocketed it and said, in a none-too-friendly fashion, 'Police. We're here to arrest Peter Winifred and search these premises. This search warrant entitles us to look where we like.'

Winnie jumped up and walked to the door. The uniformed police grabbed his arms, forced them behind his back and clapped on the cuffs.

'Dad!' Harry's distressed call shook Winnie to his core.

'Mimi, ring John Baker.'

The detective holding the warrant snapped, 'No you don't!'

In his coldest voice Winnie said simply and irrefutably, 'Yes, she does. Her name is not on the warrants.' Mimi showed no emotion and put her arm around Harry's shoulders.

Winnie looked at the two detectives and remembered that he'd seen them before. It came to him in an instant — they were the cunts he'd seen with old man Gibbs and Twister. The uniformed pigs re-cuffed his hands in front so the detective could hand him the warrants. Winnie threw them on the kitchen table and leaned over them to read what he could. They were specifically looking for drugs, money and guns. The arrest warrant was for a trafficable amount of amphetamine. He said nothing, just stood in the kitchen and listened to doors opening and closing. The two uniformed cops looked uneasy. Winnie asked them to stick the warrants in his back pocket.

A detective called out, 'Search him.' They went through his pockets. 'Now drop your pants.'

He hesitated.

'Got something to hide?'

Winnie struggled with his buckle and let his jeans hit the floor. He looked at the Pig. 'I haven't had a shit yet. Which one of you wants to stick his finger up my arse?'

'Think you're a smart cunt, don't you?'

'I do the best I can.'

'Put him in the van.'

While searching the garage they found his handgun but no drugs. He didn't mind about the gun; he'd rather be caught with it than without it. Mimi called John Baker in front of the cops, who were still ransacking the house and turning the drawers out. The uniforms took him to Central police station where he was fingerprinted, photographed and charged. Then they put him into a cell by himself. He heard a voice.

'Hey, Prez.' It was Kev.

He went to the cell door. 'They got you, Kev?'

'Yeah, mate.'

'Who else have they got?'

'Don't know.'

'Say anything to you?'

'Nothing, Prez.'

They heard another cell door open. Winnie spied Tony Mario being led into another cell. 'Tony! Tony!'

'Who's that?'

'Me, Winnie.'

'What the fuck's going on, Prez?'

'Don't know yet. John Baker should be on his way.'

One by one they were taken to the interview room, where John Baker sat at a table with the two detectives. Winnie sat next to John. He answered

'No comment' to each question. He signed the interview sheet. When they were done, John asked them for a moment. 'I want a word with my client in private.' The cops left the room.

'What's going on, John?'

'They say they have evidence of you trafficking in speed and they claim to have witnesses. They're going to oppose bail.'

'What? They can't, can they? I'm not a flight risk.'

'They say that you'll try and intimidate the witnesses.'

'Who are they?'

'They're not saying.'

'Well, how can I intimidate them if I don't know who they are?'

'They also say it's because they suspect you of dealing in commercial amounts. What can they have on you?'

Winnie sat back. 'I don't know, John. Have they been to the shop?'

'I'll let you know when we go before the magistrate.'

He hoped they hadn't. He was worried about Kev's 'toys'.

'Have the blokes made statements?'

'No.'

'They never mentioned my handgun in the brief?'

'No, but for Christ's sake don't say anything about it. You know what they're like; let them keep it for themselves. Obviously they think they have enough on you.'

'When do we go to court?'

'I'm putting in bail applications this afternoon.'

As it turned out, the three were denied bail and sent to the remand centre at Long Bay Jail. While they were being processed Winnie saw his old acquaintance Kero Ken. Kero winked at Winnie, then raised his finger to his lips and smiled.

'Heard you were coming, Winnie.' Kero handed Winnie his towel and bedding.

Big Kev was next in line. 'Kero, I can't say I'm glad to see you here, mate.'

'Stop your talking!' a guard shouted.

They showered and donned their prison uniforms. Winnie and Big Kev were put into their cells.

'Who do you think they might have as witnesses, Prez?'

'It seems strange, Kev. I saw the pigs that arrested me with old man Gibbs and Twister. I wish our Pig was around; he'd know what's going on.'

'Maybe Kero knows something, Prez. This is my first time in jail but I bet it'll be just like the Army. Full of stories. You have to pick which ones to believe.'

A bell rang and the cell doors swung open. 'All out!' the screw screamed.

'I'm going to hate this, Kev.'

'Don't fight it, Prez, just go with it. Here's Tony.'

The Mario brother walked in front of them. He gave them a 'What the fuck is going on?' look. Winnie shot back his own 'What the fuck?' look. Anyone watching would have understood and laughed at the pantomime.

The guard barked orders. 'Back! Stop! Forward!'

'They all sound like Pommies and Scots to me, Prez.'

They entered the food hall and grabbed a plate each. Winnie stared at the food. It looked like his mother's cooking, overdone and under-flavoured.

Big Kev whispered, 'The inmates all know who we are.'

They sat at an empty table and Winnie noticed all eyes around the room were fixed on them. There were many bikies in there; some he recognised as customers from the shop. 'How are you going, Tony? What have you been up to?'

'Fuck-all, Prez. Those pigs said that you supply me and I sell it on. You haven't made any admissions, have you? They tried to trick me by saying you said you supplied me. I thought to myself, these cunts have no idea. This is a set-up. What happens now, Prez?'

'Fuck knows, Tony. What happens on television? I haven't been inside before. We wait and see what John Baker does. That's why we pay him.'

After ringing John Baker, Mimi contacted Brian. Brian sent Gina over to keep her company as soon as he could.

'Thanks for coming, Gina. I have no idea what this is about.'

Brian and Ocker sat in the office and tried to work out what was up. 'What a time for the Pig to be away, Ocker. Bernie can run the shop but I think I'll give her the day off and close the shop while we find out what this is all about.'

'What do you know, Brian?'

'Fuck-all at the moment. I'll call John Baker later. Mimi told me she rang him at around seven this morning so I bet he's at Long Bay. Is the shop clean?'

'As far as I know. Kev would have his toys hidden away somewhere. I know the combination of the safe so I'll stash what I can in my hidey-hole. Got anything you want disappeared?'

'Good thinking,' said Brian. 'I've got a few ounces of pure in my office — they're supposed to be picked up this morning but I cancelled. I want to get it out of this shop, but I don't fancy driving around with it in my car. Take it with you.'

'Do you think they'll hit us?'

'Just believe that they will, Ocker. We'd better have a Club meeting. I'll ring Little Tony.'

The Prez, Big Kev and Tony Mario paced up and down the exercise yard; the other crims kept a respectful distance. An announcement over the address system told the new-arrival prisoners to report to the gate. Winnie followed the guard to the common room, where the prison superintendent addressed them, flanked by a couple of arselickers.

'New arrivals, sir,' the guard said pompously.

'There are a few rules in here you should be aware of,' said the superintendent. 'No violence, no drugs, no swearing at the officers. It is up to your solicitor when he wants to see you. Visitors are allowed on weekends. You are allowed one monitored phone call a week. Your daily routines are posted on the noticeboard outside — familiarise yourselves with it. Any questions?'

'Yes: where can we buy a beer?' That cracked everyone up.

The superintendent walked over to the little bloke who'd spoken out of turn. 'We don't take kindly to smart cunts,' he roared. 'You follow me, son?' The little bloke took a small step backwards. 'Okay, dismissed.'

They lined up for their sandwiches at lunch then marched back to their cells to eat.

Tony Mario muttered something about it being worse than being back at school.

Kev laughed quietly. 'Yes, mate, it's much worse — it's fucking jail.' The boys chuckled.

At two o'clock the doors opened and they filed out to the courtyard, where they met Tony and the little bloke who'd wanted a beer. They let him talk.

'This the first time you fellas been in here? Do you want to know what the go is?'

'Keep going,' Kev said.

'One of you has to get the sweeper's job.'

'How do you get that?'

'Ask the guard. They try to give it to the hard-looking one. That's you.' He stared at Winnie. 'You get to have your choice of the food, you don't get locked up as long, and sometimes you get to talk to prisoners from the main wing in the kitchen.'

That got Winnie's attention. 'Why are you telling us this?'

'It's good to keep the big fellas onside.'

'At least you're honest.'

'No, I got done for car theft.' That raised another laugh. 'My name's Parker.'

'Number 5173,' the guard called. 'Phone call in the office.'

Winnie hardly recognised his number. Kev read it and said, 'That's you, Prez.'

'Hello, Peter, it's Mimi.' She tried to control her sobs.

'It's alright. It's alright.' He spoke gently.

'How is it?'

'Okay. How's Harry? Are you okay?'

'We're fine. I'm due to see the doctor tomorrow.'

'I hope I'm out before the birth. What did John Baker learn?'

'He's coming to see you today.'

'This is just all bullshit.' He was suddenly annoyed with himself, so he lowered his voice. 'Visiting day is Sunday, babe.'

'I'll be there, Peter.'

'Don't bring Harry.'

'Time!' the guard called.

'I love you,' he whispered. The guard walked him back to the exercise yard and Winnie decided to strike while he had a chance.

'What are the chances of getting the sweeper's job?'

'We're going to need one. Wilson goes to trial tomorrow. Go with him this evening and he can show you what to do.'

He rejoined the other boys and let them know the good news. 'I'm the new sweeper.'

'That was quick, Prez.'

'Right place, right time. John Baker will be here this arvo.'

When John Baker arrived he saw them together. 'What's going on, John?' asked Winnie. 'When can we get bail?'

John slumped backwards in his chair. 'You seem to have made some serious enemies, Peter. They're playing hardball. They won't tell me anything except that they're conducting ongoing enquiries. They have informants.'

'Why hardball?'

'I have no idea, but they appear very cocky. Someone wants you in here. So we wait while they gather their evidence. I'll prepare your bail applications and say you're involved in legitimate business, you and Kev in the bike shop and Tony with the pubs.'

'When will we go to court?'

'Monday morning.'

'What do you think our chances are?'

'No promises, Peter.'

Back in the yard the sweeper, Wilson, turned up.

'Are you Winifred? You're to come with me. You're the new sweeper.'

Winnie followed him past the checkpoints to the kitchen, where he saw Kero. Kero had been in jail nearly two years and obviously knew his way around. When Winnie went to pick up his dinner, Kero called out for him to come and have a chat. 'We have about five minutes.'

They went into the vegetable locker. Winnie'd always liked Kero; he would have made a good Miner. 'How are you handling it in here, Ken?'

'It's a piece of piss once you get used to it. Do you know why you're in here, Winnie?'

'No, tell me.'

'Twister.'

'Isn't he your mate?'

'Yeah, like fuck. He left me to carry the can for the hash deal. It was a fix from the start. Fucker put me in here and never visits or puts any money in my buy-up account — I get nothing.'

'I guess you don't like him any more?'

'He's the reason I'm in here, so what do you reckon?'

'What do you mean he's the reason you're in here? You got caught with the hash.'

'Yeah, you're right, Winnie. I was the sacrificial lamb. The hash is still out there in storage waiting to be sold and guess who has access to it? Fucking Twister. That's it, Winnie, you'd better go. I'll talk to you more tomorrow.'

* * *

On the Friday night the Miners turned up for the big meeting. Brian, Ocker, Little Tony and Boris talked beforehand. Brian spoke first. 'Until we find out what's happening we should all pull our heads in.'

'It's in all the newspapers,' said Tony.

Ocker spoke up. 'I reckon Brian should run the Club until the Prez gets out. Agreed?'

Everyone agreed. 'Boris, tell the boys to come in.'

The boys were worried about the busts. Brian addressed them.

'There's not much we can tell you except anybody in business should keep their heads down until we find out what's going on. I want our colours to be seen — no weakness — because you all know that other clubs are waiting to pounce if they think we're just a one-person Club. Now's the time for everyone to stand up, take no shit off anyone and keep in touch. Me and Ocker are going to Long Bay tomorrow.'

'Give them our regards, Brian.'

Winnie and Wilson pushed the food trolley together. Winnie's job was cleaning up after spills. He served massive portions to Kev and Tony because the boys were locked in their cells to eat so he reckoned they deserved a good feed. Winnie stayed out for an hour longer and ate in the common area.

He told Kev that Kero had confirmed that the two bent pigs worked with old man Gibbs. 'Kero reckons the pigs stored the hash and now's the time for it to hit the streets. We were in the way and I bet you Gibbs will move into our market.'

'But we haven't got much left.'

'They're not to know that, Kev. That vengeful Gibbs cunt has it in for us. I'll bet they're moving into the eastern suburbs already. It's going to be tough if they have the pigs onside.'

Kev grew quiet. He thought about Twister and Kero and the predicament Twister had left Kero in. 'Twister uses Kero, Gibbs uses him. If Twister doesn't understand that he must be brain-dead.'

Winnie's mind drifted off as he thought about the Gibbses' deviousness. Secretly he admired its pure evil and vindictiveness. He decided never to underestimate an enemy again.

Some time passed in silence before Kev sang out in a hoarse whisper, 'Sandy rang. She and Mimi are coming on Sunday. Maybe we can get word to Ocker and Brian to get on the case.'

'How's Sandy?'

'Okay, mate.'

Winnie hoped the Pig had heard what had happened. He'd know who the Gibbses had on their side.

Brian and Ocker rode their bikes to Long Bay and parked. A group of four guards on their way to shifts glanced at the bikes as they passed. Ocker said loudly, 'What sort of a man do you think would lock people up?'

A guard's head swung around. 'It will be a pleasure to see you in here one day, laddie.' The four guards laughed as one.

'Yeah, like fuck you will, you queer cunts.'

The guards kept laughing and walked on.

'That'll make it easy for us to get in.'

'Sorry, mate. I couldn't help myself.'

They came in through the visitors' entrance, filled in the forms and waited.

'Oh no, look who it is.' The Scotsman from the car park walked over and smiled.

'I told you I'd see you in here. Come with me. Empty your pockets and take your belts off and lock them in here.'

Winnie and Kev heard their numbers called. They went to the visitors' gate and waited for a guard to open it. Brian and Ocker sat at a table together, waiting. When they saw Winnie and Kev they stood and wrapped them in big hugs. 'I never thought I'd be so glad to see you two.' Brian's voice faltered. People at other tables stared at them.

'Come on, let's sit down.'

'What's going on, Prez?'

'Not too sure, Brian.' Winnie bent forward and retold the chat he'd had with Kero.

'Fuck, Prez, they aren't the only ones to have pigs onside.'

'We go for bail again on Monday. We'll find out more then. Our Pig called yet?'

'Not a boo.'

'How's everything going?'

'We shut the labs down, just in case,' said Ocker.

'We can't do that, mate; we have to keep supply up. Just be careful. If we lose our market it'll be hard getting it back. Gibbs probably thinks we'll shit ourselves and close shop, fuck him. I want to show this cunt what we're made of. Talk to Nestor, too — if there's going to be a hash shortage after the pigs sell theirs we should start hydroponic growing in a big way. Ocker, you're the technical man. Talk with Nestor and get it started. Are you still giving Squizzy's mate tips?'

'He's had six winners out of six so far, Prez.'

'The next time you tip him have a talk with Squizzy. Just get him to have a poke around to see if he can find out anything through his Minister. Brian, make sure Mimi and Sandy get looked after, even though we should be out of here on Monday. How's the Club?'

'We met Little Tony yesterday. Don't worry, Prez, we're staunch.'

'Time!' the guard yelled.

As Ocker and Brian emptied their locker the Scotsman walked by. Ocker said as he passed, 'I still can't understand why you do it.'

'It's just a job, laddie.'

Winnie pushed the food trolley towards the kitchen, hoping to continue his conversation with Kero. The coolroom door opened and Kero stuck his head out and motioned Winnie over. Winnie parked his trolley, walked in and Kero slammed the door. It was pitch black and for a half-second he thought the lights might come on. They didn't. He was struck simultaneously by two wooden vat stirrers. Over and over the blows to his head, arms and knees fell. He likely didn't feel the blood gushing from his nose and mouth. He fell to the floor unconscious, but still the beating continued. Kero opened the door.

'We're not finished yet.'

'Yes, you are, the food's ready. Get out.'

The assailants dropped their weapons and Kero closed the door on Winnie and collected his trolley. When the head cook called for the remand trolley boy and no one had seen him he notified the guards. They went straight to the cool room.

'This is a job for the nurse.'

Winnie was carted away and woke up in sick bay. A male nurse was swabbing blood from his face and neck.

He asked the nurse, 'How do I look?'

The nurse put a hand on his hip. 'Oh, real pretty.'

Winnie gritted his teeth; everything ached. 'Listen, you queer cunt, how bad is it?'

The queer's voice changed. 'It's not too bad. Possibly broken ribs and lots of blood and bruising. I'm keeping you here overnight. It's the rule, and head injuries stay for observation.'

Big Kev and Tony waited for word. Everyone had known about it within minutes, but details were invented. Kev asked the prisoner pulling the trolley, 'Have you heard about our mate?'

'Word is he had an accident in the kitchen. He's in the hospital.'

Big Kev was incredulous. 'What do you mean by accident?'

'That's enough!' the guard shouted.

'That's all I know, mate. The guards questioned everyone in the kitchen.' He lowered his voice. 'I think he got bashed.'

Kev kicked his door. The guard reacted immediately. 'Settle down. In your cell now.' Big Kev heard the cell door slam behind him then his guard said quietly, 'Your mate will be alright but no hot meal for you. Cool it, son, for your own good. You're going to be here a while.'

'You're trying to tell me something … Who are you?' The latch opened and Kev stared at the man's face and the row of combat ribbons on his uniform.

'Sergeant White! You were in the Regiment.'

The guard tipped his head a degree. He was a hero to his men in Vietnam.

'You were a good soldier, Kevin. I'm sorry to see you here.'

'I won't be here long.'

'You can't tell anyone about our connection — they'll move me if they know. I won't be corrupted but I'll keep an eye out. The word is you won't get bail. Lights out, soldier.' He closed the flap and through it Kev heard him walking away singing, 'Left, right, left, right.'

Kev remembered the parade ground and his time in the Army; it wasn't the worst time in his life.

When Winnie tried opening his eyes he found he could only see through a slit in one eye. The pain was constant and enormous; a doctor gave him shots. He lay almost motionless for a day and a half before he could extend his arms, which had been badly bruised when shielding the blows. He drifted in and out of consciousness.

The nurse rattled something and it startled Winnie. He woke up disoriented. The nurse leaned over Winnie and said, 'You're awake! Back in a minute.' Less than a minute later Kero Ken appeared at the door.

'Come to finish me, you dog cunt?'

'I had to let them in, Winnie. They're Irish cunts, muscle for the Gibbses. I should have warned you but then they would have done me. Yesterday I got my first visitor ever from the Tigers in two years and they told me to arrange it. I'm sorry it went so far, honest.'

'Fuck, Kero, they almost fucking killed me.'

'I know, Winnie, but you're alive and you're still going to need a friend in here.'

'I want to know who done it, and no bullshit.'

'I've got to go now. I'll get their names.'

The door closed. What to believe? he wondered as the door opened again.

The nurse held a cup of tea at an angle so Winnie could have a few sips.

Winnie tried to grasp the cup in his hands but he had difficulty bending his fingers. An old doctor smelling of stale grog examined him. 'Had an accident, eh, boy?' He pulled at Winnie's face roughly.

Winnie gritted his teeth trying to smother his pain, which escaped with every breath. When the doctor examined his ribs and traced the broken one Winnie almost howled — the most excruciating pain he'd ever felt.

'You'll be right, only one rib broken. Some tape and we can have you out of bed tomorrow, but first you have to get out of bed now.'

Winnie slid his legs off the bed onto the cold floor. He steadied himself while the doctor gave him a needle. The taping hurt and his sole consolation was returning the next afternoon to the remand centre. He shuffled along slowly, accompanied by a guard.

'Come on, we haven't got all day!'

Big Kev and Tony rushed to help. 'Come and sit down, Prez.' They tried to help him but Winnie wanted none of it.

'No, don't, I'll follow you.'

'What happened, Prez?'

He told them about Kero luring him into the coolroom.

Kev's face turned blank and his eyes burned. 'I'm going to get that cunt.'

'Hold on, Kev, that's not all of it. This morning Kero visited me in the sick bay. He had visitors yesterday from his club, and they told him to set it up for a few of Gibbs's boys to do the work, if you can believe him. He said he wants to help us; he's been fucked over by Twister and he's had enough. He reckoned in this case it was him or me and, in the end, he knew it had to be me.'

'Can we trust him?'

'I don't think we have a choice, Kev. Christ, that sun feels good.' Winnie stretched out. 'Fuck, I ache all over.'

'We're going to have to bash Twister, Prez.'

'Let's see what the Club does without us.'

Tony Mario had heard from his brother that young Gibbs was in the pub. He'd said to tell Kev that Gibbs has a bad limp. Kev had a good laugh.

'Don't make me laugh, Tony.' Winnie wrapped his arms around his ribs and tried hard not to laugh. 'Is everything under control with the pubs?'

'Bruno got a couple of cousins in to help and they fucked young Gibbs off out of the pub.'

Kev had had a call from Ocker, who already knew the score.

'How?'

'The nurse is a mate of a mate of his; he rang him when he finished his shift. He's meeting Little Tony and Boris this arvo.'

'As long as it doesn't fuck up our bail application.'

'I told them to wait to hear from us.'

Winnie heard his number called, for a phone call. He shuffled slowly to the gate.

'Peter, is that you? Your voice sounds strange.' Mimi was upset. 'What's going on?'

'Don't worry, babe, I'm alright. I just don't want you to visit on Sunday.'

'Why not?'

'We go to court on Monday for bail. Come to court.'

'Are you sure I'll see you in court?'

'No doubt. John will represent us. How's Harry?'

'I told him the truth. He doesn't quite understand, but I said you'll be home soon. Peter, I saw the doctor. I'm six weeks and I feel fine. Marge comes and helps me with Harry — she's a good lady.'

The guard called, 'Time!'

'I love you, Peter.'

Winnie slowly made his way back to the yard.

'Prez, when do you go to the sick bay next?'

'Don't know, Kev, why?'

'Ocker gave the nurse a block of hash for me. If you see him, get it, will ya?'

'The things I do for you, Kev.'

That night the nurse poured out two painkillers into a little paper cup and handed it over. 'Here, take these.' He slipped the hash to Winnie while he examined him in front of the guard.

Back in their cell Kev rolled a hash joint and exhaled the smoke outside his cell.

'You better hide that, Kev. The last thing we need is to get caught.'

Monday morning they dressed in civvies. The guards handcuffed them and loaded them into a van and took them to the court's holding cells, where John Baker waited. 'Jesus, Peter, you've had quite a beating. Are you okay?'

Winnie's face looked awful. 'It's nothing. What are our chances, John?'

'I don't really know much; the prosecutor won't tell me everything. I'll do my best, but there's something I don't quite get. You follow me?'

Winnie said, 'See?'

Ocker and Brian sat with Mimi and Sandy in the back of the court. They tried to prepare Mimi for how Winnie might look. Words could not do it justice, and she gasped when she saw him. The ferocity of the beating was obvious from his puffy, purpled eyes and nose. Bloody scabs covered his distended face and neck. Bloody, bandaged, and with his hands held before him, Winnie shuffled into court ahead of Kev and Tony. He searched for Mimi and beamed a smile.

The prosecutor started by reading the charges. 'The police are continuing with their investigations and oppose bail because there is serious concern for the safety of witnesses. The police allege trafficking of large amounts of drugs.'

The judge stared over his glasses. 'Mr Baker?'

'Your Honour, these men are totally innocent of these as yet undefined charges. One is a married man with a pregnant wife, one a Vietnam veteran, and the other a hotel proprietor. All work full-time, none has a record of any involvement with drugs, there are no prior convictions and, as you can see, Mr Winifred has suffered grievous harm in jail.'

The judge cleared his throat then looked at the prosecutor. 'Mr James, how long do you need to prepare the brief?'

'A month, your Honour.'

'In view of the seriousness of these charges, bail is denied.'

Mimi tried to remain composed but called out involuntarily, 'No!'

'What the fuck is going on, John?'

'I just don't know.'

Winnie lowered his voice. 'John, talk to Squizzy. Ask him to find out.'

Outside the courthouse, Brian, Sandy and Ocker comforted a distraught Mimi. She left with Sandy and the boys went to the clubhouse. That night all the boys turned up to be told the news and they weren't too happy. Little Tony and Brian sat and chatted. 'What do we do, Brian? We can't let Twister get away with this.'

'They're not, we're going to give it to them. We have to wait and do it good and proper. They'll go to ground and when they think it's safe they'll start riding again. There's no hurry, we'll get them.'

'I know where to find a few.'

'No, that'll just bring us trouble,' said Brian. 'There's got to be a plan.'

After the meeting some senior members sat around talking.

'How do you want to do this — shoot them?'

'No guns, just bats, Ocker. When do you see Squizzy?'

'Thursday — that's when we know what horse gets the boost. This Minister cunt is going to owe us.'

'How about giving me the tips?' Boris asked.

'You'll fucken tell everybody.'

'No I won't, mate, and I'll put money into the boys' legal fund for every winner. What do you think, Brian?'

'We have to keep this quiet, for the Prez's sake. This horse caper never happened; mum's the word.'

'Don't we even bet on them?' Boris's disappointment was obvious.

Ocker pulled out his portable phone and threw it on the table. 'I'm going to smuggle one of these in for them.'

'Will they work in there?'

Brian gave it thought. 'Only one way to find out — we can ring him.'

Ocker had it sussed. 'No! Imagine it going off in there. No, it's only for him to ring out.'

The prisoners' van raced them back through the remand centre gates and they went through the procedure of stripping. Kero Ken handed the reissued uniform over. 'We have to talk.'

'How?'

'Don't worry, I'll find a way.'

The boredom of the remand centre set in immediately. Tony Mario taught Kev chess and backgammon and Winnie read books on building.

461

Kero strolled into the common room pushing the library basket. Kev watched him. 'This cunt must have the run of the jail.'

Kero Ken joked with the guard.

'Now he's the librarian,' Kev said.

Winnie picked up a book. 'What do you have for me?'

'The names of the blokes who bashed you. Those two Irish boys are due for release in two weeks.'

He handed Winnie a piece of paper. 'I wrote down the name of their pub. Your boys'll find them.'

'What about us?'

'What I heard is that two blokes signed statements claiming they bought drugs off you.'

'Who are they?'

'I don't know. I'll find out.'

The guard turned and stared at them. 'Come on, you two.'

Kero held a book up. 'Yeah, that's the book for builders.'

The guard stood behind Winnie and looked at the cover: a DIY builder's manual.

'How long does it take to select a book?'

'Finished, boss.' Kero pushed his basket away.

Winnie opened the note and read the names: Kieran Foley and James Clout, Three Weeds, Rozelle. Winnie had no recollection of their faces but he smiled in anticipation of their homecoming party. While the boys played chess, Winnie filled them in.

The guard called out a number. 'Phone!'

'That's me.' Tony went off with a guard but that night at lockdown had still not returned.

In the morning Kev's Vietnam sergeant mate was on duty, and Kev asked him about Tony.

'I'll find out for you, soldier.'

Next morning, while Kev ate his porridge, true to his word the sergeant walked by and told him quietly, 'He's been sent to Parramatta Jail.'

'Can they do that?'

'You're prisoners, remember?'

Kev told Winnie what the sergeant had said. 'What do you think, Prez — divide and rule?'

'He won't talk, mate.'

A guard collected Winnie and took him off to sick bay.

The nurse checked his stitches. 'Yes, it's time for them to come out.' He whispered, 'I have something from your mate,' and dropped a phone into Winnie's sling.

'Fuck, how do I use it?'

'There's a note with it. If you get caught don't mention me.'

'You just do your job.'

'It seems simple enough, Kev. Ocker says it needs to be charged every week.'

'I can't wait to try it, Prez.'

Seven o'clock that night Winnie dialled Ocker and waited.

'Good, it worked, Prez. Get it to the nurse to recharge it.'

'You don't know how hard that is, mate. Every week? It's too big. Get pen and paper and write these names down. They're the blokes who bashed me for old man Gibbs. They get out in two weeks.'

'We'll look after them, Prez.'

'They moved Tony to Parramatta. Go and see him, find out what they're trying to do, Ocker. Speak to Squizzy yet?'

'Thursday, mate.'

'You have to put a bit of pressure on him. The Minister owes us by now.'

'I will, Prez.'

'What does the Club think of me getting flogged?'

'Everybody got the shits. They want to hit the Tigers.'

'If they do, make sure they do it right. Give Brian and Little Tony those names.'

'What's it really like in there, Prez?'

'We get fed, we get told when to go to bed, and we get told when to get up. It's easy. It's probably harder for Mimi and Harry, Sandy and you blokes. There are some different cunts in here but, mate, I'll tell you, I know where I'd like to be. Make sure you see Squizzy.'

'I will, Prez. Can I talk to Kev?'

Winnie passed the phone over to Kev.

'Hello little fella, orright?'

'Good, mate, I miss you.'

'Don't worry, mate, we'll be out soon.'

'Tell the Prez no one has the number except me. Hide it well.'

'I'll tell him. There are fuck-all places to hide a phone, though. Seeya.'

In the yard Parker walked up and down with them. He nodded at a group of Asians playing cards. 'What do you think of the slope-heads, boys?'

Every now and then, one threw himself on the ground and did a set of push-ups.

'That's what they do when they lose. I heard you blokes are in for trafficking.'

'What's that?' Winnie stared at him.

'I'm only repeating what I heard.' Silence. He lowered his voice. 'That your Club manufactures and supplies most of the gas in Sydney.' More silence.

'You shouldn't believe everything you hear,' said Big Kev. 'Now why don't you just fuck off somewhere else?' Parker quickly walked away. 'I don't trust that cunt; he knows everybody and thinks he knows everything. So that's what they're saying about us.'

'Remember what Kero said — they have two informants against us. Everything'll come out eventually, Kev; no use banging our heads against the wall until we know. Let's play chess.'

Ocker worked in his spray booth on a petrol tank. He looked up and saw Brian pointing at his watch. He finished spraying and joined Brian and Squizzy. 'I thought we were going to meet in the pub.'

'I know, Ocker, but the Minister is going to Melbourne for the Cup.'

'Is that all you're here for, tips?'

'Listen to him, Ocker.'

'I spoke to the Minister's chief of staff. His mate works in the Attorney-General's office. He's looking into it.'

Ocker looked dismayed. 'Is that fucking all you can tell us?'

'Hold on, Ocker.'

'Shut up, Brian. Squizzy, we've been friends a long time. The Prez helped you out while you were in university. We give you solid gold tips that make you look good with your fucking Minister, and I'm sure he doesn't think you pull them out of the form guide with a pin. We're relying on you to talk to the fucking Minister and not some fucking chief of staff. Lean on the cunt. It's not much for him to find out. Otherwise I might let the papers know about his run of good luck.'

Squizzy paled. He pushed his rimless glasses back onto his forehead and rubbed his eyes. 'Fuck, Ocker, you wouldn't do that.'

'I'll do whatever I have to do to get them out, mate.'

'Well giving the papers that story would ruin him and then we'd all be fucked.'

'Here's your tip in the Melbourne Cup: number seven, and when it wins, you tell him we need a fucking white knight.'

After promising to help, Squizzy left.

'You wouldn't go to the press would you, Ocker?'

'No, but he's not to know that. I'm going to visit Tony Mario this afternoon to find out why he was moved to Parramatta. The Prez also has a job for you and Little Tony. I have the names of the blokes who bashed him — they get out in a couple of weeks. Wait until we see Little Tony and I'll give you both the drum at the same time.'

Ocker was denied a visitor's pass, no reason given. He went straight to see John Baker. 'How come Tony Mario was moved?'

'He rang me this morning. It's one of their games — they think by separating them he'll roll over.'

'He won't.'

'I know that. We have to wait until they finish their brief.'

'When can they apply for bail again?'

'I'm working on it. Maybe a month.'

'Fuck me!' Ocker was shocked. 'This is a set-up.'

'We can't prove that.'

Ocker stood. 'We will, mate.'

Chapter 38

On Friday night — meeting night — tension filled the clubhouse. Both Chapters turned up. Brian took over.

'We're hitting the Tigers tonight. Nestor knows they're meeting at the Callan Park Hotel. It's perfect — small pub, street parking. No colours and no guns. We go by car.'

Little Tony went ahead to check how many Tigers were inside. He called Ocker's portable phone to let him know. The Miners drove up to the front of the pub and left their drivers double-parked. Suddenly thirty baseball-bat-wielding Miners charged into the Tigers, who didn't stand a chance. They tried to retreat further into the pub and threw chairs to defend themselves but in five minutes all of them lay on the floor, moaning or unconscious. It was Twister's lucky night — he was elsewhere. The boys piled into the waiting cars. As a last act of bastardry Nestor kicked over one of their bikes and opened the petrol cap, lit a box of matches then casually tossed it under the bike. As they drove off, the glow from the explosion was reflected in all the shop windows. Nestor said to the blokes in the car, 'That'll teach them to bash our Prez.'

Back at the clubhouse the boys got on the piss. Brian sat down with Ocker, Little Tony and Boris.

'That was a good job tonight, boys. Pity about Twister not being there. The Prez told me to give these names to you and Brian.'

Little Tony studied the paper. 'I've been thinking. You two have enough on your plate now. Why don't me and Boris look after this? You won't even know till after it's done. If they take you in for questioning you'll have no problems — that's if they make a connection. Kieran Foley and James Clout,' Little Tony read slowly, 'rest in peace.'

* * *

Kev stepped away from the window. 'Let's hire a television, Prez. It looks like we're going to be in here a while. What are you reading?'

Winnie showed him the cover of the book. 'I want to have our house built before the baby arrives. There are a lot of good ideas in here.'

'Are you building a castle?'

'No, just a nice home and a cosy flat for you and Sandy when you visit.'

Kev rolled a hash joint. A full moon rose over Long Bay.

'Why would they put a prison in such a beautiful spot?'

'Torture, Kev, pure torture. Don't look at it. That must be good shit, you're going all sentimental on me.'

'Top quality Afghani hash.' Eyes glazed, Kev climbed down. 'You know, Prez, instead of giving the phone back we should try to hide it in the rented television. I'll look after getting it charged, don't worry. I'll just strap it to my leg and wait until my Vietnam mate's on duty.'

Late in the afternoon they were let out to use the phone. 'Keep it short!' the guard called. 'One minute each.'

Winnie called home and Harry answered. 'Dad! When are you coming home?'

'Soon, mate. How's school?'

'Real good.'

'Is Mimi there?'

'She's in the shower.'

'Okay, you take care of her.'

'I will, Dad.'

'Tell her I rang.'

'I love you.'

'Time!' the guard called.

Winnie went out to the yard and a moment later Kev followed. 'Fuck, a minute goes quick. Sandy said she'd ring Mimi and meet to visit on Sunday. Come on, Prez, let's rent that television. The buy-up shop's open.'

Kev got the set and took it back. He pried one corner open and found room for the portable phone. They played chess in the common room and Kero came in pushing the basket loaded with books.

'Twister rang. He wants a truce. It's bringing too much heat.'

'What are you talking about, Kero?'

'Your boys gave it to the Tigers in a pub on Friday night. They burnt seven bikes.'

Winnie smiled. Kero was not real impressed. 'Some of those blokes are mates. The only one I wanted you to bash was Twister and your blokes missed him. Now, is there going to be a truce?'

'I'll talk to the Club, Kero. It'll be alright, trust me. But you can tell Twister this: if the Tigers move into our market he won't know what hit him.'

On Sunday afternoon inmates waited for their visitors. There wasn't much privacy. At the sight of Mimi, shivers shot up Winnie's spine. His face still looked awful. The bloody bruises had given way to mottled purple and yellow patches. He hugged her while she cried then he kissed away her tears. They held hands and he gently rubbed her bulging stomach.

'How's our baby?'

'Growing, just like Harry. How is it in here?'

'Monotonous. I play chess with Kev, the food's shit and I'm reading up on water tanks and solar energy. I think we could do it ourselves. I try to keep busy so I don't think too much about you.'

'That bashing at a pub on Friday night looked very bad on television. Someone said it was the Miners.'

'I knew nothing about it, Mimi. I can't be responsible if I'm in here, can I?'

'I spoke to Murray at John Baker's office. If he can't get you bail, nobody can.'

'I hope you're right, baby. Did Harry tell you I rang?'

'Yes. He thinks he's man of the house now.'

He slid his hand up her dress and rubbed her. 'I miss you a lot, baby.'

Mimi blushed and kissed him. 'I love you so much.'

The portable phone kept them up to date. Ocker told Winnie that the two Irish boys, Kieran Foley and James Clout, on their first night out, went to their old pub, the Three Weeds in Rozelle, and someone shot them as they left at closing time — no witnesses. A story in the newspaper said they were hard men, allegedly hiding out in Australia.

'I gave Squizzy the winner of the Cup. The Minister'd better deliver when it wins.'

'Let's wait to see if it wins. I don't want to get my hopes up.'

'Don't worry Prez, we haven't missed on a tip yet.'

'I spoke to John Baker about Tony Mario. Apparently the pigs are trying to get him to roll over on you and Kev.'

'No fucking chance.'

'That's what I said, Prez.'

Kev and Winnie were playing chess when they heard the sound of Kero's wicker basket. Kero wasn't smiling. 'I thought you said there'd be a truce. Twister thinks I'm bullshitting him.'

'Slow down, Kero, what are you talking about?'

'Kieran Foley and James Clout were killed yesterday.' Winnie feigned surprise. 'Twister is shitting himself; he thinks he'll be next. That old cunt Gibbs is probably winding him up. He's capable of anything.'

'Tell him from me, the war is over, and he's okay as long as they don't try taking our business. I want to get out of here. We don't need any more drama or headlines. Now, do you have the names of the informants?'

'No, nothing yet, Winnie. I'll find out. It takes time. I brought another book on design ideas for you; you can't read too many. Melbourne Cup's tomorrow — having a bet?'

'I don't bet.'

'Neither did I till I came in here. It's a business. How do you think I can get around?' he whispered. 'I take bets off everyone.'

'Guards too?'

'Fucken oath, mate. I do alright.'

'Now I know why you like it in here.'

'When I get out of here I'm buying a farm and getting away.'

'Good luck, Kero.'

Winnie walked up and down in the yard with Big Kev. 'Did you know that Kero's the SP bookie in here?'

Kev laughed. 'That's what I heard.'

'Even the guards?'

'Yep.' Kev laughed.

'This place runs on favours. Do you think we should tell Kero about the hot tip?'

'No, fuck him, Prez. I'll tell my old Army mate it's a good bet, but no one else.'

Everyone was happy when their horse won the Cup. Everyone but Squizzy. It meant he had to front the Minister on his return from Melbourne. He turned up at the shop the next day.

'Well, Squizzy, it won. What's the story?'

Brian put up his hand. 'Hold on, Ocker. Did you speak to him, Squizzy?'

'Yes, Brian. I wasn't sure what to say, so I just told him the truth: I went to school with two blokes who worked hard, a Vietnam vet and his married partner who own a successful motorcycle shop. I mentioned Mimi's pregnancy and then I told him what the charges were. I said they can't get bail because the prosecutor won't release the names of the informants and that they'd been denied natural justice.'

'What did he say?'

'He asked for their names, then he told me not to put anything in writing.'

Ocker put his arm around Squizzy's shoulder. 'You done good, mate, real good. You never mentioned about me spilling me guts to the newspapers?'

'Don't be silly, mate.'

'Good. Come on, I'm going to give you the biggest line.'

The boys were hopeful, but three weeks dragged by very slowly. They kept in touch with Ocker and got news by phone.

A not-too-confident John Baker arranged a meeting to go over their next hearing. 'It's a different judge this time — that might help us. I don't know yet if the director of prosecutions has any new evidence. We'll have to wait until Monday.'

'Will Tony Mario be there?'

'Of course. You're all charged together.'

Winnie decided over the weekend to give the portable phone to Kero Ken, on the condition that they'd get it back if they were denied bail. Kero was excited.

'Here's the charger. Now remember, only ring out.'

Kero put it in his basket. 'Good luck, boys.'

On Monday morning they were woken early for their day in court. Kev's Army mate took them down to the van. 'Good luck, soldier.'

Big Kev just winked and they shook hands.

At court they met Tony Mario in the holding cells.

'How are you, Tony?'

'Good, Prez. I've been waiting for today.'

'So have we, mate.'

When their names were called, the policeman led them up into the courtroom and into the dock. Mimi, Sandy, Gina, Brian and Ocker sat with others packing the courtroom. John Baker stood and appealed for bail. The prosecutor reared up in opposition. 'Your honour, we strongly oppose the granting of bail.'

John continued. 'Your Honour, my learned friend at a previous bail application said they have more evidence. They say it is coming but I see none. I ask you to grant these men bail today so they can prepare their defence and get on with their lives.'

The judge looked the prosecutor and the defendants up and down. 'Mr Baker, I see no reason to keep these men locked up. Bail is granted and set at fifty thousand dollars each, with a similar surety.'

Mimi and Sandy hugged. Ocker held up a bag containing the cash, and after the paperwork had been taken care of, the three were freed. Winnie kissed Mimi; tears welled up in her eyes, and she held his hand tightly. Winnie thanked John for all his work, though it might have had something to do with Squizzy and his Minister. 'It's my pleasure, Peter. Let's sit down next week.'

Chapter 39

When they arrived home Mimi opened the door to reveal little Harry shyly holding a cake.

Winnie felt like crying. He kissed Harry. 'Come on, mate, let's cut it. I haven't had cake in ages.'

Later, lying in bed together, Winnie gently stroked Mimi's stomach. 'I plan on finishing our new house before the baby's born. There was plenty of time in jail to study and now I know exactly what I want.'

'What about what I want?'

'I'm not going ahead on anything until you've seen the plans. I'll show you in the morning. Anyway, most of the things I want are underground or in the roof.'

'Thanks, Peter.'

'Do we know if it's a boy or a girl?'

'No, and I don't want to know. Does it matter?'

'The only thing that matters is that you're both healthy.'

When Winnie started his bike the next morning, Mimi felt good for him as she listened to his Harley thumping. 'He's home,' she said out loud.

Winnie rode to the shop and pulled up next to Kev, who was bent over his bike adjusting a carburettor.

'I knew you'd be here today,' said Winnie. 'Seems like an age, doesn't it?'

Ocker shouted out to them, 'About time you blokes came to work!'

'Get fucked.'

They hugged.

'Where's Brian?'

'Out the front with Bernie. We never expected you today. Look who's here, Brian.'

Bernie went watery as she hugged them both.

'We didn't want to hang around yesterday, Prez. You were all Mimi's.'

'Thanks, mate. Now who put up the bail?'

'Ocker.'

'Thanks, mate. I'll fix you up for my share.'

'There's no rush. What do you think about portable phones now, Prez?'

'They're the go, Ocker. I gave it to Kero Ken. He's my ears; he'll find out who they have as witnesses. We can't very well go and visit him. Did the Pig ever ring us?'

'No, Prez.'

'He'll find out soon enough. How's the shop been going?'

Brian was very excited about the shop. 'Our sales have been increasing each month. All that free advertising in the newspaper kept people coming. I saved the clippings.'

Winnie looked through all the sensational news stories. 'Fuck, they sure laid it on thick. Our Club and this shop got a lot of ink. You'd think we sell drugs across the counter right here.'

'They have no idea, Prez.'

'Meanwhile, the Tigers are selling hash and you know where it comes from? The shipment Kero got hung for. That's why he's helping us. That Twister is a real cunt.'

'Too right he is.'

'Brian, did Nestor set up the hydroponics yet?

'He did. Wait until you see it, Prez. He'll get three crops a year if everything goes to plan. He rented an old bottling factory in St Peters.'

'Who's working with him?'

'Doc and his nephew, Nick.'

'That's good. Is everybody getting an earn?' Brian nodded. 'What about the speed?'

'Like clockwork, Prez. We still buy the pseudo off Rastus and we haven't touched our supply yet. I spoke to Bruno Mario about getting cocaine. He says the eastern suburbs crowd prefer coke and they can afford to pay for it.'

'Where would we get it?'

'Have you ever had it, Prez?'

'No. You, Kev?'

'A couple of times. It doesn't do anything for me.'

'Do you want to try some, Prez?'

'Sure, I'll try it.' Brian poured out a small mound and divvied it into six lines with a credit card. 'You pay big money for this.'

'How much?'

'Two hundred a gram.'

'Fuck, that's a bit rich.'

'Here, Prez.' Brian passed a rolled note. 'Have them both.' Winnie snorted both lines. 'They say the first time you have it is the best.'

Winnie leaned back. 'What's it supposed to do to you?'

'Make you feel good.'

'But I already felt good.' That got a laugh.

A steady stream of members turned up at the shop to welcome Winnie and Kev back. Even Little Tony and his Southside members rode over.

'It's getting a little crowded here, Kev. We should go to the clubhouse.'

'We won't get home tonight, Prez.'

'You're right. I'm ringing Mimi.' The phone rang and rang until at last Mimi picked up. 'Hello, babe.'

Mimi heard laughing and men's voices in the background. 'Are you at a party?'

'No, at the shop.'

'You're going to party though, aren't you?'

'Looks like it.'

'Will I see you tomorrow?'

'Don't get the shits.'

'I'm not. It's alright, have fun. I was half expecting it. I love you.'

Winnie smiled as he hung up. 'Let's go for a ride and a party at the clubhouse.' The boys cheered.

Boris looked at Winnie's scarred face. 'The blokes responsible paid for that, Prez.'

'Are you growing, Boris?'

Little Tony sang out, 'It's all the fucking doughnuts he eats. You want a line of coke, Prez?'

'No, thanks. I had some before.'

'You need a top-up?'

Winnie remembered what Brian had said about cocaine — the first line is the best and it never gets better, no matter how much you snort. He declined.

Bernie stayed behind to look after the shop as Winnie and Kev led the ride to the clubhouse. A banner welcomed them home. Even though it was the middle of the day, someone cranked up the music and the booze started flowing. Big Kev toked on a fat joint and shared it with Ocker. Nestor tried to tell Winnie about the hydroponic set-up but the music was too loud.

'Don't worry, Prez, you can come and see it one day.'

Winnie just nodded. 'Fuck, Nestor, I'm feeling terrible.' He started to sweat and feel dizzy and bolted for the toilet. When he closed the door he spewed his heart up. He washed his face in cold water and suddenly felt much better. He walked outside and joined Nestor. 'I don't think cocaine likes me, mate.'

'Are you alright, Prez?'

'I am now, mate. I had to spew.'

'It's that cocaine, Prez — sell it but don't use it. It fucks people up. There might be good money in it but it's a shit drug.'

Squizzy turned up and gave Winnie a long hug. 'I heard you were out. I rang the shop and they told me you were here. I'm sorry you were in so long.'

'Did the Minister ever say anything to you?'

'Nothing, Prez. I wonder if he had anything to do with getting bail, but I'm too scared to ask.'

'No, don't, Squizzy. Come on and have a drink with me.'

'Ocker told me he organised some party girls. You want one, Prez?'

'No, Squizzy, just being here with the boys is enough for me.'

Winnie nabbed Little Tony. 'Come outside, Tony. Let's talk about cocaine. How much can you get?'

'Not much, Prez. I get an ounce now and then off this airline steward.'

'That's no good, mate.'

'I know, Prez. I could get rid of heaps of it if I had it.'

'I'll look into getting a supply.'

'Where from?'

'I don't know yet.'

'Be careful, Prez. There's a lot of shit around. They cut it too much, but you can test it.'

'How?'

'Kits from the States are foolproof. You put coke in a vial with some chemical in it, shake it and the coke turns blue and the rest sinks to the bottom. A colour scale tells you the percentage of coke.'

'I'll keep that in mind.'

* * *

475

Winnie hadn't seen Tony Mario for a week so he decided to go over with Kev and have a drink in the pub before they all went to see John Baker. The pub was fully renovated with new carpets, lighting, chairs and tables — all very up-market. He and Mario admired the empty pub. 'Any sign of the Gibbses?' asked Winnie.

'Not since the Irish left town.'

'How's business?'

'It's been packed. It's real trendy now. Wait until the gaming machine laws come in. That's when we'll make a motza. Here's Bruno. He wants to show you the books.'

'Good to see you, Winnie, Kev.' Bruno plonked down the books on the table and opened them up. 'We're making a profit but we have to repay the investors first. You're entitled to be paid now, Winnie, if you need it.'

'No, mate, I can wait.'

'This is the first pub we renovated. Part of the cash flow will go towards the other two pubs and they definitely need work.'

'Can we just buy the other investors out?'

'I can ask.'

'It'd be better for us. We'd have the control then. Keep me informed.'

Winnie checked his watch, and the three of them went to their meeting with John Baker.

'Right, John, what's the go?'

'We still don't know yet. We have to wait for the committal hearing to see what evidence they have. Do you know what they might have on any of you?'

'Whatever it is is bullshit.'

'They have to prove it. That's all I can tell you, boys. There's no date set down for it yet.'

Winnie dropped Tony off and headed back to the shop with Kev.

'You're really into the pubs, Prez.'

'It's legal, Kev, that's why.' They pulled into the shop's parking lot and Ocker rushed out to tell them that the Pig had rung.

'About fucking time. What did he say?'

'He wants to talk. Here's a number.'

The Pig answered after half a ring. 'Winnie, how are you?'

'In trouble.' The Pig laughed. 'It's not fucking funny.'

'I know, mate, we need to talk. What about tomorrow? You can buy me lunch. Do you remember Fritz's? See you around one o'clock.'

The Pig sat in his usual seat. 'Winnie. Good to see you.'

'Have you found out what's happening to us?'

'I only got back this week. Old man Gibbs has Quirk and Brown in his pocket.'

'They're the two who are investigating us.'

'That's what I mean. They work for Gibbs.'

'How can we get around that?' asked Winnie.

'We have to discredit their evidence. Is there a way of you finding out who their witnesses are?'

'That's your job, isn't it?'

'No, I have a mate in Internal Affairs. It's his job. It's going to cost you.'

'How much?'

'Five grand.'

Winnie raised his voice. 'Fuck!'

'Settle down. Either we do it my way or not at all.'

'What have we been paying you for?'

'I can't cover all angles,' said the Pig. 'You're lucky you know me or I guarantee the three of you would get five years each.'

'We don't have much choice then, do we?'

'The money has to be up-front.'

'How good is your mate?' asked Winnie.

'Don't worry about that.'

'How come you never knew about the hash being knocked off by Gibbs and your mates?'

'There were only rumours. They kept it hidden for two years. I was out of the loop.'

Their meals arrived. 'This'd be better than prison food, eh, Winnie?' Winnie just glared. 'You had some strife in there. It's a bit of a coincidence that the two blokes who did you over had an accident when they got of jail.'

'I have a perfect alibi. Besides, they were involved with the IRA. The papers said so.'

'Do you believe everything you read?'

'I don't give a fuck.'

'I just want to keep you out of Long Bay.'

'You only want your money.'

The Pig wiped his mouth with his napkin. 'But you knew that from the start. I still have a soft spot for you, Winnie. So when can I get the money? Sooner I get it, the quicker Internal Affairs is onto it.'

'How about tomorrow?'

'Where? We have to be careful. Let's make it out in Hornsby, the pub opposite the railway station. Do you know it?'

'Won't be hard to find.'

'I hear you got married — my invitation must've got lost in the post. I'm disappointed, Winnie. I've known you since you were a kid.'

'We're not that close.'

One month after their meeting a headline in the *Sydney Morning Herald* screamed: 'Police Corruption'. The report began: 'Internal Affairs suspend two Sydney CIB detectives over alleged links to Sydney underworld figures.'

John Baker called Winnie early in the morning on his portable phone. 'Have you seen the newspaper?'

'I'm reading it now — do you know who it is?'

'It's our friends Quirk and Brown. It's too early to get excited but this is good news.'

'I know, John. Let's just see how it plays out. Seeya, mate.'

Winnie rang Big Kev and Tony Mario and filled them in. Winnie thought about the Pig — one thing about him, he was true to his word.

Mimi was folding clothes in the laundry. Winnie slipped his arms around her. 'That's nice,' she said.

Up close to her, he whispered in her ear, 'I just got some good news.'

Mimi backed into him and rubbed her bum against him. 'Go on.'

'Internal Affairs are investigating Quirk and Brown. You know what that means?'

Winnie was grinning from ear to ear and Mimi turned to him smiling as he reached for her breasts and felt their plumpness. Mimi stepped out of her undies and leaned on the washing machine. Winnie dropped his jeans to the floor and gently slid into her. It was a first for the laundry.

The next weekend they drove down in the Ford Customline to see the progress on their house. Toothpick had given them the car as a wedding present. Winnie glanced in the rear-view mirror and watched Harry playing in the back seat. It made him happy and sad at the same time — happy that Harry felt secure but sad because he'd had such a short time with his mother, and no father in his early years. Winnie had a lot to make up for.

'What are you thinking about, Peter?'

'Just wondering if the house will be finished before the baby arrives.'

The builder waited on-site with the plans. 'It's a big house, Winnie. I've got all my boys trying to get it finished on time.'

'I know, Dave. Just take your time. I don't want any fuck-ups. Better to be late a few weeks than have problems later, eh?'

At the shop the Miners had their annual Open Day, and during the excitement Kero Ken rang. 'Hello, Winnie, it's Kero. Do you have a pen handy? I have the names.'

'Fuck, Kero, I paid for these names a month ago.' Winnie listened as Kero recited the names: Col Sheppard and Cyril Bronski.

'Sheppard claims to have bought off Tony Mario. The other bloke is just some junkie cunt.'

'Do you know where we can find them?'

'I know Sheppard drinks at the Horse and Cart.'

'That's the Marios' pub.'

'Yeah, I know.'

'You've done well, Kero. Look me up when you get out. I owe you.'

'Kero Ken gave me the names of the dogs.' He showed Kev the names. 'Do you know them, Kev?'

Kev thought about it. He'd never heard either name before.

'Tony Mario will know Sheppard, if he's a regular.'

'How will we deal with it, Prez?'

'I want to talk to the Pig first.'

Brian walked around in the Open Day crowd, sniffling. 'Look at this crowd, Prez.'

Winnie wasn't sure why, but he didn't tell Brian about Kero's call.

'Tell me, Kev, have you noticed Brian is always sniffling these days? How much coke does he snort, do you reckon?'

'Haven't noticed, Prez, but I'll keep an eye out from now on.'

Rastus and Spike arrived from Melbourne and greeted Kev and Winnie warmly.

'You boys have been in a bit of trouble, I hear.' Rastus stared at Bernie moving back and forth.

Spike whispered to Kev, 'Bernie's all he talked about on the plane.'

'Rastus, you can have her if she wants you.'

'I'm going to try.'

Kev laughed at him.

'Come on out to the workshop, mate. It's private.'

Ocker opened the fridge. 'Here are the drinks, boys. Take what you want. I'm going out the front.'

'Do you want some barbecued sausages?'

Ocker smiled. 'No mate.' He rubbed his cock. 'There are girlies out there that I want to slip the sausage into.'

The boys laughed.

'Ocker never changes. He's still a dirty little cunt.'

'A dirty rich little cunt now, Spike. His portable phone investment is making him millions.'

'Goodonya, Ocker.'

'So Rastus, what's the story in Melbourne?'

'Good, mate, better than here.'

Winnie told him enough, but not everything. Rastus and Spike listened carefully. Rastus leaned back in his chair and puffed on his cigar.

'An old Italian friend reckoned old man Gibbs should have tried to work with you.'

'He did try, but I told him to get fucked. I didn't like him. You don't work *with* Gibbs, you work *for* him.'

'That's no good, mate.'

'Now we're just waiting for the committal hearing.'

'How do you feel?'

'We'll be right.'

Big Kev and Spike wandered off to talk bikes.

'How's business, Winnie?' Rastus asked.

'No hash left.'

'Yeah, I know. I buy it off some Tigers — they're the only ones with any. They don't know it's me buying, otherwise they'd jack up the price. Besides, I don't like doing business with them either.'

'What about cocaine? Do you have much to do with it?'

'It's expensive. I can get good quality and the price depends on how much you want. A Russian is a hundred grand.'

'Alright, Rastus, what's a Russian?'

'A kilogram of the best, a KGB. Sell it in grams and see how it goes. Just don't cut it and you'll do alright. I'll take the money when I go back and I'll send it up the usual way. A bloke I know brought a shitload in but doesn't know anyone. He's my mate now.'

'When are you going back?'

'Tomorrow. Ocker's taking me out tonight for a look at some girls.'

'On your way to the airport, drop in to my place and pick up the money.'

'I'm going to find Bernie,' Rastus said.

'You won't get her.'

A few days later Winnie's parcel came by interstate truck. He waited until the shop closed before calling the boys together. 'I think we're onto another good earn. This is a kilo of top-quality coke from our mates in Melbourne. It cost us under $100,000 so we ask $200 a gram and we'll do alright.'

'We better see how good it is.'

Winnie opened it and Brian flipped open his knife and dipped into it. 'It's nice and rocky, Prez, a good sign — no filler. But the best test is to taste it.' He rolled up a note and he and Ocker snorted a line. 'That's good, Prez; we have another good product.'

'Who'll buy it? I think it's too expensive to sell out here.'

'Tony Mario says the Eastern suburbs are the go.'

'What about the Rat, Prez?'

'Can you talk to him, Ocker?'

'Now I've paid for this we'll split the proceeds four ways.'

Brian rewrapped the parcel. 'I'll weigh up the ounces, Prez.'

'Bring a couple in for Tony Mario. We're meeting tomorrow.'

Chapter 40

Winnie arranged a meeting with the Pig near a bridge on the Georges River. The Pig arrived dressed for fishing. He brought out a fishing rod and tackle box from his car and walked over to Winnie.

'It's a good spot this. I fish here a lot. Now, my mate, this is what you have to do. Quirk and Brown were suspended for their links to Gibbs, and are still under investigation. Guess who's taking over the case against you? That would be me.'

'So it's over?'

'No, the informants made statements; I can't do anything about that. You have to persuade Sheppard not to turn up in court. Bronski can appear, because he's a scattered concept at the best of times. I'll make sure he has a good taste of something before he appears, then John Baker can tear him apart in court.'

'Will it be that easy?'

'That easy.' The Pig cast his baitless line into the river. 'There's no other evidence; the judge will have no choice but to knock it on the head. I'll see you in court, Winnie. I'm going fishing. Remember that Sheppard has to disappear before we can serve him a summons. If he doesn't turn up he's in strife and we're off the hook.'

Winnie drove straight to the pub to find Tony Mario and talk about Sheppard. He knew it wasn't as simple as just knocking him — that that could come back to haunt them. Winnie explained the plan to Tony.

'If the cunt moves over to West Australia and ignores the summons to appear in court, he's subject to arrest and whatever he had as evidence won't count.'

'Let me and Bruno look after this one. We know Sheppard. He'll listen to reason.'

'Good. Now Tony, you asked about cocaine — well, I brought you a sample. Do you know how much of a market there is for good quality?'

Tony poured some out and had a line. 'That's top notch stuff. I can sell whatever you have, no worries. You want some, Prez?'

'None for me, mate.'

'You don't like it, Winnie?'

'I spewed when I had it.'

Tony sniffed another line then dipped his finger into the residue and wiped it on his lips and gums. He waited a few moments and let the numbing feeling sink in. 'Top grade. I'll let my boys know.'

The day of the committal hearing Mimi was past her due date by three days. She was having a hard time but was determined to attend. Tony Mario, John Baker, Sandy and Big Kev waited outside for Winnie and Mimi. Winnie helped Mimi out of the car.

John Baker gathered his troops. 'This is it, boys, let's go.'

John went after the junkie, who kept changing his story and admitted in the end that he only said what the police told him to say. Of course Sheppard never turned up and the judge held him in contempt of court in his absence. The Pig was right: the case was tossed out of court and all charges were dropped. The boys were so stunned at their victory that they just shook hands with John and each other and went their separate ways, promising to get together later to celebrate properly.

Mimi was so excited that she began a long labour that ended that night when Lucy Frances was born. Both mother and daughter were healthy. Winnie rang Mimi's mother with the good news.

'I thought she'd have a girl. We'll come over to see them tomorrow morning. Lucy Frances is my mother's name. Tell Mimi she's a darling. I'm so happy for the both of you.' It meant a lot to Winnie — for the first time he felt wholly accepted by her.

Winnie and Harry visited Mimi the next morning. Her room was flooded with flowers from practically everyone in the Club.

'I can't wait to come home to rest, Peter,' said Mimi, who had Lucy Frances in her arms. 'I feel as if I'm up all night and all day.' She kissed him and Harry. 'How do you like your baby sister, Harry?'

'She's great, Mum. Can I hold her?'

'Let's just wait till we get her home, mate.'

'Sure, Dad.'

Life felt good, although the new house was still not finished. Winnie drew on his patience, knowing a good job took time. They decided to have Lucy's christening at Mimi's parents' house. It was a pretty low-key party, with just a few friends and family. Brian and Gina arrived with Kitty, who ran off with Harry to look at the baby. Gina gave the Prez a kiss. She held a present for the baby.

'Where shall I put this? I don't want it to get lost.'

Winnie took the gift and gave it to Mimi in the kitchen.

Brian and Gina disappeared into a bathroom to powder their noses. Kev watched them go and said to Winnie, 'I reckon they're both using too much coke, Prez.'

'As long as it doesn't interfere with our business, Kev, who are we to preach?'

After the christening Mimi's father came over to Winnie. 'Peter, when you're not busy I'd like you to meet an old family friend.'

'I can come now.' They walked down to the lawn area overlooking Sydney Harbour. A distinguished-looking gentleman gazed at the yachts crisscrossing the water.

'John.' Mimi's father's voice startled him, and John swung his head around.

'I'd like you to meet my son-in-law, Peter Winifred. Peter, this is John Clarke.' They shook hands. 'We're old friends; we served in the Navy together. We call him the Minister.' Straight away Winnie's ears pricked up. Could it be *the* Minister?

'You married a great girl there, Peter.'

'You're right there, John. Have you known Mimi long?'

'I've known the family a long time, way before Mimi was born.'

Mimi's dad walked away. 'I'll leave you two to talk. I'm needed in the house.'

John looked at Winnie. 'You're lucky, you know. These people are the closest to family I ever had. They're good people; you'll be right with them.'

'Why do they call you the Minister?'

'After the war I studied to become a priest. I never finished, but it didn't stop my friends from calling me the Minister.'

Winnie relaxed and followed the Minister's gaze to the harbour.

'You see those yachts? They're eighteen-footers. In the old days there used to be a lot of money spent gambling on them. I used to go out in ferries to watch and place a few bob with the SP bookies on board.

Maybe they still gamble on them. I don't know; it's been a long time for me.'

'So are you a banker too?'

Clarke laughed. 'Good God, no. I could never have that temptation. I'm a punter and a politician.'

Winnie looked at him, uncertain what to say. 'Are you trying to tell me something?'

Clarke smiled and nodded. 'You'll find out who I am soon enough, I'm sure. Would you please not mention our arrangement to Mimi?'

Winnie smiled. 'So you're our Minister, the one who gets race tips?'

'One and the same.'

'I'd like to thank you for what you did for us.'

The Minister sipped his wine. 'I did nothing, Peter.' He turned to walk away then stopped. 'Oh, and leave our friend Squizzy out of this. You follow me?' He walked back to the house.

Stunned, Winnie stood alone. He gave it thought then spoke aloud to no one: 'I wonder if he did it for Mimi or for me?'

He wondered if he should tell the boys about the meeting and decided against it. They'd spend all afternoon staring at the poor cunt and that would serve no purpose at all. He joined Mimi and Lucy, who were the centre of attention, and the afternoon went past in a round of kissing relatives, drinking and eating.

On the Monday morning Winnie arrived at the shop and was surprised that Brian was absent.

Bernie sat at Brian's desk and sorted invoices. 'Brian won't be in today, Prez. Kitty called.'

'Thanks, Bernie.' Winnie found it odd, so he went out to the workshop to talk to Kev, who was working on a chopper. 'Brian's not in today, eh?'

'You should have a talk to him, Prez. I definitely reckon he's using too much. Haven't you seen the change?'

'I never noticed. I'll have a talk to him. Now don't get up me, but I'm taking a week off because we're moving down to the new house this week.'

'That's different, Prez.'

'I'll talk to Brian.'

Winnie rode out to Brian's place before going home. He knocked on the kitchen door, startling Brian and Gina. She tried to hide a mirror with cocaine on it under the table cloth but little balls of cocaine scattered over the table. When she saw Winnie she relaxed.

'Aren't you worried about Kitty coming home?'

'She stays at Mum's on Monday night. Off to your new house, eh, Prez? That must be exciting. You want a line?'

'No thanks, Gina.' Winnie was embarrassed. Gina had bent over to snort the line and her brunch coat opened, revealing her tits. Winnie looked away, at Brian. 'We need to have a talk, mate. I'll be taking a week off to settle into the new house. Let's go outside.'

Gina, high on the coke, mimicked Winnie's voice. 'Got to talk bikie club business, eh?'

Brian rolled his eyes. 'Come on, Winnie, don't mind her.'

They went out to the shed.

'The boys are worried about you and so am I.'

'Winnie, it's only one day a week. From now on I'm taking every Monday off. You blokes take time off whenever you like, so it's my turn.' Winnie said nothing. 'I mean, who looked after everything when you were inside? I did. Who did all this business? I did. The money was there for you and Kev. Because I've finally found something that Gina and I both like to do, all of a sudden I'm a problem. Well, you can all get fucked.' His defensive tone startled Winnie, but it shocked Brian. He shut right up.

Winnie just stared. 'Brian, there's no way you're a problem. Take every Monday off — you deserve it. Just let Bernie know. The shop was your dream. Don't neglect it. If it's a problem we can sell it. We don't need it.'

'No, Winnie, we won't need to do that.'

'I wouldn't without talking to you. I know how much it means to you. But it's up to you; we don't want to run it.'

'It'll be good, Winnie, I promise you.'

'Okay, Brian, I'll see you next week. Don't use too much — it really fucks you up. They don't call it the great delusion for no reason, you know.'

Chapter 41

The removal truck took all their furniture to the new house and Winnie, Mimi and Harry followed.

When they arrived, Harry jumped off the bike to open the gate.

'How do you like moving here, mate?'

'I reckon it'll be terrific, Dad. Can I get a trail bike?'

'We might get two and ride together.'

'That'd be fun.'

That night Mimi and Winnie lay in bed. 'What were you and the Minister talking about at the christening?'

'Just getting to know one another. Why's that?'

'Just wondering.'

After spending the week moving furniture and setting up the property Winnie was glad to be riding to the clubhouse. The little town of Picton must have thought all their Christmases had come at once. All the shopkeepers were familiar with them after they'd dropped a lot of money in the bike shop, nursery and antique furniture store. Mimi had an eye for fine furniture and she bought bits and pieces to make their home look just right.

Winnie rode into the clubhouse and found some of the boys already there. Big Kev and Ocker arrived together a little later, looking very unhappy. 'Prez, we need to have a talk,' said Kev.

'What is it?' They looked at one another. 'Come on, what is it?'

Big Kev started. 'We're pretty sure all our cocaine and nearly three hundred thousand bucks is gone for good.' Winnie immediately felt sick as the sudden jolt of adrenalin sank into his guts. 'We think it's Gina.'

'Fuck off! Brian wouldn't wear it.'

'Coke fucks people's minds, Prez. We didn't want to believe it ourselves but Gina was shooting her mouth off, saying how if it wasn't for her organising the cash and the books we'd be nothing. It was news to us, so we talked to Brian and he admitted he took the coke home, cut it with baby laxative and sold it off as top stuff. He gave the money to Gina to bank and the stupid cunt gambled it away in two nights.'

Winnie's head spun. Nothing like this had ever happened to him, not with Brian. He'd never trusted Gina but he'd been sure Brian hadn't either.

'We can't let this go on, Prez. We'll all end up in strife. She knows too much and she tells everyone everything.'

'Where did you hear that?'

'From Sandy, and she has no reason to bullshit us.'

'I know, Kev.' Silence engulfed them. 'We have to be two hundred per cent sure of this, you both know that. What proof do you have?'

'Ocker, you tell him.'

'The last shipment from Melbourne, Brian got a few kilos of top quality. I know for sure what the quality was like because I tried it when the package arrived. We divvied it up into ounces and started selling it, then we heard people saying it's not the same as before, it's been stepped on. I got hold of some and it had definitely been diluted.'

'So what you're telling me is, Brian takes what he wants of pure and adds filler.'

'That's it, Prez. He gets the pure for nothing and sells the shit. That'll stuff up our business if it continues. Our word is our bond, and if we fuck up, we're fucked.'

'Why would he do that?'

'She's made him greedy. We don't know what she tells him but it's fucked his head up.'

'How long has this been going on — any idea?'

'Fuck knows, Prez.'

'Well, what do you both think we should do?'

There was a long silence. Ocker and Big Kev looked at one another. 'It's not just the money, Prez,' said Ocker.

'I know. What a stupid cunt. Let's just think about it over the weekend. We'll make a decision on Monday at the shop.' Winnie's mind was in turmoil. It was one decision he didn't want to have to make. No one in the shop was happy.

Winnie fronted Bernie, busy setting up a display. 'Brian's on his day off?'

'Yes, Prez, he needs it. He hasn't been himself lately.'

Winnie forced a smile. 'He'll come good. You still enjoy working here, Bernie?'

'It's always been my dream to run a bike shop.'

Big Kev and Ocker met Winnie to tell him their decision.

Before Winnie said a word, Ocker started. 'Prez, we talked about this and if you don't want to be involved in what has to be done, we understand.'

'No, we do what has to be done together. What have you come up with?' In his heart he knew what they were going to say.

No one said a word for a moment, then Kev said it. They had no option, Gina's big mouth could put an end to it all. They nodded.

'We do it tonight, little Kitty's not home. This is never to be spoken about again, not even to be thought about. If it ever comes out it'll be the end of us and my family. Mimi would leave me. We have to carry on as normal. We'll leave the shop separately and meet at the clubhouse tonight.'

Winnie waited in the darkened clubhouse for them. The prospect of making Kitty an orphan played on his mind. When the boys arrived he'd worked it out. 'Now, we have to make this look like it's a robbery gone wrong. Do you know where he keeps the coke, Ocker?'

'He has a safe in his garage. I know the combination — I went and got a couple of ounces on Saturday and he opened it in front of me. The silly cunt uses his birth date: ten to the left, twelve to the right, then forty-nine. At least he won't forget it.'

'While you do that, Kev and I will look after them.'

Big Kev produced two pistols fitted with silencers and handed one to Winnie. He checked to see if it was loaded and that the safety was on. 'It's right to go, Prez.'

No one said a word on the drive to Brian's house. The sign that said Snow's Mountain brought back memories of their youth. Winnie tried to find the bike trails they'd ridden but with new trees and all the new houses it was all obliterated. Late on a Monday night most homes were in darkness. They parked around the corner from the house and made their way there individually, meeting in the backyard. Winnie pointed Ocker towards the garage and he and Kev crept in the back door. Winnie thought Brian was a silly cunt making it so easy for anyone to walk in and help themselves.

Gina slept on the lounge in front of a blaring television. Winnie tapped Big Kev, pointed at him to do her. It was his job to look after Brian. He tried not to think about what he was about to do and went to their bedroom. He paused for a few seconds to let his heart rate slow down so he could think clearly. A sudden muffled thud, followed a few seconds later by another, meant there was no turning back now. He was glad Brian was asleep. Winnie lifted the gun to point-blank range, aimed at the back of Brian's head and fired three shots in succession. Only the recoil let him know the gun had fired. Blood oozed immediately onto the pillow. He felt nothing as he backed out of the room. He couldn't look at Kev as they headed for the back door, where Ocker waited. He held up a bag, nodded, and they left, all taking separate paths to the parked car. They said nothing on their way back to the clubhouse.

Winnie handed the gun back to Kev. 'I want you to go right now and make sure these are never found. I'll see you blokes at the shop tomorrow. I want to be by myself.'

After they left Winnie sat at the bar and cried uncontrollably. He put on a brave face the next morning at the shop and tried to show no emotion until Brian and Gina were found.

Bernie wandered around with a customer and finally asked for some help when the phones rang. 'Prez, can you give me a hand? I don't know where Brian is. He never rang.'

'Don't worry, Bernie. He'll ring if there are any problems.'

There was nothing worse than waiting for bad news when you knew it was coming.

'Prez! Phone.'

'Thanks, Bernie.'

'Hello, I have some bad news for you.' It was the Pig's voice. 'Your mate Brian and his wife are dead.'

'What? Where?'

'At their house, both shot. What have you been up to? Who would have done it?'

'I haven't got a clue. Is their daughter alright?'

'His mother was dropping her off and found them.'

'Fuck me,' was all Winnie was prepared to say.

'You'd better expect a visit.'

At that moment Winnie looked up to see two uniformed police standing talking to Bernie. 'They're here now. I'll talk to you soon.' He hung up.

'Bernie, what's up?'

'These coppers want to talk to you.' She was crying freely. 'Brian and Gina were murdered last night.'

'What?' Winnie said loudly. 'How?' The truth once out allowed Winnie to let loose his emotions. His eyes welled and he collapsed onto the couch, mumbling 'Jesus fucking Christ' over and over.

'We can't tell you anything while it's under investigation. The detectives will be talking to you. We're just letting you know they were found this morning by the in-laws.'

Big Kev and Ocker tried to comfort Bernie but Winnie locked the shop doors behind the coppers and told her to go home. He rang Mimi before she could hear it on the radio.

Ocker rang as many members as he could and got the word out. 'Let's go to the clubhouse for a wake.'

Bernie was distraught. 'Can I come, Prez? I don't want to be alone today.'

'Sure, Bernie.'

A lot of the members arrived at the clubhouse, all of them filled with questions. 'Is it true, are they dead?'

Winnie nodded. 'It's true. We don't know anything yet.'

'They were shot, Prez.'

'How do you know?'

'It was on the radio. They also said police were fearful of war breaking out between bike clubs.'

'Don't believe everything you hear on the radio. We don't have a clue yet who it was. We're not going to play into their hands.'

'Phone, Prez.'

'Hello, Winnie, it's Twister. I just heard what happened to Brian and his missus — is it true?'

'Yes.'

'I just want to say I'm sorry to hear that. On my mother's grave I swear we had nothing to do with it.'

'What about old man Gibbs?'

'He's not even in the country. He's in Ireland, on holidays.'

'That means fuck-all, Twister.'

'Winnie, that would be between you and him. It has nothing to do with the Tigers.'

'I believe you. Thanks for the call.'

For the rest of the day a procession of callers expressed sympathy, and most motorcycle clubs called with condolences.

'Rastus called to say he's bringing his whole club up from Melbourne for the funeral.'

'The pigs are here, Prez. They want to talk to you.' Big Kev followed Winnie outside to two waiting detectives.

'My name is Sergeant Dawson, this is Senior Constable Rourke. We're investigating the deaths of Brian Corrigan and his wife Gina. Are you Peter Winifred?'

'That's me.'

'What do you know about it?'

'First I heard about it was from two uniforms that came to our shop, and then we heard a report on the radio.'

'Have you any idea who could be involved?'

'Brian never had an enemy in this world. Everyone loved Brian.'

'Not everyone, by the look of it. What about other clubs? Have you been having trouble with the Tigers?'

'I doubt it. There's no reason for them to be involved.'

'What about drugs? Don't bullshit us that you're not involved. We're in the homicide squad, not the drug squad. We just want to solve your friend's murder. If you just stand there and resort to your code of silence, you won't help us. Or don't you care?'

'We care alright. It could have been a robbery for all we know. He handled the cash from the shop and I never knew how much cash he had.'

'Believe me, it was not just a robbery. If you hear anything, leave it to us. Don't go taking the law into your own hands.'

Winnie watched them leave.

'Born to Be Wild', Brian's favourite song, was playing on the radio. 'Turn it up!' yelled Big Kev.

Winnie left the organising of the funeral to Ocker and Little Tony while he went back home to Picton. Riding down the driveway he admired their new home, with the sun setting behind it. The funeral and the new house spelled the end of an era. He felt the energy drain from his body; he felt black inside.

'Dad, Dad!' Harry ran out of the house. 'Dad, Uncle Brian's dead.'

'Yeah, I know, mate.'

Winnie wrapped Harry in his arms and let the tears pour from his eyes. He thought of Brian. It just had to be. You would have understood, Brian. It wasn't personal; it was business and you fucked us. We couldn't allow either of you to rob us.

'It's okay, mate.' Winnie held Harry tightly. 'We all die someday. It was Brian's time.'

Mimi watched her two men for a moment, then rushed into Winnie's arms. Harry hugged Winnie's leg and they all stood and cried. Winnie felt genuinely sad, not for Brian and Gina, but for Mimi and Harry. Then he remembered young Kitty. He felt awful for her. He thought of baby Lucy Frances and suddenly longed to hold her. 'Let's go inside.'

Marge was feeding little Lucy at the table. Lucy saw her old man and got all excited. Winnie took her from Marge and rocked her in his arms. Lucy was pure, his little innocent angel.

Mimi told him the Minister had called to offer his condolences.

'You two really hit it off. What's going on, Peter? I'm worried.'

'Do you want me to get you a gun?'

'I'd rather divorce you than carry a gun or even have one in this house.'

'Settle down, honey. We're not sure yet what happened. We don't know what shady characters Gina hung out with at the casinos. We're thinking she might have reneged on her gambling debts or something.'

'I told her she was heading for trouble, Peter.'

'When?'

'Heaps of times. She used to borrow money from me but I stopped lending to her about twelve months ago.'

'You never told me.'

'It was my money and she always paid me back. So what do the police say?'

'They say it was over drugs. They're just fishing. We don't know.'

'I'm just glad that Kitty was with Brian's parents. Have you spoken to them yet?'

'So much has been going on I completely forgot. Fuck, I feel bad about not ringing. I'll call first thing in the morning.'

Mimi wrapped him in her arms. 'Peter, I'm so sorry for you.'

As hard as he tried, Winnie could not picture Brian's face. His mind turned blank.

The day of the funeral Winnie arrived early at the clubhouse. 'What's the plan, mate?'

'We pick the casket up at the funeral home,' said Ocker, 'then form a procession to the cemetery, where the priest will do the service at the grave site. That's what his parents wanted.'

'We spoke to the pigs,' said Little Tony. 'They're going to fix the traffic lights.'

The sound of a lot of bikes came from the road. It was the Commandos, up from Melbourne. They rode into the clubhouse in single file.

'Prez,' said Ocker, 'Twister wants to come to the funeral.'

'Funerals are neutral.'

'That's what I told him.'

Rastus and Spike walked over. They hugged the boys. 'What can we say, Winnie? Any idea who it was?'

'We just don't know, mate. We don't know what Brian was up to or if his missus and her gambling got them into strife. I've been asking around but no one knows a thing.'

'It's one of life's little mysteries.'

'Prez, I organised a couple of stretch limos to take the wives.'

'Good one, Ocker.'

The Redbacks arrived from Newcastle, followed by the Sharks, down from Brisbane.

Kev was in charge of the procession and he let the visiting clubs know where their place was, in line behind the Miners. Little Tony and Winnie led as they rode to the funeral home for a viewing of Brian, dressed in his Club colours. Members filed past the open coffin. Some leaned in and kissed the cold body.

'Are you going in, Prez?'

'No, Kev, I can't.'

'Me neither. Gina's being cremated — they're going to sprinkle her ashes around his grave.'

Twister and the Tigers arrived while the mourners waited for the hearse. A few Miners appeared tense at their arrival until Winnie and Big Kev walked over and shook Twister's hand. True to their word the police set the traffic lights to green and over three hundred motorcycles followed the hearse to the cemetery. Winnie, Big Kev, Ocker, Nestor, Little Tony and Boris lifted the coffin onto their shoulders and, followed by the rest of the Miners, slowly made their way to the grave, where the priest, Brian's parents, the wives and family members stood. Winnie saw Little Kitty, tears streaming down her cheeks, carrying a single red rose. She stood next to Mimi and Sandy, both wearing dark glasses and dressed in black. Brian's Club colours were draped over the coffin.

The priest's sermon was a blur of God-speak and mystery. At its end, the pallbearers gently lowered the coffin into the grave, accompanied by loud wails from some women. Winnie noticed the smell of freshly dug soil in the air. He picked up a shovel and threw soil onto the coffin. The members stood in line to take a turn until all that remained was for Little Kitty to bend over the grave and place her single rose on top. She stood alone then turned to Mimi and Sandy. Winnie made his way over and took Kitty in his arms and hugged her.

'Come on, let's go and see your grandma and grandpa.'

In between sobs she said, 'Okay.'

Mimi and Sandy followed.

The Corrigans were never pleased to see him. Mrs C mumbled that she never did take to Gina. Winnie turned to Mr Corrigan, who was much more emotional. 'Hello, son.'

Winnie shook his trembling hand. 'Are you coming back to the clubhouse for a drink?'

'Yes,' Mrs Corrigan answered. 'Brian would have liked us to.'

Winnie grasped Mimi's shoulder as they passed the grave where members gathered in groups.

Big Kev walked past with Sandy. 'What do you say, Prez?'

'Leave in ten minutes?'

'Okay, Prez.'

'Are you coming back to the clubhouse, Mimi?'

'No, Peter, I'm going home to the kids. You go.'

'Alright, I'll see you tomorrow.' He walked her to her car. 'Tell the kids I miss them.'

After a fast ride back to the clubhouse the nominees opened the bar and got the snags onto the barbecue.

'Come on, Winnie, let's go and have some drugs.'

'Rastus, you never change.'

'Do you want me to?'

'No, come on.'

They went out the back and Rastus poured out a line each. 'Do you know who done it?'

'We just don't know. The only thing it could be is her gambling.'

Rastus said nothing. Winnie handed him a rolled note and they both snorted their line.

Winnie knew Rastus thought he was lying, and at that moment he wanted to be as far away from him as possible.

'I've got to mingle, mate. I'll catch up with you later.' He found Big Kev. 'Come with me, mate.'

They found Sorrow from the Redbacks and Gina's cousin from the Sharks. Everyone had a question.

Winnie held up his hand. 'Don't ask, boys. We don't know. But if you hear anything, let us know. Whoever did it will talk for sure.'

Ocker came over. 'How are you feeling, Prez?'

'Sick in the guts.'

'Me too. Brian's parents are here.'

'Okay, mate. I'll catch up with you later, boys.'

They took Brian's parents and family into the clubhouse and cleared a table for them. 'Ocker, tell the bar they're to have free piss — anything they want for as long as they want.'

'Okay, Prez.'

Brian's father introduced Winnie to the family. A nominee came over to get their orders.

Winnie turned to Brian's father. 'Mr Corrigan, what would you like?'

'Call me Jack, Peter. Just a beer, and one for the wife.'

'Jack, when everything's settled we'll sit down and work out Brian's business. John Baker, our solicitor, is trustworthy. He'll arrange a meeting to work out what's best for Kitty, and there should be something there for you and Mrs Corrigan.'

'Don't worry about us.'

'Jack, I think you'll find that Brian did quite well in business.'

'Well, if Gina hadn't gambled a lot away he might have done better. We don't even know if they owned their home because the police still have all their paperwork.'

'Don't worry, Jack, I'll have a talk to John Baker. Brian left all his details with him; he'll know. How's Kitty faring?'

'Pretty good, considering she lost both her parents.'

'Did Mimi tell you? We'd love to have her down on the farm whenever she likes. I know Harry would love that.'

'Tell Mimi to call my wife.'

'I'll do better than that — we'll come over and show you our new baby.'

'I know Brian wanted more kids but Gina was happy with just Kitty. I always thought she trapped Brian, you know.' Jack's voice faltered. 'If it weren't for her, perhaps he'd still be alive.'

Winnie wandered around the clubhouse thanking members of other clubs for attending the funeral.

When he noticed Rastus and Bernie having a laugh together he made his way over. 'What are you two laughing about?'

'I was just telling Bernie about our parties in Melbourne, and how she should move down.'

'Yeah, like fuck she should. Bernie, you wouldn't leave us now, would you? We need you.'

'Don't worry, Prez. I'm just playing with him.'

'I thought you were fair dinkum for a moment. Now Brian's gone, it's up to you to run the shop and we'll even give you a pay rise.'

'That won't be the reason I'm staying. I love working in the shop.'

'Yeah, but you've got to take more responsibility. I want you to do Brian's job. Anyway, you don't fancy Rastus, do you?'

'God no, but he's funny.'

Winnie saw Mrs Corrigan readying to leave, and winked at Bernie. 'I'll talk to you later.'

He joined Ocker in saying goodbye to the Corrigans. Jack looked broken, but his wife wore a steely look that warned anyone nearby to stay away.

Back at the clubhouse Winnie asked Ocker if he still passed on tips to Squizzy for the Minister.

'Yes, Prez.'

'I thought Squizzy might have come.'

'I don't think so, Prez. The coppers were there with telephoto lenses — he didn't need that.'

'We're going to have to sit down with John Baker and work out a percentage of the business for Kitty and put it in trust for her. She'll be looked after.'

The shop got lots of play in the newspapers, which was free advertising, and it soon became busier than ever. Winnie didn't know what he would have done without Bernie — she flitted from task to task and did it all with a smile.

Winnie made his way out the back to meet the Pig.

'Get in, Winnie. Let's go for a drive.'

'What's up?'

'Have you heard anything about the shooters?'

'What makes you think there was more than one?'

'Five shots from two different guns, a very professional job. They found no drugs except marijuana residue and traces of cocaine on the kitchen table. Someone emptied her purse and Brian's wallet, so maybe it was about the money, but we can't be sure. Anything you want to add?'

Winnie's face darkened. 'I haven't got a fucking clue.'

'Don't get the shits with me. I'm just telling you what they think. There's something else, too: your phones are probably tapped, so be careful what you say. So, have you got something for me?'

Winnie passed over an envelope. 'Now I want you to do something for us. All Brian's files and paperwork, including those of the shop, were taken by a detective in charge of the homicide investigation. We need it; it affects Kitty, the Corrigans and us. Can you find out how long before we can get it back?'

'I'll talk to the boys in homicide. Just remember about the phones.'

'Okay. Thanks for the tip.'

Winnie called Ocker and Big Kev over to say the phone was tapped.

Ocker pulled out his mobile.

'I don't know, mate. I wouldn't trust them either. Be even more careful what any of you say on them. Maybe they can listen.'

'We'd better let the members know about the taps, Prez.' Ocker leaned in closely. 'No one but the three of us knows anything.'

'I'm more concerned that the blokes who do deals on their mobiles might say too much. Now's not the time to relax.'

'I follow you, Prez. I'll talk to as many now as I can and we can bring it up at the meeting on Friday night.'

'If they have to, tell them to set up codes. The pigs aren't stupid, they'll know something's up. One more thing: at the meeting on Friday

I'm making an announcement that affects everyone in the Club.' Winnie stared at the floor for a moment. 'I'm stepping down as President.'

'You're joking?'

'He's not,' said Kev. He'd seen the look in Winnie's eyes.

'Why, Prez?'

'Ever since Lucy was born it's all I think about. I look at Harry and realise how much I missed, and there's no way I want to repeat that with Lucy. Anyway, I'm not retiring from the Miners — I'm just stepping down as President, and you'll have to elect another. As for the shop, well, you don't need me there. I do fuck-all, don't I?'

Ocker smiled, 'Whoever said that, Prez?'

Winnie gave Ocker a big hug. 'I love you blokes.'

'Look out, Ocker, he'll want to kiss you next.'

'We've been through a lot for a long time. I'll keep my hand in with our private business but now that I'm into the pubs with the Marios I can't see myself doing this any longer; it's too much. Besides, it's time we all went legit and lived normal lives — we're not kids any more.'

Kev understood at once. The constant high levels of adrenalin were beginning to take their toll. He was feeling his age for the first time and he agreed: maybe they should all look at their lives and decide to do what was most important.

'The Marios bought some cheap land from some government release. They're thinking of holding on to it for a few years and then developing it or selling at the right time. They need investors and I said I'd be in it.'

Kev slapped Winnie on the back. 'Goodonya, Prez.'

'What about a new President, Prez? Who do you reckon?'

Winnie thought about it. 'What about Nestor?'

Ocker sifted through the likely candidates. 'What about Big Kev?'

'You wouldn't want it, would you, Kev?'

Kev looked suddenly pissed off. 'No, but it would've been fucking nice to be asked before Nestor.'

Ocker went silent because Kev rarely got mad with him. He had no idea if Kev was serious, and so he backed up a step.

Then Kev smiled. 'That got youse going, didn't it?'

'Fuck me, Kev, I thought you were fair dinkum.'

The tension broke and the boys laughed as one.

'Well, what about me?' Kev and Winnie looked at Ocker incredulously.

'Do you want it, Ocker?'

'No.'

Kev grabbed Ocker in a headlock and mucked up his hair. 'You're a cunt, Ocker. What are you?'

'A dirty, rich little cunt, but I reckon Nestor might be a good choice. He treats everyone well, the boys like him and he's an ace organiser.'

Winnie shook hands with them both. 'Alright, if that's agreed, I'm off to the farm.'

Winnie suited up. 'What's up with you, Ocker? You look sad.'

'I'm sad.'

'Yeah, a sad, dirty, rich little cunt alright.'

Ocker beamed. 'Ride carefully, Prez.'

Winnie kicked the Harley into life and rode away slowly, nothing much else on his mind except the long ride home, back to Mimi and the kids. As he headed down the highway he had a feeling of relief. No more the Prez, he thought, the wind blowing in his face. The Club will grow without me. Then thoughts of his best mate Brian flashed through his mind. How did it get to this, you silly cunt?